Library of
Davidson College

Corporatism and National Development in Latin America

Westview Replica Editions

This book is a Westview Replica Edition. The concept of Replica Editions is a response to the crisis in academic and informational publishing. Library budgets for books have been severely curtailed; economic pressures on the university presses and the few private publishing companies primarily interested in scholarly manuscripts have severely limited the capacity of the industry to properly serve the academic and research communities. Many manuscripts dealing with important subjects, often representing the highest level of scholarship, are today not economically viable publishing projects. Or, if they are accepted for publication, they are often subject to lead times ranging from one to three years. Scholars are understandably frustrated when they realize that their first-class research cannot be published within a reasonable time frame, if at all.

Westview Replica Editions are our practical solution to the problem. The concept is simple. We accept a manuscript in camera-ready form and move it immediately into the production process. The responsibility for textual and copy editing lies with the author or sponsoring organization. If necessary we will advise the author on proper preparation of footnotes and bibliography. We prefer that the manuscript be typed according to our specifications, though it may be acceptable as typed for a dissertation or prepared in some other clearly organized and readable way. The end result is a book produced by lithography and bound in hard covers. Initial edition sizes range from 400 to 800 copies, and a number of recent Replicas are already in second printings. We include among Westview Replica Editions only works of outstanding scholarly quality or of great informational value, and we will continue to exercise our usual editorial standards and quality control.

Corporatism and National Development in Latin America
Howard J. Wiarda

This provocative volume emphasizes the necessity of coming to grips with historic and contemporary corporatism in order to fully comprehend Latin American and Iberian development on its own terms and in its own sociopolitical context. Professor Wiarda fully explores corporatism--its theory and practice (and the vast gap between the two), its ideology and historical roots, and its sociology and political economy. Providing background materials, comparative and empirical data, and case studies, he uncovers new areas of research for historians, social scientists, and area specialists. Although the focus of this potentially controversial book is on Latin American development, it shows as well how corporatism has relevance for our understanding of recent changes in the United States and other advanced industrial societies.

Howard J. Wiarda, professor of political science, adjunct professor of labor relations, and chairman of the Program in Latin American Studies at the University of Massachusetts, is also visiting scholar at the Center for International Affairs, Harvard University. Professor Wiarda has written and edited numerous books and articles, including <u>The Continuing Struggle for Democracy in Latin America</u> (Westview, 1980).

Corporatism and National Development in Latin America

Howard J. Wiarda

Westview Press / Boulder, Colorado

A Westview Replica Edition

All rights reserved. No part of this publication may be reproduced or transmitted in any form or by any means, electronic or mechanical, including photocopy, recording, or any information storage and retrieval system, without permission in writing from the publisher.

Copyright © 1981 by Westview Press, Inc.

Published in 1981 in the United States of America by
    Westview Press, Inc.
    5500 Central Avenue
    Boulder, Colorado 80301
    Frederick A. Praeger, Publisher

Library of Congress Cataloging in Publication Data
Wiarda, Howard J., 1939-
    Corporatism and national development in Latin America.
    (A Westview replica edition)
    Bibliography: p.
    1. Corporate state--Latin America--Addresses, essays, lectures.
2. Latin America--Politics and government--1948-   --Addresses, essays, lectures.   I. Title. II. Series: Westview replica edition.
JL960.W49   321.9   81-2097
ISBN 0-86531-031-9   AACR2

Printed and bound in the United States of America

Contents

List of Figures and Tables ix
Preface xi

PART 1   INTRODUCTION: THE STUDY OF CORPORATISM AND DEVELOPMENT IN IBERIA AND LATIN AMERICA

1   THE MAKING OF A LATIN AMERICANIST: A NOTE ON CORPORATISM AND ITS SOCIOLOGY OF KNOWLEDGE 3

2   IS LATIN AMERICA DEMOCRATIC AND DOES IT WANT TO BE? THE CRISIS AND QUEST OF DEMOCRACY IN THE HEMISPHERE 11

PART 2   CORPORATIST THEORY AND THE CORPORATIST MODEL

3   THE LATIN AMERICAN DEVELOPMENT PATTERN 31

4   TOWARD A FRAMEWORK FOR THE STUDY OF POLITICAL CHANGE IN THE IBERIC-LATIN TRADITION: THE CORPORATIVE MODEL 51

5   ALTERNATIVE PARADIGMS: THE "CONFLICT" AND "CONSENSUS" MODELS 73

6   CORPORATISM AND DEVELOPMENT IN THE IBERIC-LATIN WORLD: PERSISTENT STRAINS AND NEW VARIATIONS 95

7   CORPORATIST THEORY AND IDEOLOGY: A LATIN AMERICAN DEVELOPMENT PARADIGM 117

PART 3   COMPARATIVE STUDIES: THEORETICAL AND EMPIRICAL

8   THE STRUGGLE FOR DEMOCRACY AND HUMAN RIGHTS IN LATIN AMERICA: TOWARD A NEW CONCEPTUALIZATION 139

9   THE CORPORATIVE ORIGINS OF THE IBERIAN AND LATIN AMERICAN LABOR RELATIONS SYSTEMS 157

10   DOES EUROPE STILL STOP AT THE PYRENEES? POLITICS AND THE PARTY SYSTEMS OF SPAIN AND PORTUGAL 185

11 DOES THE FUTURE STILL LIE IN BOLIVIA? POLITICS AND THE
    STAGES OF CORPORATIVE DEVELOPMENT IN LATIN AMERICA 211

12 COMPARATIVE AND THEORETICAL RESEARCH IN PROGRESS 235

PART 4   COUNTRY STUDIES

13 A DOMINICAN CASE STUDY AND THE CORPORATIST MODEL 251

14 THE BRAZILIAN CATHOLIC LABOR MOVEMENT 273

15 THE CORPORATIST TRADITION AND THE CORPORATIVE SYSTEM IN
    PORTUGAL: STRUCTURED, EVOLVING, TRANSCENDED, PERSISTENT . 289

16 CUBA: IS IT ALSO CORPORATIST AND BUREAUCRATIC-AUTHORI-
    TARIAN? 317

17 THE LATIN AMERICANIZATION OF THE UNITED STATES 323

PART 5   CONCLUSION

18 CORPORATISM IN IBERIAN AND LATIN AMERICAN POLITICAL
    ANALYSIS: CRITICISMS, QUALIFICATIONS, AND THE CONTEXT
    AND "WHYS" OF THE DEBATE 343

References and Bibliography 357

Figures and Tables

3.1	Structure of Spanish Society and Polity	36
3.2	Contrasting Traditions and Time Periods in the Colonization of Latin America and North America	41
10.1	Spain and Portugal: Voting Percentages	202
10.2	Distribution of Votes by Region and Size of Place: Portugal, 1975	202
11.1	The Stages of Corporative Development in Latin America	219
11.2	The Corporative Structure of Latin America, circa 1890–1930	228
11.3	The Modern Corporative Structure of Latin America	231

Figures and Tables

Preface

Occasionally, an entire discipline and field of study, or even two or three, may be shaken to their foundations and forced to reexamine their earlier assumptions by the impact of a single concept. In this instance, the fields are political science, sociology, and Latin American and Western European comparative development studies, and the concept that has forced the rethinking is corporatism.

Among the reasons why corporatism as a concept, frame of reference, and pattern of institutional arrangements has created such a stir are the following:

1. Corporatism, once thought dead, a product of the interwar period whose time had come--and gone!--has now reemerged or been rediscovered in a great variety of modernizing nations: Brazil, Chile, Mexico, Peru, Tanzania, and many more.
2. Corporatism, we have rediscovered, is not merely a "smokescreen" or "confidence trick," as the early literature on Italy sometimes argued, but a complex and often quite rational way of organizing diverse nations, of structuring both political society and public policy, of institutionalizing consultation between the state and societal groups, of filling the organizational void in fragmented transitional societies, of integrating new groups into political society and/or controlling their participation, of serving as an alternative model of national social and political development. These functions can neither be ignored nor easily dismissed as anachronistic.
3. Corporatism, once thought to be synonymous with fascism and reaction, is now viewed as a national organizational form that may take liberal, Christian-democratic, and syndicalist directions as well as bureaucratic-authoritarian ones.
4. Corporatism and the corporatist framework, like the dependency concept, have spread beyond the area where they have recently been utilized, Latin America, to have their impact on European and general comparative studies as well. The flow of social science ideas and concepts, historically from Europe outward, may now have begun to be reversed.
5. A new nexus has been discovered between corporatism and capitalism and between corporatism and large-scale

bureaucratic organization. Some have argued that corporatism may be the organizational component of the modern, centralized, administrative state, whether capitalist or socialist.
6. While corporatism may in a Spain or Portugal take more liberal and pluralist forms than heretofore thought, we have recently also discovered that the polities priding themselves on their liberal and social-democratic forms may practice a certain disguised form of corporatism. Corporatism seems present not just in modernizing nations but in advanced industrial democracies as well, including the United States.
7. The corporatist focus has precipitated a major reexamination of many ethnocentric social science assumptions and of the presumed universality and unilinearism of the development process by positing other alternative routes to modernization and by questioning the feasibility of applying "Western" assumptions and models to non-Western areas where they have little relevance. The "corporatist framework" has helped challenge numerous Euro-centric notions and stimulated another social science "great debate."

With particular reference to Latin America and the broader culture area of Iberic-Latin civilization, this book explores these and other issues that have grown out of the new emphasis on corporatism. The volume draws together a series of theoretical, comparative, and empirical case studies written over the past decade. The essays were meant to be provocative and to stir debate, and there is no doubt they have stimulated much discussion and controversy on a new or rediscovered theme that has by now assumed major importance. The book shows the development and utility of a concept that has, we have discovered, relevance not just for Iberia and Latin America but for other societies as well, both Third World countries and advanced industrial ones.

One of the main arguments of the book is that, if we are to comprehend Iberian and Latin American political society and development on their own terms rather than through the ethnocentric notions of North American social science, we must come to grips with corporatism. Corporatism may well be to Iberia and Latin America what liberalism has been to the United States: the dominant political-cultural and institutional framework within which political and social life is organized. Of course, corporatism has both multiple causes and multiple effects, and it may exist in more-or-less pure form or in combination with liberal, socialist, and republican features. Nevertheless, it seems clear one cannot, in Iberia and Latin America, come to grips adequately with patterns of labor relations, interest groups and associational life, the role of the state and state-society relations, class structure and public policy, the nature of representation and the role of such agencies as the army or Church, decision-making and change, without coming to grips also with corporatism.

This study focuses on corporatism and national development in Latin America. But like many scholars who have studied that area,

I have concluded that, to understand fully the Latin American systems, one has to get back to their roots and origins in Iberia. Hence, the inclusion here of several studies of Spain and Portugal or that treat Iberia and Latin America as a single culture area.

But it is not just in Iberia and Latin America where corporation is strong or resurgent. For in the growth of statism and officially sanctioned interest associations in the United States and other modern industrial nations, the looming possibility of corporatism is also apparent. The troubling implications of these trends toward corporatist and state-technocratic rule, and whether corporatism can be transcended, are questions to which the discussion repeatedly returns.

The studies collected here contribute, from varying perspectives and research undertakings, to the analysis of corporatism and the corporatist framework as both theory and practice. Most have been published previously in scholarly journals; a few appear for the first time. One feels somewhat embarrassed and presumptuous in drawing together a collection of one's own studies; but in this case the importance of the subject, the controversy that has swirled about the corporatism theme (and sometimes the deliberate misrepresentation of the issues raised), the fact these writings have appeared in such scattered and diverse journals, and the urgings of colleagues and editors would seem to provide justification.

The book presents in an ordered and coherent fashion a series of arguments, probings, essays, and research findings that otherwise would have remained dispersed and that could not, therefore, be read as part of a single, integrated, ongoing body of work. The collection has been lightly edited to update some comments and references and to remove major repetitions, and the footnoting system has been modified to put all references at the end; but essentially the individual pieces remain as they were originally written. As such, they reflect a certain evolution of thought, the gradual refinement of concepts and definitions, expanded empirical testing of the model hypothesized, and an effort to deal with the differences and disputes surrounding the corporatism concept. The collection also reflects the wrenching conflicts and self-examinations that we all went through during this past troubled decade that, along with other features, saw a new questioning of numerous political science, sociology, and developmental concepts. Thus, while the study of corporatism tells us a great deal about Iberia and Latin America, it may also tell us something about ourselves, our society, and our profession as well.

The author wishes to express his thanks to the many scholars here and abroad who have commented on this body of corporatism writings over the years and, in both public and private forums, have thus contributed mightily to the elaboration of this concept and the author's understanding of it. Most of these intellectual debts are duly noted in the references; special thanks go to friends and colleagues Charles Anderson, John Bailey, Douglas Chalmers, David Collier, Kenneth Erickson, William Glade, Martin Heisler, Robert Kaufman, James Malloy, Richard Morse, David Scott Palmer, Stanley Payne, Frederick Pike, Susan Kaufman Purcell, Keith Rosenn, Kalman Silvert, Evelyn Stevens, Iêda Siqueira Wiarda, and Edward Williams. A number of sponsoring agencies also helped support the research on which these writings are based. These agencies were always mentioned in the original articles and monographs, but it seems just to acknowledge again their contribution here: American Council of Learned Societies, American Philosophic Society, Center for International Affairs at Harvard University, Fulbright Program, Labor Relations and Research Center of the University of Massachusetts, Mershon Center at Ohio State University, National Endowment for the Humanities, National Institutes of Health, Research Council of the University of Massachusetts, Rockefeller Foundation, and Social Science Research Council. As always, the author remains wholly responsible for what appears in this volume.

Howard J. Wiarda
Cambridge, Massachusetts

Corporatism and National Development in Latin America

Part 1
Introduction: The Study of Corporatism and Development in Iberia and Latin America

The materials in Part 1 provide an introduction to the study of corporatism. The first essay, which takes an autobiographical form, provides an understanding of the origins of the corporative approach and its sociology of knowledge. The second raises the troubling question of whether Latin America is democratic or wants to be, traces the literature on Latin America's supposed quest for same, explores the implications of our democratic biases as applied to Latin America, and suggests alternative avenues of approach to our understanding of the area.

1 | The Making of a Latin Americanist: A Note on Corporatism and Its Sociology of Knowledge

Corporatism and its study have acquired a certain vogue of late; corporatist interpretations are now "in," a part of the prevailing "moda." But these changes do not happen by accident; rather emphases and interpretations of societal and political phenomena have a "sociology" of their own, a "sociology of knowledge." Hence, the first statement in this book is concerned with the issue of where the new corporatist focus and interpretation came from, how and why it has replaced "liberalism" or "developmentalism" as a dominant explanatory paradigm. Though the discussion that follows is written in the first person, a genre with which I feel uncomfortable, that is the story and life history I know best. Justifying this autobiographical statement also is the impression that my own experience and "journey" in the realm of these ideas may be not altogether unique. In fact, it may be quite common.

I began life, politically that is, as a liberal and social-democrat just like the majority of the academic community. I believed liberalism to be ethically good, to represent the wave of the future, and to be universally applicable. At the University of Michigan where I did my undergraduate work, I studied Latin America chiefly with the distinguished historian (and passionate partisan of the Spanish Republic) Irving Leonard, learned international relations and comparative politics under Harold Jacobson and Martin Needler, whose writings on Latin American development I later, with great reluctance, critically reviewed (549),* and, together with Tom Hayden, helped lead the campaign in The Michigan Daily to force fraternities and sororities to remove discrimination clauses from their constitutions! Supporting Kennedy in 1960 and the creation of the Peace Corps and Alliance for Progress, I grew up believing liberalism and U.S.-style democracy could be brought to Latin America by "right"-thinking people.

At the University of Florida from 1961-63 my liberal and social-democratic predilections were reinforced. That was an

---

*The numbers in parentheses in the text refer to specific references listed alphabetically at the end of the book; the small letters in parentheses refer to substantive or explanatory notes that follow each chapter.

intense period in the South of marches, demonstrations, and sit-ins to achieve racial equality, and I identified with and, albeit peripherally, was involved in the struggle. My mentor at Florida was an old-time, Norman-Thomas, League-for-Industrial-Democracy socialist, Harry Kantor, whose lead and enthusiasm I followed in supporting the Latin American democratic-left. My Master's thesis on the Trujillo dictatorship in the Dominican Republic and its methods of control was strongly condemnatory (555).

But thinking back over those years, there were other currents also present, which had a secondary place in my mental processes at the time but which would later assume greater importance. For although my major was political science, my minor was history; and at Florida, which then had an especially strong Latin American studies program, I worked closely with A. Curtis Wilgus, Donald Worcester, and Lyle N. McAlister, and was especially influenced by Professor Worcester's analysis of the Spanish past as an "enemy of change" and by Professor McAlister's studies of the "fuero militar" and the historic corporate role of the armed forces in Latin American politics (569, 570, 286-92). Teachers such as T. Lynn Smith, Raymond Crist, John V. D. Saunders, Alfredo Pareja, H. W. Hutchinson, Hugh Poppino, and Robert Bradbury--all with long experience in the field--were also skeptical of the "inevitability-of-democracy" framework and were more inclined to take Latin America on its own terms rather than through the lenses of a North American or European perception. Fellow graduate students at the time, such as Murdo MacLeod, Ronald C. Newton, Anthony Maingot, Burt English, Lawrence S. Graham, Warren Dean, Jack Hopkins, and Ièda Siqueira also viewed Latin America in nonethnocentric terms and from several quite varied political and sociological perspectives.

Reinforcing the liberal and social-democratic bias many of us held was the literature on political development, then emerging as the dominant paradigm in comparative politics. Almond and Coleman's <u>Politics of the Developing Areas</u> (14) seemed not only to provide an integrating framework but also to argue that development toward pluralism and social and political democracy was both morally correct <u>and</u> an inevitable process.

Armed with these "certainties" about the evolution and proper role of political parties, labor unions, churches, the armed forces, etc., in a pluralist democracy, I went to the Dominican Republic for a year to study these "developments" and write my doctoral dissertation. I believe it is fair to say that many graduate students of my generation, a sizeable number since we were the first products of the post-Fidel and NDFL-sponsored boom in Latin American Studies in the early-to-mid-1960s, went to other Latin American countries equipped with the same intellectual baggage of "developmentalism." It would be an interesting exercise to study the doctoral dissertations we all wrote at that time, the conceptual frameworks used, the conclusions reached, and the gravitation subsequently of our thought (a).

The Dominican experience was an eye-opener--and not just because it was my first extended research period abroad. I found, perhaps surprisingly given what has already been said, a good deal of "political development" in the Dominican Republic in the early

1960s in accord with the research design of my dissertation--emerging political parties and a competitive election, developing labor unions and peasant associations, a growing pluralism of groups and ideologies, social mobilization, and the like. But there were other aspects that didn't fit: workers' associations that failed to follow the "Western" model of trade unionism, a democratic government under Juan Bosch that was closer to the model of organic syndicalism than any democracy I had previously seen, major corporate groups such as the Army, Church, or oligarchy that insisted on dominating and monopolizing the system entirely rather than accepting their place as only one group among many in a pluralist structure (512, 515, 516, 528, 532, 533, 546). In addition, I began to see that the liberal-capitalist model of development and foreign aid, based largely on U.S. New Deal and Marshall Plan experiences, had little relevance for and often produced damaging and unanticipated consequences in countries like the Dominican Republic.

During that same period I rethought, did further research, and rewrote my earlier thesis on Trujillo, hardly excusing his brutalities but portraying him more sympathetically in the context of Dominican realities and aspirations rather than from a North American perspective (529, 530). I also included a chapter, that had not been a part of the original thesis, on Trujillo's organicist, corporatist, and authoritarian political ideology.

The prospects for democratic developmentalism in Latin America suffered a severe blow when John F. Kennedy was assassinated in 1963; in the Dominican Republic in 1964-65 I watched as the United States recognized and aided the military-oligarchic junta that had overthrown the democratic Bosch. As the atrocities and corruption mounted and the repression of the democratic forces increased, I wrote an article for the New Republic strongly critical of the existing government and U.S. support of it (554); for my pains, I was summoned to the American embassy and threatened with the revocation of my Fulbright-Hays fellowship unless I ceased writing such materials. My faith in democratic developmentalism then suffered a devastating and perhaps irreversible blow when the United States militarily intervened in the Dominican Republic in April 1965 to snuff out a democratic social revolution led by the pro-Bosch forces, and when we subsequently proceeded to help eliminate the very groups and agencies for development--labor unions, peasant associations, democratic political parties--that I had recently studied. Dominican friends and colleagues were killed and permanently scarred by the American intervention, the country was partially destroyed, and the natural course of its social and political development was retarded and stymied. Early in 1965 I had therefore become both very skeptical of the assumptions of the liberal-developmentalist model as applied to Third World countries like the Dominican Republic and thoroughly disillusioned with and alienated from my own government's foreign policy, some time before the larger intervention in Southeast Asia would similarly disillusion my colleagues. At the time of the Dominican intervention I wrote that the United States had already lost the Cold War as far as most Third World countries were concerned, a comment that I was not entirely sure I believed myself at the time but now from a longer perspective may well have been borne out (b).

In 1966 and 1968 we were in Brazil for extended periods conducting research for a monograph on the Catholic labor movement. In that research I was exposed to the same corporatist concepts that I had seen in Trujillo's ideology, although representing a somewhat different shading on the corporatist spectrum. I was also fascinated by the relations of the Brazilian Catholic labor movement to employers and to the state, the role of the Church and the clerical advisers within the organization, its nonmilitant emphasis on class harmony rather than conflict. These interests in turn led me to a close study of Vargas's corporative system, the nascent syndicalist scheme that Goulart had in mind, and the return to a more authoritarian and conservative corporatism by the Brazilian armed forces following the 1964 revolution (513, 560).

In the meantime I had also spent time in Mexico examining the corporatist structure of the PRI. I went to Nicaragua and to Paraguay where I was fascinated by the parallels with the Trujillo regime. I was particularly interested in the Paraguayan Council of State, a corporately organized and functionally representative body incorporating the major sectors of Paraguayan political society(c).

Since I thought I had a clue to their true nature, I was amused also by the early literature which was unable to decide whether the Paraguayan Febrerista Movement, the Bolivian Movimiento Revolucionario Nacional (MNR), or the Peruvian Apristas were "fascists" or "socialists." In Argentina about the same time I did work on the Peronist version of corporatism (or justicialism), and in Peru both the government of Belaunde Terry and the military regime that replaced him contained strong corporatist ingredients. In the meantime my wife was completing her doctoral dissertation on political parties in Venezuela, offering a corrective to some interpretations by showing how the Venezuelan partidos were a mix of both democratic features and more traditional Venezuelan ones (561). I was finding corporatism, or sometimes fusions of corporatist and more liberal-republican aspects, to be ubiquitous, present in traditional regimes as well as diversely modernizing ones, in regimes of the left (Cárdenas, Goulart, Bosch), which displayed various syndicalist-corporatist features, as well as regimes of the right (Trujillo, Vargas, Somoza, Stroessner). Many others (Perón, the MNR, some others) could not entirely accurately be labeled left or right. Moreover, contrary to the "development" literature, these corporatist-organicist features did not seem to disappear as modernization went forward; if anything, they were strengthened.

During 1969-70 I received a post-doctoral grant to spend a year in research and writing at the Mershon Center at Ohio State University. That year was a turning point since it enabled me, free from the usual teaching and academic committee obligations, to think through more thoroughly than previously the results of the diverse research projects in which I had been engaged and to explore more fully the theory, sociology, and background of the corporatism phenomenon. I rewrote my findings from the research in Brazil on the Catholic labor movement, stressing the more theoretical and corporatist aspects (514). I had the opportunity for the first time to rethink and rewrite my doctoral dissertation on the

Dominican Republic, a study that, reflecting my own ideas then in transition, stressed both the liberal-democratic and the corporatist forces at work there (531). I also had the time to read a great deal, in history and sociology, and it was at Ohio State in early 1970 that I first presented the paper on "The Corporative Model" of Latin American development that was subsequently refashioned for presentation to the American Political Science Association in 1971 and that became the <u>World Politics</u> article of January 1973 (551).

In the meantime I had also published two preliminary studies, one on "Law and Political Development in Latin America" (542) and the other exploring the "New Developmental Alternatives" (539) in the area, that from distinct perspectives also stressed corporatist themes. Another essay, entitled "Elites in Crisis" (536), designed as a companion to the <u>World Politics</u> piece and containing all the qualifications and discussion the latter could not, remained unpublished for a time after the editor's contract for a volume on Latin American Elites in which it was scheduled to appear was cancelled unexpectedly. That essay was eventually published (531) and most of the material is also contained in this volume; but had it appeared at the time it was written (1970), many of the misunderstandings and misconceptions concerning "The Corporatist Model" (i.e., that it is "tautological," that it provides a "culturalist" explanation) could have been avoided.

During all this period, of course, there was the Viet Nam War, Nixon, and Watergate. None of these events or persons would serve to increase one's faith in a democratic future, either at home or abroad. Meanwhile, the critiques of American liberalism as old, biased, and outdated were gathering momentum; the ethnocentrism of the development literature as regards Third World nations also came under broader strong attack. My contribution to this critique was included in the "Elites in Crisis" essay (536) which included an assault on the alternative "conflict" and "consensus" paradigms.

There was another factor operating in the late-1960s-early-1970s that also helped influence my decision to offer "The Corporative Model" as an alternative or supplemental explanation of Latin American development. The fact was that the decline of the developmentalist perspective had paved the way for the rise and growing acceptance of more radical, "structuralist," and Marxist interpretations, to the point where among students of the area this new orthodoxy seemed likely to supplant the older liberal-developmentalist paradigm. Finding useful and necessary features in both these approaches but opposed to orthodoxies of whatever stripe and not convinced either the liberal or Marxian paradigms provided a complete and sufficient explanation, I felt it was necessary to correct what I saw as a growing imbalance in the literature. Strongly critical myself of the biases in the developmentalist approach, but not entirely persuaded either by the Marxian categories, seeing both of these as starting points but not end points of explanation, I thought it important to fashion something of a middle way, to take what was useful from the development literature but also to incorporate into it the insights of class analysis and the "structuralists," while simultaneously incorporating materials and concepts from Latin America's own history and traditions.

"The Corporative Model" was hence offered not as a monocausal "culturalist" explanation, as is sometimes alleged, but as a way of complementing other explanations and of reemphasizing the importance and relative autonomy of historical, sociological, and political-cultural variables and the "distinctiveness" (that is, "distinct" from the dominant U.S. liberal-capitalist model) of the Iberic-Latin tradition, points which appeared to me to be almost ignored in much of the new literature. I sought to stress some "unique" (again as compared with the United States) features of Iberian and Latin American development and particularly the all-important role of the state and its efforts to manage and control the corporate group life that swirled about it (hence, the rather loose and broad formulation of "corporatism" in the early statement of the model); but this emphasis was not intended to exclude other explanatory variables or to stress the corporative aspects to the exclusion of all others. Nor did I mean to imply that corporatism was sui generis, only to be found in Latin America. Rather, I left open the possibility for corporatism to exist in other forms in other areas, and used that term as a shorthand or ideal type to help emphasize how and why Latin America diverged from the prevailing developmentalist models, themselves derived heavily from the Northern European and United States experiences.

Doubtless in making the case for "The Corporatist Model" I exaggerated it somewhat, and in criticizing alternative approaches I was perhaps too strong. But my actual purpose was to try to restore balance and perspective to the explanations then gaining currency, and my own methodology and research, as shown in this collection, remained eclectic, borrowing from diverse approaches, and utilizing the useful perspectives of the developmentalist and/or class-based explanations as well as the corporative one. I thought these points were clear (and to most readers they were) in my early statements of the corporative framework, particularly if one read the "Elites in Crisis" essay in conjunction with the better-known World Politics piece. But to some, apparently, the matter was not clear and gave rise to considerable misunderstanding and even some misrepresentation of what the corporative model was intended to convey. Hopefully, the explanation, chronology, and complete collection of writings presented here will help serve to correct such misconceptions.

In the summer and fall of 1972 we returned to the Dominican Republic, Brazil, and Venezuela; and during the remainder of the 1972-73 academic year we did research in Portugal for a book on the purest, in a formal-legal sense, and longest-lasting of the corporatist regimes established in the interwar period (519). Research in Spain during that same period provided an added comparative perspective. Returning to Iberia in 1974, 1975, 1977, and 1979 enabled us to study further the corporative aspects of both the Franco and Salazar-Caetano regimes and the more change-oriented (in the Spanish case) and revolutionary (in Portugal) governments that followed. Several articles, a monograph, and an edited volume on these themes were subsequently published (523-5, 545, 550, 552).

The broader European experience (England, France, Belgium,

Germany, Austria, Holland, Switzerland, Italy, and Greece in addition to Spain and Portugal) during this period helped provide a better understanding of the persistence, even resurgence, of corporatist forms and institutions in the advanced industrial societies of Northern Europe, in nations that had long prided themselves on their social-democratic structures, and not just in the Catholic cultures of Southern Europe and Latin America. Meanwhile a plethora of unsolicited letters (one of the joys of writing in a public forum) had begun to come in from diverse scholars working in other areas stating they had read my studies of corporatism and had found them useful in examining such widely scattered countries as Japan, Canada, Indonesia, Viet Nam, Yugoslavia, the Soviet Union, the Philippines, Zaire, and Tanzania. In turn, the Nixon-Ford experience with wage and price controls, the concentration of central authority under an "imperial presidency," the growth of officially sanctioned interest associations in American society, the emergence of central planning and state capitalism, and the spread of bureaucratic-technocratic rule led me to explore the growth of a corporatist structure in United States political society as well (541). Reading on Eastern Europe and the sense that, since I had studied corporatism in various state-capitalist systems, I should also see if it existed in state-socialist systems led me to a preliminary exploration of the structure of the Cuban state (527); another research project begun in 1979-80 involves a comparative study of labor and industrial relations in Southern Europe (Greece, Italy, Portugal, Spain), particularly the transition from state corporatism to a more liberal form and even, in two cases, to what might be called neo-syndicalism.

The published record of this conceptual and research journey is available in the public domain and a goodly share of it is collected in this book. What is not so easily available are the motives, history, and causes described here which helped shape the "sociology of knowledge" of corporatism and its rediscovery, at least in terms of the odyssey of one person. But it is worth noting also the number of scholars who have undertaken a journey somewhat parallel to my own--that is, beginning as Latin Americanists and then seeing that to comprehend the roots and origins of the Latin American systems they would have to undertake the trans-Atlantic journey to Iberia: Charles W. Anderson, Kalman Silvert, Paul Lewis, Philippe Schmitter, Juan Marsal, Lawrence Graham, Sidney Greenfield, doubtless others as well. Not all of them went by the same routes, nor did they necessarily arrive at the same ends or conclusions. Nevertheless the parallels and comparable experiences exist.

My own studies and research over this period have led me to some conclusions I would not even have thought about, let alone entertained seriously, as a graduate student oriented toward the use of models of democratic development fifteen years ago. I now find the general development literature of limited utility as a conceptual framework. It served to stimulate research in comparative politics and provided some useful heuristic tools, but as a comprehensive model to explain change in the Third World it takes us only part of the way. I am thoroughly disillusioned also with the effort to apply the representative-democratic model of the United States to culture areas where it does not fit, or fits only partially (518). I am no longer certain the model applies even to the United States or to the Western European nations from which it derived. And as a trained social scientist, I am even at the point of doubting whether a social science, properly so-called, exists or ought to exist, since I no longer have faith that very many of the social science maxims we hold to be universal are, in fact, universal. The fact is that virtually all our models derive from the Northwest European and United States experiences, and are only of marginal utility in helping us comprehend the quite different context of development today and in exceedingly diverse Third World nations. I am almost ready to call for the growth of a distinct social science for Latin America, or for other culture areas, since I find the general and universal models in which social scientists are ordinarily steeped to be so culture-bound and ethnocentric as to retard clear thinking about Latin America and its sociopolitical dynamics rather than enhance it (526, 537, 540). Meantime, I have begun to rethink, refine, and reanalyze some of my and others' earlier work on corporatism (521, 522).

The ideas and arguments are controversial and provocative and purposely so. They are meant to challenge old views and to suggest some potentially useful new approaches. But the journey is obviously not over and the ouvre still incomplete. In the collected essays and studies that follow, the discussion begins but does not end.

NOTES

a. Florida, North Carolina, Columbia, Wisconsin, maybe Berkeley, or one or two other places were the main centers for the study of Latin American politics during this period. An interesting survey could be done not only as regards the common impact of the development literature on the young Ph.Ds of that period, but also of the differences between the distinct perspectives these several graduate programs imparted.

b. Writings on the revolution include 517, 535, 538, 556. Some of my comments then on the United States intervention made headlines throughout Florida and even in the New York Times, and members of the Florida legislature demanded that I be investigated and removed from my teaching job. Although there are by now a number of useful books on the intervention written largely from a United States perspective, much remains to be said on these events from a Dominican perspective. Having researched and been closely involved in internal Dominican politics during the year immediately preceding the revolution, I intend one day to write an article analyzing what this research reveals the revolution was all about and what its goals were. I believe this will add a perspective not yet available in any of the published accounts and may contain some fresh and perhaps surprising research findings.

c. This research has never been published, and at this stage considerable updating and reassessment would be required.

2 | Is Latin America Democratic and Does It Want to Be? The Crisis and Quest of Democracy in the Hemisphere

> The United States seems destined by Providence to plague America with misery in the name of liberty.
> — Simón Bolívar

Everywhere in Latin America democracy seems to be dead, dying, or under siege. Twelve of the twenty republics (and the vast majority of the Latin American population) are presently governed by military regimes (a), and in five of the remaining countries the military is so close to the surface of power as to make the civil/military distinction nearly meaningless (b). It has now become commonplace to point to the decline of civilian democracy throughout the continent, the rash of military coups since the 1960s, the rise of corporate-authoritarian regimes in such formerly democratic nations as Chile and Uruguay, the use of torture and repression in Argentina and Brazil, and widespread violations of human rights. Meanwhile the number of genuinely democratic regimes has shrunk to a mere handful: Colombia, Costa Rica, Venezuela. And even these are often perceived to be elite-directed democracies (Colombia and Costa Rica) or else the product of such fortuitous circumstances (the vast quantities of oil in Venezuela) that their experiences are unlikely to be imitated elsewhere.

The problem is not just the rising tide of military-authoritarian-corporatist rule, however, but of a growing body of literature and interpretation that sees authoritarianism, corporatism, and elitism as essential, almost "natural" aspects of the Latin American tradition (304, 400, 545). Democracy and its usual accompanying paraphernalia (checks and balances, elections, separation of powers, free press, and the like) are often viewed in the newer interpretations as foreign and inappropriate, Anglo-American imports artificially imposed on a culture and society where they do not fit, ill-suited to Latin America's needs. In some of the overly deterministic and simplistic expressions of this argument, democratic reformism is hence viewed as futile, since if Latin America is <u>inherently</u> elitist and authoritarian no amount of democratic reform-mongering is likely to succeed. Democracy is in

---

From <u>The Continuing Struggle for Democracy in Latin America</u> (Boulder: Westview Press, 1980).

trouble in Latin America, therefore, not just because of spreading militarism but also because a whole new school and generation of Latin American historians and social scientists have pronounced it as irrelevant to or outside the main currents of the Latin American tradition. Sometimes these interpretations, by rationalizing it, have also provided, most often inadvertently, justification and legitimacy for military-authoritarian rule.

This essay and others collected here wrestle with these themes. They trace the preoccupation in Latin American studies with the issue of democratic development, the biases that perspective has given our understanding of Latin America, and the possibilities for a Latin American democracy based on its own rather than North America's conception of the term. They analyze the causes and manifestations of democracy's decline, as well as the possibility that the present wave of authoritarian-military regimes may, like others in the past, be a passing wave, ephemeral and not permanent.

The essays collected in this volume seek to clarify the meaning of the recent corporatist and bureaucratic-state interpretations of Latin America and whether these approaches militate against the possibilities for Latin American democracy or may be compatible with it. We shall also be examining the blends and fusions that may exist, for while corporatism and authoritarianism represent one, heretofore largely neglected aspect of the Latin American tradition, it is not the only one. There are strong liberal, democratic, and socialist currents as well, which should not be ignored or swept aside in our new preoccupation with these other themes. The fact is Latin America remains a mix, an amalgam of a corporatist-authoritarian tradition, a liberal-democratic one, and a newer socialist one. Much of politics centers on the conflict between these contrasting traditions and the various compromises and accommodations used to reconcile them. Among these are various democratic possibilities, though as we shall see, the form democracy takes will likely be closer to a Latin American understanding of that word than the North American. The struggle for democracy in Latin America will therefore continue, and it behooves us to know both the older and now largely outdated meanings of that term, the newer conceptions, as well as the elements in the struggle itself.

LATIN AMERICAN STUDIES AND THE QUEST FOR DEMOCRACY

Latin American studies in the United States have long been preoccupied with the presumed quest of the Latin American nations, whether real, imagined, or wishful, for democracy. From the early Puritan preoccupation with the "black legend" of Spanish--and Catholic!--atrocities, to the famous (or infamous) doctrine that bears the name of President Monroe, to Henry Clay's and John Quincy Adams's efforts to assist in separating Spain from her colonies, to the advocates of "manifest destiny" who in the name of democracy and progress deprived Mexico of half her national territory, to Teddy Roosevelt's and Woodrow Wilson's undoubtedly sincere efforts to bring, missionary-style, the "benefits" of democracy to "our little brown brothers," using a "big stick" or the Marines, if necessary, to Kennedy's Alliance for Progress and Carter's concern for human rights, the United States has consistently sought to export and impose its own democratic political institutions on an area which it has seen as mystifyingly authoritarian, chaotic, nondemocratic, Catholic—inquisitorial, "oligarchic," "feudal," or "underdeveloped" (165). Latin American studies in the United States, unhappily, have historically not only served as the handmaiden of this design and effort but have frequently provided the rationalization and intellectual justification as well (349, 469, 502).

The attempt to bring democracy U.S.-style to Latin America is not just a recent or ephemeral preoccupation but stems more basically from the historic drives, ambitions, and presuppositions of the North American nation. It reflects our Protestant and Lockean heritage and, conversely, our insensitivity and hostility toward the oftentimes nondemocratic and nonegalitarian assumptions of historic Catholic political culture (349). It reflects United States great power ambitions and it clearly also serves our foreign policy designs for hegemony in the Western Hemisphere.

Perhaps most important, it mirrors our sense of superiority, the notion that we are the most modern and developed of nations, the Churchillian idea that Anglo-American democracy is the "worst form of government except for all others," and the parallel presumption of the social sciences that the nations of the North (Europe and America) represent the leading cutting edge of "advanced" sociopolitical change whose experience can only be repeated and palely imitated--generally much later--by the nations of the South. Marx's dictum that "the more developed nations only show to the less developed the mirror of their own future" is perhaps the most well-known expression of this latter sentiment, though the belief is widespread in the social sciences among both Marxists and non-Marxists alike. Hegel provided an early, not a-typical, and particularly devastating comment which relegated the entire New World to pre-history, or non-history:

> What has taken place in the New World up to the present time is only an echo of the Old World--the expression of a foreign life--and as a Land of the Future, it has no interest for us here, for as regards History our concern must be with that which has been and that which is (201, 157).

Hegel (and much European and North American thinking since that time) left Latin America with only two possible alternatives: either becoming an echo of the old world and placing hope in the continent's future realization, "developing" toward and perhaps one day catching up with the model and example of the advanced nations; or, working for the assimilation of advanced "civilization" into Latin American life. But note that nowhere in either alternative does Latin America and its civilization have any value or worth of their own, let alone something that they could teach to the rest of the world; Latin America is only derivative. In short, we both as northerners (North Americans and North Europeans) and as social scientists <u>believe</u> the myth of our superiority and Latin American inferiority. Our social science and our policy initiatives all reflect this fundamental ethnocentrism (377, 474, 531, 537).

Despite the historic European and North American efforts--and sometimes because of them--the quest for democracy in Latin America seems not to have proved very successful. For as the quote from Bolívar with which we began this chapter implies, in the name of liberty and democratic development, we have as often plagued Latin America with misery as with good deeds. Democracy, as North Americans understand it, is in retreat, under attack from both the Right and the Left. A host of authoritarian-military regimes have substituted themselves for civilian representative rule. Elsewhere Left-authoritarians have taken power and effectively subverted the middle way of social-democracy. Human rights are frequently violated, coups occur with the same regularity as before, and the optimism for democracy that accompanied Kennedy's original Peace Corps and Alliance for Progress conceptions is now dead. Across the board, democracy appears to be faring badly; some would go so far as to pronounce Latin America's quest for the same--and by extension all of Latin American history--a "failure" (c).

It is difficult to think of history as a "success" or "failure," however. History is, rather, a neutral process, and unless one imposes a set of preconceived moral standards on it, it can hardly be branded a "success" or "failure." But perhaps that is part of the trouble with Latin American studies and helps explain why we so often think of Latin American history or development as "failed," "dysfunctional," or in terms of other euphemisms. Perhaps we have applied the wrong or inappropriate standards. Perhaps we have judged Latin America by U.S. standards and expectations rather than its own. Using U.S. standards or criteria of development and democracy, one would almost necessarily conclude that Latin America's history has been a "failure," for it has not developed the separate and coequal parliament or courts, the system of local government, the traditions of party politics, loyal opposition, regular elections, and so forth that we deem to be necessary for democratic growth. But are there other criteria that might be used, criteria that reflect Latin America's own expectations instead of North American, measures by which Latin American history may be judged a "success" and not a "failure"?

Latin Americanists have been of several minds on this issue, reflecting a debate that rages widely in the humanities and social sciences and with important policy implications, as to whether and to what degree there exist universal principles of "right" moral behavior (or developmental criteria) or whether these must be determined on a national, regional, or culture area level. Some scholars have cast their analyses within "the struggle for democracy" universal- or United States-style tradition. Others are skeptical whether "the struggle for democracy" theme is the proper and correct way to interpret Latin American history and politics and are frankly hostile to an approach they see as derived from the United States and with little relevance to the Latin American culture area. They would agree that it is impossible to label any history a "failure" and argue that our doing so reflects merely our own ethnocentric biases and not the realities of Latin American development.

Still others, while recognizing the biases and ethnocentrism that pervade a "struggle for democracy" focus that derives its chief assumptions from the United States's experience, have sought nonetheless to analyze what is, after all, a still genuine and deep-rooted Latin American desire for democracy. But these writers have tried to discover an indigenous Latin American sense and meaning of democracy, different from and perhaps not altogether inferior to the North American one. It is a critical and important debate, with major implications for Latin America, for our understanding of the area, and for policy. Building upon this discussion, a number of the studies collected here seek to reformulate and reconceptualize the "struggle for democracy" issue as it relates to Latin America.

LATIN AMERICA AND ITS "STRUGGLE FOR DEMOCRACY"

To what extent is Latin America democratic? To what extent does it wish or aspire to be? To what extent can Latin America be interpreted through a liberal and democratic model of development? These questions have from the beginning preoccupied both Latin Americans and outside students of the area. They continue to concern us today.

It is probably to be expected that the United States should seek to interpret--and remake--Latin America in terms of its own democratic ethos and institutions. We like to think of ourselves as "the greatest democracy on earth" and the tendency is probably natural to interpret the political affairs of others in the light of our own behavior and expectations. Nor is the tendency to view the rest of the world through its own ethnocentric biases entirely confined to the United States.

So long as the United States remained a minor power, our fervor for democratic rule was largely confined to moral suasion and righteous injunctions. We sympathized with the struggles of Latin America for independence from Spain and the efforts of these early "new nations" to write democratic constitutions and to fashion representative governments. But beyond that we seldom went, and our trade and contacts with the area in the early nineteenth century remained limited. The era of "manifest destiny" was probably the first large-scale effort to bring the "benefits" of democracy to territories that once belonged to Spain, to blend our desires to expand democracy with our self-interest and power ambitions and to use force if necessary to implement these goals. The Spanish-American War of 1898, in which under the guise of freeing Cuba, Puerto Rico, and the Philippines from the yoke of some supposed Spanish cruelty and oppression, we annexed them as colonies, represents another clear-cut effort on our part both to export our brand of democracy while simultaneously acquiring a series of client states and territories to serve our ambitions for major power status.

Although it would be easy to dismiss the speeches of our leaders regarding our concern to export democracy as mere rationalizations for baser motives, such a view would be too simple. There can be little doubt that William Jennings Bryan, Teddy Roosevelt,

and Woodrow Wilson were sincere in their desires to bring the
"blessings" of democratic rule to Panama, Haiti, Nicaragua, Cuba,
Mexico, the Dominican Republic, and other lands that we annexed or
landed the Marines. To dismiss our moral fervor for democracy as a
mere smoke screen for imperial designs and colonialism is to fail
to understand the American tradition and its, admittedly self-
righteous and ethnocentric, democratic ethos. Even Lyndon Johnson,
when he sent 20,000 troops into Santo Domingo and then even greater
numbers into Viet Nam in the two major interventions of the 1960s,
was operating, by his own lights, from the same liberal-democratic
premises (238). And who could doubt the sincerity of Jimmy Carter's concern for human rights, or the indignation of members of
the Latin American Studies Association in passing resolutions condemnatory of authoritarian regimes?

The issue would be simple if it only involved the attempt of
the United States to impose, by example or force, its particular
democratic conception on Latin America. The matter is complicated,
however, by the fact that in their laws and constitutions the Latin
American nations have apparently also adopted the democratic model.
"Checks and balances," "federalism," "bills of rights," and the
like were incorporated into the basic law of every Latin American
nation. Moreover, among Latin American intellectuals, particularly
during the nineteenth century but continuing to exist as a strong
strain today, liberalism and republicanism seemed to lie also at
the heart of Latin American aspirations (d).

The apparent quest of the Latin American nations for democratic representative rule--and the constant thwarting and frustration of those goals--produced several important results. Among
Latin American intellectuals and often the general public, it gave
rise to what may be termed the "myth of democratic incapacity," a
certain national inferiority complex, the belief that because of
some character or culture flaw Latin America was incapable of democratic rule, and hence a search for villains and scapegoats (364,
540). In some of the classic writings of Latin American sociology
the villains included the Church, caudilloism, the Spanish past,
the "hybrid" racial mix of the population, the Indian subculture,
independence from Spain, "feudalism," "capitalism," the United
States (e). The myth of democratic incapacity and the national
inferiority complex also inspired a frenetic search for other hol-
istic solutions also imported from the outside: republicanism,
positivism, socialism, communism, even fascism. Implied in the
search for outside solutions was the widespread belief in Latin
America, bolstered by the North American sense of superiority and
corresponding disdain for things or peoples Latin American, that
there was nothing of value in their own society, culture, and institutions. Only in relatively recent times, with the rise of
newer progressive and nationalistic movements, do we begin to see
developing new and innovative efforts to take, critically and
selectively rather than with the blind enthusiasm of the past,
what is useful from the outside and blend and fuse it with indigenous Latin American institutions and practices (f).

North Americans, too, looked at Latin America in terms of its
presumed quest for democracy. Scholars and journalists often took

at face value the articles in the Latin American constitutions providing for democratic rule. Naturally, since few of the Latin American states lived up to constitutional expectations, their histories were usually written in terms of their "frustrated" or "thwarted" march toward representative democracy. Latin America was pictured as "struggling" for democracy; but it was clearly a slow, pained, uphill, frequently reversible process. In perhaps the classic statement of this point of view, in a 1950 special edition of the <u>American Political Science Review</u>, the "Pathology of Democracy in Latin America" served as <u>the</u> focus. Only one of the contributors seemed troubled by that focus, pointing out that of the words in the title only "of" and "in" were neutral, while "Latin America" was itself a misnomer and "pathology" and "democracy" can get us into water as hot and deep, in his words, "as any that lies under the thin ice over which the social sciences skate" (100, g).

The "pathology of democracy" view shaped an entire generation--and more--of serious students of Latin America, perhaps the first to study the area in a serious way (h). Their interpretation, based strongly on the North American experience, was that Latin America represented a "flawed," "imperfect," "incomplete" yet "evolving" or "progressing" area for democratic growth. Few in the social sciences questioned whether democracy U.S.-style was desired, let along appropriate or functional for Latin America; that was simply assumed, not entirely unexpectedly in the light of the United States position as the world's leading power and influence in the post-World War II period. Even those who pointed out that Latin America was "different" still continued to hold out hope that one day it would develop more democratic institutions. The criteria used to evaluate Latin America remained strictly U.S.-based.

The "pathology of democracy" approach is interesting not just as an historical relic, however, but also because it helped determine the questions asked and conclusions reached. To a large degree this legacy still remains powerful. Thus, if democracy a la the United States is an ethical "good" to which Latin America also aspires, then military coups and interventions in civilian affairs are necessarily "bad" and to be condemned (264). If separation of powers is a superior moral principle, then the centralized organic systems of Latin America cannot possibly function well or democratically. If separating Church from state is similarly a sine qua non for democracy, then the Church's influence has to be curbed and pervasive Catholic culture eliminated (321). Along with the Army and the Church, the oligarchy, hierarchy, and elitist rule were viewed as the "enemies" of democracy which had to be overcome. Personalism, <u>continuismo</u>, caudilloism, executive predominance also had to be exorcised.

If some institutions were villified by ostensibly unbiased historians and social scientists and condemned to obsolescence or irrelevance, others necessarily had to be praised and elevated to a position of importance out of proportion to their real influence in Latin America. Thus, if personalism and a national patron-client system were "bad," political parties were "good"; and Russell Fitzgibbon admonished an entire generation of political scientists to study them. If caudilloism and all-powerful executives were "bad," then a stronger parliament, court system, and local government were all "good"--even though these institutions had seldom played much of a role in the Latin American tradition or were specifically assigned a weaker position than was true of North American constitutionalism. Based in large part on indices such as these (strong parliaments, courts, parties, local government, etc.), Professor Fitzgibbon published a series of articles purporting to measure the "progress of democracy" in Latin America every five years (148-52).

The point of these comments is not to disparage democratic values or institutions. The difficulty comes when scholars apply what are personal or particular values to Latin America. First, this emphasis has given rise to a great deal of what we may term "wishful sociology"--that is, analysis based more on our North American hopes for the area rather than on the actual experience of Latin America. Second, it reveals the pervasive ethnocentrism of our usual approach to Latin America, one based on liberal-Lockean and Anglo-American conceptions rather than one derived from Latin America's own experience. And third, the "pathology" focus has biased the questions raised and answers given in our study of Latin America, literally painting some institutions in the "blackest" of terms, glorifying others undeservedly, and meanwhile, because of these blind spots, ignoring the dynamics and realities of how politics and change in Latin America do, in fact, occur.

The most recent expression of the democratic bias in our approach to Latin America is the development literature, particularly that of the 1960s. Beginning with Almond and Coleman's enormously influential volume, The Politics of the Developing Areas (14), and finding expression also in the writings of the recent giants of the social sciences--Seymour M. Lipset, Karl Deutsch, Talcott Parsons, Reinhard Bendix, W. W. Rostow, Edward Shils--the mobilization of the democratic bias took a new and more sophisticated turn. Whereas the emphasis of the "older school" had been placed chiefly on institutions (congress, elections, courts, etc.), the newer approach heavily stressed political-sociological factors (the "input" functions). But interestingly, the "inputs" stressed as critical for a "modern" nation (political parties, a pluralist interest group structure, an informed citizenry participating in regular elections, and so forth) once again posited a political system that looked "just like us" and toward which other nations presumably inevitably "developed." The development literature emphasized "social mobilization" and such "prerequisites of democracy" as "middle-class societies" and broad (electoral) participation.

Again, few of us would quarrel with these ideals and certainly the development literature offered some new perspectives. But what bears emphasis are the familiar biases built into the approach. The "developed" society posited in the literature consistently bore a striking resemblance to the United States: democratic, pluralist, secular, achievement-oriented, and so on. "Traditional" institutions in Latin America and elsewhere, such as the Church, personalism, militarism, ascriptive behavior, familism, particularism, and the like, were condemned to disappear in the wake of "modernization." Although the terms are different and the biases somewhat less manifest, the dichotomies of the development literature bore a striking similarity to the older idea that U.S.-style democracy was "good" and everything else "bad."

The model of political society envisioned also derived largely from the United States experience, based on pluralist and democratic theory and assumptions (377). Not only were the major Latin American institutions dismissed as "backward" and "underdeveloped," but no thought whatsoever was given the possibility that "democracy" and "participation" might mean different things in different cultural contexts or be organized through distinct institutional mechanisms. And so an entire generation of graduate students, armed with this conceptual baggage, descended upon Latin America looking for a form of "development" that could not possibly exist. They studied political parties and "interest aggregation," political groups and "interest articulation," the emergence of "pluralism," elections, etc.--almost always from a U.S. perspective. Of course, few found these institutions and patterns functioning or even existent in most Latin American countries. It is no wonder that many of them wrote dissertations and learned articles pronouncing Latin America "underdeveloped" or "dysfunctional," for in the absence of institutions conforming to their preconceived notions of what a "developed" society looked like, they were bound to reach that conclusion. The same concepts and presumptions dominated our AID and foreign assistance programs during the 1960s and there the results were even more nefarious. For not only did AID seek to create institutions which had no solid grounding in Latin American realities (for example, community development programs based on the U.S. conception of strong, active local government) but it also served to undermine those Latin American institutions that did work by consigning them to the category of "traditional" and hence to the dustbins of history.

Although some, more experienced Latin Americanists were skeptical of the new approach from the beginning, it was not until later that the biases of the development model were examined. Then in a remarkably revealing autobiographical note published in 1970 that has not received the attention it deserves, Gabriel A. Almond, probably the most influential advocate of the developmentalist approach, stated explicitly the values and assumptions that had undergirded his earlier formulation (13). He writes that his first field experience in a developing nation came in 1962, several years <u>after</u> his basic theories had been advanced in <u>The Politics of the Developing Areas</u>, apparently <u>a priori</u>. And instead of the supposedly "neutral" and "scientific" variables used for analyzing the transition from "traditional" to "modern," we receive confirmation from Almond that the development concept also involved his personal "search for grace and redemption," that his concern was as much with promoting democratic development as analyzing it, that his model and the policy recommendations following from it were based more on a <u>faith</u> in democracy than on empirical research, and that he and the other members of the Social Science Research Council's Committee on Comparative Politics, whose concepts dominated the field during the 1960s, were caught up in what Almond calls the

Kennedyesque "Peace Corps mood" of the times--the effort to <u>bring</u> democracy and social justice to the less-developed nations.

From the foregoing it is clear that Almond and his colleagues were advocating not just "development" as a neutral process amenable to scholarly analysis but development as an ethical "good." Furthermore, development as they conceived it was tied intimately to the North American, or perhaps Northwest Europe-North American, experience and practice of democracy. Now, none of us could be against "development," just as we would not be against "democracy." Our point is not to question these values as values. But it is to show the biases of that approach, its grounding in a particular (United States and European) political tradition rather than on more universal principles, its biases and its fundamental ethnocentrism. For the terms are not "value free" and social-scientific but heavily charged and prejudicial; they have elevated our own political experience into a reified model for others to emulate, meanwhile dismissing the existing institutional arrangements of Latin America as outdated and irrelevant.

But other scholars have become convinced Latin American institutions cannot so easily be dismissed, and at the least the question of the universality of North American or Northwest European democratic norms and their applicability to Latin America should remain open instead of closed. One is tempted indeed to rephrase Bolívar to say that it is no longer in the name of liberty that the United States is destined to plague Latin America but in the name of "development." The questioning and assessment of just how relevant the democratic-developmentalist model is to Latin America lie at the heart of this discussion.

IMPLICATIONS OF THE DEMOCRATIC BIAS: A CRITIQUE

Viewing Latin America through the democratic prism of United States values and social science assumptions offers numerous advantages. It is a simple approach and easy to understand, and does not involve the complexities of mastering a foreign language and coming to grips with a foreign culture on its own terms rather than our own. It helps make us feel superior and "modern" by positing the United States as a moral and democratic society to which all other nations both aspire and inevitably develop. It is also a useful device for getting students interested in the area and, for a time, for prying foreign assistance funds from an often reluctant Congress. Moreover, on the surface, it seems to correspond to the goals of the Latin American nations, as expressed in their laws and constitutions.

While the approach that sees Latin American development in democratic or would-be democratic terms, based on the United States understanding of that term, is the historic, hallowed, and still venerated one, sentiment is now growing that it is a wrong and misleading focus. Among younger scholars especially, an attitude of severe questioning of the moral "superiority" of U.S. institutions has emerged, and a corresponding new appreciation of Latin American culture, civilization, and the special nature of its development processes. The sense is now widespread that the U.S.-inspired

democratic focus has not only perpetuated our misunderstandings of
Latin America but, in serving frequently as a smoke screen for
other U.S. purposes, has wreaked downright harm on the area. Some
of the criticisms and ramifications of the "democratic" bias may be
summarized as follows:

    1. The approach is ethnocentric, patronizing, preachy. The
U.S. model is no longer widely admired abroad, nor is United States
society any longer viewed as the ideal end-product of the development process. Any approach that sees the rest of the world exclusively through North American eyes is bound to be biased and false.
Such moral superiority may have been appropriate when the United
States was the world's greatest power, widely admired and emulated,
but those times have passed. A large dose of cultural relativism
is now required, a new <u>verstehen</u> approach, an ability to deal with
other societies on their terms and in their own language (127,
383). That obviously does not mean that we stop making moral judgments or that cultural relativism be carried to the point of
accepting a Hitler. But it does imply that we avoid knee-jerk
judgments, that we hold our moral righteousness in abeyance until
we fully understand the phenomena we would otherwise be quick to
condemn. We may even want to empathize with the policies of a
Fidel Castro or an Omar Torrijos, for example, instead of condemning them as "Caribbean despots" or "tin horn dictators." For the
efforts missionary and Peace Corps style to bring the "benefits" of
"democracy" to "our little brown or black brothers" a la Teddy
Roosevelt, Wilson, Kennedy, or Carter will no longer do; in fact,
such efforts in the present context not only won't work but may
well prove counterproductive. President Carter's efforts to
impose a United States-centered concept of human rights on Latin
America provides a major case in point: not only will such pressures not change the attitudes of Latin America's governing elites
but, as the ruptures with Argentina, Brazil, Chile, El Salvador,
and Uruguay indicate, they may produce a harmful backlash. In
short, the U.S. model will no longer wash, and efforts to impose it
are almost certain to produce harmful and unanticipated consequences.

    2. The view that sees Latin America as struggling toward democracy, or pictures its political evolution as a constant conflict
between "democracy" and "dictatorship," "enlightenment" versus
"reaction" is far too simple and unidimensional. Thinking in such
terms is too confining. It not only glosses over the realities of
Latin American politics and change but it ignores the various
alternative positions and types of regimes spaced out between these
polar extremes, where in fact <u>all</u> the Latin American nations are
situated. The "dictatorship"-"democracy" framework restricts the
range of developmental alternatives and ignores other possibilities. Forcing Latin America to choose between the one and the
other imposes a constrictive straitjacket on the area and implies a
series of false choices instead of realistic ones. Latin America
has historically demonstrated a genius for improvisation and compromise between its abstract stated goals and the actualities of
its social, political, and economic life. The time has come when
we may begin to appreciate the genius and functionality of such

halfway houses, rather than belittling or condemning the area out of hand or forcing it to choose artificially among unrealistic alternatives. Even the terms in which we discuss Latin America and attempt to impose our preferred solution on it, are, in short, a form of cultural imperialism (520).

3. Viewing Latin American history as a "struggle for democracy," one must almost necessarily brand that history as "unsuccessful," since few if any countries of the area have fully lived up to the goals their constitutions proclaim. But history, we have already said, cannot be "successful" or "unsuccessful" unless we impose some "higher" criteria on it--in this case the biased, ethnocentric criteria of U.S.-style democracy. By these criteria Latin American history may indeed be a "failure" but by others--to be advanced below--it may be considered about as "successful" as that of other nations. The moral conclusions reached depend obviously on the measures used and the values underlying them.

The "history-as-failure" theme also finds recent manifestation in the development literature, where the term "dysfunctional" is used instead. Thus, if political parties in Latin America fail to develop or perform the functions ascribed to U.S. political parties, they must be "dysfunctional." If the trade unions fail to adopt a nonpolitical, collective-bargaining orientation, they must be "dysfunctional." If a "middle-class society" fails to develop on the U.S. model, several things may be "dysfunctional." If the armed forces refuse to remain subservient to civilians, they must be "dysfunctional." The same goes for AID programs, based similarly on the U.S. model. If the agrarian reform, administrative "modernization," family planning, and other programs introduced largely through U.S. initiative fail or produce unintended consequences, it is not the programs or their assumptions that are at fault but the Latin American systems which are again "dysfunctional." But note the "dysfunctional" label in all these areas is always used with regard to North American criteria. Furthermore, what North American social science has pronounced "dysfunctional"--personalism, nepotism, coups, political trade unions, military intervention, and the like--may be quite functional, albeit not necessarily attractive, in Latin American political society. We need obviously to examine the functionality of numerous Latin American institutions, but the criteria to be used must be theirs, not ours (i).

4. Looking at Latin America not through its own eyes but through our culture-bound perspectives serves not only to perpetuate myths about the area but also to retard our understanding of how Latin American institutions actually do function. Instead of simply lamenting or condemning the irregularity of democratic elections, it may be suggested we should instead examine the dynamics and regularities of coups and the coup process (526). Instead of our usual knee-jerk condemnations of the "oligarchy," we might more appropriately examine the realities of elite circulation and renewal (551). Instead of expressing wishful thinking about the future pluralist-participatory role of peasants and workers in the political process, we might, perhaps more importantly, concentrate on the corporative control mechanisms used to structure their

participation, as well as the structured violence these same groups in turn use to make their influence felt (384).

Hence, instead of speaking about the "pathology of democracy" in Latin America, let us look carefully at the actual functions of elections, parliaments, parties, and the like. And rather than condemning the military out of hand as a "predatory force," let us examine realistically the overlaps and dynamic crosscurrents of military-civilian politics. Instead of dismissing as "false consciousness" the conservative attitudes peasants and workers frequently hold, let us consider why such values remain so strong and often quite rational. A host of such challenging questions and research areas exists for which answers will not be found if we continue to study Latin America in the light of the U.S. experience. But we can begin to deal with these issues if we start to treat Latin American institutions and political practices realistically, without condescension, in terms of how these institutions function within the Latin American context and not by some presumed "universal model" that upon close examination derives directly from the United States (469, 537).

5. The use of a "democratic model" of development derived from the United States would not be so dangerous if it involved merely ethnocentrism. The trouble is the "democratic smoke screen" has been used as a cover for far more dangerous acts. Under the banner of "democracy" we have invaded, occupied, and sometimes pillaged various Latin American countries. Using the same "democratic" cover, we have helped overthrow governments in Brazil, Chile, Ecuador, the Dominican Republic, Guatemala, Honduras, and other nations. Our CIA has subverted and helped ruin the Latin American labor movement; our military missions have myopically strengthened the one institution in Latin America that hardly needs strengthening; we have assassinated heads of state and numerous others; we have inflicted violence by hired street thugs, strafed and napalmed rural villages, taught modern torture techniques. Under the guise of reform and democratization, we have reorganized the land title systems of several Latin American nations chiefly to the advantage of U.S. investors; those same rationalizations have facilitated the economic penetration and machinations throughout the continent of the big corporations and multinationals. Whether we approve of any or all of these actions or not, and though many of our policies have produced positive as well as negative results, there can be no doubt that "democracy" and "development" have frequently been useful handmaidens of United States imperialism in Latin America. They give "democratic" legitimacy to actions that would otherwise be seen as nefarious and self-serving (47, 187, 200).

6. The use of the "democratic" label implies not just political and economic imperialism but cultural imperialism as well. Is it not the ultimate in arrogance that we should presume to judge Latin America not by its values but by our own? How presumptuous of us to force our criteria of the just society on a culture area where the beliefs and traditions are quite different! Is it not a form of cultural imperialism to impose the norms and formulae derived from European and North American social science on an area

where they fit imperfectly at best? Why should we expect Latin
America to imitate our institutions or live up to our criteria when
its history and background are distinct? Do we really know what's
best for the rest of the world and is it not terribly conceited of
us to think that our form of government is the best for all times
and places? The assumption that we do have all the answers and
that it is our right and duty to export them seems to constitute a
form of imperialism as much as the economic sense of that word.
What perhaps is the ultimate in such cultural imperialism is the
fact that so many Latin Americans themselves "bought" these same
myths of the natural "superiority" of the United States and the
inferiority, incapacity, and lack of worth of their own culture and
institutions. But that is another story that deserves full-length
treatment of its own (157, 317, 540).

THE "STRUGGLE FOR DEMOCRACY" THEME: A REEXAMINATION
AND A LOOK AHEAD

Up to this point we have been rather harsh, both on the
"struggle for democracy" literature as it is applied to Latin America and on those who have advanced such views. Let us look at some
more complex dimensions of the issue.

The fact is those who look on Latin America exclusively
through the ethnocentric perspective of the United States experience, or those who use "democracy" as a smoke screen to disguise
less glorious pursuits deserve all the lumps and condemnation here
given. And it is true that for a long time the "pathology of democracy" approach dominated much academic thinking on Latin America.
But the situation is not so simple. For there is a tradition of
genuine struggle for democracy in Latin America, and it should not
simply be set up as a straw man all that much easier to knock it
down.

In the first place, there is a powerful current of Latin American thought and action--although probably not a majority current
anywhere in the area--that remains committed to democratic, representative government in the liberal-Lockean sense. This element
takes seriously the principles of separation of power, checks and
balances, an a-political military, etc., as articulated in the laws
and constitutions. It believes in political parties, regular elections, limited government, the classic human rights, and representative government in the Anglo-American sense. Like the older generation of U.S. political scientists concerned with Latin America,
it sees the struggle for democracy there as a long, uphill process.
But it remains committed to the struggle while also recognizing
democratic theory and practice in Latin America may never be fully
reconciled (j). Except in a mere handful of countries, this concept of democracy is limited to a generation that is now fading
from the scene.

A second, newer current in Latin America remains committed to
social and economic democracy, but political democracy has been
largely abandoned. This posture is strong among intellectuals and
university students, where the admiration for the United States
political system has waned or disappeared but where the demand for

redistribution of national resources is powerful. The assumptions of this group tend to be Marxian rather than Lockean; it usually dismisses or denigrates the political variables and institutions about which North American political scientists write and concentrates on the themes of dependency, class structure, colonialism, and imperialism. "Democracy" has not been entirely abandoned as a national goal but it has been redefined in socioeconomic terms instead of political (k).

A third group, both within Latin America and with its counterparts in North American academe, has abandoned democracy as a goal all across the board. It tends to emphasize Latin America's authoritarian tradition and dismiss its democratic one as mere concessions to foreign fads. Beneath the democratic facades of those laws and constitutions, this argument runs, are a host of provisions that provide for authoritarianism and special privilege. The extensive powers of the president; the weakness of courts, congress, and local government; the special privileges given the Army and the Church; the restrictions on the franchise and popular participation--all point to the conclusions that Latin America's founding fathers intended from the beginning not to enshrine democratic principles but authoritarian, elitist rule. The principles of separation of powers and so on were merely "para ingles ver" ("for the English--or Americans--to see") but were not meant to correspond to actual reality. In this view the Latin American tradition has never been, or aspired to be, democratic but rather authoritarian and, in Glen Dealy's words, "monistic" to its core (113). This frankly authoritarian tradition finds present-day expression in the authoritarian-technocratic regimes of Argentina, Brazil, Chile, Mexico, Nicaragua, Peru, Uruguay--regimes that are not just authoritarian but often take pride in same and laud it as an integral, "natural" part of the Latin American tradition.

Still a fourth position--and one that may well now represent the dominant one, although with ample room for variation within this category--tries to blend and reconcile the democratic with the more authoritarian traditions. This view sees both currents operating simultaneously in Latin America and seeks to analyze the blends and overlaps as well as the conflicts that may exist between them, the various intermediary types. It rejects the simplicities of the "pathology of democracy" approach, based as it is on North American perspectives, but it also recognizes the democratic tradition in Latin America--in its sense of the word rather than ours. It seeks to understand what Latin America means by such terms as "rights," "participation," "pluralism," "representation," even "democracy" itself, and to relate that to the broader Latin American political tradition, rather than imposing a U.S. understanding on the area.

At the same time this approach seeks to understand coups, military intervention, patron-client relations, and the like in the light of Latin American expectations and political behavior, not just condemn these features out of hand. It may favor "pluralism" and "social justice" but it does so on Latin American terms, not North American. It seeks to comprehend what elections or the voting act means in the Latin American context and how and why these are different from the U.S. conception. It comes to grips with civil-military relations not from the point of view of a more "advanced" political culture where coups do not occur but in the light of a Latin American political culture where these and other forms of violence are a normal, regular part of the political process. This approach, in short, shows how the democratic and the authoritarian traditions, both strongly present in Latin America, may be combined and reconciled, fudged over, and sometimes ignored altogether. Alternatively, it shows how the presence of such conflicting traditions may lead to violence, fragmentation, and a situation of long-term crisis. Probably the majority of the papers in this collection could be characterized as within this tradition of seeking a more realistic interpretation of Latin American politics and social change, of reconciling or seeking to show the crazy-quilt patterns of an area where both democratic institutions and authoritarian, elitist, and corporatist ones have been strong (1).

Seen in this light, it may yet be possible to reconcile a concern for democracy in Latin America with the sophisticated and realistic scholar's recognition of the strength of other currents, or the special meaning democracy carries in Latin America, or the ingenious overlaps and blends that exist. We shall be approaching these issues from distinct perspectives. Throughout, however, our concern remains the viability of democracy in Latin America, the appropriateness of the democratic focus, the special meaning democracy carries in that culture context, and the possibilities for dynamic and development-oriented fusions of the democratic and the corporatist traditions.

NOTES

a. Argentina, Bolivia, Brazil, Chile, Ecuador, El Salvador, Guatemala, Honduras, Panama, Paraguay, Peru, Uruguay.

b. Cuba, the Dominican Republic, Haiti, Mexico, Nicaragua. Cuba and Mexico may be special cases.

c. The "history as failure" theme dominates much popular, official, and journalistic thinking on Latin America, as well as the more scholarly works with titles such as "One Minute to Midnight in Latin America," "Latin America: Evolution or Revolution," "One Spark from Holocaust: The Crisis in Latin America," or "Latin America: The Eleventh Hour."

d. Although the democratic ideas were widely diffused through Latin America during the nineteenth century, incorporated in the basic laws and constitutions, and seemed everywhere triumphant, the precise meaning of that term remained unclear. Writers such as Bolívar, Sarmiento, Alberdi, and Herrera remained skeptical of the suitability of democratic, representative government in Latin America, and as early as the 1830s the democratic ideas had been redefined in terms of a more conservative, elitist, and authoritarian vision. Beginning in midcentury with the influence of positivism, the conservative and elitist revision of the earlier democratic idea was further reinforced. On this, see especially 111.

e. Some of the classic statements include Tibor Mende,

America Latina Entra en Escena; Francisco García Calderon, Latin America; Manuel Ugarte, Destiny of a Continent; Alcides Arguedas, Puebla Enferma; Julio Ycaza Tigerino, Sociologia de la Politica Hispanoamericana; José E. Rodo, Ariel; German Arciniegas, The State of Latin America; Antenor Orrego, Pueblo Continente; Luis Alberto Sánchez, Examen Espectral de America Latina.

    f. The Apristas, for example, sought to borrow from democratic and Marxist theory but to adapt it to the realities of Latin Amerida (232). Other interesting efforts during this period to blend outside ideologies with indigenous realities include Vargas's Brazil, Perón's Argentina, Mexico and the PRI.

    g. Professor Crawford went on to say, "The term 'pathological' suggests too strongly a complacent superior attitude on our own part that may fit the propagandist or the naive and uninformed man on the street, but not the social scientist. The world does not fall into the patterns of perfect democracy and the outer darkness as Mr. Churchill has supposed. Can we not accept a certain relativity in these matters and remember the large-sized mote in our own eye?"

    h. In the 1940s and 1950s one thinks particularly of the general works by Asher Christensen, Russell H. Fitzgibbon, Austin MacDonald, J. Lloyd Mecham, William S. Stokes, Harold W. Davis, Rosendo Gomez, Miguel Jorrín, and William Pierson and Federico G. Gil.

    i. As L. N. McAlister argues, military intervention in politics in Latin America may be neither "pathological," "aberrant," nor "dysfunctional" but a normal, regular, quite functional part of the political process (292).

    j. Based on my own research experience in the Dominican Republic, I am consistently surprised to find how strong the liberal-democratic tradition is there, despite the unhappy history of dictatorship and American intervention and the spreading popularity of other, more radical solutions.

    k. Many of the "dependencia" writers fall within this school, such as Fernando Henrique Cardoso, Pablo González Casanova, Anibal Quijano, Julio Cotler, Octavio Ianni, Theotonio dos Santos.

    l. These themes also lie at the heart of both the general analysis and the country-by-country treatments in 557.

Part 2
Corporatist Theory
and the Corporatist Model

In Part 2 the theoretical background and main concepts of the corporatist model are discussed. The first essay discusses the history and context of Latin America and places its developmental pattern in comparative perspective. It provides useful background on the origins of corporatist forms of social and political organizations in the area. The second presents one of the earliest outline statements of corporatism and the "corporative model." The third discusses the alternative "conflict" and "consensus" models while further refining and qualifying the corporative approach. The fourth essay analyzes both the persistent historical strains as well as the newer manifestations of corporatism in a variety of regimes. The final essay specifically traces the historical theory and ideology of corporatism, as a complement to the sociopolitical analyses presented earlier.

3 | The Latin American Development Pattern

Much of Latin America is today in ferment. Profound social and economic transformations are shaking and undermining the traditional structure of society, and in the political sphere the rising tide of revolutionary pressures threatens to sweep away or inundate the efforts of various kinds of regimes--military or civilian, conservative or reformist--to cope with and manage these changes and to promote national development. This is not to say, however, that revolution a-la-Castro's Cuba is an immediate prospect for Latin America, for in most of these countries, it is generally agreed, the conditions are simply not ripe for a <u>Fidelista</u>-like revolution (310, 325). But there is a growing realization, or fear, that <u>no regime</u>--be it Christian-democratic, military-Nasserist, democratic-Left, Castroite, or whatever--will be able to deal successfully with the interlocking vicious circles of Latin American underdevelopment. For despite--and sometimes because of--a greater United States foreign assistance program for Latin America during the 1960s, despite our Alliance for Progress and Peace Corps, despite the efforts of various Latin American regimes to promote development, and despite the designation of the 1960s as the "decade of development," it is clear that the majority of the Latin American states did not develop as expected or as anticipated, that in many areas living standards have declined and the gaps between haves and have-nots widened, that stagnation, immobilism, and decay rather than development have been the hallmarks of many of the Latin American nations in recent years, and that the prospects for the future appear dim. Moreover, none of the great developmental panaceas advanced during the previous decade for resolving these problems seem any longer to offer the great promise they once did (130, 299, 413, 539).

Rather than any great or "glorious" revolution, therefore, or very much successful "develop-mongering" (to borrow Hirschman's apt phrase--206), what we are likely to witness at least in the near future is continued muddling along, exceedingly slow and gradualist

---

From "Elites in Crisis: The Decline of the Old Order and the Fragmentation of the New in Latin America" (Columbus: Ohio State University, Mershon Center, 1970); published as Chapter 1 of 531.

change by fits and starts, at a time, however, of rising revolutionary pressures and of growing impatience with the traditional methods. Thus, the immediate prospect in many of the Latin American countries, it may be suggested, is neither a radical restructuring, on the one hand, nor a sound and successful development strategy, on the other, but a growing incapacity on the part of government to respond effectively to the new pressures that have been thrust upon it. This is likely to result in increased societal and political division and polarization, the growth of tension, conflict, and violence (which, however, falls short of full-scale revolution), accelerated instability and chaos, the aggravation of crisis until it spirals into a widespread phenomenon and becomes a virtually constant feature of these Latin American political systems, and, perhaps ultimately, the ever-present possibility of society-wide collapse and disintegration. This is a rather dismal prognosis, to be sure, but one suspects that for at least some of the Latin American countries it may be a fairly accurate and realistic one. Indeed, that may already be the situation in countries as diverse as Argentina, Bolivia, Chile, Guatemala, the Dominican Republic, Uruguay, and perhaps others (136, 211, 224, 372, 373, 467).

The difficulty would seem to lie in the fact that, while the traditional elitist order in Latin America is currently in decline, this has not been accompanied by the rise and consolidation of a new and more "modern" one to replace it. Instead, what we are seeing is the continued coexistence of old and new, of traditional and modern, in a hodge-podge, heterogeneous, frequently crazy-quilt pattern that not only defies our common conceptions of the development process but is also actually inhibitive of genuinely national growth (135). No one group or ideology can command unquestioned legitimacy or wholly dominate these societies any more; rather, there is a growing plurality and differentiation of ideologies and social groups. But whereas in the context of North America or Western Europe, greater pluralism proved generally to be a dynamic and positive force for development and increased democratization, in Latin America it has resulted in the growth of increasingly fragmented, disjointed, and dysfunctional sociopolitical systems. There has thus been precious little "development" in Latin America in either a Marxian or Weberian sense; on the contrary, the trend has been toward rising anomie and alienation, toward institutional atrophy and decay, and toward what Ortega y Gasset referred to as invertebrate societies. The argument of the present essay is that the familiar models of socioeconomic and political change have been of limited use to us in comprehending the peculiar nature of the change process in Latin America, but that by recasting our thinking and analysis somewhat in terms of what is referred to here as the "corporative model," we gain some new perspectives and perhaps a fresh insight into the distinctive aspects of Latin American development.

In the discussion that follows, an effort is made, first, to trace briefly the pattern of Latin American development and then to offer an interpretation as to why the development process has proceeded the way it has. There is little in this first and

historical section that is strikingly new or original, especially
for Latin Americanists; but it does provide an indispensable base
for the more theoretical considerations that follow and may contain
some ideas and suggestions that will be of interest even to the spe-
cialist. The approach of this section is analytic and interpretive
rather than detailed and exhaustive. The heart of the argument,
however, is contained in the following chapters, where an attempt
is made to fashion a conceptual framework that is more in accord
with and helps us better explain the unique features of the development and/or change process in Latin America. The framework presented is as yet in the formulative and preliminary stage, subject
to a great deal of further refinement and explication. But it
does, I believe, have certain advantages over the other major general theories that have been used to explain Latin American development (or the lack thereof), for it not only encompasses what is
useful and relevant in these other approaches but at the same time
goes beyond them to reflect more accurately the realities of power
and society in the Latin American context. The conceptual schema
here outlined also points us toward some heretofore largely
neglected areas of research and suggests some patterns and interrelationships that have thus far not been treated adequately in the
literature. What remains to be done, therefore, is both a more
detailed elaboration of the model as well as its further investigation and testing in field situations and with greater empirical
data.

   Latin America has always been woefully misunderstood, not only
in the United States but in much of the rest of the world as well.
One suspects that the reason for this is that we have almost always
looked at Latin America through our own rose-colored glasses and
have tried to apply our own criteria of the "good" society and polity to a region where the traditions are quite distinct. This is
perfectly understandable, for we all tend to impose a framework
derived from our own socialization experiences on the world around
us; indeed, it is virtually impossible for us to avoid bias and
preconceived notions when examining political behavior in societies
other than our own. However, as social scientists we are obligated
to try to be as neutral as possible, without prejudice--or at least
making our biases explicit where they do impinge upon the research
and analysis. We must, this essay argues, seek to understand Latin
America <u>on its own terms</u> and <u>in its own context</u>. Our obligation is
to try to comprehend the Latin American experience within its own
framework and to derive more general propositions from that experience, not bring to bear a set of expectations, concepts, and categories derived from outside the hemisphere which are ill-suited to
an understanding of the nations of Latin America (a). We cannot
seek to impose some narrow, preconceived general theory on a society where it does not fit or comprehend Latin America's unique
development pattern exclusively in the light of our own or of that
of Western Europe. This essay does not entirely avoid these parochial and ethnocentric pitfalls, but it does attempt to come to
grips with the realities of Latin American development on its own
terms and using a model of change that grows out of the actual
Latin American experience. Only by continuous efforts in this

direction can we begin to comprehend adequately a region that we
have only weakly understood in the past and develop a model of
political development that is genuinely comparative and scientific.

THE COLONIAL ERA: THE ESTABLISHMENT OF THE
TRADITIONAL STRUCTURE

A good starting point for the study of Latin American society
and politics--not just of its traditional order but of much of its
present-day style and structure as well--is to think in terms of a
fairly well-defined, rigid yet adaptable, hierarchically and vertically segmented system of class and caste stratifications, social
rank orders, estates, juridical groupings, corporate bodies,
elites, and <u>intereses</u>, revolving around, tied to, and deriving
legitimacy from the authority of the central state or its leader.
The historical origins of this system lie in the remote Iberic
past, most particularly the Roman era with its corporative group
structure; the late-medieval and early-modern growth of corporations
such as the Church, the military orders, towns, and the state itself; and the early-modern attempts to blend and accommodate the
medieval-Catholic concepts of hierarchy, natural law, and estates
with the newer requisites of centralization, absolute monarchy, and
the Conquest. The intellectual-religious rationalizations for the
structure derive chiefly, in Richard Morse's analysis (348), from
organic and Catholic principles as found in Aristotle and Thomas
Aquinas, and from the concepts of hierarchy and the functional and
corporative organization of society. Socially and economically,
the pattern stems in large measure from the peculiar development of
the Spanish economy and society during the <u>Reconquista</u> and on into
the period of social consolidation that followed (172). Politically, the model derives from the emerging pattern of royal absolutism and from the structure of the Spanish administrative empire.
The Latin American systems have thus traditionally been based upon
a social and political order that is hierarchical, authoritarian,
elitist, patrimonial, Catholic, stratified, feudal, corporatist,
and patriarchal to its core; and any attempt to comprehend the
Latin American experience must take these fundamental factors into
account.

At this time--that is, roughly 1500--the elites of Europe,
particularly those of Spain, conceived of society chiefly in terms
of "orders" or "estates." If one prefers, one can also use the
word "class," though it should be remembered this term often carries a different meaning in Iberia and Latin America, referring not
just to economic classes but to the military "class," the medical
"class," etc. Further, by concentrating on but one albeit crucial
dimension of social structure, its horizontal layers, the term does
not adequately convey how Iberian and Latin American society is
organized vertically in terms of major corporate groups as well.
Social structure there must be viewed as organized along <u>both class
and corporate lines</u>. At this stage, therefore, it seems useful to
think of Iberia and Latin America as structured both horizontally
by classes and vertically in terms of a variety of corporate entities, groups of people bound together by similar functions,

interests, occupations, locations, etc. In much of Europe these corporate groups--Church, guilds, Army, artisans, craftsmen, merchants, traders, farmers, universities, municipalities, and so on--came to be represented through constituted assemblies, parliaments, or estates general. In Spain, however, with the dissolution of the Cortes, what representation existed was organized directly and through a compartmentalized vertical arrangement centering in the Crown (188, 297, 408). Though oversimplified, the system may be envisioned schematically in terms of an inverted cone or pyramid, structured vertically into its component corporate units, organized horizontally so as to form a series of layers or classes with the lines between them rigidly drawn, and with a broad base, narrowing sharply as it reaches the top, and reaching the apex in the Crown, as shown in Figure 3.1.

Each corporate group, as well as each layer in the hierarchy, had its own legal status and its own special privileges ("<u>fueros</u>") and responsibilities, which were believed to correspond to Natural Law or to God's just ordering of the universe. There could, therefore, be no questioning of the system, no bridging of its boundaries, no mobility, and little overlap. Men were simply expected to accept their respective stations in life. One tended to identify with his own small locality or corporative group, and there were few contacts outside one's own "class" or corporate unit. One was born into his parents' notch in the system, lived and married into the same class or social group, and died there. One's children followed the same pattern. In this way there was little crossover and mobility, few possibilities for improvement or advance; society was viewed as fixed and immutable. Little fundamental change could or did take place.

When men began to talk of "liberties" and "rights," they were generally speaking not in the same terms as their Anglo-Saxon counterparts but in what they saw as nonpolitical terms concerning inalienable fiscal or juridical privilege, a chance to occupy the specially favored place within the system to which they felt they were entitled. "Feudalism" thus meant primarily the system of peasant and mass obligations under the patrimonial, manorial system and the differences between the nobles, the commoners, the clergy, and eventually the Army and other groups in such areas as taxation, landholding, and the various sociojuridical distinctions by orders and estates generally. This system, much of which remains intact today, though frequently dressed up in "modern" apparel, was quite different from that which England transferred to her colonies. In fact, many of the differences between England and to a lesser extent France, on the one hand, and Spain, on the other--and between the English and the Spanish colonies in the New World--may be explained by the fact that at the time of the conquest of the Americas the institutions and practices on which English liberalism and eventually a <u>bourgeois</u>, industrialized nation were built were virtually nonexistent in Spain and her American fragments. At the same time, the regime of corporate privilege and hierarchy remained largely intact in Spain and her colonies at a point when it had all but disappeared from Britain and her colonies (197, 198). This structure and tradition have died hard in the nations of Latin

FIGURE 3.1
Structure of Spanish Society and Polity*

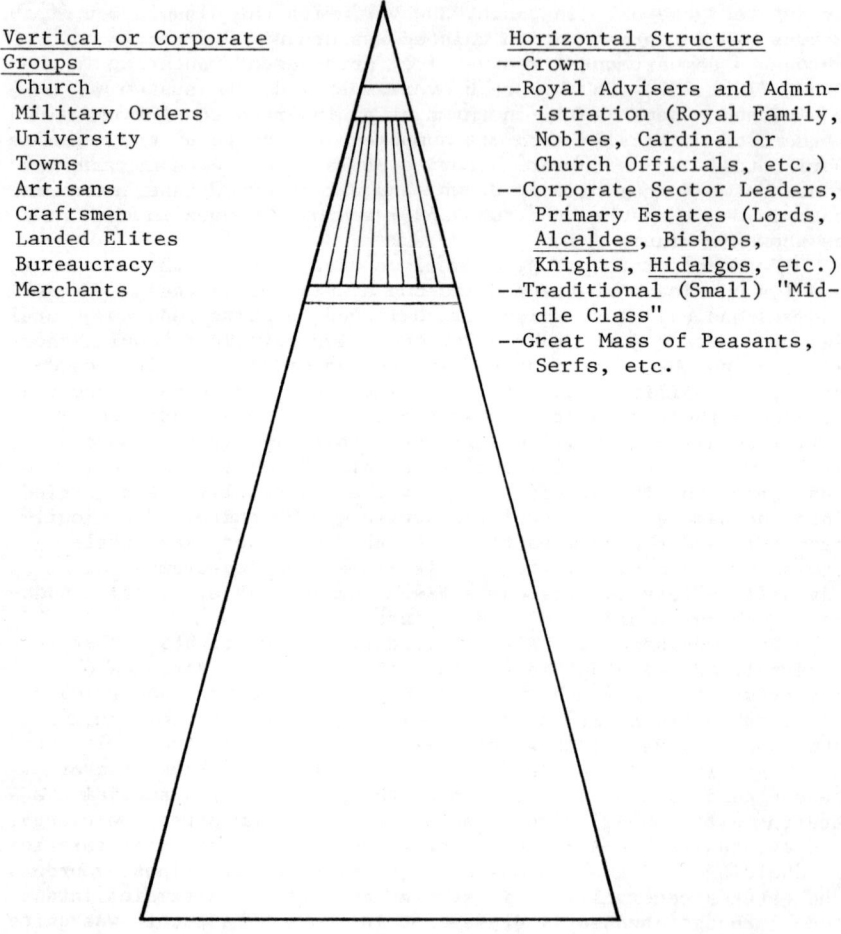

Vertical or Corporate Groups
- Church
- Military Orders
- University
- Towns
- Artisans
- Craftsmen
- Landed Elites
- Bureaucracy
- Merchants

Horizontal Structure
- --Crown
- --Royal Advisers and Administration (Royal Family, Nobles, Cardinal or Church Officials, etc.)
- --Corporate Sector Leaders, Primary Estates (Lords, Alcaldes, Bishops, Knights, Hidalgos, etc.)
- --Traditional (Small) "Middle Class"
- --Great Mass of Peasants, Serfs, etc.

*These structures naturally fluctuated somewhat with time and changing power relations. Horizontally, the relations between the crown, nobles, cortes, and primary estates varied depending on dynamic circumstances. Vertically, the relative fortunes and juridical status of the corporate units also waxed and waned. The basic pyramidal, hierarchical, and corporative structure, however, remained intact.

America; indeed, in many respects they are still the dominant patterns even now.

Much of the history of Latin America all the way to the present may be understood in terms of the persistence of the institutions and behavioral patterns that Catholic, corporate, feudal, authoritarian, elitist, patrimonial Spain carried with her to the Western Hemisphere. On the eve of the conquest the constituent elements of Spanish society fell into two general categories, the vestiges of the medieval estates and the functional corporations (291, 569, 573). The estates consisted of nobles, clerics, and common; and within these, further hierarchies of social rank existed. The major corporative elements, each with its own juridical status and code of conduct, we have already enumerated. There was, of course, some overlap between the estates and the corporate bodies--the Church, for example, was both a functional corporation and one of the primary medieval estates; and as a society in itself whose power at times exceeded that of the temporal authority, its position in the social order often transcended both. But generally the pattern was one of rigid hierarchy and compartmentalization.

The various groups and associations constituting the Spanish system were sharply identifiable in terms of ascribed functions and/or statuses, patterns of shared values and activities, and distinct orders and ranks, the roles of which were defined in elaborate legal codes. The "natural" inequities inherent in the universe implied each person's acquiescence in his particular status and its obligations. But society, though inflexible and compartmentalized, was also viewed as an organic, integral whole, tied together through natural law, the Catholic-corporate world view, and royal authority. The Crown emerged as the center of authority from which favors and position were derived. From this tradition, it seems certain, derives the fact that juridical recognition by and administrative subordination to the central state is still the sine qua non of social legitimacy for any group or would-be political power contender in Latin America (359).

Suárez stands as the chief codifier and expositor of the conflicting doctrines and overlapping historical epochs that marked this period. He was able to blend the Christian underpinnings of Spanish society with a corporate organizational form that also included justification for a modern and centralized state. Though the reconciliation of these aspects of Suárez's theory involved some rather elaborate juggling, his entire schema and the structure it justified proved to have remarkable staying power, providing the rationale for the Spanish colonial system for the better part of three centuries and more. Suárez's state was based on the principles of hierarchy and order, and it proved to be a remarkably efficient agency for maintaining the existing order (191, 263). How different this tradition of Iberian and, by extension, Latin American thought is from the liberal-Lockean tradition as it developed in England and North America!

In Latin America, however, the sociopolitical structure evolved somewhat differently from the peninsular prototype. This was due, on the one hand, to the influence of the Crown, which frequently intervened in the process of social formation. The

Crown's contrived and pervasive presence perpetuated what Claudio Véliz has referred to as a system of "vertebral centralism," which has carried over into the present era as the central, all-embracing, all-powerful, paternalistic but authoritarian state. The overriding importance first of the Crown as the symbol of authority and legitimacy (even though it was far away and its mandates frequently more honored than obeyed) and after independence of the caudillo and later the bureaucratic state has, in the Latin American context, tended to militate against the growth of local government and initative, "modern" interest associations, governmental checks and balances, party politics, delegation of authority, or any of the other strong intermediary and linkage structures that have grown up in the North American-Western European tradition (491-4).

On the other hand, the presence of such large numbers of indigenous elements that they could not possibly be fully integrated into the dominant Iberic-Latin cultural pattern, the large-scale importation of Negro slaves, and the widespread miscegenation that took place between the three races led to an even more elaborate system of stratification that was as much based on caste considerations as it was on class factors. Though economic considerations, narrowly defined, clearly shaped the patterns of Indian exploitation, slave importation, and landholding, considerations of social status, race, culture, juridical rank, even religion were, it may be suggested, perhaps equally important. And though the Latin American class-caste pattern developed in an ad hoc fashion that frequently had little to do with an explicit political theory, underlying the Spanish conception was a whole set of moral, legal, social, religious, and political values--usually all tied up together--that laid great stress on considerations of social origins, hierarchy, estate, status, and corporate "place," that promptly devised ways of justifying de jure what already existed de facto. In other words, the prevailing notion of functional social hierarchy, so powerful in Spain, became even stronger in the New World, for there the overriding importance of position, wealth, education, corporate affiliation, juridico-legal status, and economic-professional activities was reinforced by racial and ethnic considerations (291, 347).

Once the system was firmly established during the first eighty years or so of the Spanish conquest, it remained largely intact for the better part of three centuries of colonial rule--and even survived with some reordering on into the independence period. Of course, some change occurred: new laws and regulations were promulgated; Spanish authority waxed and waned; some reorganization took place; foreign interlopers had to be dealt with; a number of revolts had to be put down; a new mercantile and entrepreneurial "bourgeoisie" eventually began to grow in strength; vast demographic changes occurred; some Enlightenment ideas began to filter in; the Bourbon kings of the eighteenth century initiated a variety of reforms; the North American and French revolutions had their impact. Nonetheless, the colonial structures developed by the mother country proved to be flexible and adaptable enough to accommodate themselves to these changes and yet to persist virtually intact and with only minor modifications in the fundamental structures of power and society. An essentially corporative sociopolitical structure and its religio-juridical legitimation remained, as Newton concludes, unchanged in its essentials during the entire colonial era and on into the independence period as well (359).

Since "the system" we are referring to here had such a pervasive and lasting impact on the course of Latin American development, it merits somewhat greater explication. For in many respects the social and political systems of today's Latin America are the direct descendents of the Spanish colonial pattern of organicism, patrimonialism, manorialism, corporatism, and feudalism. Thus, the political structure was one of bureaucratic patrimonialism, of authoritarianism and paternalism, of a strict hierarchy of absolutisms. The patrimonial structure is highly centralized, and in it one finds a number of orders and estates tied personally and absolutely to the ruler, who not only provides it with direction but also gives it meaning. The power of the king or lord or <u>hacendado</u> extends to all his subjects, and all relations of authority are considered the personal prerogative of the ruler, whether it corresponds to his domestic power or his possessions. The ruler exercises seignorial and tutorial power over his subjects, yet the relationship is two-way: he owes them protection and official favor and they in turn owe him fealty, loyalty, and service. In many ways, the traditional pattern of patrimonial rule, the <u>patrón-clientela</u> relationships, remains the dominant tradition throughout Latin America today (448).

At the same time Catholic hegemony and orthodoxy in Europe were still intact, and their traditions and practices were likewise spread to the New World. The long Spanish crusade against the Moorish infidels and, later, the efforts of the Hapsburg kings to preserve Catholic unity and the purity of the faith helped make Catholicism in Spain more fanatic and intolerant than elsewhere in Europe—and much of this intolerance, the Inquisition, and religious fanaticism was transferred to America. The Church was marked by an authoritarianism that matched the state concept and by a set of traditional values and ideas that were inhibitive of modernization. Catholic beliefs undergirded the political culture and its assumptions (321).

The social structure, as we have seen, was equally unyielding. A small group of colonial officials, nobles, clerics, and wealthy or landed interests existed at the top, monopolizing wealth, property, power, privilege, and status. The noble or <u>hidalgo</u> class was usually divided sharply between creoles (those born in the New World) and <u>peninsulares</u> (those born in Spain), or between the <u>hidalgos de primera</u> (those of pure European descent) and <u>hidalgos de segunda</u> (those high-ranking officials whose family or ethnic credentials were not quite so noble). Below this, a small number of artisans, soldiers, lesser officials, craftsmen, traders, and so on formed what might be termed the "old middle class." Not a dynamic or enterprising "<u>bourgeoisie</u>," these middle-sector elements aspired to and aped upper-class ways and sought to acquire wealth or wheedle favors, special privileges, and monopolies that would enable them, too, to live the life of an <u>hidalgo</u> or grandee. At the bottom of the social scale (though with some distinctions between them) was a large mass of laborers, smallholders, landless serfs, indentured servants, and slaves, serving the interests of their masters, exercising deference toward those above them in the social scale, and hoping for favors and the paternalism of the lord in return. Few moved from one social level to the next (291, 571).

The economy was founded on a "colonial trader" or get-rich-quick philosophy and based upon the monopolistic exploitation of the New World's readily available mineral wealth and its human resources. The ownership of land, slaves, and other possessions served as a symbol of status, to be simply held onto and possessed rather than being worked in a dynamic, entrepreneurial fashion. The <u>encomienda</u> and later the <u>hacienda</u> and plantation systems that were established became a way of life, a structure that not only served to perpetuate the essentially two-class nature of Latin American society but to keep its people poor and to retard development as well (79, 476).

What there was of educational and intellectual life centered around the Church. Revealed truth, natural and God-given law, Thomistic philosophy, and Aristotelian logic formed the core of knowledge. Rote memory of unquestioned truth, a deductive method of reasoning, and scholasticism served to perpetuate an immutable, unchanging, closed system of knowledge and to bolster the established sociopolitical order. For the central religio-sociopolitical ideas in this tradition imply the unquestioned acceptance of each man of his place in the hierarchy together with its attendant obligations, and the organization of the entire system along hierarchical, corporatist, integralist, and authoritarian lines (350). The Inquisition helped keep out other, possibly conflicting ideas. The religious ideology of traditional Catholicism thus helped legitimize the traditional power relationships, of which it was an integral part.

The isolation of the entire area during the colonial period and on into the nineteenth century and the maintenance of the closed and absolutist system outlined above meant that Latin America, in contrast to North America, only marginally participated in the great revolutionary transformations that we associate with the beginning of the modern age. Much of this was due to the peculiar pattern of the Spanish historical experience, which was then transferred to the New World, but much of it was simply an accident of history: the fact that the Spanish conquest and establishment of a far-flung colonial empire took place early in the sixteenth century while that of England occurred more than a century later. During this intervening period, between roughly 1500 and 1600, so much had happened in Europe that the base on which the Spanish colonies were founded--essentially feudal, medieval, corporative, mercantilist, patrimonial, traditional, two-class, closed, authoritarian, elitist, rigidly hierarchical, and compartmentalized--was right from the start fundamentally different from that of the North American colonies, whose history was marked by the absence of a dominant feudal tradition and whose foundations were essentially in the early modern era. These sharply contrasting starting points and traditions profoundly shaped the course of development in the two parts of the Western Hemisphere and determined right from the beginning that North America would move ahead while Latin America vegetated and lagged behind. The contrasting traditions are outlined in Figure 3.2.

FIGURE 3.2
Contrasting Traditions and Time Periods in the Colonization of Latin America and North America

	Latin America (c1500)	North America (c1600)
Political Tradition	Bureaucratic-Patrimonialist, Absolutist, Hierarchical	Limited Government, More Representative and Participatory
Religious Tradition	Catholic Hegemony and Absolutism	Protestant-Pluralist
Social Structure	Closed, Rigid, Two-Class, Little Mobility	More Open and Multi-class
Economy	Feudal-Patrimonialist, Monopolistic, Mercantilist	Capitalist, Industrialist, Bourgeois
Education and Intellectual Life	Scholastic, Closed, Deductive, Rote Memorization	More Scientific and Empirical

Source: Derived from Irving A. Leonard, "Science, Technology, and Hispanic America: The Basis of Regional Characteristics," Michigan Quarterly Review 2 (October 1963): 237-245. It should be noted that these descriptive classifications represent simplified "ideal types" rather than precise mirrors of reality.

The political structures of Latin America thus remained authoritarian, absolutist, and narrowly based, and the region was bypassed by the trend toward limited government, government of law and not of men, checks and balances, and more representative and democratic rule. The rise of capitalism, the industrial revolution, and the growth of an ambitious, achievement-oriented bourgoisie had but indirect and limited effects in Latin America. The social pattern based on class, caste, hierarchy, rank, and ascribed status, and strictly segregated by rank, corporation, and estate, also remained largely intact. Society was divided into privileged and nonprivileged, haves and have-nots; a strong middle class, either urban or rural, failed to develop. Nor did the scientific revolution, ushered in with the empiricism of Galileo, Newton, and others, have much effect on Latin America. Similarly, Catholic hegemony remained intact, and Latin America was largely untouched by the Protestant Reformation and the age of rationalism and enlightenment and thus never experienced the processes of religious and intellectual pluralism and of secularization that these movements gave rise to. Latin America, therefore, was condemned to stagnate, behind the rest of the modernizing Western world and cut off from it, to remain on the fringes and in the shadows while the North American colonies passed her by. In this way Latin America remained fundamentally feudal and "traditional" at a time when elsewhere in the West an entirely new and modern order had begun to emerge (164, 195, 343).

THE INDEPENDENCE PERIOD: THE REORDERING AND CONTINUITY OF THE TRADITIONAL STRUCTURE

The wars of independence by which the Spanish and Portuguese colonies separated themselves from their mother countries between roughly 1810 and 1824 were great and dramatic events, but few sharp changes occurred in the structure of society. It must be emphasized that these were wars of separation, not social revolutions. The scattered Indian and mass uprisings that accompanied the independence struggles were brutally suppressed. The withdrawal of the Spanish crown left a void at the very top of the political pyramid, but the rest of the hierarchy remained largely intact and there was little fundamental alteration in the underlying social and economic substructure. Indeed, in many ways the independence struggles represented an effort on the part of creole elites to restore and expand the ancient system of special privileges against the liberalizing reforms of the Spanish Bourbons and the inability of incompetent monarchs to preserve and protect the traditional order. The result of independence was that the king and his agents were removed as the symbols and locus of political power, but the base and intermediate levels of the system were largely unchanged and a new elite sought to fill the vacuum created by the withdrawal of the crown (40).

This quest initially proved to be chaotic and divisive. There was no agreed-upon conception of a state idea and, hence, loyalties were weak and fleeting. In some of the countries the heroes of the independence movement or the creole aristocracy stepped in to fill the breach. But their rule generally proved short-lived, and they were only temporarily able to hold in check the disintegrative forces at work. The federations of Central America and Gran Colombia split up almost immediately; other nations were torn by conflict and revolutions. The result of the continuing legitimacy crisis, of the absence of effective indigenous institutions and of a new head who could step into the vacuum created by the withdrawal of royal authority and hold the conglomerate of corporate units together, was frequent political and administrative breakdowns into <u>caudillo</u>, man-on-horseback politics, strong-man rule, frequent civil war, and alternate periods of chaos and dictatorship. For most of the Latin American nations, the first forty years or so of independent life were a period of incipient nationhood, of economic stagnation and often ruin, of frequent dependence on Europe, and of political disorder and instability. Only Brazil, which solved its legitimacy crisis temporarily by continuing as an independent monarchy, escaped this period of upheaval (190).

Despite the frequent revolutions, the social and economic substructure of these new nations remained largely unchanged, and so did many of the political practices and institutions, though now organized under somewhat different forms. New governing procedures were devised and new institutional arrangements grafted on, but the underlying political realities and the socio-cultural-economic base on which the entire system rested were semifeudal, corporatist, patrimonial, and authoritarian. The rigidly hierarchical pattern of class and caste, the compartmentalized vertical structure of society, the system of "fueros" and special privileges (now extended to include the newly created national armies as well as the older colonial corporate elements), the agrarian-patrimonial-seigneurial system centering around the hacienda, the power of the Church and the values of a preeminently Catholic religio-political culture, the Hispanic-Latin tradition--all these were in the main unaffected by independence (143).

Among the institutions grafted on during this early period were the constitutions written for these newly independent nations, as well as one or another version of the French Code Napoleon. It is practically a truism to point out that both the new constitutions and the new codes were ill-suited to the countries which adopted them and that the "grafts," hence, failed to "take." The constitutions, for example, provided for representative and democratic institutions, separation of powers, bills of rights, etc., in societies where these traditions were largely lacking and where the dominant structures had always been closed, authoritarian, centralized, and highly personalistic. Similarly, the law codes derived from France were in many ways inappropriate in Latin America. The Napoleonic Code was in essence antifeudal, while Latin America remained a creole-feudal area. The French law was utopian and revolutionary, built not only on the dramatic concepts of the Enlightenment and the French Revolution but also on the gradual and frequently less dramatic revolutionary modernizing movements that had been occurring in Western Europe in the two or three centuries prior to the promulgation of Napoleon's famous code. In Latin America, however, these movements had only had but limited effects and, therefore, a legal system derived from them was bound to be largely irrelevant (328). One finds, for example, a rejection of the old order in the codes but not in the way Latin America continued to be governed, a rationalization of the law but not a concomitant rationalization and modernization of society and polity. Of course, both the new constitutions and the new codes were based upon a series of abstract universal formulas--just as were Latin America's own earlier Roman and Thomistic "basic laws"--and, though irrelevant in many ways, they could thus be grafted on rather easily without altering either the sociopolitical or even the philosophical bases of the society. As a further result, however, a truly national legal system never developed in Latin America; the law remained isolated from the society it was intended to serve (542).

There has been a great deal of nonsense written about the inappropriateness and the supposed dysfunctionality of the legal-constitutional models adopted by the Latin American nations in the nineteenth century. First, one must keep in mind the very few alternatives open to Latin America's early "nation builders." Monarchy was considered and rejected; republicanism seemed to be the wave of the future. At the time, there seemed to be no other solutions, no "middle way." So the framers of these new constitutions did the next best thing: they adopted charters that were republican and democratic in form but not in substance, that provided a superficial veneer of representative self-government while maintaining the colonial aristocratic ethos virtually intact.

Second, one must note the intentions of the men who drafted these constitutions. They were not, as Glen Dealy's research has shown, naive and inexperienced men, seeking unrealistically to emulate the French or North American constitutional-legal models and to impose them on societies where they did not fit. Nor did this quite give rise to such a strict separation of "theory" from "practice" as is supposed to characterize the Latin American political tradition. In point of fact, the men who drafted these charters were eminently reasonable and highly qualified. Nor did they seek to divorce themselves from 300 years of colonial rule and a Hispanic-Latin tradition that stretched back even further. Rather, they consistently tried to adapt the new laws to prevailing custom and history, showing what Dealy calls a "remarkable genius" for incorporating the republican forms and language of the day while retaining their nondemocratic and nonrevolutionary heritage almost intact (111).

One need only examine the view of human nature found in the new constitutions (Thomistic, not Lockean), the distinctive meaning given the word "rights" (implying privileges or special "<u>fueros</u>," group rights rather than natural individual rights), the privileged place accorded the Church and other corporate elites, the subordinate position of the legislature and judiciary, the role of the military as the "moderating power," the extensive authority of the executive, etc., to demonstrate that these founding fathers did not wish to repudiate the past but to preserve it, while at the same time assimilating some elements that were new. Democratic theory was not embraced at that time, for even though the language sounded familiar, the content and meaning were decidedly Latin-Hispanic and authoritarian. The former colonies of Spain and Portugal in the early nineteenth century were clearly still thinking more in medieval terms, of estates and corporate bodies, of hierarchy and authority, than they were in modern, democratic concepts; and the content of their laws and constitutions was similarly derived more from their own than from the experiences of others. They did not simply take over, as numerous legal and political commentators have proclaimed, the frameworks of the West but consciously sought to borrow what was useful in these newer schemes and largely rejected the rest. They chose, as Dealy concludes, to implement a system of government and of laws which in <u>both theory and practice</u> had much in common with their own tradition and was consistent with it (111).

The independence period, thus, did not mark such a sharp

change from the past as is often believed. Scholars have long pointed out that the wars of independence in Latin America were not "true" revolutions because there was little change in the socioeconomic substructure; now it appears there was precious little change in the political-constitutional-legal sphere as well. The garb was changed as new liberal, democratic, and representative dressing was added on, but the character of political society underneath remained much the same. In fact, the dominant tradition of the past, one which was Catholic, authoritarian, stratified, elitist, semifeudal, corporate, and patrimonialist, was retained.

The vision of society and polity held by the leaders of that time was essentially nondemocratic, and it remains so today. The direction of political thought, Dealy again reminds us, has maintained a remarkable continuity since 1810 as well as before that date. At virtually every step, the reality of Latin American society and politics has been supported by constitutional and legal provisions that authorize, legitimize, and enshrine authoritarian, hierarchical, and corporate practices and thus continue the venerated tradition. In short, Latin America does not seem to suffer, as so many North American writers have proclaimed, the "pathological condition" brought on by a relentless but frustrated search for democracy, by its effort to bring theory and practice together. The writers who hold that position are necessarily bound to consider Latin American history to the present largely a failure, for the democratic quest they envision Latin America embarked upon has not been accomplished. But that evaluation rests on the assumption that democracy North-American-style was in the 1820s and remains a century and a half later the goal to which Latin America aspires. The argument of the present essay, however, is that that was not the case--and probably still is not today. Thus, it would seem, to paraphrase Dealy once more, that the supposed "failure" of the Latin American countries to achieve democracy in the 1820s or again in the 1960s was not really a failure but in fact a triumph for the major ideals and aspirations that had been theirs since the sixteenth century--however <u>undemocratic</u> these might be (111).

The patriarchal state had thus lost its head, but the main body still stood and the residual holders of juridical, social, and economic status maintained--even enhanced--their positions. Given the fact that the underlying social system tended to be static and closed rather than dynamic and open, however, it was unable to adapt adequately to the changed circumstances--at least immediately. In the absence of the Crown, political life often became a raw, naked, contest among a number of elites for control of the patrimonial state apparatus. Politics usually turned upon dynastic feuding among major families or clans and their retinues, involving one region against another, the capital versus the provinces, rival rag-tag <u>caudillo</u>-led bands competing against each other, clerical versus anticlerical factions, and the like. Political power was determined by the often-tentative maintenance of a dominant coalition among these particularistic solidarities (359).

Revolutions, <u>pronunciamientos</u>, civil wars, barracks revolts took place regularly and the political system was generally unstable, but it must be remembered that there was an order to the chaos, that it took place within fairly well-delimited boundaries and under gentlemanly rules. The elites circulated in and out of office, thereby giving off the appearance of change when, in fact, there was practically no change at all. This process of elite rotation may be viewed as serving more of a renewal function for the elites than of effecting any structural metamorphoses; it was more a process of adaptation and substitution than of transformation (143). The underlying structure of society, of group and class-caste relations, and of the polity, therefore, remained stable, despite the surface manifestations of frequent upheaval. Repeated cries for liberalism and democracy, on the one hand, and eventually in the following century for militant class struggle, on the other, had little appeal in societies where authority and hierarchy are widely accepted as natural and where, as Morse writes, "all groups look separately to the patrimonial structure for accommodation, tutelage and salvation" (347).

By the 1870s or 1880s in nearly all the Latin American countries, some semblance of order and stability had been brought out of the earlier chaos. In some countries this took the form of the firmer consolidation of oligarchic or elitist rule; in others a new breed of "order and progress" dictators replaced the men on horseback of the past. Throughout Latin America the last decades of the nineteenth century and the first decades of the twentieth were a period of national consolidation, increased urbanization, institution-building, resolution of the Church-state controversy and of the conflicts over federalism, immigration, massive influxes of foreign capital, emergent nationalism, mechanization, communications and transportation development, and considerably greater resource exploitation, trade, and commerce. A new political equilibrium was forged based often on the alliance of foreign interests with the native <u>criollo</u> landed oligarchies and a rising business-commercial elite (frequently the same people) and generally supported by the new, more professionalized armies and eventually by the Church. For most of the Latin American countries, this was a period of economic expansion, infrastructure development, stability, and continuity which, with Mexico as the major exception, lasted until 1930 (568).

The early stirrings of industrialization, the expansion of trade, and the overall quickening of the economic tempo tended to give rise to a greater variety of social groups than had existed in the old stratification system, and new escalators of social mobility appeared. A new business and commercial elite rose up alongside and frequently intermingled with the older landed oligarchy; a number of prospering foreign colonies also appeared. The middle sectors expanded and began to demand a say in national political affairs. Peasants were uprooted and either employed in the new capitalistic enterprises or forced to eke out a subsistence existence in the more infertile rural areas. At the same time, the increases in foreign trade and commerce, the establishment of diplomatic relations with the outside world, and the overall opening up of the previously closed and isolated Latin American nations exposed them to a variety of new political forms and ideas, to different educational and intellectual currents, and to competing ways to organize social and political life. The boom of the prewar years, the war period, and the 1920s further stimulated these developments. After nearly four centuries of stagnation and lack of much real progress or development, the changes ushered in in the late nineteenth and early twentieth centuries marked, in the words of Maier and Weatherhead, "the twilight of the Middle Ages, the waning of feudal customs, the debilitation of the colonial legacy" (301).

Through adaptation, accommodation, and cooptation on the part of the ruling elites, however, the basic structure of power and society in Latin America remained largely as it had been in the past. The traditional elites and ruling groups adjusted and accommodated themselves to the gradual shift from the sleepy and self-sufficient hacienda to the more dynamic, capitalistic plantation; and in most instances, they were able to coopt the rising merchant and commercial elements into their system of dominance--or to go into these businesses themselves (114). The franchise was later extended to include the emerging new-rich and middle-sector elements, somewhat greater respect was paid to the classic nineteenth-century freedoms, and a variety of new political parties and interest associations began to come into existence. These changes did not involve a revolutionary reordering, however, but implied, in Morse's terms, a means of readjusting the system, of adapting a Catholic, patrimonial, corporatist, and hierarchical structure to the necessities of the modern world (348). A number of pragmatic adjustments were made, but the basic landholding pattern remained intact; the fundamental two-class structure of society continued; the values and behavioral patterns of the past were largely preserved; the system of "fueros" and special privileges was retained; and the structure of society remained hierarchical, authoritarian, elitist, corporative, and closed (131).

THE ACCELERATION OF THE CHANGE PROCESS AND
THE CRISIS OF THE OLD ORDER

In many of the Latin American countries, give or take a few years, the traditional order suffered a severe blow in 1930, along with the collapse of the world market prices for the products which the region exports. The 1930 collapse marked a watershed in the histories of many of the Latin American countries, for it signaled the beginning of the end of the absolute monopoly of social, economic, and political power that had been held by the landowning oligarchies since the nineteenth century and the gradual extension of the corporate structure to encompass some of the rising new groups, such as the middle sectors and the urban laboring class, who had risen to prominence in the preceding decades. Except in Mexico, the traditional order was not destroyed, however, but some new layers were added onto it. Moreover, the very fact that some new ideas and concepts, a number of new social groups, and a variety of new institutional arrangements were incorporated or grafted on meant that these would no longer be quite the simple, traditionalist, nineteenth-century societies that they had been before. The dominant elitist structure had not been superseded, but it was forced to absorb some new elements into the prevailing power structure and to come to grips with an increasingly secularized, pluralistic, complex, and socially differentiated national system (21, 140).

In some countries the old order held on or quickly reconsolidated its control following the 1930 crisis and tried to snuff out forcefully the newer currents then stirring. In others, populist leaders, both civilian and military, rose to power, often reaching their accommodation with the old elites but assimilating some of the newer concepts and rising social forces as well. In still others, powerful new middle-class, liberal-<u>bourgeois</u>, and, eventually lower-class, social-democratic, and even socialist movements sprang up to challenge the power of the traditional elites--in some cases coming to power alone or in coalition, in others provoking a violent counterrevolutionary surge by the more status quo-oriented elements. Many countries oscilated between these various kinds of regimes and were torn apart by the accompanying violence, instability, and rising social and political conflict; some--like Argentina--have still not fully recovered from the devastation and discord that the crisis of 1930 ushered in. But whatever the short-range effects, the long-term result was the acceleration of the decline of an older elitist order based on status, hierarchy, authority, and corporate privilege, and, if not its replacement, then certainly its modification in order to adjust to and accommodate the broad-scale social and political transformations that the economic thrust, the gradual movement toward national modernization, and the increased international contact of the late nineteenth and early twentieth centuries had ushered in.

The decline of the old order and its at least partial eclipse--and particularly the acceleration of these disintegrative processes in the last decade or two, albeit at different rates of speed and in varying degrees, depending on the country involved--have left a legitimacy vacuum in Latin America of a far more profound sort than that caused by the withdrawal of the Crown in the early nineteenth century. That older crisis was chiefly an administrative-political one, while the present crisis is social, economic, ideological, moral, and behavioral as well. For though the change to independent status was often a wrenching one for the Latin American nations, the socioeconomic structure and the underlying value system, as we have said, had remained largely intact. Despite the disruptive and frequently chaotic conditions which prevailed in the political sphere--as reflected in the frequent revolutions, civil wars, and the comings and goings of successive <u>caudillos</u>--a sense of continuity and systemic stability prevailed. In the present crisis, however, there is little sense of continuity and, since it affects virtually all areas of life, little systemic stability either. The undermining of the traditional socio-religio-political order has left the Latin American nations with little in the way of an institutional infrastructure, a disrupted and disordered social system, floundering and stagnant economies, little sense of social purpose, virtually no consensus on the ends or means of political action, and few commonly shared values other than nationalism itself (and frequently very little of even that).

The established ways are being abandoned for uncertain new ones, and the paternalistic and other traditional remnants of mutual interest and cooperation between have's and have not's are collapsing. The Catholic-Thomistic world view no longer enjoys unchallenged acceptance, the newer and rising social groups have become increasingly impatient for reform and for a greater share in national decision-making and in the national wealth, while contact with and pressures from the outside have also grown. As these new social forces increased and as the pressures for change accelerated in the 1950s and especially the 1960s, it is small wonder that instability, revolution, discontinuity, and frequently sheer chaos set in. Since 1930, in fact, a number of the Latin American countries have been living through a period of virtually permanent crisis (1).

Latin America is thus an area in transition from underdeveloped to developed, from old to new, from traditional to modern, but it has not yet permanently, completely, or irrevocably bridged that gap. It has begun the great leap from a traditional, backward, semifeudal system into the modern industrialized, twentieth-century world, but done so only partially, unevenly, and in a patchwork fashion. Furthermore, these changes have come largely through the mediating institutions of Latin American traditional society and not through the "Western model." While new and more modern practices, behavioral patterns, and institutions have been introduced, the vestiges of the older traditional, semifeudal order thus remain strong; indeed, there is even yet some reason to believe that these traditional structures will not wither away but will again prove capable of managing and absorbing the new pressures and thus surviving the present crisis, as they have others in the past. While the older order is thus declining and in the process of decay, it has by no means disappeared; and while a new order is rising, it has not yet been firmly established or acquired the requisite legitimacy. Moreover, the modernization process itself--the eclipse (even if partial) of traditional society and the rise (even if incomplete) of a modern one--implies discontinuity and disruption. Traditional patterns are thus sometimes being repudiated before reliable substitutes have been created, and the "traditional" institutions themselves often stubbornly refuse to go away.

At the present time, therefore, Latin America is neither the one nor the other, neither traditional nor modern, but a confused, chaotic, overlapping pattern of both, jumbled together in a way that seems almost to defy not only all "reason" and ideological consistency but also our commonly accepted schemes and frameworks for analyzing the development process. Latin America, in fact, is torn between conflicting tendencies, not only between its traditional and its modernizing forces, <u>between</u> those who demand change and those who would preserve the status quo, but also <u>among</u> those who would like to have both at the same time but who disagree violently as to how this reconciliation can best be accomplished (b). The conflicts seem to have become increasingly intense in recent years and not susceptible to the traditional reconciliationist techniques; it may be in fact, as the common basis of understanding has been undermined and as class and ideological lines have hardened, that these issues are no longer reconcilable. In any case, it is the absence of <u>either</u> a solidly entrenched and still intact traditional order or a firmly organized and legitimized modern one, coupled with the fact that there is no middle way on which all these divisive factions can agree, that accounts for much of the instability, chaos, and revolutionary potential of present-day Latin America.

Ironically, it is this very tendency toward crisis and breakdown in Latin America that has helped precipitate the resurgence of corporatism. One must, therefore, distinguish, as we do more sharply later in the book, between the historic and cultural affinity for corporatism in Latin America, and the newer forms of more manifest and militant "corporatism." Whereas the former is integrally a part of a long Latin American cultureal and institutional tradition, the latter tends to emerge as a response to economic crisis, to lower-class challenges to existing institutions, and to elite efforts to preserve the status quo while locking the newer claimants, such as workers and peasants, in place. In these essays we shall be exploring both the older and the newer forms of corporatism, the relations between them, and the implications that the pervasive presence of corporatism has for Latin American social and political life.

NOTES

   a. One of the primary examples of this is the Latin American contribution to the influential volume edited by Almond and Coleman (1). Indeed, Latin America has always fit rather uncomfortably into the development literature of the last decade; see on this 246, 318, 354. The attempt to graft on a set of categories advanced in some of the early development literature to a Latin American context where they would not "take" has led a whole generation of Latin Americanists--the present author included--into some blind alleys from which we have only recently begun to extract ourselves.

   b. It should be noted that, when we use the terms "traditional" and "modern," "status quo-oriented forces" and "forces for change," we are dealing in abstractions and employing "ideal types" which need not correspond exactly to actual political realities. Every abstraction--indeed virtually every statement--of course, exacts its price in terms of simplifying phenomena that are in reality far more complex. Nevertheless, these categories provide a useful means of organizing and analyzing certain fundamental aspects of political behavior in Latin America; furthermore, the basic two-part division of society and polity implied in these two terms corresponds far more closely to the realities of political life in Latin America than at first glance seems conceivable. See, for example, 4.

4 | Toward a Framework for the Study of Political Change in the Iberic-Latin Tradition: The Corporative Model

In the early 1960s a great deal of "scare" literature was produced on Latin America. The titles and subtitles of many of the books and articles written during the period help bear this contention out: "The Eleventh Hour," "Reform or Revolution," "Evolution or Chaos." Stemming principally from the Cuban revolution, the concern of scholars and public officials alike was that Latin America was about to explode in violent upheaval, that unless democratic reformism was quickly forthcoming, the Latin American nations would soon be the victims of "Castro-Communist" takeovers. The "one-minute-to-midnight" mentality shaped not only a great deal of official thinking and policy with regard to Latin America during the 1960s but also infused the large body of development literature dealing with the area.

More recently the counterarguments have gained prominence. Latin America is seen as an "unrevolutionary society," a seemingly inherently and permanently conservative region (310). Neither peasants, workers, nor students are very revolutionary; the guerrilla movements have achieved neither widespread support nor great success; the old-time Communist parties are by now outdated, tired bureaucracies; the traditional structures and institutions have not collapsed but proved remarkably resilient; and the profound social revolution predicted for the area has not occurred and probably will not (255, 325, 493, 494). Midnight has not tolled--or if it has, little happened; the choice of reform or revolution has proved to be a false, or at least not an all-inclusive, choice. And in Washington, this interpretation of the essentially conservative nature of Latin America, and particularly of the absence of threatening Castro-like movements, has been reflected in a new period of official neglect and indifference.

This essay contends that neither of these scenarios, or models, accurately delineates the nature of the Latin American development process. The "eleventh hour" theme is probably useful for raising the level of public concern regarding Latin America, but it does not reflect the sociopolitical realities of or main forces at work in the Latin American countries, or in Spain or

---

From World Politics 25 (January 1973): 206-235.

Portugal. Moreover, the "scare" tactics and verbal overkill that
accompanied this era have now produced the inevitable reaction, in
the form of public and official unconcern and a body of literature
that, in seeking to correct past misinterpretations, overcompensates by focusing solely on the static, conservative aspects of
Latin American development. But this approach does as much injustice to the complexities involved as does the earlier reform-or-
revolution alternative. These interpretations have not only inaccurately portrayed the Iberic-Latin development process but, in so
doing, they have rendered a disservice to our better comprehension
of this culture area (a).

This brief critique of some of the conventional "wisdom"
regarding Latin America serves as the point of departure for the
main theme of the paper: that there are some unique aspects to the
process of sociopolitical change in the Iberic-Latin tradition that
do not correspond to the models ordinarily used to analyze national
development. These nations are not adequately or completely explained by a Rostowian "stages of growth" analysis, by Eastonian-
Almondian systems theory and the functionalist development literature, nor by class analysis or the "power elite" paradigm (47, 72,
314, 479, 494). Rather, because of their peculiar tradition and
antecedents, the Iberic-Latin nations are subject to special imperatives and interpretations and have evolved some distinctive developmental patterns which seldom find expression in our studies of
the history of political thought or the literature on social and
political change. Indeed, it may well be that the Iberic-Latin
tradition represents a "fourth world of development," a peculiar
way of managing the great transformations of modern times that has
not yet received the attention it merits (b). It is toward the
explication of the Iberic-Latin developmental model that this paper
is directed.

THE TRADITIONAL STRUCTURE OF
IBERIC-LATIN SOCIETY

The Iberic-Latin nations were largely bypassed by the great
revolutions associated with the making of the modern world. The
Protestant Reformation, the rise of capitalism, the scientific revolution, the rise of socially more pluralistic and politically more
democratic societies, the industrial revolution and its many-faceted ramifications--all of these had little effect on the nations
of the Iberic-Latin culture area. They remained cut off from these
modernizing currents, at the margin of the ideological trends and
sociopolitical movements taking place elsewhere in Europe, fragments of a peculiarly Iberic-European tradition circa 1500, with a
political culture and a sociopolitical order that at its core was
essentially two-class, authoritarian, traditional, elitist, patrimonial, Catholic, stratified, hierarchical, and corporate (198).
Given the times and circumstances, it should not be surprising
that the Latin American region should also be structured on the
model of and as an extension of the Iberic metropoles; what is
remarkable is the incredible durability and perseverance of this
structure on into the present. For, despite the recent,

accelerated onslaught of modernization, the traditional political culture and institutions have proved permeable, accommodative, and absorptive, bending to change rather than being overwhelmed by it, and thus in many respects retaining their traditional essence even under the strains and currents set loose during this century. Since the weight of history and the past is still so heavy in virtually all the Iberic-Latin nations, and since what seems to have evolved is a unique, peculiarly Latin mode of coping with the change process, let us examine this traditional structure in detail.

The Theoretical Dimension

One looks in vain in the standard works on political theory for more than brief mention of the Iberic-Latin tradition. We treat of medieval Christian thought; but other than Machiavelli, once in the modern era attention turns to the Northern and more dynamic, developing areas of Europe: Locke and the Anglo-American experience, Rousseau and the Revolution, the Germans Kant and Hegel. By the nineteenth century our focus has become even more circumscribed: English utilitarianism and liberalism, socialist thought, and the ideological concomitants of rising nationalism and industrialization. Later, we may trace the evolution of democratic thought, the varieties of socialism, and the ideological underpinnings of modern totalitarianism. All of these are peculiarly Western conceptions, however, and conceptions borne of a particular part of Western Europe. The point merits further elaboration (537), but it seems likely that part of the bias and ethnocentrism that pervade the development literature stems from this conception of the evolution of political thought in the West and our selectivity as to what themes and movements are worthy of mention and support and which are not. In structuring attention along these lines, however, we miss an important thread of thought that remains dominant in the Iberic-Latin nations, that lies at the heart of their peculiar national histories and development processes, and that, because we ignore or reject it out-of-hand, contributes to our miscomprehensions concerning the area. As Morse suggests in explaining the deficiencies of Latin American studies in the United States, ours has been a Protestant and now pluralist nation and our academic disciplines of an increasingly secular and scientific orientation, with the result that we are "insensitive and vaguely hostile to the sociological and psychological foundations of a Catholic society" (349).

If modern political analysis in the Northern European and Anglo-American tradition was to lead to the glorification of the accomplished fact and of political pragmatism, to materialism and the success theory, and to a unilinear, stage-by-stage conception of development, which was also derived principally from the experiences of these nations, then Iberic-Latin culture can surely claim as its basis a moral idealism, a philosophical certainty, a sense of continuity, and a unified organic-corporate conception of the state and society. This conception derives from Roman law (one can still with profit read Cicero and Seneca for an understanding of the Iberic-Latin tradition), Catholic thought (Augustine, Aquinas), and traditional legal precepts (the "<u>fueros</u>" or group charters of medieval times, the law of the <u>Siete Partidas</u> of Alfonso the Wise). The foundations for these organic-corporative systems lie in what Morse called the "Thomistic-Aristotelian notion of functional social hierarchy" (348), and they find their major expression in the political thought of Spain's Golden Century.

In pursuing paths other than those of Protestant or secular thought, such thinkers as Vitoria, Soto, Suárez, Molina, and Mariana, the chief intellectual architects of the sixteenth-century Spanish state and of the transfer of its essential features to the New World, laid the foundations of a modern theory of Christian society (394). In contrast to the separation of politics and morality, which dates from Machiavelli and which we usually take to be the beginning of modern political analysis, the ideal of Spain remained the integration of the ethical and the social. Empirical facts had to show the credentials of logic, rightness, and relation to abstract justice. From the modern, secular viewpoint, such scholasticism shackled Spanish thought and removed the Iberic-Latin nations from the mainstreams of modern history. But from another, less utilitarian perception, it helped give Spanish life its firm moral pattern, its philosophy of behavior and dominant political culture, and its peculiar mode of adjusting to the pressures of modernization.

Vitoria and Suárez stand as the great systems-builders on which the Spanish empire and Iberic-Latin society were constructed. Their genius was to fuse the older Thomistic conception and the system of juridical estates derived from Spanish customary law with the newer concept of absolute, state-building royal authority. There were important differences among the several writers mentioned (191), but equally striking are the common, unifying themes. All assume an ordered universe; all adopt the Thomistic hierarchy of laws; and all base their theories of state and society on Christian assumptions. All share, furthermore, a disdain for the common man; what they mean by "popular" government is feudal and aristocratic, based upon a restoration of the privileges or <u>fueros</u> of the middle ages, the power of the traditional estates, dominated by "natural" elites, and without popular suffrage. Their view of society and the state is an organic one--that government is natural, necessary, and ordained by God for the procuring of harmony among men. This conception is an almost inherently conservative one. In contrast to contract theory, which except in Hobbes is individualistic, democratic, liberal, and progressive, organic theory subordinates human law to natural and divine law, is more tolerant of authority, slights the individual in favor of group "rights" or a superior "general will," accepts and justifies the status quo, reserves extensive powers for traditional vested interests, and leads intrinsically toward a corporate system which subordinates man to some allegedly higher end and unity (263).

The best form of government is thus an enlightened monarchy (or all-powerful executive), required to keep peace and maintain the "natural" order. Extensive powers are also reserved for such corporate entities as the Church, the municipalities, the landed and commercial elites, the guilds, the military hierarchy, and other vested and chartered interests. Organic theory in both Church and state rejects liberal individualism and the materialistic and secular conceptions that accompanied development in Northern Europe. Although this repudiation does not **necessarily** follow from the organic, Catholic, and scholastic premises, it certainly has a powerful basis in them (191, 263).

It is not surprising that this view of the proper ordering of sociopolitical relations should be articulated and strongly established in sixteenth-century Spain, Portugal, and their New World colonies, but that it should endure so long. In the metropoles, with their nonrevolutionary traditions, it persisted through the decline of Spanish power in the seventeenth century, the Bourbon reforms of the eighteenth, the divisive currents of the nineteenth, and the period of challenge and conflict in the twentieth—only to be reestablished in almost pristine form in the Spain of Primo de Rivera and Franco and the Portugal of Salazar. In Spanish-Portuguese America, it not only survived some three centuries of colonial rule but also, in reordered and rebaptized form, the separations from the mother countries in the early nineteenth century, the tempestuous histories that followed (where the **restoration** of the Spanish system remained often the operating ideal), and on into the period of accelerated industrialization, social change, and ideological challenge of the present. Despite these newer pressures—discussed in greater detail later on—one still finds powerful echoes and manifestations of the earlier corporate-organic framework in virtually all contemporary regimes and institutions in Latin America and in their underlying political-cultural foundations. As Newton writes, sixteenth-century Spanish political theory endowed the state "with a remarkable stability, a stability achieved through the delicate balancing of opposing and ultimately antagonistic forces, . . . a system admirably designed, out of very disparate components and different traditions, for the preservation of the status quo" (359).

Space here does not permit elaboration of all the nuances and challenges to this dominant tradition. The Laws of the Indies, derived from both the *Siete Partidas* and the newer sixteenth-century concepts, provide a remarkable example of and bulwark for this tradition, albeit modified and reinterpreted many times over. In the eighteenth century the newer ideas of empiricism and the Enlightenment began to have their impact, but their influence was superficial, limited chiefly to a small circle of royal advisers and an occasional daring intellectual. In the early nineteenth century came the break with Spain and Portugal, but in the New World this implied mainly a redefinition and reformulation of the classic Iberic-Latin tradition, not its repudiation. Historians have long argued that the wars of independence were not true social revolutions because the fundamental nature of society remained largely intact; now, as the research of Dealy has demonstrated, we know there was also precious little change in the political order (111). The constitutional **forms** were representative and democratic, but in **substance** the nondemocratic, elitist, corporate, hierarchical, authoritarian heritage was retained almost intact.

The direction of political thought maintained a remarkable continuity both before <u>and</u> after 1810.

By this time, however, the commercial success of the English, the growth of the natural sciences and technology, the inspiration of representative rule in North America, the glitter and glory of France and the ideals of the Revolution, together with the restlessness for change on the part of the Latin American creoles themselves, had begun to have their impact. New, agonizing questions were asked: Who are we? Spanish? New World? What? What shall be our relations with North America, Europe, Spain, or Portugal? How did we become what we are, and what is our destiny as a continent and a people? (99). In the absence of restraints imposed by the Spanish Crown on the questioning of established truths and on contact with the outside world, the dominant tradition was subjected to the increasing challenge of new ideas and conceptions. In Spain and Portugal, too, this was a period of unprecedented challenge to established ways and frequently of bloody conflicts. In both the Iberian Peninsula and Latin America, subsequent intellectual history would hence be written in terms of the dialectical interplay between the prevailing organicist-corporatist framework and the gradually more numerous adherents of alternative systems.

Throughout the nineteenth century, liberalism was the foremost challenger in the attack on corporate privilege (188). It managed, at least in law, to abolish or disestablish some corporative agencies, but others such as the army were quickly established and the more fundamental <u>corporative order</u> was retained. Liberalism's impact varied from country to country, but one can safely say it was seldom very successful and nowhere dominant. Positivism, with its emphasis on order and progress, was accommodated and assimilated within the prevailing rubric. Later, the ideologies of socialism, communism, nationalism, social democracy, Christian democracy, populism, developmentalism, Third Worldism, and others also made their presence felt. Except in rare, probably unique circumstances, however, such as Cuba, the older tradition has been able to maintain its paramountcy even in the face of these challenges. It has done so by absorbing that which is useful from the newer currents and rejecting the rest. Much of the traditional, organic-corporatist philosophy has thus been retained, albeit in somewhat diluted form, while its challengers have been repeatedly thwarted or coopted. This is what Anderson means by his characterizing Latin America as a "living museum" (21), for in the absence of any genuine social revolution in all but two or three of the Iberic-Latin nations, which would have resulted in the discarding of the older structures, virtually all the systems of society that have ever governed men's affairs continue to coexist--a blend of Thomism, divine right monarchy, feudalism, autocracy, republicanism, liberalism, and the rest.

This discussion of the dominant Iberic-Latin ideological tradition has up to now portrayed it as a conservative, reactive, closed ideology that has shut out those currents it could not usefully absorb. This, however, is only partially true. As a set of what we might term traditional and nonrevolutionary beliefs, the Iberic-Latin heritage <u>has</u> often been a reactive one, excluding the "dangerous," heretical ideas of Protestantism, empiricism, the Enlightenment, rationalism, liberalism, socialism, and the like. But beginning in the mid-to-late nineteenth century, there began to be articulated in the Iberic-Latin nations a new developmental ideology, uniquely attuned to their own tradition, positive, progressive, and serving as the Iberic-Latin counterpart to the modernizing ideologies evolved elsewhere. This tradition remains almost wholly ignored in our intellectual histories, but it is crucial for an understanding of Iberic-Latin development (466, 523).

Spain, Portugal, and their former New World colonies had also begun to be affected by industrialization, urbanization, accelerated social change, and the newer ideological currents of that period. In turn, their major thinkers--such as Donoso Cortés, Balmes, Menéndez, Antonio, Unamuno, Maeztu, Ortega, to cite only those most prominent in the Spanish tradition--began to grapple with the same fundamental questions that concerned Marx, Durkheim, Weber, and other more well-known analysts. The Iberic-Latins built upon the newer and reformist currents emanating from the Church and also drew upon their own historical tradition. Still within the corporate-organic mold, they sought to fashion a framework for thought and action blending the traditional regard for order and hierarchy with the newer imperative of change and modernization. They attempted, for instance, to deal with the phenomenon of mass man by erecting corporate structures that provided for class harmony rather than conflict, structured participation rather than rootlessness and alienation. Representation was generally to be determined by functions (labor, business, agriculture, religion, etc.) rather than through divisive interest groups and political parties. The state was to regulate and harmonize the entire process. In this way, the Iberic-Latin nations sought to face up to modern realities but without sacrificing the organic-corporate structures of the past (65, 99, 394).

By the third and fourth decades of this century, these ideas had been diffused widely, not only in Spain and Portugal, but also throughout Latin America. They helped give rise to a variety of at least semimodernizing movements--the corporate state in Portugal, the _Falange_ in Spain, the _Estado Novo_ in Brazil, integralism and Christian democracy in a variety of countries, _Peronismo_ in Argentina, the MNR in Bolivia, the PRI in Mexico, and numerous others. Despite the significant differences that marked these regimes and movements, the common ingredients were at least equally impressive: a common historic and philosophic tradition, some agreed-upon assumptions about the way the sociopolitical order ought to be arranged, new but similar social and political forces to be dealt with, a shared predisposition not to destroy the old order but to inherit it, bending it sufficiently to accommodate the newer forces but maintaining inviolate the essential corporate, hierarchical, and organic structures. With World War II, many of these movements and corporately organized schemes suffered ignominy and were discredited; some were overthrown, others rebaptized under different names, still others continued much as before. It matters little what labels are applied, however; the important fact is that the same fundamental and historical conception of the state and society still remains, powerful and almost all-pervasive, finding contemporary expression in the ideology and actions of old-style <u>caudillos</u> and new-style military "Nasserists," in the evolving structure of the PRI, in the traditional authoritarian regimes and in the newer "syndicalist republics," perhaps even in revolutionary Cuba. There is obviously room for considerable variation within this framework, but there can be no doubt that it remains crucial for a proper understanding of the Iberic-Latin tradition (19, 450, 453, 513).

More work remains to be done in this area. However, it should be stressed that the movements mentioned here were and are by no means all wholly reactionary or "fascistic," but often represented and continue to represent forward-looking, dynamic efforts at achieving modernization. They attempted to evolve a uniquely Iberic-Latin ideology and mode of action, one which sought to deal with contemporary pressures but to preserve those traditional features considered valuable in their own heritage. It is this strand of thought which our studies of political theory and of social change have neglected but which must be recognized if we are to comprehend the Iberic-Latin development process. There is a distinctively Iberic-Latin model of development whose complex dimensions fail to accord with our more familiar developmental paradigms and whose functioning these other models are, by themselves, incapable of fully explaining. Some aspects of this framework may be ideologically distasteful to us, but as scholars and/or developmentalists we ignore what is probably the still-dominant conception within the Iberic-Latin tradition at the cost of continuing fundamentally to misinterpret the experience and present-day realities of the nations that are a part of this culture area. What is required, therefore, is a counterpart volume for Latin America of, say, Hartz's <u>The Liberal Tradition in America</u> (197), a study which traces and analyzes these political-cultural variables and provides us with that integrative view of the whole that is so sorely needed.

The Sociopolitical Dimension

The Iberic-Latin sociopolitical tradition goes hand-in-hand with its religio-cultural tradition. Again, a useful point of departure for the discussion is to picture the Iberic-Latin nations as structured horizontally in terms of distinct and fairly rigid classes and vertically in terms of a number of corporate elites and <u>intereses</u>. The Crown rested at the apex of the sociopolitical pyramid, regulating, through its power over financial affairs and its authority to grant charters and legal recognition, the corporate and group life that swirled about it. The central administration was the focus through which these units related to each other, rather than directly or across class lines. The Iberic-Latin model of political authority is thus essentially a traditional-patrimonialist one, where the wealth of the realm, its subjects, etc., are all a part of the ruler's own domain (42, 144, 172).

The institutions of the two metropoles—a corporate and hierarchical social order, an authoritarian-patrimonialist polity, an exploitive, semifeudal-early-capitalist, "colonial trader" economic system, a fixed and immutable law--all formed part of the structure that Spain and, in a more easy-going form, Portugal first established at home and then transplanted in the New World (291, 448). What would soon be anachronistic and dying institutions in the rest of Europe and North America remained largely intact in the Iberian Peninsula and Latin America where they not only received a new lease on life but thrived and persisted. This is obviously not to say that no change took place within the prevailing structure but that these were generally accommodated within the prevailing system. As Newton concludes, "the social and political patterns and juridical legitimation of the corporate regime remained substantially intact to the eve of independence" (359).

Though the separation from the mother countries in the early nineteenth century brought on a severe politico-administrative legitimacy crisis, no sharp changes occurred in society's basic structure. Indeed, the wars of independence were largely conservative movements, designed to preserve corporate privilege and elite, centralized rule against the revolutionary, democratizing currents then at work. The pyramid's apex had been lopped off, but the underlying base and the governing mores and institutions remained constant. Once the legitimacy vacuum created by the withdrawal of Spanish and Portuguese authority had been filled by the creole aristocracies, caudillos, and armies, the traditional structure reasserted itself. New "republican" institutional arrangements were grafted on; but, in essence, the hierarchical patterns of class and caste, the system of "fueros" and corporate privilege, the seigneurial system of patrón-clientela relations, the power of the Church and of a preeminently Catholic religio-political culture, the patrimonialist political structure--all these elements of the Iberic-Latin tradition were mainly unaffected by independence (40, 111, 143).

The nineteenth century was characterized by the attempts to create nations out of the disparate, fragmented factions that made up society. This was the classic era of Latin American caudilloism, of rival men on horseback vying for national power and galloping in and out of the National Palace with frequent regularity. By the 1880s and 1890s in virtually all the Latin American nations, the long quest to restore order and unity had largely succeeded; power had been consolidated in the hands of the oligarchic interests, the merchant-entrepreneurial elements bound up closely with them, and a new breed of order-and-progress caudillos. A period of stability, prosperity, and national infrastructure-building ensued. These changes helped stimulate an economic take-off, gave rise to a greater variety of social groups than had existed in the old stratification system, and provided new escalators of social mobility. But again, these changes--and those that followed in the twentieth century--implied little fundamental reordering in the basic structure of power and society. Through the techniques of adaptation, accommodation, and cooptation, the two-class, corporate-patrimonialist system remained unaltered except in peripheral ways. The established groups adjusted readily to the shift from the self-sufficient hacienda to the capitalistic plantation or commercial enterprise; and usually they were able to coopt the rising merchant-business elements into their system of dominance--or to go into these activities themselves, thus welding the older and newer bases of wealth and power (114).

Later, the franchise was extended to the rising middle sectors; greater respect was paid to the classic nineteenth-century freedoms; and a variety of new middle-class associations and parties emerged. From roughly the 1920s onward, new pressures were felt upon the traditional elitist structure, and in several countries the new <u>bourgeois</u> parties and movements came to power. But the pervasiveness of the historic political culture and legacy remained strong: the new middle sectors lacked any sense of class consciousness; they aped elitist ways; once in power they acted in much the same way as had the traditional elites; and eventually they forged an alliance with these elites or were fused into the dominant elitist structure, so as to preserve the privileges and place in the system that they had recently won against the rising pressures from the awakening masses (2, 501, 563). A number of new corporate interests were thus accommodated and some new institutional pillars grafted on, but the basic order of society and polity remained intact.

More recently, some newer interests began to make their presence felt. From the 1930s on, organized labor, usually incorporated in the form of official, government-controlled syndicates, directed and often organized by the elitist and middle-sector ruling groups, was assimilated into the prevailing structure. Now, albeit in the same paternalistic fashion, it has become the peasants' turn. The extension of the labor laws to the rural areas, the enactment of agrarian reform laws, the structural innovations in the countryside being carried out in Peru and elsewhere provide ample illustration of this. Frequently, these changes in labor's or the peasants' position have been introduced as a result of structured violence, or the threat of violence, emanating from the workers and rural masses themselves; but more often they have come about through the action of the ruling elements seeking to ensure their hegemony and control of the change process. Moreover, once these techniques of structured violence and frequently revolutionary posturing have helped the labor and peasant leaders to secure their place in the system, the tendency has been for them also to become conservative and guard their positions against new encroachments (254, 384).

Change in the Iberic-Latin context, as Morse states, has been not so much a matter of "fundamental" change in the European or North American sense (that is, implying a revolutionary transformation, the substitution of one ruling class for another, or the obliteration of the past) as it was the mediating and gradual accommodating of the accoutrements and rallying cries of industrial civilization to a political culture that remained in its essence Ibero-Catholic, creole-feudal, and patrimonialist (348). A number of adjustments were made, but the basic pattern of ownership and wealth was perpetuated; the fundamental two-class structure of society continued; past value and behavioral norms were preserved; the system of "<u>fueros</u>," patronage, and privileges was retained; and the structure of power and society remained hierarchical, elitist, authoritarian, and corporative. Some new social groups were assimilated, but this has generally been accomplished under the tutelage and containment of the older ruling groups and norms. These latter elements have also been the chief beneficiaries of development. Thus, as an ECLA study concluded, the "traditional structure" of Latin America, "far from having been rigid and impenetrable, has had sufficient permeability for a good many of its component parts to be modernized, without this having implied a swift and radical process of 'modernization'" (131).

THE CHANGE PROCESS

We have been considering the religio-theoretical aspects of Iberic-Latin political culture and provided an overview of the sociopolitical system and its modifications, but we have not so far addressed ourselves explicitly to an analysis of the change process.

In keeping with the Catholic-Thomistic conception, society and the state in the Iberic-Latin context are thought of as an organic whole with a profoundly moral purpose. Attempts are thus made, through personal and family ties, the compadrazgo, and personal identification with the leader, to construct various linkage mechanisms so that a sense of "belonging" is engendered and all are integrated into the prevailing structure. Branches, associations, and official syndicates now exist for nearly everyone. The national system is often conceived in terms of the family metaphor--implying strong, benevolent leadership; assigned, accepted duties, privileges and status; a purpose greater than the sum of its individual parts. It is now the state, replacing the Crown, that serves as the instrument of national integration, incorporating diverse groups and interests, and functioning as the regulator and filter through which new social and political forces have their legitimacy recognized and are admitted into the system. Power tends to be concentrated in the executive and in the bureaucratic-patrimonialist state machinery; the president is viewed as the personification of the nation with a direct identification with and knowledge of the general will of his people. The bureaucracy serves to dispense the available goods, favors, and spoils to the deserving. The traditional patrón-client relationship thus remains strong, with the government and its many agencies playing the role of national patrón, replacing the caudillos and local hacendados of the past. The same paternalistic clientela system persists, dressed up in new and more "modern" forms, but retaining its traditional substance and mode of operation (412, 491).

The same traditional hierarchical, corporative, elitist, and authoritarian orientation and structure is also still present today, modified by twentieth-century changes but by no means destroyed by them (223, 391). Politics still centers around the old, hierarchically organized and vertically compartmentalized system of corporate intereses and elite groups, now broadened somewhat to include the newer elements, but still authoritarianly controlled from the top and linked together directly through the government. The "corporative framework" thus refers to a system in which the political culture and institutions reflect an historic hierarchical, authoritarian, and organic view of man, society, and polity (140, 144). In the corporative system, the government controls and directs all associations, holding the power not only to grant or withhold juridical recognition (the sine qua non for the group's existence) but also access to official funds and favors, without which any sector is unlikely to succeed or survive. Group "rights" or "fueros," hence, take precedence over individual rights; similarly, it is the "general will" and the power of the state that prevail over particular interests. The government not only regulates all associations and corporate bodies but also seeks to tie those that have earned their place in the existing system into a collaborative effort for integral national development. Obviously, the system works best where the number of interests is small and within a context of shared values, but it is not necessarily incompatible with a growing pluralism of ideologies and social forces.

In the virtually inherently corporative systems of the Iberic-Latin nations, the effort is made to ameliorate social and political conflict, to deal with it bureaucratically, rather than to provoke divisiveness and breakdown. In both theory and practice, administration supercedes politics; thus, society is represented functionally in terms of its component segments and organized bureaucratically, with the government seeking to maintain the proper balance between the various interests coordinated into the state apparatus (101). Political issues are dealt with more through the process of elite integration and the granting of access to the spoils and privileges that accrue with acceptance into the system, rather than through program enactment and implementation. The greatest need is social and political solidarity; there can be no room for divided loyalties, autonomous political organizations, or challenges to the system's fundamental structure. The personnel of government may shift, new groups and ideas may be assimilated, and the elites may rotate in power (thus giving the appearance of change more than its substance); but the essentials of the sociopolitical order and the base on which it rests must remain steadfast (143). The newer groups may be coopted in, but they cannot challenge or seek to topple the system per se. Those that do will likely be crushed--unless their goal is merely the limited one of trying to demonstrate a power capability and the right to be admitted as a bargaining agent in the larger system. This kind of limited and usually carefully orchestrated violence may be tolerated, even accepted; a movement aimed at toppling the entire structure, in contrast, can expect to and will likely be suppressed (21).

In the corporative system, considerable change can and does take place, but it usually comes from the top downward and not necessarily as a result of pressure from below. A culturally conditioned form of "democracy" may be established, as in Venezuela, Colombia, Uruguay, Chile, or Costa Rica, but its structure is that of tutelary or guided democracy directed from above. The state system is founded on a structure of institutionalized popular movements. An attempt is thus made to transfer the traditional elitist values to the rising newer groups through example and education. First, the business-commercial elements were "civilized" in this way, then the rising middle sectors, now the lower or popular classes. That helps explain the persistent presence in the Iberic-Latin context of government-supported and -run trade unions, political parties, peasant leagues, professional associations or "colleges," etc. Through these agencies, often bureaucratic appendages of the state, the prevailing systems have sought to institutionalize and thus contain the rising social forces. Middle and now lower-class elements are offered marginal benefits and a stake in the system as a means of diffusing discontent and of putting them directly under the paternalistic direction of the state. "Agrarian reform," for example, has become more an instrument of social control than of social change. In this way the dominant elements have skillfully managed the historic unfolding of the development process, channeling it in preferred directions and either coopting in or snuffing out new challenges to their power and way of life (391).

It is the duty of the state and its líder to organize public opinion and maintain the proper societal equilibrium through the delicate balance of domestic interests and, increasingly in the 1960s, foreign pressures. Decisions are usually made by a cadre of elite-group representatives, linked by formal and informal ties to the administrative hierarchy and centering, ideally, in a single individual who personifies the national values, knows the general will, and is the best and most-qualified leader. The U.S. ambassador and the various U.S. mission heads may also be included in this coterie. Traditionally, patronage, status, and access to the channels of influence and wealth, rather than concrete benefits, served as the chief media of political currency; now, however, at least lip service (and sometimes more than that) must be paid to program enactment and implementation. Patronage, privileges, even programs are doled out by the state in exchange for support and acquiescence to official policies by groups who might otherwise attempt organized opposition (140). Hence, the public service becomes a huge "social security" system—a haven for friends, relatives, party hacks, and dissident oppositionists, as well as for a large part of the middle class and now increasingly the labor and peasant leaders, who are in effect "bought off" by being put on the public payroll. Effective program implementation is difficult by a bureaucracy for which this was traditionally a secondary function (178, 460).

The corporative framework helps maintain the traditional structure while concurrently providing for limited change through the cooptation of new social and political units into the administrative apparatus of the state system. Corporate structures, reinforced by a political culture grounded on hierarchy, status, and patronage, enable the traditional sociopolitical forms in the Iberic-Latin tradition to hang on so tenaciously. The corporative framework helps preserve the status quo but also provides for the gradualist, incremental accommodation to newer currents. It helps keep the pressures for change in check by minimizing the possibilities for disruption and full-scale revolution (140, 144). The corporative state may thus respond to modernization and adopt those "modern" aspects that are useful and can be controlled, but in seeking at the same time to preserve certain traditional attitudes and institutions, it may reject the social and political concomitants that ordinarily accompany the modernization process.

It should be emphasized that the corporative structures and value system are nothing new in either Spain, Portugal, or Latin America. They did not originate in the 1920s and 1930s when the corporative states and certain "integralist" ideologies acquired self-consciousness, power, and a full-blown statement of political philosophy, but stretch back for centuries to ancient and medieval political theory and organization and were transferred by the metropoles to the New World. In the warp and woof, the dialectic of Iberic-Latin development, they have been reformulated and updated many times, but the basic organic-corporate-elitist structure of the sociopolitical system has remained steadfast.

In the Iberic-Latin political systems, new social groups and political forces, new ideas and new institutional arrangements, may be appended on in a continuous fusion-absorption process, but, owing to the absence of genuinely revolutionary transformations in that tradition, old ones are seldom completely discarded (21, 350). Only in Mexico, Cuba, and perhaps Bolivia and Peru, have there been sharp breaks with the past by destroying the power of the traditionally privileged elites; in the rest of the countries, and even in some of those that have had revolutions, the traditional structures remain strong. In the sociopolitical structure as well as in the theoretical base, one is reminded of Anderson's "living museum" concept. Organizational forms which have died off or been discarded elsewhere in the West continue in the Iberic-Latin context to exhibit a remarkable durability and viability, adapting and coexisting with those newer currents which industrialization and modernization spawned.

As a result of the tenacity of these traditional sociopolitical institutions, there has been limited "development" in the Iberic-Latin nations in either a Marxian or Almondian sense. The Iberic-Latin political process has involved not the transcendence of one "class" or "stage" over another but the combination of diverse elements pertaining to distinct historical periods in a tentative, working arrangement. The question has been not so much one of "development" or "modernization" but of reconciling, in Morse's words, the static and vegetative features of the older, patrimonial-corporate state with the imperatives of a modern, urban, industrial order. The traditional order has not been so rigid as is usually pictured but flexible, permeable, and capable of absorbing a variety of newer currents—without undermining the traditional structures in the process. It has assimilated those features of modernity that were necessary and could be controlled, but it has rejected the rest. As the newer elites and social forces have been absorbed into the dominant system, the number of participants has slowly increased, but the system itself has changed little. Hence, in virtually all the Iberic-Latin nations, there is a series of distinct social and political forms, each superimposed upon the other, with new elements continuously being appended on and adapted to an older tradition, but without that older tradition being sloughed off or even undergoing many fundamental transformations.

These distinct but overlapping layers originate in different historical eras, but in the Iberic-Latin tradition they have been combined and blended. It is the genius and on-going challenge of politics and politicians in these nations that they have been able to function and accomplish anything at all of a developmental sort, given the heterogeneous, frequently crazy-quilt political systems in which they must work (347).

In seeking to explain these aspects of the Iberic-Latin change process, Richard Adams has fashioned a theory of what he terms "secondary development" (1). Secondary development refers to the course development takes when it enters an area that was previously an isolated hinterland of the industrial revolution and of the modern world. Development in Latin America does not <u>follow</u>, as a matter of successive stages, the development patterns of Western Europe and North America but involves the <u>adaptation</u> of an older order to some newer forces. This is a process of derivation, assimilation, and reorganization, not of innovation. Secondary development, in Adams's formulation, implies the importation and adaptation of more modern social and political organizations and techniques and their superimposition on top of an already-established sociopolitical order, not the replacement of the one by the other.

In Anderson's terms (21), the key dilemma in the politics of these nations is and has been to find a formula for reaching agreement among various "power contenders" whose power is unequal and whose interests and life-styles are almost totally incompatible because they emerged from and pertain to quite different historical epochs. Characteristically, the political process involves manipulation and almost constant negotiation among these several power contenders, for elections are tentative and but one means to power, and they do not carry the definity they do in the Anglo-American context. The shuffling and reshuffling of the delicate power balance is almost an everyday preoccupation. The distinctive flavor of the change process is that new power contenders may be accommodated and admitted to the system, if they accept and conform to its rules, but old ones are not eliminated. However, because these various elites and <u>intereses</u>--landowners, businessmen, Church, army, middle sectors, students, labor, peasants--emerged from different eras, with distinct expectations and uneven bases for their power and legitimacy, the attempt to fashion an accommodation between them is exceedingly difficult. The job of the president, who must juggle and reconcile these contending forces and maintain the equilibrium between them, is complex and uncertain.

One comes to think, writes Newton, in terms of "multiple currents of cultural evolution moving at different rates to uneven rhythms, regressing as well as advancing, submerging as well as predominating, intersecting and interacting fortuitously within the framework of a given metropolis, a given institution, or indeed, a given personality structure" (359). Some modernization is possible within this context, but only within circumscribed limits. Politics, Anderson says, thus involves the capacity to combine heterogeneous and incompatible power contenders and capabilities in a conditional and continuously shifting coalition. Frequently, these efforts involve what to North Americans appear to be some incredible marriages of convenience--alliances that defy not only all "reason" but also our conceptions of ideological consistency, or the stretching or interpretation of the law and constitution so as to render them all but meaningless. Yet it is precisely these features, the application of a little "grease" here or a little cement there, that help account for the distinctive flavor of the development process in these countries and that give them their dynamism and capacity to respond. If we wish to understand this process, the focus of scholarly inquiry ought also to be toward this direction: not seeking to bring to bear categories and concepts derived from a different tradition and their application to societies where they do not fit, but trying to comprehend the Iberic-Latin systems in their own terms and context, the way traditional institutions have been modified to meet the exigencies of modern times as well as how the modernizing groups have used traditional institutions to further their own ends (140).

Kalman Silvert's analysis of what he terms the "Mediterranean ethos" or "syndicalism" also closely parallels the present framework (466-471). This ethos is founded upon a value system dedicated to hierarchy, order, and absolutes. The urge toward corporatism provides another manifestation of this ethos, since the organization of men by functions is in accord with the historical tradition and actualizes the love of order and hierarchy, serves to contain divisive class conflict, avoids the hated liberal and materialistic values, but also provides for the slow and at least partial adaptation of traditional, patrimonial society to urbanization, industrialization, and modernization. An effort is made to bring into harmonious coexistence those characteristics venerated from the past and those considered valuable in the modern world. The good society is still pictured as one where each individual is rooted and secure in his life's station, where representation is determined by functions and status and not as the result of mere citizenship, where decision-making is centered in the hands of corporate, sectoral elites who are harmonized and coordinated into an organic whole, and where the state exercises firm but benevolent authority over the whole scheme. The "City of God" still takes precedence in many respects over the "City of Man," but since a modern society cannot exist on this simple bi-institutional basis any more, the Iberic-Latin response has been to erect new institutionalized pillars to accommodate the changes taking place. Each pillar remains highly striated by social class, with recruitment into the upper levels still largely a function of social position. As Silvert concludes, "The major social purpose of the syndicalist approach is to find a way of subsuming the new class complications of modernization to hierarchy, preserving a kind of Latin 'Fuhrerprinzip,' leaving inviolate the privileges and power of the traditional, and thus escaping the secularization and, to their eyes, immorality of the nation state."

THE CRISIS OF THE TRADITIONAL SYSTEM

What we have termed the corporative framework for the

analysis of sociopolitical change in Iberia and Latin America has exhibited remarkable staying power. At present, however, the traditional system is experiencing a crisis of major proportions which may sweep away the regime of hierarchy, elites, and special privileges once and for all (209, 392).

We may use as our point of departure Bernice Hamilton's assertion that "the fabric of natural law of the sixteenth century could only remain unshaken in a homogeneous, fairly static society with no major cleavage on moral principles, or in a primitive community which had little disturbing contact with the outside world" (191). Clearly, these conditions no longer apply in the Iberic-Latin nations. They are no longer homogeneous or static; major cleavages have emerged as to the proper way of ordering society and polity; and contact with the outside world, as well as deep foreign involvement in their internal affairs, has helped break down the traditional isolation. Since World War I, particularly, to use an arbitrary and approximate cut-off date, the pace of change has been accelerated, new social forces have emerged, the older basis of legitimacy has been increasingly challenged, and the foundations on which the ancient order rested have been progressively undermined.

First, the older power bases--and the religious, social, behavioral, and economic foundations on which they rested--are in decline (2). These include the village community, the <u>hacienda</u>, the Church, caudilloism, the extended family, the landed oligarchy, the traditional cadre-type parties, and so on. Meanwhile, newer power bases have emerged, including the educated <u>tecnicos</u> and professionals, organized labor and peasants, mass-based political parties, more professionalized and development-oriented militaries, the "new" Church, and the like. The situation is complicated by the presence of various external influences--principally the United States, but also encompassing a myriad of international agencies and other foreign pressures--in the domestic politics and social programs of these countries. This is a factor with which the neatly patterned system of adding new pillars and power contenders, as described by Silvert and Anderson, does not adequately come to grips. The fact that new interests have emerged who have organized themselves around principles not previously considered the only right or legitimate ones for the society, that the old interests and corporate units are themselves undergoing transformation, that new values and organizing principles are competing for men's minds, that government is being called upon to perform services that it never provided before, that foreign pressures and influences have multiplied--all these and other changes have added a new, complex, and increasingly conflicting dimension to the Iberic-Latin potpourri.

Politics have become progressively more class-, issue-, and interest-oriented. The traditional mechanisms for accommodating and adapting to change have also begun to break down. The Brazilian "<u>jeito</u>," for instance, which may be loosely translated as "grease" and which has traditionally served as a many-faceted means to ease the cumbersome turning of the wheels of government, is no longer, under conditions of "no nonsense" military rule, quite the effective instrument that it was before. The pace of change is becoming so rapid and its extent so great that the traditional techniques of adjustment, accommodation, and cooptation are proving inadequate. The participation crisis is reaching revolutionary proportions, the level of new demands and expectations has far outstripped the capacity of the political systems to cope with them, and the older corporate-elitist structures are proving incapable of handling the new pressures that have suddenly been thrust upon them. The present Iberic-Latin political panorama has tended to become a profoundly fragmented and unstable one, marked by the absence of any single consensus, by the tenacious attempt of the traditional elements to hang onto their wealth and power, by the rising revolutionary sentiments of the masses, and by the weakness and ineffectiveness of those who might occupy the middle way. We are witnessing the erosion and at least partial eclipse of the old order but without the emergence of a sufficiently strong or legitimized newer order to take its place.

It is difficult to maintain the ideal of the nation as an organic "family" when the common basis of understanding on which the older solidarity was based no longer exists, when the earlier idea of the "harmonization" of classes is giving way to class conflict, when the number of interests or pillars in the corporate structure has multiplied beyond the capacity of the traditional mechanisms to control them, when issues are confined no longer to small elitist coteries but reach further down into the social scale and now involve the early stirrings of mass mobilizationalist politics, when new educational and ideological formulas are replacing the paternalism and accepted truths of the past, and when increased national divisiveness and polarization have set in. A framework of order and stability has increasingly been superseded by a philosophy of change. New ideologies, new interests, and new institutional forms organized internally, coupled with new pressures from the external environment, have combined to provoke a challenge of unprecedented proportions to the older, established institutions.

Yet, with all these changes, the traditional organic-corporate-elitist-patrimonialist order in the Iberic-Latin nations remains remarkably strong and viable. With one or two exceptions, it is still probably the dominant mode throughout the countries of this culture area. Moreover, its capacity to weather these newer challenges should not be underestimated. The evidence is considerable for the capacity of the dominant elites to continue mobilizing workers and peasants into official appendages of the traditional corporate structure, to thus defuse mass discontent and maintain their own privileged positions intact, to manage the pressures from the United States and other external influences chiefly to their own advantage, to articulate new developmental ideologies, and to erect new institutional arrangements which provide more the appearance of change than its substance, to continue to direct and control the essentials of the entire change-modernization process. Though we, as committed "developmentalists," may prefer other forms of change, and though our scholarly analyses, often exhibiting what we might call wishful political sociology, may focus on those groups and institutions which seem to offer the best hope for rapid modernization or democratization, it is the older and still

venerated tradition that remains dominant, whose structure and
methods of adaptation and assimilation have not been adequately
studied, but which we ignore at the risk of even longer misunderstanding the Iberic-Latin nations.

CONCLUSION AND IMPLICATIONS

The first part of the 1960s saw a great outpouring of books
and articles which offered a generally hopeful and optimistic view
of the development process in emerging nations; in the later 1960s
there was considerable disillusionment with this hopeful view and
more and more questioning of the assumptions and biases on which
the model rested. By this time we are safe in concluding that, for
all the fresh perceptions and stimulus to research which the general development literature provided, it subjected not only Latin
America but much of the so-called "third world" to too hasty interpretation and overgeneralization. The echoes of Marxian and Weberian theory, both based on the common assumption of the dissolution
of traditional societies before the onslaught of industrialization
and modernization, have reverberated widely, too widely, far beyond
the examples of those nations, principally of Western Europe, on
whose developmental experience these two paradigms are essentially
grounded. The assumption of both these models is that traditional
societies are hardened shells capable only of remaining obdurately
unyielding or else shattering into pieces. The fact is, however,
that many traditional societies, and particularly those of the
Iberic-Latin nations, have proved to be remarkably permeable and
flexible, assimilating at various points more "modern" and more
"rational" elements but without thereby losing their characteristic features (357, 441).

Granted that much of the work in comparative political development provides new and sometimes perceptive insights, the proposition presented here is that the Latin American nations, as well as
their two mother countries, Spain and Portugal, are subject to special imperatives as offshoots of a Catholic, Iberic, patrimonialist, semifeudal Europe _circa_ 1500, which never experienced until
recently the full force of the great revolutionary movements that
we associate with the rise of the modern era and whose traditional
institutions, through accommodation and assimilation, have not been
swept away under the impact of the change process but have remained
largely intact and, indeed, quite viable even to this day. It is
time to put away the concept of a unilinear path to development, to
reexamine the narrow and frequently ethnocentric models on which
these interpretations are based, to begin to examine the Iberic-
Latin nations on their own terms rather than through the lenses of
some universal scheme that, upon examination, turns out to be far
less universal than its advocates have posited (537). In the
Iberic-Latin context, the issue even now may be not the either-or
one of reform or revolution, of tradition versus modernity, but of
adjustment, adaptation, accommodation, and continued muddling
along. This remains still not so much a matter of class conflict,
in a Marxian sense, or of transcendental development, from a North
American point of view, but of reconciling, largely on an ad hoc

basis, the conflicting currents of traditional and modern that continue their interplay within the Iberic-Latin culture, and of assimilating those desirable features of the modern, industrial world to a way of life that retains much of its traditional essence (348). Perhaps it is appropriate here to suggest something of a <u>verstehen</u> approach to the study of these foreign areas, for it is clear that future developments in comparative politics are not likely to take place at the level of grand, universal theory-building but at a lower level and by culture areas (225).

The framework employed here implies that the change process in the Iberic-Latin tradition has been and remains a fairly, but by no means wholly, conservative one. The corporative structure serves the interests of the dominant elites by subordinating the rising social forces to the authority of the elite-dominated central state apparatus. The peculiarly Iberic-Latin model of development seeks to preserve as much as possible of the traditional order by structuring the participation of these newer power contenders under its control and direction (140). But while the change that takes place within this mold often seems inordinately slow and circumscribed, one should not assume that no change at all is possible. Change in the Iberic-Latin context, we have emphasized, has occurred through a special and often unique process, usually gradually and incrementally, through adaptation and assimilation, within a framework that combines and seeks to reconcile traditional and modern rather than implying the transcendence of one over the other or of one "class" or "stage" over another. In the past, most change in Latin America has come discontinuously and usually not as the result of any major quantum leaps forward, or even through much purposeful action. Change has come, ordinarily, by fits and starts, through the repeated crises and alternations of government that Latin America is popularly known for, through shifting coalitions, cabinet changes, barracks revolts, new realignments, and the circulation of elites. In all of these changes there is usually implied some subtle shift in the balance of power, the accommodation of new groups and new ideas, the demonstration of a new power contender of its power capacity and, hence, of the legitimacy of its claim to be incorporated into the dominant, corporate power structure. Change takes place not so much as the result of any great or glorious revolution but through continuous shifts in the constellation of sociopolitical forces, through disintegration and ad hoc rebuilding, from various forms of structured and unstructured violence that seldom reaches the dimension of a full-scale revolution. This may not, by North American standards, be a very "rational," ideologically consistent, or model-conforming way to achieve development, but it is often development nevertheless, cumulative and thus eventually of a structural sort (21, 75, 206). Moreover, it does seem to correspond, more realistically than those models often employed in the past, both with the peculiar nature of the historic, Iberic-Latin development process and also with the present realities of power and society in these nations.

One final consideration merits mention, and that involves the outcome of the process we have described. At this point, based on the analysis and conclusions presented, one might well arrive at a fairly hopeful and at least modestly optimistic prognosis for the future development of the Iberic-Latin nations. Up to a point, indeed, some optimism may be justified. But as the process we have been describing unfolds, as new ideologies, new frames of reference, and new power contenders are constantly added on without the older and anachronistic ones being cast off, there comes a time when a kind of saturation and national paralysis sets in, when the number of corporate interests and ideologies becomes so large and divergent that they are no longer manageable or reconcilable, when, hence, in the absence of any common consensus or of a dominant ruling coalition, the national fabric begins to unravel, when crisis becomes a constant and virtually everyday fact of life, when an almost Hobbesian war of all against all ensues, and when national politics becomes a situation of seemingly permanent disintegration and conflict. The future of the Iberic-Latin nations lies not in Bolivia or even Cuba and probably not in those others that have been mentioned as possible developmental models, but more likely in Argentina or perhaps Uruguay, by all indices among the most "modern" of the Latin American nations, but which, precisely because they are so socially differentiated and with such a wide variety of groups and interests competing in the political arena, have also progressed further along that path to virtually permanent national breakdown (224, 373, 467). The result of the change process in Latin America is unlikely to be the final triumph of a new order and epoch over the older one, nor a more-or-less peaceful transition from traditional to modern, but a series of eruptions and blockages, a continuation of the present system coupled with a deterioration in its capacity to manage and accommodate to change in the traditional fashion, a rise in tension and society-wide praetorianism, and a long-term condition of spiraling discord, institutional paralysis and decay, and recurrent breakdowns (136, 211, 433).

NOTES

a. For the argument that Spain and Portugal should be included as part of a single Iberic-Latin culture area, see 180, 466.

b. The development literature of the last decade has largely ignored or dealt only uncomfortably with the place of Latin America in these various schemes. The nations of Latin America can hardly be called "New States"; they are not "Non-Western"; they do not often identify or think of themselves as a part of the "Third World"; and there is considerable doubt as to whether they are "emerging" or "developing." For a parallel argument to the one offered here, that Latin America should be regarded "as something of a Fourth World, with characteristics of its own which entitle it to be studied in its own right and not forced to conform to whatever generalizations can be made about the Third," see J. D. B. Miller, The Politics of the Third World (London 1967), Introduction. See also 246, 318, 354.

5 | Alternative Paradigms: The "Conflict" and "Consensus" Models

In the previous chapters, we have traced the historical pattern of Latin American development, spelled out some of the dimensions of both change and continuity characteristic of that pattern, and suggested some of the more salient and distinctive features of the Latin American change and/or development process. We have also presented an early statement of "The Corporative Model" or "The Corporative Framework." In this chapter, we back up a step or two in order to offer some disclaimers regarding the model just presented, to discuss the alternative "Conflict" and "Consensus" paradigms in order to understand better the context out of which "The Corporative Model" emerged (a), and to introduce some reservations and qualifications regarding "The Corporative Model" itself.

SOME DISCLAIMERS

Before delving deeper into the discussion of "The Corporative Model" and its utility and implications as presented in this book, it is necessary to make some disclaimers. The first of these involves the disavowing of any pretensions to having fashioned a full-blown or "scientific" theory of development. Rather, this exercise has more modest goals. As political science has become more methodologically self-conscious in recent years and as the canons of scientific research have become more rigorous, the theory builders have tended to become more and more isolated from those who work in the field. Theory building for the sake of theory building, without establishing its relationship to the real world, has always bothered the present author somewhat, just as has data collection for the sake of data collection. What follows, therefore, is not to be confused with "scientific" or "pure" theory but involves the setting forth of a number of observations, guidelines, and ordering principles that seem to have some heuristic value. That is, they provide a rough and tentative method of ordering and arranging a great deal of data; they help map a research terrain; they serve as instruments of self-education; they help facilitate research; they provide a means for laying out variables and hypotheses and discussing the relations between them; and

---

From "Elites in Crisis" (Mershon Center, 1970).

they suggest why a particular approach is useful in the examination and testing of propositions. They help provide that indispensable link and feedback between data collection and the process of more general theory development that seems to the author to be at the heart of scholarly inquiry. Since heuristic theory of this sort does help develop our sensibilities and understanding and helps facilitate research and the development of general theory, it seems appropriate to have this exercise go under that label (13).

A second disclaimer involves the recognition that every theoretical construct must necessarily represent a simplification. An explanation which is as complex and multidimensional as the event it aims to describe is really of no utility at all. At the same time, to try to force all the dimensions of a complex historical event onto a single explanatory axis is bound to lead to oversimplification. We must seek to avoid elevating useful but partial explanations into exclusive and all-encompassing ones. While every scholar is, of course, free to adopt his own theoretical framework, every such schema exacts a price by its selective inattention to data that do not fit in. The approach of this study recognizes the complex, multicausality of most historical events while, at the same time, it seeks to understand these in terms of a set of theorems, propositions, and ordering concepts that can be called a "conceptual framework" or an "ideal type," a construct that represents an approximation of reality and is not intended to be its mirror (383, 505). This framework is derived, moreover, not <u>a priori</u> from some existing "truth" but from the empirical evidence that the Latin American experience itself provides.

In adopting such a theoretical schema, one must exercise caution so as to avoid ascribing to it qualities which it does not possess. That is the third disclaimer that must be mentioned. For not only does any conceptual framework and set of theorems necessarily simplify to an extent, but one must be careful not to reify one's own creation. The ideas presented here are tentative, a set of working concepts and nothing more, which are to be revised or scrapped altogether as the empirical evidence becomes "harder." Terms like "development," "modernization," and the like, we must recognize, are at best abstractions, useful metaphors that conjure up images in our mind and help us think about and order more complex events, but metaphors nonetheless (361). Some of the terms and categories used here, therefore, are at times somewhat simplified, and some of the distinctions are not so neat or with so little overlap as we would like for purposes of unambiguous categorization and strict methodological procedure. But then, in the real world these lines are often not so clear-cut either. Though these distinctions are useful for analytical purposes, we must bear in mind that the realities they serve to order and help explain are infinitely more complex; further, that some of the general propositions here presented may have to be modified or abandoned altogether as the case study evidence accumulates.

A fourth disclaimer has to do with the limited claims made for the "corporative model." It is offered not as a substitute for other approaches but as a complement to them. It aims to correct some oversights in and overemphasis on "developmentalist" or "structuralist" approaches, but not at throwing out their more useful insights. Although these other approaches are strongly critiqued here, the intention is to show that they are incomplete explanations and not that they should be scrapped altogether. The corporative model is, hence, to be used not in place of these others but along with them.

THE "CONFLICT" AND THE "CONSENSUS" MODELS

The Latin American countries are currently going through a process of change of epoch-making magnitude. These changes are not simple or of the palace coup type--a recurring phenomenon so familiar in Latin American history--but are of a far more profound, complex, and significant sort. They involve the fundamental restructuring and reordering of an entire system and way of life. The implications of these broad-scale changes--in the political culture, the economy, the society, and the political system--are enormous, affecting every area of Latin American life. Slowly, unevenly, discontinuously, the Latin American nations are beginning the great transformation from traditional to modern, from underdeveloped to developed, from old to new.

As these comments suggest, the changes taking place throughout Latin America are not entirely unlike those which other countries of the world have already gone through or are currently experiencing (407). Because the Latin American nations are not entirely unique in these regards, comparison with other nations may be possible; and for that reason, at least some of the general theoretical literature developed in the comparative politics field in the 1960s may be usefully employed. Yet one cannot, after examining the evidence, conclude otherwise than that the Latin American experience is somewhat distinct, that its developmental pattern is somewhat unusual, and that the classic, unilinear models of development simply do not apply.

In the past two decades, a period in which an unprecedented amount of scholarly research and official attention has been devoted to Latin America, two major models--a "consensus" model and a "conflict" model--have been widely employed to analyze the processes and vicissitudes of Latin American development and underdevelopment. Although there is much disagreement between the advocates of these two models, differences that are elaborated below, there are also some shared understandings. Scholars and public officials alike have demonstrated a level of agreement concerning some of the fundamental processes involved that, at least at the most general level, is quite remarkable. This reflects, in part, the growing interdependence, interchange, and feedback between the scholarly community and the government, particularly during the early-to-middle 1960s, and also a certain shared basis of understanding of "development" based on the European experience. As regards Latin America, it is generally agreed that change is occurring throughout the hemisphere; that a traditional, agrarian, two-class society, commonly referred to as semifeudal, is dying or fading away; that Latin America is undergoing the processes of modernization and development; and that it behooves both the U.S. and the

Latin American nations involved to recognize and get on the side of those changes.

While a considerable measure of agreement exists as to the general nature of the changes taking place in Latin America, there is also considerable--and growing--disagreement as to the selection of appropriate models to interpret these changes and, hence, in the prescriptions and policy recommendations that should follow (376). The reason for the growing scholarly discord--and for the current confusion as to what the proper U.S. policy should be--stems in large measure from the inadequacy and irrelevancy of the models we have used heretofore to try to explain Latin American development and, hence, of the policies based upon them. The argument of the present study, in fact, is that neither the "consensus" model nor the "conflict" model are, in themselves, sufficient for the assessment of present-day change in Latin America--or as bases on which to make policy recommendation. An attempt is here made, therefore, to suggest a framework for analysis that does seem to reflect more accurately the historical and contemporary Latin American experience. For convenience sake, we have termed this the "corporative model" and have tried to test its applicability and relevance in the Latin American context.

The "consensus" or "equilibrium" model of social and political change sees Latin America as gradually evolving from an agrarian to an industrialized society, from a rural to an urban one, from a society which was essentially particularistic, ascriptive, parochial, and functionally diffuse to one in which more universalistic values hold sway, where achievement considerations become paramount, which is functionally more differentiated and specific, and which is increasingly pluralistic, participatory, and democratic. The structure and legitimacy of the old order are giving way, and a new, more modern equilibrium is coming into existence. Without belaboring the point or elaborating further on themes that are already familiar, it is clear that these formulations owe a great deal to the seminal work of such sociologists as Max Weber and Talcott Parsons (382, 505), and they find specific applicability to the political sphere in the writings of such prominent "systems analysts" and "developmentalists" as Gabriel Almond, David Easton, A. F. K. Organski, Karl Deutsch, C. E. Black, Seymour M. Lipset, W. W. Rostow, and others (14, 46, 118, 128, 271, 370, 438). As applied to Latin America, the consensus model finds its expression in the essays of such writers as John J. Johnson, Martin C. Needler, and others (222, 353). This paradigm has undoubtedly been the dominant one in the political development field in the past.

The consensus model is derived largely from the modernization-development experiences of the already highly developed Western European and North American nations--and surely it is not coincidental that the foremost proponents of this approach have been socialized in and derived many of their intellectual conceptualizations from the experiences of these same nations. Briefly (and somewhat oversimply) stated, the consensus theorists argue that with modernization and development comes a progressive trend toward social equality and a concomitant decrease in class and ideological conflict. As a result of industrialization, growing prosperity, greater social mobility, and democratization, the old class stratifications are giving way and a generally moderate, egalitarian, pragmatic, middle-of-the-road and middle-class society and polity are coming into predominance. Rising affluence, expanded educational opportunities, the growth of communication, etc., are bringing into existence a new and more "modern" society in which the gaps between have's and have-not's have increasingly lessened, class lines have been bridged and blurred, and class conflict blunted. Feudal structures and traditions have progressively given way to more modern ones, while increased social and economic homogeneity has rendered largely meaningless the old ideological battles of the past and given rise to a new system of consensus based on equality, democracy, and social justice. Some of the other political concomitants to these broad-scale, socioeconomic changes include the decline of political passions, the growth of a modern mass-based, political-party system, an increasingly professionalized and a-political military and public service, a more balanced and pluralistic interest-group system, and a government which is both responsive and effective in satisfying the needs of its people.

Translated into foreign policy considerations, the consensus model finds expression in the U.S. foreign aid program and, specifically regarding Latin America, the Alliance for Progress. Indeed, it is by no means coincidental that some of the foremost "developmentalists" were also among the prime architects of the Alliance. For underlying the Alliance conception is the recognition of the modernizing currents sweeping over Latin America, the necessity of the U.S. to side and become aligned with the forces for change, and the requirement of channeling these changes in a peaceful, gradual, evolutionary, incremental fashion, as in the nineteenth- and early twentieth-century Anglo-American experiences. Through the techniques of economic pump-priming, road-building, military assistance, aid to education, and other controlled social reforms, the assumption is that Latin America may enter the modern world without falling prey to violent revolution or the possibilities of a Communist takeover (43, 438).

This entire package comes wrapped in the intellectual respectability of development-systems theory, which all but guarantees that the unfolding of the historical process will result in such a desirable outcome. Surely, it must be enormously comforting to <u>know</u> that, despite the instability and disorder of the moment, the model assures a favorable final result, that inevitably and as a matter of course the Latin American militaries will become more professional and a-political, the middle class will grow and eventually acquire all the supposed middle-class virtues (e.g., moderation, pragmatism, patriotism, etc.), the parties will develop, government will become more efficient and effective, and the Communist threat (a "disease of the transition," as Rostow called it--shortly before becoming a presidential adviser and putting his ideas to work) will diminish. If only we can hang on long enough, so the argument runs, and play for time until the socioeconomic changes occurring in Latin America have had a chance to work their inevitable repercussions in the political sphere, eventually these nations will come to look just like us--modern, developed, democratic, and so forth. Given these facile assumptions, here admittedly oversimplified, it is small wonder that among skeptics, men like Lipset, Rostow, Schlesinger, and others, for all their important early scholarly contributions to the literature of development, social change, and democratization, came, through the influence of their ideas on policy-making, to be known as "Dr. Yes" spokesmen for the U.S. foreign assistance program. That the processes of change with which they had previously been primarily concerned (Western Europe, North America) had little to do with the developmental experience of Latin America was ignored, forgotten, or simply unrealized.

The "conflict" model of Latin American development, for all its manifest and obvious differences with the consensus model, is based on many of the same assumptions. It, too, sees Latin America as emerging from an agrarian, feudal, two-class past to a capitalistic, entrepreneurial, bourgeois, industrial present. Indeed, many of the same categories which serve the consensus theorists--agraria/industria, feudal/capitalistic, two-class/multiclass--also serve the conflict theorists. Both are derived essentially from a Western European-North American model and both tend to interpret political change in terms of its socioeconomic determinants (334). The end result, of course, is different, but both conceive of the unfolding of the historical process in terms of a more or less linear progression. Both the consensus and the conflict theorists tend to use their conceptual constructs as a plan of action as well as a tool of historical analysis; and both are convinced that history is on their side, that in the end it will prove them right. But whereas the consensus theorists tend to view these changes from the perspective of the possibilities for peaceful compromise, accommodation, conciliation, and the achievement of a new balance in the form of the emergence of pluralistic, peacefully competitive, and democratic societies, the conflict theorists emphasize the discontinuities and polarizations that the development process brings on, the intensification of class conflicts, the fact that the social and economic development of Latin America is incompatible with prevailing U.S. interests, and, hence, the irrelevance--indeed, the damaging effects--of the consensus model as applied in the present Latin American situation.

The conflict model, of course, derives principally from Marxian analysis, finds contemporary expression in the writings of such diverse theorists as Paul Baran, Ralf Dahrendorf, and Barrington Moore, Jr. (36, 104, 341) and is applied to Latin America in the work of Andre Gunder Frank and recently edited volumes by Petras and Zeitlin and by Horowitz, de Castro, and Gerassi (156, 209, 392). The forms and expressions that conflict theory (including much dependency analysis) takes are almost as varied as those of the consensus theorists. Moreover, like consensus theory, conflict theory has its sophisticated and its unsophisticated theorists, its "refined Marxists" and its "vulgar Marxists." If one, for example, seeks to explain Latin American development or class behavior solely in terms of the ownership of the means of production, narrowly defined, then conflict theory as a tool of analysis would seem to have only narrow and limited utility; if, however, it is expanded to encompass social and power relations and dependency more broadly defined, then its usefulness in the Latin American context is greatly enhanced. That, in fact, is the direction that much of the new, "scientific" political economy and political sociology coming out of the newly created social science departments in the leading Latin American universities is taking. The conflict or "power elite" paradigm has in recent years increasingly challenged the dominant consensus-pluralist-interest group-equilibrium approach.

It almost goes without saying that the conflict theorists often function as dissenting "Dr. No's" to the U.S. foreign assistance program. They reject the notion that the Latin American militaries, given the elitist orientation of their officer corps, can play a constructive nation-building role, that the middle class will rise above its self-serving tendencies to become the bulwark of more stable and democratic systems, that agricultural technology is sufficient to encourage economic development without a prior restructuring of the social bases of rural society, and that Latin American aspirations are compatible with either private or official U.S. interests. Conflict theorists tend instead to put the emphasis on the fact that Latin America exists in a "neo-colonial" or dependency relationship vis-a-vis the U.S., that domestic socioeconomic and, hence, political relations are also dominated by a form of "internal colonialism" that is related to and closely bound up with the international marketplace, and that only by a revolutionary transformation of the bases of power can the Latin American nations succeed in breaking out of the colonial-dependency relationship in which they have been cast. The conflict theorists reject the notion of the Alliance for Progress that the moderate middle way of the social democrats can succeed in meeting the problems of underdevelopment, and they dismiss the assumptions on which U.S. assistance has been based as at best illusory and more than likely founded on bad faith and self-serving intentions.

It is easy to overstate the differences between the consensus and the conflict theorists, to caricature them and set them up as straw men so as to knock them down more easily. The fact of the matter is, however, that many scholars, whether consciously or not, explicitly or implicitly, employ one or the other of these paradigms or use some combination of them. Indeed, even those scholars whom we have here mentioned as belonging to one group or the other generally recognize at least some merit in the arguments of those whose approach is contrary to their own. Allowing for these gradations, therefore, and recognizing that this twofold classification is grossly oversimplified, it is still useful to distinguish rather sharply between the two models here discussed and to classify research in terms of which approach its author takes.

Both the consensus and the conflict models have much to offer the student of Latin American development, but neither model is adequate by or in itself. These approaches should be viewed not as providing final "truths" but only an opening threshold for research. Thus, the consensus model has helped us better understand changing patterns of legitimacy, some of the political implications of social and economic change, some implications of the growth of the mass media, and so forth. The systems approach, which has served as the handmaiden of consensus theory, has enabled us to see the relationships among the various parts of the system that we only weakly perceived before, forced us to deal as much with the informal "input" as with the formal-legal aspects of politics, helped us to incorporate functionalist theory and the findings of the other social sciences back into political science, and carried us at least part of the way toward the development of a comparative, more scientific, and less ethnocentric theory of societal change. The consensus theorists have also provided us with insights which help us better explain the process of development in such relatively stable, developed, democratic, and functional systems as Costa Rica and Venezuela. At the same time, as Latin America has industrialized, urbanized, and become more socially differentiated, and as its politics have become increasingly class- and interest-oriented, class analysis has provided us with a number of useful concepts and insights. Furthermore, as the U.S. presence has grown so enormously in the countries to our south and as the heavy hand of the U.S. in internal domestic affairs has increased, and as we have become more aware of the strength of international market forces, the concepts of social, economic, political, even cultural imperialism, colonialism, and dependency have taken on some real meaning that goes far beyond mere sloganeering on the part of a "few malcontents." This by no means exhausts the list of contributions provided by the approaches of these two conflicting though frequently complementary models of change in Latin America, but it is perhaps illustrative.

The argument of the present study, however, is that, while the consensus and conflict models have both proved useful and enlightening in some respects, both provide at best only partial explanations concerning the nature of change and continuity in contemporary Latin America. This has not only continued to obscure our understanding of the processes of development (and/or decay) in that area, but the fact that both models have at least partial validity and some usefulness as research tools has perpetuated an argument in intellectual circles, but with important ramifications at the policy level as well, that often misses the mark.

Though a brief critique of this sort runs the danger of gross oversimplification, it must be pointed out that there are some fundamental misconceptions and prejudgments in both the consensus and the conflict models. The consensus model misses the mark by continuing to assume--as in the Western European-North American pattern--that gradual economic growth in Latin America will automatically lead to the establishment of more modern, "developed" societies and polities, that inevitably more moderate, stable, middle-class democracies will result in which radical ideological passions will decline, the elite will acquire a sense of <u>noblesse oblige</u>, and the military, organized labor, and other groups in the system have been conditioned to accept their "proper," a-political roles. The evidence of recent years, however, seems to offer scant support for these propositions. Changes in the economic and to a limited extent the social sphere have not automatically produced more stable, democratic systems (in fact, quite the opposite may be true); the hoped-for new equilibriums have failed to emerge; political atrophy and decay rather than development seem to have set in. The correlations between such sociodemographic indices as literary levels, spread of mass media, industrialization, degree of urbanization, even rising per capita income and the institutional capacity to sustain growth and provide new goods and services appears in many countries to be a negative one. Economic and social moderization, in fact, instead of being the handmaiden of political development, seems to be disruptive of it. The rich in Latin America are still rich and getting richer; the poor are still poor and getting poorer; the middle sectors are still weak and fragmented; the military remains prone to intervene; instability, ideological conflict, social disintegration seem to have intensified. In most of the recent studies of Latin American "development," indeed, the real subject matter has been immobility, decay, sporadic eruptions, breakdowns, etc.; Latin America has not so much "developed" as it has stagnated and even atrophied (136).

The conflict theorists miss the mark by continuing to insist that class and ideological position are exactly consonant, that class identification and solidarity are necessarily increasing, that the peasants and/or workers are becoming increasingly revolutionary, that the "anti-imperialist" forces are becoming stronger, that the state is an exact reflection of class interests, and that Latin America is soon to explode in violent revolution. In most countries, however, the evidence seems to point to the continuing conservatism of the bulk of the peasantry and much of the working class, to the rise of nationalism but not necessarily of "anti-imperialism," to the continued capacity of the older elites to adapt to change rather than being overwhelmed by it, to a considerable degree of state autonomy, and to the fact that revolutionary movements have not been notably successful. Indeed, almost none of the cataclysmic predictions that accompanied Castro's rise to power and the renewed interest in Latin American affairs on the part of the U.S. in the early 1960s has come true: the Andes have not been set aflame, Castroism has not proved to be exportable, and the hemispheric showdown between capitalism and communism, the status quo and the pressures for change, have not, in fact, reached the showdown stage. Class analysis is of limited use even in explaining Latin American "class" behavior, and it has been of only partial utility in helping us comprehend the special role played by the state or by such corporate interests as the Church or the military. Class considerations, of course, play a part in any examination of Latin America--and, as these societies have modernized, an increasingly important part--but class is not the mirror reflection of economic and social history, nor can political, ideological, and other variables, or the crosscurrents of personal and family rivalries and interrelationships that are frequently so important in shaping Latin American political behavior, be neatly subordinated to class determinants (310, 325, 494).

The evidence, it seems to this writer, is overwhelming that neither the consensus nor the conflict model entirely squares with the empirical facts or fully explains Latin American political

behavior. Despite this, and while the proponents of these two
frameworks have continued a long and vigorous debate, there has
been relatively little calm and dispassionate examination of the
assumptions, presuppositions, and biases on which the two models
are based. Instead of having our interpretation of the change process emerge logically from Latin America's own past and present, we
have continued to impose our preconceived notions upon a set of
historical events to which they do not apply. It is here submitted
that both the consensus-pluralist "liberal" growth model and the
conflict-power elite "Marxian" model have been overgenerally
applied as regards Latin American development, that both approaches
provide only partial and incomplete explanations, that both bring
to their analyses a bias that derives from their own world view
rather than deriving from the field situation they are investigat-
ing. This has given rise to prejudice, ethnocentrism, and cultural
imperialism.

How can one explain our continued misinterpretation of the
Latin American change process, of the repeated use of inappropriate
indicators to explain development there? One crucial explanation
involves the fact that <u>both</u> the consensus <u>and</u> the conflict models
are derived from the narrow Western European-North American experiences and thus explain only inadequately the peculiar process of
Latin American development here outlined. We all tend to see the
case histories of others in the light of our own, and it is thus no
accident that the most influential writers dealing with development
themes--indeed, the concept itself--have come out of the Western
European and especially North American context. Since the nations
of this area tend also to be the most "developed" and most "modern,"
it should not be surprising that our developmental models usually
reflect the experience of these nations, not only positing univer-
salist principles to our own essentially peculiar tradition but
placing ourselves at the top of the list of "modern" societies and
seeing others as occupying varying stages of "backwardness," "traditionalism," or "underdevelopment" on the way to our own achievement. It is, furthermore, an easy step from underdeveloped nations
to underdeveloped peoples--a fact that may help explain the sense
of superiority and paternalism with which we have always viewed
Latin America. Much the same criticism applies to systems theory
and equilibrium analysis. Usually, the "system" that we take for a
norm is our own--frequently idealized and distorted almost beyond
recognition--and countries whose inner workings are somewhat different are almost by definition "dysfunctional." Equilibrium analysis likewise implies competitive, interest-oriented politics on
the U.S. model, is biased toward stability and gradualism, and may,
therefore, be inappropriate for countries seeking rapid and purposeful development (356).

Even within the Western European-North American context, moreover, the range of indicators we have chosen to concentrate on is
fairly selective and unrepresentative of the range of experience
even of the nations of that area. Using, for example, primarily
the Anglo-American experience and to a somewhat lesser extent the
French and German and perhaps even Benelux and Scandinavian experiences, we have tended to assume that political parties are not

only "good" but "modern," without taking into account that the development of parties in these contexts may represent a peculiar response to peculiar needs and that their range of functions in this milieu may have something less than universal applicability. Much the same is true with regard to the bureaucracy, the military, group relations, etc. Because certain ingredients are important in the politics of one area, we have simply assumed them to be important elsewhere--even the subdivisions and chapter heads of our studies thus often represent basic assumptions about the importance of certain groups and institutions in the political society which may or may not be valid.

The conflict theorists are often as biased as the consensus theorists in this regard, ascribing an importance to class as the driving force in change that in the Latin American context does not seem to be wholly borne out by the experiences of these countries. The Latin American state systems, for example, may sometimes act independently of all classes; similarly middle-class officer corps may go in quite different political directions. A key reason for our frequent misinterpretation of these phenomena is that both Marx and Weber, the leading lights of the conflict and consensus paradigms, respectively, as well as most of their disciples, derived their main ideas and concepts from the developmental patterns of the Western European and/or North American nations, or as a negative reaction to this. Both models, reflecting the intellectual and national origins of their respective proponents, are thus fundamentally ethnocentric; as a shorthand, we may term the consensus model the "Anglo-phile fallacy" and the conflict model the "Anglo-phobe fallacy" (b). Both are essentially "fallacies" in that they ascribe a universalistic character to concepts developed out of a far narrower context; and both may be termed essentially "Anglo" in that they are based upon, or were developed as a negative reaction to, the developmental traditions of a select group of countries centering in Northern and Western Europe and North America. Both the consensus and conflict models--indeed the whole concept of unilinear development that underlies them--if not "as American as apple pie," are surely as "Western" and "Judeo-Christian," and originate and are derived principally from that same "Westernizing" experience (c). As such, neither is entirely satisfactory for such emerging and Hispanic nations as those of Latin America.

DISCUSSION, RESERVATIONS, QUALIFICATIONS

In both the consensus and the conflict models, the peculiar Iberic-Mediterranean experiences of Spain and Portugal (and to a lesser extent, Italy and perhaps other Southern European countries) have been largely ignored (19, 180, 267, 450). This has not only distorted the various frameworks used, providing them with a false universality and a relative simplicity and neatness that would be lacking if the Portuguese and Spanish experiences were taken into account, but it has also been a profound disservice to the proper understanding of Latin America. For many of the roots of Latin America even today still lie in its peculiar Hispanic (or Portuguese) past, and it is impossible to comprehend fully the special nature of contemporary societal change in Latin America through the use of models derived from a quite distinct tradition. It is, of course, axiomatic in the social sciences that models are meant to be tools of research in order to help us order and arrange our data and to provide for better understanding and analysis--they are not of intrinsic value in themselves or to be worshipped for their own sakes. The models we use are, therefore, not to be imposed on data where they do not fit, nor are the data to be manipulated arbitrarily to fit the model. Rather, the process of scientific inquiry and the expansion of knowledge occur the other way around, for it is the theory that must be revised in keeping with the data, not the facts that must be modified to fit the theory. In the case of Latin America, we have often forgotten this elemental truth, accepting the models as given and selecting our facts to fit them rather than marshalling the data to revise or reformulate the theory. Once committed to a particular model, however, scholars and public officials frequently acquire a vested interest in it and are loath to give it up. Yet in the Latin American case, we must begin to rethink our earlier assumptions or we shall be doomed even longer to relive our past mistakes and to misunderstand fundamentally the nature of the contemporary changes taking place in that area.

Given the paucity of data on many aspects of Latin American development, it is neither possible nor appropriate to construct at this stage a full-blown model for the study of Latin American society and politics. Consequently, in these pages only the barest skeletal outlines and some broad guidelines are indicated which might be useful in constructing such a model. The conceptual scheme suggested, the author believes, has the advantage of not only more closely corresponding to the realities of the Latin American development process but also of incorporating what can profitably be used in both the consensus and the conflict models. Relatively little of what is contained here has not been said before in various places, but it may include some ideas of which we perhaps need to be reminded. Beyond that, it is hoped that the collecting of these scattered insights of various writers and the synthesis and arrangement of them in a more or less orderly fashion will lead us to see aspects of the process of development in Latin America that have thus far been largely ignored and that need to be more thoroughly researched and evaluated.

Any attempt to suggest a set of ordering concepts for the study of Latin American development must begin by recognizing the diversity of the nations of that area and of their developmental patterns. Argentina and Paraguay, for example, are as different from each other as either of them is from Italy or France; much the same could be said for the other Latin American nations. Any general statements about Latin America must, therefore, be qualified in terms of their greater or lesser applicability to the various countries.

Yet, it is really variations on some common themes that we are dealing with in Latin America, not differences in the themes themselves. Moreover, my own view is that, if we are to proceed with the fashioning of a genuinely comparative theory of political change, that goal is not likely to be well served through the use of some supposedly universal categories that turn out to be not nearly so universal and, in fact, quite ethnocentric. Rather, the process of theory-building must go forward incrementally, based on a prior thorough understanding of individual countries and areas. Of course, one cannot separate the task of theory construction from the task of gathering data, for the two go hand-in-hand; but it may be that this process will have to take place at a somewhat lower level of generalization than has recently been the case. Grandiose theories of development that encompass and purport to explain the whole world have not proved very satisfactory, and perhaps it is now time to get back to what we might term "middle-range theory" at the culture area level (225, 257, 537). If there is any area of the globe that is appropriate for genuinely comparative analysis, surely Latin America is it.

Latin America is sufficiently homogeneous that within some fairly wide bounds the most decisive and fundamental structural "types" and many of the same patterns may be observed. The similarities that exist among the Latin American countries, the regularities and comparable aspects, may be even more striking than the differences. One cannot but be impressed with the fundamental sameness of the Portuguese and Spanish colonies in the New World and of the remarkable parallels in their overall patterns of development since that time. In each colony, indigenous geographic, climatic, racial, and economic conditions blended with the institutions brought by Spain or Portugal to the Americas to shape the warp and woof of the variants that eventually evolved; but one cannot escape the fact that each of these variants, as fragments of Iberic society of around 1480-1580, had many fundamental commonalities. Throughout Latin America, the common ingredients were closed, absolutist, and authoritarian political and religious structures, rigid class-caste social hierarchies, exploitive mercantilist and agrarian-based semifeudal economies, and scholasticism and Thomism in the religious and intellectual spheres. The dominant forms of sociopolitical organization and behavior revolved around the requirements of strict centralization, order, rank, and estate, a persistent pattern of patrón-client relationships, patrimonialism, juridical definition and categorization, corporatism, and elitism.

It has only been in the past hundred years or so that the forces were set in motion that began to undermine the old order, and it is only in the past half century--in varying degrees and in varying fashions--that the traditional system has come under serious challenge. Economic, social, and political change began to accelerate. After some 400 years of relative slumber, backwardness, and stagnation, Latin America had "woken up" and begun to stir--not just at the top level, to which most changes in the past had been confined, but increasingly farther down in the social hierarchy (301).

Yet, while change is clearly affecting all areas of Latin American life, the types of changes occurring do not seem to correspond to the Western European-North American mold. Thus, while the old order seems to be in decay, to pronounce its epitaph now would surely be premature; and while a new order is rising, it has not

yet become predominant. It is, in fact, this uneasy balance and
frequent conflict between old and new, traditional and modern,
change and continuity that characterize much of Latin America today
and that accounts for much of the area's instability and disorder.
New blends and permutations are constantly being created.

Economic growth and industrialization, modern technology, increased societal differentiation, new values and belief systems,
new forms of organization, increased interdependence among men and
nations--all these and other innovations and far-reaching changes
are fundamentally altering the landscape of Latin American society
and politics, changing the face of the map, as they have of other
social and political systems before. Moreover, except for temporary and usually short-lived reversals, once this overall modernization process begins, it tends to generate its own independent
requirements and becomes its own motor force; and there is little
likelihood--despite the desires of some diehard traditionalists--
that the clock can be turned back and the old order restored. Allowing for appropriate time and regional lags, the sweep of these
changes is all-encompassing, cumulative, and probably irreversible.

Even accepting all this, however, what has occurred in Latin
America is that the dominant and historic elites have generally
been able to manage and control this change process, channeling it
in preferred directions and coopting or snuffing out those who have
risen to challenge their hegemony. By being adaptable, the traditional order, instead of being swept away as the change process has
gone forward, has persisted. These and other features have helped
make Latin American "development" distinctive.

It is precisely the lags and discontinuities, furthermore, the
pattern of uneven development, and the overlapping of social and
political phenomena stemming from quite different epochs--all factors that are usually dismissed in the general theoretical literature with a qualifying phrase--that are at the heart of the Latin
American development process. Accelerated change is occurring
throughout the length and breadth of Latin America, but in many
ways the traditional order and ways of doing things remain dominant. For anyone who has done field research in Latin America, it
is hard to believe that the aristocratic ethos and the social and
political institutions that go with it are dead or dying. The national economies are still organized essentially on a mercantilist
basis that presently goes by the label of "state capitalism." Social and political structures are most often organized even today
on hierarchical and authoritarian principles and bases. The patron-client system remains intact, even though its forms may now be different and more complex (412). Corporatist forms of organization,
functionalist representation, and vertically and horizontally compartmentalized systems are still powerfully present. The number of
corporate elites has been increased, but the fundamental structures
of society remain largely intact in most countries of the area.
The persistence of these institutions and practices has been remarkable.

While the traditionalist structures and ideal are still powerful, the immense pressures of the contemporary period have placed
an unprecedented burden upon them and there is no longer any

assurance that they will continue to be able to adapt, coopt, and
assimilate. In State Department jargon, it may be that the old
order and the political process that is a reflection of it are
about to be "overtaken by events," that the rapidity and pervasiveness of the changes presently sweeping the area have rendered the
traditional accommodation mechanisms obsolete, and that the ancient
and venerated structures and the older established interests are
soon to be overwhelmed and cast aside in favor of uncertain new
ones (223, 391). The established order is now being challenged,
both from below and from without, by the pressures emanating from
its own people as well as those from the international environment.
Whether the traditional structure can last in the face of these
pressures is at this moment still an open question.

The breakdown of Latin America's traditional isolation, further, has meant increased contact with and influence by the forces
and modernizing trends of the outside world. Concurrently, the
growing international role played by the United States in the post-
World War II period led to the rapid growth of the North American
presence and influence throughout the hemisphere. One of the major
dilemmas of the Latin American elite groups in recent years has,
thus, been how to acquire the "fruits" of the modern outside
world--such as the Alliance for Progress and U.S. aid--without in
the process destroying the base on which their power, position, and
wealth rest. This involves an enormously difficult juggling act--
one which the elites have managed with varying degress of success,
for it entails paying lip service to and giving the appearance of
democratic reformism without providing much of its substance (260).
The other side of this coin is that, with its preoccupation with
preserving stability at all costs, with "anti-communism" and the
"second Cuba complex," the U.S. and its aid programs have most
often been aligned with the traditional, status quo-oriented groups
and against the forces for change.

Though traditionalist outlooks and institutions remain strong
in all the Latin American countries, new ideologies, interests, and
institutions are rising to challenge them. In many cases, the
newer forces and institutions have simply been grafted onto the
older structures, overlapping with them in often-confusing and unsystematic fashion and yet not really replacing them. These include "republican," "bourgeois," and "popular" forms. There has
been growth in the number of sectoral participants, but little
change in fundamentals. As a result, most "development" in Latin
America has been merely the repeated grafting on of new layers in a
way that has become increasingly disjointed and unmanageable.

With the, at least, partial undermining of the traditional
order and yet its continued coexistence with more "modern" forms,
with the system of successive layers piled up, the one upon the
other, and with the absence in most of the Latin American nations
of a fully consolidated, newer sociopolitical order, no single set
of ordering principles or ideology and no new institutional infrastructure have acquired sufficient legitimacy or developed adequately to fill the vacuum that exists. The nations of Latin America, with only a few exceptions, are now existing in a state of almost perpetual discord. A wide variety of regimes--reflecting the

vast panoply of ideologies and movements uncomfortably coexisting there--have come and gone. The crucial problem of these societies has been not so much achieving modest economic growth as the lack of development of new political institutions capable of governing, the absence of a new set of national values to replace the one that is in decline, the lack of new regulative and accommodative mechanisms to handle the new pressures now being thrust upon them, and the absence of new instruments of solidarity and reconciliation (211). At the same time, the absence of genuine social revolution in all but two or three of the Latin American nations has enabled the traditional elites to preserve and enhance their fortunes, power, and way of life instead of their being discarded along the way, as was the case in Great Britain, France, the Soviet Union, and other nations. New types of specialized agencies and "corporations," such as trade unions and professional associations, and more differentiated social systems have come into existence; but this has not resulted in the creation of a viable new institutional structure or necessarily implied the triumph of the modernizing elements.

This heterogeneous, overlapping pattern calls into question one of the fundamental assumptions of both Marxian and developmental systems theory--that change in one sphere of life, the economic, is <u>bound</u> to have a predetermined reflection in the social and political. Considerable economic growth has been and is taking place in Latin America, but social and political forms have not developed apace. Some change has occurred, but certainly one of the more striking features of Latin American social and political life is the conspicuous durability of traditional institutions and patterns of behavior.

As the legitimacy of the older order has been undermined, as the ancient contractual ties have been broken, and yet as no new order has so far emerged to replace it, the Latin American nations have reverted to a situation of endemic civil war, pitting one faction or group of factions against another, almost literally one epoch against another. That helps explain why elections in Latin America are frequently so divisive, for the opposed candidates often represent wholly different and uncompromisable ways of life-- Bosch vs. Fiallo or Bosch vs. Balaguer in the Dominican Republic, or Allende vs. Tomic vs. Alessandri or Frei vs. Allende vs. Duran in Chile, etc. If one prefers the Marxist lexicon, one can say that in Latin America feudal, capitalist, and now, at least in some countries, increasingly socialist orders all exist side by side; or one may say Latin America has gone from a system of relatively few corporate interests or elites to a system of multiple elites; or, in political terms, the continuum may be said to run from authoritarian-patrimonialist to liberal-representative to populist-participatory. Reflecting the fact that they pertain to quite different epochs and life styles, the ideologies and parties arrayed on most of the Latin American political spectrums are too much at variance to be easily amenable to compromise and frequently so evenly balanced that no one of them wholly predominates any more or is even able to command a working majority. Again, Chile provides an excellent example; but so does Argentina and, increasingly, Uruguay,

Brazil, Peru, and a number of other countries.

Yet, through various subterfuges and often with the assistance of the U.S., which is afraid that the collapse of the traditional order may lead to Castro-like takeovers, the older established elites have generally been able to survive and cling to their privileged status. Meanwhile, new ideologies and movements have continued to grow that are subversive of the traditional order. Latin America has become, thus, a "conflict society," a "mosaic of discord," a society that has become unhinged and which lacks the unifying institutions to hold it together or a common set of rules of the game which a majority of participants could accept as binding. The result has been frequent instability and alterations in the ruling groups, institutional atrophy, the emergence of stagnative regimes with little capacity for promoting sustained growth, and, hence, the recurring vicious circles of eruptions, blockages, violence, coups, countercoups, and revolutions (135, 224). Argentina, for instance, has been in a state of almost permanent breakdown since 1930 with no regime--civilian or military; left, right, or center--able to put it back together. Arthur Whitaker's comments, thus, take on particular poignancy if we think of Argentina as the most "modern" nation in the area:

> Socially and politically, Argentina is a highly fragmented country. Its fragmentation is different from the pluralism which many of us think is one of the best attributes of society in the United States. In Argentina, the divisions are sharper, deeper, and more numerous, and the several fragments either do not communicate with each other at all or else do so mainly to quarrel and fight. Hence the widespread feeling of frustration and loss of direction that embitters domestic differences and tends to perpetuate them (511).

The general frameworks of social change and political development generated in the comparative politics literature of the past have been of questionable utility for the study of these aspects in present-day Latin America. The various indices of modernization provide useful guidelines to measure the extent to which educational and transportation facilities are being extended, for example, but not the degree to which these opportunities are being manipulated by the traditional holders of power. They do not tell us how the elites have frequently been able to turn modernization to their advantage rather than being routed by it. Furthermore, such indices tell us little concerning the new order that is supposed to develop, what its contours and institutional arrangements will be. Many of the measures of social and economic modernization, in fact, seem in Latin America to correlate positively with political decay and negatively with political development. Moreover, with due consideration for time lags, the "stages of growth" and political development literature--based upon the Western European and North American models--presume a regular, step-by-step progression from one "stage" to the next with new social and political forces becoming dominant at each and old, anachronistic ones being discarded. In Latin America, however, where various epochs continue to coexist and to function concurrently for different sectors of the population, the usual "stages" or "development" models simply do not apply.

There has been too much generalization in the literature on national development, and the claims put forth by the major interpretations have been too sweeping. Both the Marxian and the Weberian-Parsonian-Almondian models, derived from the developmental experiences of Western Europe and the United States, assume that with social and economic development the breakup of traditional society is bound to occur. Both interpretations see traditional society incapable of reforming itself sufficiently to withstand the impact of modernizing changes. It must either give way peacefully or it will be overwhelmed through revolution. Both these dominant models sell short the strength and durability of traditional institutions which, throughout the Third World, have proved to be remarkably long-lasting. We have forgotten Pareto's dictum, particularly applicable to Latin America, that elites may not only circulate in power but, by assimilation and accommodation of newer elements, may renew themselves as well.

Corporatism is one of the means by which this is done. The term has been used to describe some of the key institutional and organizational aspects of the Southern European and Latin American nations, and "the corporative model" has been employed as a designation for the way they have dealt with and managed the change process. While Marx and Weber and their disciples were analyzing the modernization-industrialization experiences of the Northern European countries, the Southern Europeans were trying to come to grips with some of the same kinds of changes. The kinds of solutions attempted often took a corporative form. There has long been a strong prejudice on the part of Northern Europeans and North Americans, found in scholarly analysis as well as in popular sentiments, against the Southern Europeans and the Latin Americans, both as regards their political sociology and their institutions. But surely as our own societies are racked by increasing discord, violence, crime, hatred, breakdown, and incapacity to cope, these deep-rooted prejudices concerning the "superiority" of our institutions and the theories on which they are based must be brought into question. Who are we to claim that ours is a superior, more "developed," or more "modern" civilization, or that the Northern European-North American path to progress is the best or only one?

In Iberia and Latin America, what we are witnessing is largely the attempt to deal with the pressures of modernity in terms of the institutions of tradition--the extended family, humanism and personalism, order and coherence. The institutional mechanism for achieving this reconciliation has, more often than not, been some form of corporatist organization, or perhaps a blending of corporatist forms with other institutional arrangements: republicanism, liberalism, socialism. The processes, dynamics, and functioning of these corporative or mixed-corporative forms are our main focus here.

RECAPITULATION, CONCLUSION, AND IMPLICATIONS

The framework we have proposed for the study of socioeconomic development and political change in Latin America may be termed the "corporative model." Corporatism as here used refers to an historic and continuing aspect of political culture and sociopolitical organization that appears to be an integral part of the Iberic-Latin tradition. It involves a system of national organization in which the component social and political groups are organized functionally and in terms of the major <u>corporate</u> units and bodies that are a part of the national life: religious bodies, military orders, economic groups, municipalities, parishes, universities, and the like. The social and political order is generally organized on an authoritarian, organic, centralized, and elitist basis that, at least originally, was thought to conform to God's immutable order. The monarchy, or more recently the state, serves as the arbiter and ultimate decision-maker, exercising its authority over the complex of competing interests and corporate groups that are part of the system. Policy is usually made by a strong ruler through a council of state or similarly functionally representative body presuming to speak for and in the name of the several corporate sectors of society. The corporate organization of society served as a means to increase centralized control and direction in societies long known for their "invertebrative" tendencies, to provide a system of national organization in polities whose "<u>falta de organización</u>" was often lamented, and to help preserve elitist rule-from-the-top, especially during periods when that was being challenged. It is not surprising that the corporate organization of the political system should be the preferred, even "natural," mode not only during the period of nation-building in the fifteenth and sixteenth centuries but also in the chaotic era of the nineteenth century and the strife-ridden politics of the twentieth.

The terms "corporative" and "corporative framework," however, are only catchwords, shorthand ways of describing and analyzing an increasingly complex set of relationships, which likely could just as easily be called by another name--the "clientelist system" or the "Mediterranean ethos," for example. The corporatist framework, furthermore, is more a way of conceiving of and looking at things, more a matter of emphasis than a full-blown model. It is, we have emphasized, a heuristic device. The corporatist framework helps us get at a number of questions that neither class analysis nor development analysis adequately answer, and it may also serve to help reconcile some of the fundamental differences that exist between the proponents of these two models. By looking at the Latin American nations in terms of their corporatist structures and in terms of the complex mixture and overlaps of modern and traditional, we may be able to explain better why both institutionalized consensus and institutionalized conflict may be present at the same time, why the norms of legitimacy and of illegitimacy may exist side-by-side. This may also help explain why looking at Latin America in terms of the concepts that have become commonplace in the Northern European-North American setting--"liberals" versus "conservatives," "democracy" versus "dictatorship," "class" versus "class"--so often provides such weak, unsatisfying explanations.

Using the corporatist-clientelist-patrimonialist framework here proposed forces us to reconsider--in their terms and not in ours--the peculiarities of the institutions that the late-medieval, Iberic nations of Spain and Portugal transferred to the New World and the unique developmental experiences of Latin America. It helps us comprehend better the concepts of rank, order, hierarchy, juridical estate, and so forth that have traditionally been so characteristic of the Latin American societies and may help explain the seemingly inherently corporatist and vertical structures that persist there even today. It is fairly obvious that many traditional regimes of the area may be profitably looked at in terms of the corporatist model; what is less obvious is the usefulness of examining such distinctive modernizing nations as Chile, Argentina, Brazil, Venezuela, Peru, Mexico, and probably even revolutionary Cuba in terms of the way in which the various groups and sectors relate directly to and revolve around the central state apparatus and its paternalistic, technocratic guidance, and of the means by which the government and ruling elites have sought to adapt and utilize corporatist techniques to control and coopt the newer, rising groups into their system of rule.

The emphasis here suggested may encourage students of Latin America to study continuity as well as change, to investigate the adaptability and permeability of traditional institutions as well as tracing the rise of challenging new ones, to turn their attention to such important (particularly in the Latin context, though often neglected in our own) research areas as comparative jurisprudence and public law, historical political theory, national self-interpretation as found in art and literature, comparative organizational theory and structure, and, of course, the nature of intergroup relations as defined in law and through contractual obligations and "rights" and other more traditional patterns. These are only a few of the many subject matters which are extremely important in the Latin American context but which the frameworks emerging from the Northern European-North American contexts often lead us to ignore.

A conceptual scheme such as the one here presented that more closely reflects and is adapted to the peculiar realities of political change and development in the Hispanic-Latin tradition is more useful than those based upon foreign models and arbitrarily imposed on a social setting where they do not fit. What we have termed the "corporative model" of Latin American society seems especially relevant for understanding the present-day political and social life of the region. The "corporative model" has the advantage of emerging from the empirical data we have concerning Latin America's past and present, not of being forced upon them.

At the same time, we must keep our concepts and frameworks open to new phenomena and to new combinations of interpretation. For clearly the insights of class analysis are useful in Latin America--and increasingly more so as the Latin American nations have undergone greater industrialization and their societies and economies have modernized. Similarly, systems theory and development analysis have become increasingly useful as the Latin American nations have become more like "systems" and as they have begun to "develop" more rapidly. But neither of these two frameworks by themselves is adequate to explain why the experience of Latin America and its development have been unique. It is for this reason that we need an open rather than a closed model for analyzing Latin American development, one that is flexible and adaptable enough to include the insights and ideas of other approaches, one that is attuned to the uniqueness of the Latin American experience and yet helps us understand where that experience is comparable to that of other nations.

The approach and general framework here urged is an eclectic one, designed to shift the focus of scholarly attention somewhat, but also to include the useful insights of other approaches. As Latin America has become more class-, issue-, and interest-oriented, for example, the value of class analysis and group theory has increased; similarly, as the "world culture" imposes itself more and more, development analysis and systems theory have taken on more relevance. But both of these frameworks must be employed alongside of and in conjunction with an ancient and yet still revered model, one which emphasizes hierarchy, elites, order, and corporatism. For just as the Latin American nations themselves are a patchwork of social and political phenomena belonging to distinct historical epochs, so the frameworks we use to study the area must also be derived from and reflect these mixed, overlapping patterns. Different kinds of systems, as Abraham A. Kaplan reminds us, require different kinds of theories for explanatory purposes (233).

To the present author, this is a pragmatic, not an ideological matter. Where class or group analysis is useful and yields new insights, let us use these frameworks; where they are not and do not, let us use a framework that does better explain that particular event or behavior. All models ask different questions for different purposes, so that, if we are interested only in the economic class structure of Latin America, let us use a model--probably Marxian or a variant thereof--that helps us explain this. But if we are interested in such a complex matter as development and its political as well as social and economic ramifications, then we had best use a more complex, multidimensional framework adequate to the task. What is proposed here, therefore, is an open and practical approach, one which does not foreclose on the possibilities for new and as yet unforeseen relationships, which utilizes the insights of various conceptual schemes that are relevant and appropriate, and which corresponds more closely to the realities and actual development experience of Latin America itself than do the several imported and rather foreign models used in the past. Clearly, the "corporative" framework proposed here requires a great deal of refinement and further explication, but it may serve as a useful starting point for thinking about, conceptualizing, and analyzing these in many ways unique features of the Latin American change and/or development process.

NOTES

a. The term "paradigm" is used here in the same way that Kuhn uses the concept: as the way a scientific/professional community views a field of study, identifies appropriate problems for study, and specifies legitimate concepts and methods. See 251.

b. These terms were felicitously coined by John Newman, see also 442, 475.

c. Nowhere does this come out more clearly than in Gabriel Almond's autobiographical introduction to his recent collection of essays; see 13. Among scholars generally, in fact, political development and modernization have proved to be among the more popular goals of what has been termed the "American ideological offensive toward the emerging nations" (187). One cannot fault the democratic and pluralistic values Almond emphasized as values--indeed they correspond closely to this writer's personal values--but they are values nonetheless, rather "Western" and ethnocentric ones at that, which Almond failed to acknowledge explicitly as such, while offering his categories as a neutral and more "scientific" way to analyze political development. Now categories and classifications they are--and in many ways useful--but neutral and scientific they are not. Had Almond acknowledged the source of his ideas in 1960 rather than waiting a decade to do so, we could likely have avoided much of the confusion and false starts that have marred much of the literature on the emerging nations written in the past few years. This, however, is as much the fault of Almond's followers, again the present writer included, who were caught up in much the same ambiente as he and with many of the same values, as it is of Almond himself.

6 | Corporatism and Development in the Iberic-Latin World: Persistent Strains and New Variations

Wherever one looks in the Iberic-Latin world, corporatist or neocorporatist forms of authority and sociopolitical organization appear to have staged a resurgence. One is used to thinking about such traditional countries as Nicaragua, Ecuador, and Paraguay in terms of their authoritarian and corporatist structures, and Portugal was a self-proclaimed "corporatist state" for some forty years. We shall have more to say regarding these "persistent strains" later on; what concerns us now is the apparent reemergence of corporatist ideology and organization in a variety of rapidly modernizing systems. Brazil, for instance, has always been less corporatist than Portugal in theory and in law, but even today is probably just as corporatist in actual practice (432, 457). Research on Mexico has by this time largely abandoned the approach that stressed its quasidemocratic character or its supposed democratic aspirations in favor of an approach that takes it on its own terms and analyzes its frankly authoritarian and corporatist structures (418). The resurgence of <u>Peronismo</u> in Argentina clearly carries with it echoes of the corporatist, in this case "justicialist," solutions of an earlier time. In Peru the military elite has vowed to carry through a "revolution from above" employing corporatist ideas and organizations to structure popular participation at the grass-roots and intermediary levels and reaching up to the Council of Ministers and the central state apparatus (379). And in Chile we have seen both Allende's abortive design to install a unicameral legislature based on "syndicalist" functional representation, as well as the plans by the generals that overthrew him to inaugurate a similarly functionally representative congress (though obviously the groups represented and their weights would be significantly different in these two designs) and to deal with price, wage, and production issues through a government-regulated and controlled corporative system of <u>gremio-sindicato</u> relations.

What is occurring? Is there really a "resurgence" of corporatist theory and organization, not only in those countries mentioned but elsewhere in the Iberic-Latin world? How is that possible, given the general discrediting of corporatist and integralist ideas

---

From <u>The Review of Politics</u> 36 (January 1974): 3-33.

during the war and in the Nuremberg trials, and also given the fact that we generally associate corporatism with a specific time period, whose high point had already passed in Latin America? Perhaps most disturbing is the fact that corporatism, which we identify with right wing and reactionary regimes, has, in Brazil under Goulart, the revolutionary military regime in Peru, and maybe even in Castro's Cuba, provided a form of organization and ideological component for the Left. Corporatism, thus, can be identified not just with traditional and conservative regimes but with a great variety of diversely modernizing ones. How then does one begin sorting out these conflicting currents, the "persistent strains" and the "new variations" of corporatism, the seeming reemergence of a system we had previously thought to be discredited or gone? This essay attempts to respond to some of those issues. Although it draws illustrative materials chiefly from the Luso-Brazilian world, the theme has important implications for the Hispanic one as well.

THE CORPORATIVE FRAMEWORK: APPROACHES AND DEFINITIONS

In 1936 Mihaïl Manoïlesco proclaimed that the twentieth century would be "the century of corporatism," just as the nineteenth had been the century of liberalism (312). That prediction has not been borne out by subsequent history, although in the context of the 1930s, with the apparent breakdown of liberal capitalism and the unacceptability of Stalinism, it was more understandable than it is now. The 1930s were probably the high point of corporatist ideas and movements, not just in the Iberic-Latin world and in the fascist systems of Italy and Germany, but throughout much of Europe and even North America as well. In such diverse nations as Holland, Belgium, Switzerland, France, Norway, Austria, Poland, Sweden, and the United States (clearly not just the Latin and Catholic countries), a great variety of corporatist agencies and institutions was created. These included wage-and-price agencies, labor relations boards and tribunals, councils of state, and functionally representative organs of various sorts. While none of these countries ever became a full-fledged corporative state, as occurred in Southern Europe, their corporative structures have both persisted and expanded. Indeed, it was one of Portugal's arguments in response to European criticism of its corporative system that, since the war, the other European countries were practicing a disguised form of corporatism and that, even in the U.S., corporatism finds expression in the Wage and Price Board, the Cost-of-Living Council, and a variety of other agencies (39, 138, 435, 452).

In the Iberic-Latin context, corporatism found an even more hospitable environment. In Spain the Falange provided some of the initial rationalizations for the Franco regime, and while the Falange as a political movement and corporatism as an ideology were later relegated to distinctly secondary roles in the Spanish system, corporatist ideas and organizations continued to lie at the heart of the system of labor relations, representation, and the like (60). Portugal remained the only openly and often proudly corporatist system extant, the only one of the numerous corporatist experiments initiated in the interwar period to have been carried through to full fruition--though later corporatism in Portugal evolved in ways not altogether different from the Spanish system. In Brazil under Vargas the operative agencies of the Estado Novo and the structure of labor relations, social assistance, and the like were all patterned after the model of a corporate state. In Argentina, Mexico, Chile, the Dominican Republic, and elsewhere, similar forms of corporatist organization were attempted, though in the American context they seldom called themselves by the corporatist name. It shows how pervasive corporatism was in the 1930s and 1940s, indeed (and also how confusing for foreign observers), that even such left-of-center movements as APRA in Peru and the MNR in Bolivia embraced some of its principal ideas and were, hence, often stamped--mistakenly and often ludicrously--with the "fascist" label.

It should be made clear at the outset that, when we use the term "corporatism," we are using it in two distinct, but often interrelated, senses. The first refers to the manifestly corporatist experiments and regimes of the 1920s, 1930s, and 1940s and may be defined as a system of authority and interest representation, derived chiefly (though not exclusively) from Catholic social thought, stressing functional representation, the integration of labor and capital into a vast web of hierarchically ordered, "harmonious," monopolistic, and functionally determined units (or "corporations"), and guided and directed by the state (452, 138). The second sense in which we use the term "corporatism" is broader, encompassing a far longer cultural-historic tradition stretching back to the origins of the Iberic-Latin systems and embodying a dominant form of sociopolitical organization that is similarly hierarchical, elitist, authoritarian, bureaucratic, Catholic, patrimonialist, and corporatist to its core (551, 545).

These two definitions and perspectives on corporatism overlap and are interconnected at various points. For one thing, many of the corporatist theorists of the interwar period sought to ground their systems in the historic structures and forms of organizations which had their roots in Roman and canon law, the Thomistic tradition, the feudal system of guilds and professional associations, and the characteristic, Suárezian, sixteenth-century political forms which persisted so long (65, 69, 94). For another, the corporatist experiments of the 1930s may, in part, be looked upon as a twentieth-century extension of that historic tradition, a way of handling the new "social question," of absorbing the rising labor elements into the system, in the same characteristic hierarchical, elitist, and corporatist fashion that the Iberic-Latin systems had been absorbing new elites for centuries (524). Despite these overlaps, the distinction between these two definitions and senses of corporatism is useful for our purposes in that it helps us understand what occurred in the Iberic-Latin world in the postwar period. Thus, while the discredited forms or labels of corporatism associated with fascism were submerged or rebaptized under different names, the older <u>corporatist tradition</u> remained both intact and paramount. It goes a long ways toward explaining the supposed "resurgence" of corporatism presently in Latin America if we understand that beneath the democratic facades of the postwar constitutions and the liberal posturing, frequently so as to appear more acceptable to the outside world or to qualify for Alliance for Progress assistance, the historic political culture of corporatist values and the system of corporatist organization was present all the time, disguised but still extant and perhaps even dominant. Corporatism has now reemerged full-blown to the surface.

There are a series of neglected hypotheses, at this stage mere suggestions, relating to the evolution of corporatist ideology and institutions in Latin America in the postwar period, and the U.S. presence there, that ought to be explored. For if corporatism is a dominant sociopolitical tradition in Latin America and about the only one of the three great "isms" that closely corresponds to her history and political culture, then why, in Octavio Paz's words, is Latin America in 1973 still a continent "in search of a system"? Why is it that neither liberalism nor socialism has effectively taken hold; why does Latin America remain a "heap of ruined [liberal and social-democratic] ideas and victims' bones" (Paz); why has it failed to develop its own patterns of political thought and to evolve, at least up to now, its own indigenous developmental models (388)?

A key reason is that World War II, Fascism, the Nazi experience, and Nuremberg so poisoned our thinking, not only as regards the manifest atrocities of the Italian and German regimes but also as regards all corporatist- and integralist-type experiments, that Latin America was largely forced to set aside or submerge the one "ism" that was true to its own traditions and with which it could function effectively. Corporatism was viewed as synonymous with "fascism" and, therefore, all traces of it had to be eliminated. This is, in essence, a new twist on the Cold War-dependency thesis. By totally and indiscriminately discrediting corporatism in World War II's aftermath, the U.S. and international public opinion forced Latin America to choose artificially between liberalism U.S. and European style, on the one hand (the Alliance for Progress, the Peace Corps, U.S.-conceived developmentalism), which was not in accord with Latin America's own character and tradition, and revolutionary socialism a la the Soviet Union, on the other, which was equally unacceptable. Latin America was obliged to select between false alternatives since the middle way of corporatism, an indigenous solution that might have enabled the continent to escape some of the upheavals and chaotic civil-military alternations of the postwar period, had been ruled out. The development literature then gaining currency supported this thesis by positing that modernization and the growth of a liberal democratic polity went hand-in-hand.

But corporatism is an adaptable system, not so rigid as the literature suggests; and left to her own modes of organization, Latin America would likely have more peacefully and orderly bridged the gap between the traditionalism of the pre-1930 period and the participatory demands of the present. But our discrediting of corporatism, together with the unilinear, ethnocentric developmental models we used, disallowed that possibility and thus helped precipitate the violent oscillation and swinging of the political pendulum during this period. It is only now in the 1970s, with the decline of the U.S. cultural, economic, and political influence throughout the hemisphere, along with the general discrediting of the U.S.-based developmentalist model, that Latin America is again, as it did in the 1930s, searching for indigenous solutions to its own social and developmental problems. It is probably no accident that it is precisely at this time that corporatist and neocorporatist solutions should reemerge (113, 395).

Corporatism, thus, is not to be equated with Naziism or Fascism, nor are the Latin experiments with corporatism to be considered as merely "less-developed" versions of the Fascist model. The interpretation that the Latins "just aren't up to it" reflects a typically Northern European and North American prejudice toward the Southern Europeans and especially the Latin countries, and finds expression in a host of anthologies and studies--all compiled by North Americans or Northern Europeans, attempting to look at Iberic-Latin "Fascism" in this biased perspective (363). For, despite some rather obvious and usually superficial parallels, corporatism in the Iberic-Latin tradition is a distinct and separate type, fundamentally different from the Fascism and Naziism of the popular stereotypes. Authoritarian surely, as in the Linz formulation regarding Spain, which posits that authoritarianism is a distinct political form, neither liberal nor totalitarian, with dynamics and characteristics of its own, and without necessarily implying a transition to the one or the other of these other ideal types (267); but fascist not. "Fascism" and "Fascist" may still be useful labels, but they cannot be applied in the Iberic-Latin context with much precision or accuracy. As an analytic term, "fascism," like "totalitarianism," may have outlived its usefulness.

But if corporatism is not to be equated with fascism, it cannot be seen as a wholly or necessarily reactionary, backward-looking ideology either. That idea, too, comes out of the earlier fascism studies, the belief that corporatism represents a turning back of the clock on the part of elite and bourgeois elements, an effort to restore the status quo ante, a reaction to unstable, chaotic republicanism and liberalism, a means of preserving or restoring traditional privileges and of keeping the rising lower classes from overthrowing the system from below. There is some degree of truth in these allegations, but we have already seen that corporatism may take a distinctly modernizing bent and, in fact, there is a great variety of options and alternatives open within the corporatist framework.

Philippe Schmitter, for example, has identified four schools of corporatist thought, and by this time in actual practice there are undoubtedly several more. Schmitter distinguishes between (1) a social-Christian form as exemplified by such thinkers as Albert de Mun, the Marquis de la Tour du Pin, and Joaquín Azpiazu, and whose ideas found expression in the encyclicals <u>Rerum Novarum</u> of Leo XIII and <u>Quadragosimo Anno</u> of Pius XI, and later in a variety of Catholic and Christian democratic movements (32, 138, 154); (2) an authoritarian, bureaucratic, nationalist, secular, <u>modernizing</u> school whose theorists include Manoïlesco and many of the Italian corporatist ideologues (312, 450); (3) a Radical (in the French sense), parliamentary, bourgeois, "solidarist" tradition as exemplified by Léon Bourgeois, Charles Gide, and Emile Durkheim (124); and (4) a leftist, socialist, "syndicalist" line of thought whose spokesmen would include Saint-Simon, Sorel, and perhaps the guild socialists (83). For illustrative purposes, we could say that the Spanish and Portuguese systems under Franco and Salazar represent perhaps a combination of the first and second types, while the Allende regime in Chile and perhaps that of Bosch in the Dominican Republic and of Goulart in Brazil were closer to categories three and four. The revolutionary-nationalist Peruvian regime that came to power in 1968 may not fit any of these categories very well and may necessitate still a fifth type. In any case, what this categorization illustrates is the diversity and great variety of regimes that can fit under the corporative rubric. Clearly, there is abundant room here for progressive, leftist corporatist regimes as well as for regressive rightist ones, and a variety of shades in between.

Corporatism, thus, is not a mere throwback to an earlier and necessarily conservative model of society and polity, nor can it be lumped together with the Fascist and Nazi regimes in a blanket condemnation. Rather, what we are looking at in the corporatist model is a complex and varied form, distinct from both liberalism and totalitarianism, with a long tradition of its own and a great body of political thought and sociology which, because we have condemned it out-of-hand or rendered it outmoded in our sociological analyses, we are almost wholly unfamiliar. Moreover, corporatism can be and has been a progressive, modernizing tradition, not only in the type three and four categories but also in the type one category as exemplified by Chilean Christian democracy and the type two category as exemplified, in part, by present-day Brazil. Overall, given our deep-rooted prejudices regarding corporatism, what needs emphasis is the distinctiveness and viability of the corporative routes to development as opposed to the liberal and socialist ones, the diversity and complexity of its forms, and the fact that what we are dealing with here is literally "a fourth world of development" in the Iberic-Latin tradition, or a third "great ism," which requires analysis and understanding on its own terms and in its own context, not through some frame of reference derived from another tradition and inapplicable to the Iberic-Latin one (456).

ORIGINS AND ANTECEDENTS: THE CORPORATIVE
TRADITION IN HISTORIC PERSPECTIVE

Within the confines of the present essay, no detailed tracing of the corporative tradition and its present-day expressions can be attempted. Nonetheless, some of the origins and broad lines of this tradition can be delineated and some of its contemporary ramifications noted. In the conclusion, we shall be looking at some of the implications and problems of the corporative approach.

The political-cultural origins of the Iberic-Latin tradition of corporatism lie in the Roman period (16, 59). Indeed, one might argue that any effort to understand present-day development issues in the Iberic-Latin world must recognize the imprint that Roman

civilization indelibly stamped on its far-flung empire. Rome gave
Iberia a degree of unity it had never had before, a system (and
model) of central administration and of state bureaucracy, and its
most characteristic forms of politico-military organization. Unity
and a certain cultural coherence were also forged through a common
language and law, and eventually through Christianity. Moreover,
the Romans gave to Iberia its prevailing conception of citizenship,
its system of group rights and charters, its organization of social
hierarchy and class, its similarly hierarchical structure of laws
and orders, its stoic emphasis upon "virtue" rather than material
gain, its patrimonialist state apparatus, its conception of the
"civilizing" mission of empire. And if later ideologues like Salazar and Caetano are correct, Rome also laid the basis for the philosophical, legal, and organizational structure of the corporative
state.

Over four centuries of close association with Rome as a part
of its empire helped make the Roman influence in the peninsula permanent and provided it with the foundations on which future Iberian
civilization would develop. Moreover, the long-lasting success and
logical clarity of the administrative structure strongly impressed
the statesmen and jurists of later centuries, especially when, as
Roman law and the achievements of its empire were rediscovered, it
was fused and blended with the Christian, Thomistic-Suárezian conception to serve as the model for the modern, fifteenth- and sixteenth-century structures of the Spanish and Portuguese states.
The Roman system not only served as the basis for modern, state-
building royal authority in Iberia and for the extension of that
system to the New World, but it also served as the form of organization toward which virtually all monarchs and, later, <u>caudillos</u>
and perhaps even republicans aspired (78, 328).

Meanwhile, other characteristic forms and modes of behavior
emerged which, in terms of understanding contemporary Iberic-Latin
development issues, merit far more attention than they have thus
far received. The collapse of the Roman Empire had paved the way
for a Visigothic conquest of Iberia, which represented more an
overlay on the Roman tradition than a submerging of it. The Visi-
goths helped institutionalize Christianity through an official
state church; their rule led also to a hardening of absolutism and
of authoritarian, centralized rule. The centuries-long Reconquest
of the peninsula from the Moors was also crucial in terms of institutionalizing some other characteristic forms of sociopolitical
organization, but that is a subject area that few social scientists
have explored (172, 262, 409). During the Reconquest, the Church
became more than ever an arm of the civil authority and the civil
and military realms were fused (perhaps never again to be separated, as we imply in our use of the hyphenated term civil-military
relations). And as the Reconquest proceeded, the power of the nobility and military orders frequently became territorial, often as
a result of acquisitions by or grants to them of the lands and peoples they had reconquered. Each lord was sovereign in his own
realm, and an elaborate network of vassalage and patron-dependent
relations began tardily to grow up. The system of special "rights"
which defined the relationship of the citizen individually and of

the community collectively to the overlord, who could be the monarch, noble, Church, military order, or even municipality, became the means by which political obligation was defined. The forms of authority were organized hierarchically and in a traditional-patrimonialist fashion in which the wealth and lands of the area, as well as the persons living in it, were considered a part of the overlord's private preserve (a).

It is out of this matrix of forces that the separate kingdom of Portugal began to emerge in the twelfth century and from which stems some of the dominant characteristics of the Luso-Brazilian corporative-patrimonialist tradition (b). This period of nation-building and consolidation is also woefully understudied, but it is critical in shaping the future course of political relations, both in the Iberian Old World and in the New.

As Portugal emerged, wresting more and more territory from the Moors, on the one hand, and fending off León and Spain, on the other, its internal politics were dominated chiefly by the struggle between the king and his nobles, os senhores territoriais. In return for loyalty and service, the king was obliged to grant land, titles, privileges, and foros. The landed aristocrats, hence, derived their positions from the king and, in turn, they owed him allegiance. The Church, the military, the nobility also surrounded the king like a "college of influentials"--all came to be a part of the same centralizing, bureaucratic state apparatus. Governance came to be exercised through a number of consulting organs and councils, and through the king's ministers who served as his personal agents. The system remained one of rule from above, of elite or royal protection of those below them in the hierarchy, in return for fealty and certain obligations. As it emerged, the system was classically corporatist-patrimonialist (37, 144, 326).

Among the corporate entities, municipalities, orders, and the like existent in the emerging Portuguese system, the state became overwhelmingly preeminent. The state was the regulator of both social structure and economic life. It was the state, specifically the Crown, that granted the privileges, titles, and monopolies that bought the loyalty of the nobles, that helped centralize royal power, and that made the system work. Using this model of a patronage-patrimonialist system, a succession of kings helped make Portugal the first centralized nation-state in Europe and probably the most-developed institutionally of that time (183).

It was a system based on status, hierarchy, and royal favor. Each "class," as well as each individual, was bound to accept his assigned place in society. Eventually, a commercial-mercantile elite would grow up in Portugal alongside and overlapping with the landed nobility, and it was they, along with the Crown, who in the fifteenth century launched the conquest of the vast Portuguese empire. The patrimonialist state apparatus continued to regulate the entire process of economic and political infrastructure building, however; and, hence, as a class system began to emerge in Portugal, the structure of state patrimonialism continued to coexist along with it and even superior to and independent from the various elite rivalries and class changes occurring below. Commerce, war, and colonization were all part of the same extension of royal authority and of an ever more elaborate model of corporate-patrimonialist state organization. In the promotion of trade and commerce overseas, hence, Portugal never developed a full-fledged capitalist system, nor was capitalism the motor force driving Portuguese colonialization and development. State capitalism or mercantilism, yes; but capitalism in the sense of individual entrepreneurship, laissez faire, and free enterprise, no. Hence, while commerce and capitalism of a sort grew up alongside the traditional agrarian and feudal structure, the former never replaced the latter. The economic variable in this sense remained subordinate to the political one, and in the Iberic-Latin tradition that probably remains true today. Meanwhile, the one constant remained the patrimonialist state apparatus, around which all classes and individuals revolved and from which they derived their legitimacy (298, 320).

Because this system is so strong and omnipresent, it merits further description. One can say, thus, that the Portuguese state, traditionally, was modeled after that of the imperial Roman Caesars, overlain with Visigothic, Thomistic, and feudal influences. It is absolutist and administrative. The sovereign exercises power in the name of the general interest, the res publica. He requires all powers and prerogatives for his superior mission of governance. Society remains dominated by the idea and presence of the state. The land of the realm, its wealth, as well as its individual members "belong to" the monarch (or, in present-day parlance, the state). The Crown or the state may give part of its patrimony in the form of land, favors, or monopoly to certain groups or individuals in return for a juramento a fidelidade. The system, thus, remains highly personal and vassalistic. But these relations, it should be emphasized, are not wholly one way; rather, they are governed by rules of reciprocal favors and loyalties in the classic patrão-client pattern (37, 144).

The Crown or the sovereign exercise power in an authoritarian fashion, but that power could not be "total" without violating the system of mutual obligations and restraints. Power is also limited by natural law in the Catholic-Thomistic tradition. It is limited further by the traditional rights and foros of the orders and municipalities. When the king overstepped his authority, when he violated the charters and pacts that governed vassalage relations, he was likely to face a revolt on the part of the nobility, whose bloody uprisings continued throughout the twelfth and thirteenth centuries (c). Custom, tradition, and the family also served as constraints on absolute authority.

The king had the supreme "fiscalizing" power to regulate and pass on all contracts and agreements. He also garnered the power to confirm the acts of the senhor; e.g., his military service or his right to a place in the cortes. Thus, the king was not only supreme in his own right but his sovereignty was enhanced by his ability almost literally to handpick those who sat in his parliament or tribunal. It is not hard to understand, thus, why the principle of separation of powers never became firmly established in the Iberic-Latin tradition as it did in the Anglo-American. Another royal lever came from the fact that the same individual would frequently be the recipient of grants of land or monopoly from the Crown while, at the same time, serving as the king's personal agent in that territory or municipality. The political evolution of Portugal during this period thus served to develop and unify the state through the king and his patrimonialist state apparatus (144, 326).

The rediscovery of Roman law during this period gave special impetus to these trends. The corpus juris civis provided the model of a powerful state, absolutist in character, in which administration, not politics, assured order and justice. The Roman law favored the consolidation of the state against excesses, violence, and feudal rights. It contributed to the growth of royal power and also made it absolutist. The monarch became the focus of the "direito positivo." He was the defender of "the public interest" in return for which the nation granted him broad, virtually absolute power. This then emerges as the Iberic concept of popular sovereignty, and it finds powerful echoes in the rule of Salazar and other such "Caesarist" regimes (326, 408).

The progress of royal power resulted in the weakening of the nobility and independent military orders, the development of "general" power, limits on seignorial rights, the affirmation of civilian authority over the Church and its inclusion as still another arm of governance, the development of central administrative organs, the intervention of the Crown in all phases of political and economic life, and the widening delegation of certain goods and services in return for support and loyalty. Eventually, the doctrine of the illegality of usurping royal authority emerged, that the king is not only superior in relation to other authorities but also that he or his delegated agents have a true monopoly. The doctrine as evolved asserts that the rights and foros of the various societal and corporate units come only through concessions from the king and not from any inherent right. In the sixteenth century the extension of this idea and the full consolidation of the Crown's power led to royal absolutism. It is this conflict between royal authority, on the one hand, and the rights of the "classes," on the other, that determined so much of Portuguese history--until the nineteenth century added a new, liberal, and republican idea on top of that older conflict. This complicated political relations somewhat and forced the ancient patrimonialist state model to adapt further, but it by no means destroyed the model itself (347).

In contrast to the emerging absolutist doctrines and practices, the nobles and homens bons continued to assert the Crown's obligation to defend their traditional rights, to guard good customs, and to protect the rights of "the people." This gave rise to the concept that the relation between the Crown and the "classes" was governed by a kind of pact and maintained by mutual accords. It is this system of the magistratura judicial that the contemporary corporate state tried to resurrect in its extension of the patrimonialist state apparatus and its "protective tutelage" over the rising labor classes. In the earlier period, the inviolability of these foros was always invoked in conflicts with the king, or the state, and with varying degrees of success. The various "colleges," orders, brotherhoods, gremios, municipalities, and corporations all claimed to be governed by such pacts or charters, and they sought to reserve the right to withdraw their loyalty or foment rebellion if these norms were violated. At the same time, the king and later the state reserved the right to pass on the charters of these groups, to grant or withhold recognition and thus regulate and control the group's participation in the national life, and even to refuse to respect these privileges when the sovereign had just cause (one can see how this pattern is still characteristic of the relations of the state to the university in contemporary Latin America, for example). Throughout Portuguese history, indeed, this remained the dominant conflict: between the centralizing, absolutist forces and tendencies, on the one hand, and the defenders of autonomous corporate privilege and group foros, on the other. Those privileges and rights could be extended--first, to broaden the elite; then, to include the middle sectors; more recently, labor and peasants. But again it is the system of paternalism, patronage, and privilege, exercised through an evolving corporate structure, that remains dominant. Never in any of this long history of conflict was there a strong force arguing for genuine popular sovereignty, democratization, or participation in the Anglo-American mold (326, 453).

The Portuguese cortes would, hence, never become an effective agent for popular representation, and it is purely wishful thinking that leads, particularly, English and American writers to see the seeds of democracy there. The cortes originated in the royal curia or council of the king. Its chief functions were consultative and in the administration of the laws, not the making of them. Although the cortes at several points accumulated some modicum of authority, no real separation of powers existed and the cortes always remained secondary to the real centers of patronage and influence. The cortes existed largely at the king's pleasure and call. Represented in it were the nobles and homens bons; the Church was also represented along with the masters of the major military orders, the procuradores of the principal cities, and other corporate interests. The cortes could only be called into session by the king, and its members were required to heed this call as an obligation of their vassalage (326).

The ordinary curia became an administrative arm of the king; however, the extraordinary curia gradually devolved some modest economic and legislative functions and was involved in the great political questions of that time. But as the cortes sought to expand its powers, it was called less and less frequently. The major intereses, Church, nobility, and military, were all represented, as were some persons who were there because of their elevated positions. The franchise was always limited or entirely nonexistent; the povo were represented by their "betters." Municipalities also tended to choose local notables who "andam no governo," who "went along with the government" (just as they do today in a system of "party" representation). What vote existed was ordinarily for an assigned list of the homens bons, the elite; and the king would often suggest for whom one should vote, naturally those he trusted and who enjoyed his confiança.

The cortes met by separate estates, each jealous of guarding its own privileges. It would meet irregularly and generally for

about a month when it met at all. It gradually acquired a modicum
of power over the purse and in 1372 refused a request of the king
for the first time. It was liable to be consulted by the king on
war, gained some limited authority to suggest and modify laws, and
could even exercise some choice in the selection of a monarch in
cases where the dynasty had ended. The _cortes_ remained limited,
however, never employing the supremacist doctrine that a handful of
its members occasionally advocated. The king most often legislated
without the _cortes_ through decree-law. The power of the people,
thus, remained virtually nil, and the sovereign reserved the right
to revoke the rights even of the elites. It was the popular sectors, as Barros shows, beginning to emerge in the fifteenth century, who probably had the most interest in the meeting of the _cor-
tes_, but they were the weakest and had virtually no direct representation. The elites and _homens bons_ did have representation, but
they had no more interest in promoting popular government than had
the monarch. Hence, in the great, evolving conflicts between royal
authority and the power of the state, on the one hand, and the nobles and corporate interests, on the other, whose relative influence varied over time, the people never had any direct voice at all
(37).

Was the _cortes_ ever representative of society or the nation?
Emphatically not, at least in the modern Anglo-American sense of
representation. In the Portuguese sense, the _cortes_ was roughly
representative, however, for when a Spaniard or Portuguese speaks
of "society" or "the nation," he tends to think of it in terms of
its component corporate units: the religious institutions, the
municipalities, the corporations and _sindicatos_, the _gremios_, the
army, the grand foundations and autarchies, and the like. Not included in this conception is the general public or public opinion,
for interpreting the "general will" out of the conglomerate of _in-
tereses_ is the special province of the ruler. Hence, at best we
can say that the _cortes_ was occasionally an imperfect representation of "the classes"--as most parliaments in Latin America are
today. Its membership was limited only to certain elites, and it
was their rights that were protected. The general public was not
represented, and individual rights were protected only insofar as
they corresponded to those of the _intereses_ or to "the common good"
(as defined, of course, by the king). The _cortes_ was restrictive,
also, in its elective character, local notables or the king's
choices. However, the _cortes_ was representative of society's major
corporate elements and, more than that, it sometimes presumed to
speak in defense of the common interests. But the king also
claimed that power; and, in the long run, he won out--at least up
to the nineteenth century. The _cortes_ met for the last time in
this earlier period in 1696-98. Then divine right monarchy triumphed and the _cortes_ was replaced by nonelective secretaries of
the king and superior tribunals; the "bureaucratic-state" model had
triumphed. The _cortes_, hence, never acquired the power of the
British parliament, nor was the idea of popular sovereignty (and
all its accompanying paraphernalia--elections, party government,
separation of powers, popular rights, etc.) ever secured or to become
a fundamental principle of public law (326).

We have devoted all this space to these historic themes for several reasons. First, it is clear that the fundamental foundations of the Portuguese system show a close correspondence to the model of corporative society and of the patrimonialist political order outlined previously. Second, it is important because this structure served as the base and model on which the modern Portuguese and Spanish state systems were erected from the fifteenth century on--not only in the Old World but also in the New. These ideas were probably most clearly articulated by the Infante Dom Pedro, brother of Henry the Navigator, who artfully constructed perhaps the first full-blown theoretical and practical guide (model?) for a patronage-patrimonialist system organized on a national basis; by Alvaro Pais, the Franciscan bishop of Elvas, who articulated many of the same themes; and later by Francisco Suárez, the great Spanish jurist (who also taught at Coimbra), who is as central to the Iberic-Latin tradition as Locke is to the Anglo-American (183, 350, 359). In their rationalizations of emerging power relationships in Iberia, the king (or president, in modern parlance) holds superior power; he rules authoritarianly but justly, exercising tutelage over his people and using his power to promote the general welfare. The true king is, thus, distinguished from a tyrant (or "fascist" or "totalitarian") in that his power rests on a popular base through his knowledge of the general will (elections, thus, are not the only or even very important means for expressing that general will). Moreover, the ruler is obligated to respect the "rights" of society and of the intereses. The pacts and charters by which the nation and society are governed are tentative, however, and can be dissolved if the rights, obligations, and loyalties of each party are violated. For Portugal, it is Dom Pedro who puts these formulations all together, who shows the king how to grasp and exercise all the levers of power and patronage, and who fashions a dynamic, even modernizing model of the patrimonialist state apparatus. It is no accident that the king he instructed, João II, is recognized by all historians as the best ruler Portugal ever had. It is no accident either that the model he fashioned sounds remarkably similar to the present-day formulation of the Latin American political process of Charles W. Anderson and others (21, 247).

Third, one cannot help but be impressed with the parallels between the fifteenth-century ideas and structures and the Estado Novo of Salazar and Caetano or the military regime that came to power in Brazil in 1964. In terms of the authoritarian but tutelary role of the state, the restricted functions of the legislature, the treatment of the opposition, the "fiscalizing" and "confirming" functions of the government, the respect for traditional interests, the erection of a corporative system of social organization and representation (more formally defined in Portugal than in Brazil, but still strongly present in the latter), the low place of public opinion and popular sovereignty, the controlled and regulated way of promoting development, the leadership of the patrimonialist state apparatus, etc., the parallels are remarkable. To some extent, this is so because Salazar consciously tried to resurrect in his corporative state a model derived, at least in part, from this older system. But it also represents the continuity of a powerful and dominant historical pattern and tradition, the extension in twentieth-century form of an historic model and order which have always been characteristic of Portuguese society and polity.

The patrimonialist-corporatist state apparatus, put together so painstakingly and with so much struggle from the twelfth century through the fifteenth, remained the dominant form of Portuguese political organization. The system was based upon an organic, authoritarian, hierarchical, and corporate conception of society and polity that served to lock Iberic-Latin civilization into this mold and perpetuate it to the present. The system was further elaborated and refined in the sixteenth century into a form that was particularly durable and long-lasting, not only in the Iberian metropoles but in their New World colonies as well. Through the grants of land and authority (donatários), through the ordenações, and through the creation of a number of royal councils to help govern this far-flung empire, what Faoro calls the "estamento burocrático" was extended overseas. In this way, the Portuguese (and Spanish) colonies, allowing for local variations, came to represent smaller-scale models of society and polity in the mother countries, with the Church, the military, and the civil administration all a part of the bureaucratic state apparatus and with all the lines, however tenuously and ambiguously at times, centering in the Crown (144, 179, 393, 448).

THE EVOLVING NATIONAL SYSTEMS:
PORTUGAL, BRAZIL, PERU

It is not our purpose here to present more than a gloss of the national histories of these systems. However, recent scholarship has forced us to reinterpret some of these national histories in a new light and to analyze some of these newer interpretations as a means of suggesting further lines of investigation.

Portugal

In the nineteenth-century, Portugal represented a blending of the traditional form of "monarquia moderada" with a newer (and confused and mistakenly understood) form of British parliamentarism. The forms were constitutional and republican, but the operating realities were continuous with Portugal's earlier history. The two "parties" were, in fact, rival elite factions vying for control of the same patrimonialist state apparatus. "Elections" were the expression of classic vassalage and patrão-client relations and had little to do with democratic choice in the Anglo-American model. Caciquismo flourished, with the local notables delivering votes and loyalty in return for favors and patronage. Rather than implying any genuine democratization, politics served as a means for the newer urban bourgeoisie to rise to positions of wealth and power; the elite was, thus, expanded to accommodate nineteenth-century pressures, but the elitist system was retained. Although the remnants of feudal privileges were legally abolished, the power of strong vested interests was perpetuated while the same homens bons continued to govern (63, 363, 462).

It is tempting, as the corporatist ideologues of the 1920s and 1930s sought, to dismiss the entire century of Portuguese "liberalism" and "parliamentarism" from 1822 until 1926 as an aberration, a temporary break in what was, in fact, a far longer and stronger corporative-authoritarian tradition, a set of institutions solely "for the English to see." That interpretation is clearly wrong and misleading, but so, too, is the opposite and liberal one which sees the "republican" era as a steady march toward "progress," the inevitable growth of liberalism and pluralism, the historical unfolding of an evolutionary but unilinear democratizing process (313). First, it is clear that the "progress" of the period can easily be exaggerated and would have come anyway, no matter the nature of the regime. Second, the "liberalizing" and "democratizing" influences have been overstated, for we have already indicated that Portugal remained an elitist system without any notions of genuine popular rule. Third, it is important to see that even in the most "liberal" of regimes and documents, such as the numerous constitutions of the period and in the 1891 "magna carta" of Portuguese associational life, the authoritarian, elitist, patrimonialist, and carefully regulatory features of the Portuguese tradition were preserved, thus implying that Portugal was consistently far less democratic even in intention than republican historians like Oliveira Marques care to admit. Indeed, as Oliveira Marques's own research has shown, the only time the parliamentary regime worked at all effectively is when it was least parliamentary; i.e., when it was governed by a strong monarch or president.

Finally, having said all this, it must also be said that some new currents and social forces had emerged in Portugal during this period, that a new elite had grown up, and that, alongside the traditional pyramid of power and only partially integrated with it, there had grown up a parallel structure, nascently liberal in character, in some sense assimilated into the traditional system but in another representing a challenge to it (240, 508). The liberal current was, and remains still, a minority current, still secondary to the dominant corporatist and patrimonialist tradition. Hence, as the republican regime broke down into disorder and chaos in the 1920s, the army stepped in to exercise its "moderating" function, paving the way for the coming to power of the corporatists who promised a means of dealing with the rising "social question," of responding to twentieth-century urgencies without sacrificing traditional institutions.

Superficial suppositions to the contrary, the Portuguese Estado Novo was not just a poorer, atrophied version of European Fascism, nor was the Salazar regime merely a reactionary effort to turn back the clock or to preserve the status quo ante. Rather, it represented an effort to come to grips realistically with the new social forces emerging in Portugal but without sacrificing its traditional institutions, to correct the false starts and excesses of the republican period, and to prevent the currents it had set loose from getting completely out-of-hand. Its intention was not to reverse the process by which the ruling elites had been expanded or that under which the working class had achieved certain benefits.

The Estado Novo, hence, stood for change and development, but only those features of it that could be carefully controlled and regulated. Thus, if the nineteenth century was not so "liberal" as we have often assumed, so the corporative system was not so "reactionary." In fact, one might argue that those who see the issues in terms of a struggle between liberal and reactionary forces may be fundamentally misunderstanding the nature of the Portuguese system, which even to this day remains elitist and hierarchical and has always dealt with change in that same characteristic manner.

In practice, the harmonious and coequal status of employers and workers, which the corporative ideology posited, remained a myth, for as one would expect the homens bons and the already-established interests dominated right from the beginning. Moreover, in the classic patrimonialist fashion, both labor and capital and, indeed, the entire corporative institutional network were subordinate to the central state apparatus. Furthermore, by this time it was no longer possible to resurrect a fully corporative system in the classic pattern, since new groups had already grown up organized around principles distinct from those previously considered the only legitimate ones. Cast in the rigid Catholic-corporatist mold of the 1930s, the Estado Novo could only deal with these elements who rejected "the system" through repression, because by definition they were subversive, heretical, and pernicious and had to be destroyed to preserve the "natural" order. That this repression also helped to maintain the regime in power and to protect those elites profiting from it was not merely coincidental. The same rigidities served to prevent Portugal from modernizing more rapidly in the post-World War II period during which all such corporate-integralist solutions had been discredited and when the Portuguese concept clearly required reformulation and reconstruction. That, indeed, is precisely what Marcelo Caetano had been attempting, to provide for the evolution and restructuring of the Portuguese system, a further broadening of the elites and greater benefits for the lower classes, but within a traditional framework of order, hierarchy, corporatism, and authority (519).

Brazil

Recent interpretations of Brazilian development have also emphasized its inherently corporative, elitist, and patrimonialist features. Building upon the earlier formulations of Faoro, for example, Riordan Roett has stressed the elitist nature of the Brazilian system historically, its low levels of social mobilization, its bureaucratic nature, and its clientelist, patrimonialist, and corporative features (432). These structures were institutionalized during some three centuries of colonial rule and were perpetuated on into the independence period when Brazil, alone among the Latin American nations, retained the monarchical form of government and the traditional "moderating power" of the Crown. When Brazil became a "republic" in 1889, the constitutional forms were changed, but the basic structure of society and polity was retained and the army stepped in to play the moderating role formerly reserved for the king. Despite the republican façade, politics remained in the hands of the elites who rotated in power periodically so that the benefits accruing with control of the patrimonialist state apparatus could be shared more broadly. The franchise remained limited, and coronelismo served for Brazil what caciquismo served for Portugal, a local means for delivering electoral support and loyalty in return for favors and patronage. These institutions were related to the agrarian, rural, semifeudal society that Brazil remained.

The 1930s marked a key turning point, necessitating a corporative structural reorganization in Brazil, as in Portugal. Already the new men of industrial and commercial wealth and much of the rising middle class had been and were being assimilated into the prevailing structure; now it became the turn of the trade unions. Although Vargas was more a pragmatic politician and never the corporative ideologue that Salazar was, he and his key advisers were also influenced strongly by the Catholic-corporative ideas then current. Vargas's Estado Novo constitution never went into effect, but the strategy of dealing with the "social question" through the erection of official syndicates and labor tribunals and through the incorporation of this new social force into the prevailing corporative system under the control and direction of the state was remarkably similar (140, 503, 513).

The Vargas system of officially sanctioned labor structures and trade union activities survived the restoration of republican government in 1945. Indeed, Roett demonstrates that the entire republican structure in the postwar period was not nearly so liberal and democratic as it is often portrayed and that the basic structures of the corporative-patrimonialist state remained intact. In terms of the moderating role of the army, the patronage role of the parties, the perpetuation of coronelismo in the countryside, the power of traditional vested interests, the all-encompassing regulatory role of a now even more-centralized and bureaucratic state apparatus, it is the continuities that are important as much as the changes. However, as the change process accelerated, as social mobilization went forward, as labor began to seek genuine autonomy and independent bargaining power, and as a government came to power sympathetic to labor's goals and willing to turn over the traditional patronage and control mechanisms to labor itself, the traditional elites rebelled, determined to reinstall a regime capable of managing and controlling the change process in the historic, orderly manner (560).

Roett's analysis is especially useful in showing the perpetuation over centuries, despite changes of regimes and constitutional systems, of a sociopolitical structure dominated by a powerful patrimonial state and controlled by the elite. In emphasizing the present-day continuities with an earlier tradition, he shows that Brazilian corporatism and patrimonialism cannot be understood in terms of either the pluralist or the totalitarian models but must be looked at in terms of a distinct tradition and body of literature. Roett also indicates the varieties of forms that the corporative-patrimonialist system may take in Brazil: the "preservatory" form of President Dutra in the late 1940s, the left-syndicalist form of Goulart in the early 1960s, and the military-developmentalism form of the post-1964 period. What Roett does not deal with fully, however, is the present-day blending and overlap of the traditional elitist and corporative currents with the newer strains of liberalism, socialism, and mass mobilization; the fusions and, frequently, patchwork compromises and accommodations between them; the associational and institutional mixes; the disjointed dissensual polities that exist; and the ever-present possibility for national disintegration and breakdown. Fortunately, in Kenneth Erickson's and Philippe Schmitter's works, we have considerable interview, archival, and other data to show the blends and crosscurrents present, their relative strengths and dynamics, and some of the implications for Brazil's development for continuing to operate within the corporative-patrimonialist mold (140, 453).

Peru

What calls our attention to Peru is the effort by the military elite to fashion a revolutionarycorporative model for the 1970s, in contrast to the more static and conservative (Models 1 and 2, according to the Schmitter categorization) types of Brazil and Portugal. Peru represents an updated and restructured corporative model, participatory at least in theory and now extended to the rural as well as the urban poor, but still (unabashedly and unashamedly, in the new climate of the 1970s) tutelary, corporatist, and patrimonialist in form.

The Peruvian regime proclaims itself nationalist and has taken considerable pains to fashion an ideology of corporatist development which it proudly presents as being uniquely Peruvian rather than derived from the outside. It has promised and moved partially to implement a broad range of social and structural reforms. It proclaims itself revolutionary and, in fact, has eliminated certain elites from a dominant voice in national affairs. At the same time, its ideology stresses popular participation for the Peruvian masses in the system, and freedom within a context of social democracy (30, 133, 213).

The Peruvian regime clearly represents a left variant on the corporative model, although the degree of its revolutionary fervor is open to much debate. Julio Cotler has referred to the regime as one of "military populism," while Carlos Astiz has written of its technocratic and bureaucratic way of managing change (95, 31). In perhaps the most complete analysis so far available, David Scott Palmer has pointed to the inherent conflict between the military goals of internal security and full participation for the masses. He shows that, to date, the government's tendency has been to emphasize the tutelary and control mechanisms rather than the participatory and potentially revolutionary ones, to use the corporative framework and ideology as a way of coopting, institutionalizing, and, hence, defusing revolutionary pressures within an orderly and carefully regulated structure. The military has sought to preempt the leftist and nationalist positions, but to do so within the confines of the older statist and corporatist lines. Meanwhile, where the corporative mechanisms have remained closed or too tightly regulated, the tendency for local forces has been to seek out other channels and means of influence, forcibly bypassing the corporative framework (379, 329). The Peruvian regime, thus, represents an attempt by a military elite to guide and lead the revolutionary pressures that had been building in the country for a long time and that threatened in the 1960s to get out-of-hand. This change can take place, however, only within a controlled and regulated framework, for which the corporative model has long been ideally suited. Meanwhile, the processes of social modernization, of conflicting group pressure, and of the capacity ultimately to go outside the system for recourse remain (539).

AN ASSESSMENT

There can be no doubt that corporatist models and experiments are resurgent in the Iberic-Latin world. In addition to the systems described here, Mexico, Spain, Argentina, Ecuador, the Dominican Republic, Chile, and others are all experimenting with one or another form of corporative theory and organization. Although some analysts have seen in the new wave of corporatist experimentation a retrogression to earlier political forms and a reemergence of "Fascism," another quite different interpretation of corporatism's resurgence, as the present analysis suggests, is also possible. One can see in this an effort by the Iberic-Latin systems now for the first time in several decades to come to grips with their own indigenous realities and historical traditions, to devise new developmental ideologies and forms of organization suited to their own political culture and social structure rather than the older imitation of U.S. and European models, a nationalistic response and attempt to rediscover what is unique and distinctive in their own tradition and to update and fuse that model with the requisites of modern twentieth-century life. There is a direct and sustaining continuity, regardless of the constitutional forms and labels used, between the older, historic tradition of corporatism on which the Iberic-Latin systems were originally erected, and its more contemporary manifestations.

Corporatism, thus seen, represents an effort by the Iberic-Latin nations to rediscover their own "third way," to evolve their own particular "world of development," distinctive from either the socialist or the capitalist one. The corporatist resurgence also reflects, one suspects, the declining influence of the U.S. in the area and of the U.S. model of development, a spurning of the false alternatives (U.S.-style liberalism or socialism, Soviet-style) imposed on the Iberic-Latin nations by the U.S. in its Cold War considerations, and a rejection of that era, the 1960s, particularly, of such immense U.S. influence and interference in Latin American affairs. That era has ended or is ending throughout the hemisphere and, in the present period of U.S. "benign neglect" toward Latin America, new indigenous developmental solutions are sprouting. Many will find that a welcome and healthy development. And though the corporatist label may still be an unfortunate one, conjuring up unpleasant, hateful connotations of Nazi atrocities, we must begin to recognize that the mainstreams of corporatism in the Iberic-Latin world were always fundamentally different from and opposed to the Nazi and Fascist models and that the nations of the Iberic-Latin culture area are not accurately described by resort to "Fascist" or "Neo-Fascist" brands.

Having said this, a word of caution is also in order. Corporatism and corporatist models have achieved a certain "in-ness" of late which needs to be kept in perspective. The corporatist model is useful as a partial explanatory tool in examining the Iberic-Latin development tradition, but it must be remembered that it is merely a heuristic device, helpful up to a point, and providing answers to certain questions. We must recognize that other models and approaches must be employed to provide answers to other questions. In the minds of most observers, for example, the relative weights to be assigned to a corporatist political cultural approach as determining Iberic-Latin political behavior, as opposed to a structural or class-based approach, have not been fully sorted out or finally decided (171). The "delayed development" and "dependency" theses, for instance, are also reasonable and useful (456). The corporative model cannot explain all of Iberic-Latin political phenomena, since these nations are at best only incompletely corporative systems, since the real centers of power and influence (even in Portugal, perhaps the most completely rationalized, in a formal-legal sense, of the corporative systems) often lie outside the corporate structures and institutions, and since the recourse to revolution or to political action beyond the boundaries of the corporative legal order are always possible. Indeed, it would seem that some of the most exciting areas of research lie precisely in that murky area where our models overlap, where corporatist attitudes and organizations are mixed and jumbled together with liberal and/or socialist ones, where the traditional institutions are modernizing and the modernizing ones employing traditional techniques of spoils, patronage, and the like. In all of this, both the scholarly dispute as to how best to interpret these events, as well as the political dynamics of change and conflict, will go on.

Corporatist theory and institutions can clearly take a great variety of forms and range from left to right on the political spectrum. Given this apparently dominant political culture, much useful research can be done on its national variations, the structural reasons why the Brazilian military took a rightist corporatist direction and the Peruvians a leftist one, the dynamics of modernization and development both within and outside the corporative framework. The question as to why corporatist solutions are reemerging at precisely the time of declining U.S. influence throughout the hemisphere is also an intriguing one. Perhaps part of the answer lies in the growing recognition that, while the U.S. cannot be the policeman to the world, it cannot be its political example either. Surely U.S. social scientists, long imbued with their own ethnocentric and culturally biased models of development, must also begin to recognize that fact.

NOTES

    a. Patrimonialism is one of Weber's forms of traditional authority; see 42. The Iberic-Latin systems, in a sense, have turned Weber on his head, for not only have they remained cast in the corporate-patrimonialist mold without evolving other forms of authority in the Weberian scheme, but patrimonialism itself has proved flexible and capable of modernization.

    b. It should be noted that, at this point, the focus of the article shifts to Portugal and to the use of Portuguese terms; although much of the emphasis here is on an <u>Iberian</u> tradition and though the parallels and differences with Spain are well worth developing, it was my assignment in this collection (<u>The Review of Politics</u> [January 1974]) to focus on the Luso-Brazilian world, leaving the Spanish and Hispanic to other contributors. Nonetheless, the thrust of the article remains toward exploring corporatism and development in the broader Iberic-Latin world.

    c. Later corporatist theorists, in harking back to the supposed order, stability, and unity of this era, largely ignored its violence, terror, conflict, and misery. In fact, the medieval era and guild system, which the corporatists so romanticized, was not always very pleasant; see 37.

7 | Corporatist Theory and Ideology: A Latin American Development Paradigm

> What is not in the [North] American tradition but is very deeply embedded in the Portuguese and South American tradition is the corporate organization of society.
>
> Marie R. Madden
> Letter to New York Times
> August 7, 1941

Corporatism, until recently, had been widely dismissed as both anachronistic and irrelevant. Defeated in World War II and apparently discredited by its practice in the Axis nations and its supposed affinities to fascism, corporatism as an ideology and form of sociopolitical organization seemed, for a time, to have been erased and forgotten as one of the major alternative "isms" of the twentieth century. Based largely on the Italian and German experiences, corporatism was also seen as a post-hoc rationalization that had little to do with the real locus of power, or as a "confidence trick." And because the manifestly corporatist experiments in Iberia and Latin America were never fully implemented and few regimes called themselves "corporatist," the tendency has been to describe corporatism as mere window-dressing, or to disregard it altogether as a philosophy and form of national organization whose historical epoch had been superseded (358, 452).

Such judgments as regards corporatism's alleged passing and irrelevance are premature and ill-founded. Corporatist ideology and sociopolitical structure are clearly not anachronistic. They manifest continued strength throughout the Iberic-Latin culture (and elsewhere), not just in the traditional regimes but in various modernizing ones as well. In many respects, indeed, corporatism remains the dominant mentality and form of sociopolitical organization throughout the Iberic-Latin world, at the base of its political culture and history. Nor is corporatism irrelevant; its functions are many and diverse. It has provided the ideological bases for many contemporary movements and regimes; it forms an integral part of Iberic-Latin political culture and tradition with roots deep in the past; it may also serve as an agency of class rule.

From Journal of Church and State 20 (Winter, 1978): 29-56.

Corporatism has served as a means both of change and of control. Distinct from fascism, corporatism may be viewed as an Iberic-Latin counterpart to the other "great isms" of liberalism and Marxism, a particularly (but not exclusively) Southern European and Latin American response and alternative to the problems of emerging capitalism, anomie, alienation, and mass society. Surely, if we take liberalism and Marxism seriously, if we see Locke at the heart of the North American tradition and Marxism-Leninism at the heart of the communist one, then we are also obliged to examine corporation and its chief advocates in Iberia and Latin America in the same scholarly light.

The sociopolitical dynamics of corporatism are treated elsewhere by the author; it is the purpose of this chapter to trace the history of corporatist thought and ideology, to present an ideal-typical model of the modern corporatist political society, and to offer some comments on the taxonomy and praxis of corporatism. For despite the by-now generally recognized importance of corporatism, it remains a tradition of thought that is wholly neglected in our histories of political theory, anthologies on social change, and studies of developmental alternatives. Even Latin Americanists have seldom given it much attention since, it may be speculated, corporatism's assumptions often run counter to prevailing North American liberal beliefs and since it does not always fit into established categories (a). Corporatism is, however, a tradition that is crucial for understanding Iberia and Latin America and with which we must come to grips if we are to comprehend the nations of this culture area on their own terms rather than through the biased, often ethnocentric perspectives of North American social science.

THE HISTORIC TRADITION OF CORPORATISM: ORIGINS AND ANTECEDENTS

The key distinction made earlier between the formal-institutional corporative systems of the 1920s and 1930s and the sociocultural tradition of corporatism which has a far longer history bears repeating here. The corporatist experiments of the interwar period involved the drafting of new, manifestly corporatist constitutions, such as that of Portugal in 1933 or Brazil in 1937; the establishment of functionally representative (in whole or in part) legislative bodies and councils of state; the restructuring of worker-employer relations along corporative lines and frequently the creation of official, monopolistic syndicates for each with the state enforcing the corporatist principle of class cooperation; and the organization of official agencies of economic coordination and regulation, or corporations (hence, the term "corporatism"), designed to restructure national social and economic life. Some of the corporative legislation never went into effect and much of it was implemented unevenly. But there is another meaning of corporatism that has gained usage, referring to an historic pattern of sociopolitical organization--authoritarian, elitist, hierarchical, patrimonialist, and corporatist--and that seems to form an important part of Iberic-Latin political culture. In this latter, broader sense, the nations of Iberia and Latin America may be a part of a general "corporatist tradition," whether they adopted the more manifest corporatist institutions of the interwar period or not.

These two meanings have frequently been confused in the literature. For example, some scholars call Brazil a patrimonialist-corporatist nation in the political-cultural sense, while others, using the formal institutional definition that gained prominence in the 1930s, dismiss the notion that Brazil is "corporatist," since its corporatist constitution never went into effect. The distinction made here helps clarify the two senses in which Brazil may be considered corporatist. But while analytically separable, the relations between these two meanings of the term should also be noted. For in many ways the manifest, institutional, corporatist experiments of the interwar period represented newer elaborations of earlier corporatist traditions, a modernized, updated way of responding to and managing new social pressures that exhibited numerous parallels with the past. Indeed, what made the modern corporatist arguments and institutions so attractive was both their affinity to the older corporatist tradition and the fact that under "corporatism" an existing elitist, hierarchical order could be maintained. Corporatism, in short, was both an important part of Iberic-Latin political culture, as well as a tradition that could be manipulated for class or political advantage. Separating out these two meanings of corporatism enables us also to see that, while the manifest corporatist institutions of the 1920s and 1930s may have disappeared in the postwar period (although now enjoying a resurgence in Argentina, Brazil, Chile, Peru, and other countries), the older, underlying, corporative political culture may have remained dominant, continuing to shape social and political behavior. Hence, corporatism as a political-cultural tradition <u>and</u> as manifest ideology and institutions of a certain time period both command our attention, as well as the complex relations between them (b).

Four main currents of thought and institutions--the Greco-Roman, the Christian-Thomistic, the feudal-medieval, and the Spanish-Portuguese during the era of nation-building and consolidation from the fourteenth through the sixteenth centuries--may be considered as critical in shaping the Iberian and Latin American corporatist tradition.

Corporatist theorists trace the origins of their ideas to ancient Greece, even to the origins of civil society in the family, clan, tribe, and organic local community. Greek philosophy and social organization generally form their base points, however: the earliest professional associations, the notions of order and hierarchy, concepts of organic unity in state and society, society as a reflection of its "natural" corporate bodies, etc. (68, 279).

In the Roman structure of <u>colegios</u> and in the system of professional, military, and religious institutions, corporatists see the precursors of both medieval and contemporary corporative agencies. Each colegio had its own legal status and was monopolistic in character. The state governed the relations between them. From Rome also the corporatists took the concepts of a monistic state, a hierarchy of laws and group rights, the principle of the "common good." Mihail Manoïlesco, one of corporatism's foremost modern theorists, saw it as a direct extension of the Roman system: the state as a civic and moral authority, harmony between state and society, society's organization on the basis of "natural" social and civic associations, representation by class and corporate group, etc. (311).

From Thomas Aquinas and their own national Christian traditions, the corporatists took the organic conception of state and society; the concepts that property had a social function and should be used for the good of society as a whole; the theory of just price and a fair wage (set presumably by the state), the principle of a hierarchy of men, laws, and institutions; a feudal-patrimonial natural order; the idea of a state based on Christian assumptions of mutual rights and obligations; and the principle of corporate and functional social organization. Purchaser and seller, employer and employee, should reap mutual advantage from their relations, which were to be governed by Christian brotherhood, not class conflict. Updated and sometimes secularized, many of these concepts still undergird the Iberic-Latin systems. Manoïlesco contended that it was the Roman statist and the Thomistic-Christian influences that were most important in shaping the corporative tradition, even that the various blends of these two largely determined the national variations among corporative states in modern times (311, 297).

Among feudal-medieval institutions, the guild was particularly important for modern-day corporatists. The guilds helped provide an acceptable answer to Catholic disapproval of commercial enterprise, for they were compulsory and monopolistic agencies with strict rules for admission and for regulating economic activity. The guilds implied cooperation between masters and workmen, not conflict as in the Marxian tradition, and the function of choosing one's own "class" representatives in the guild council. Membership was defined hierarchically: apprentice, journeyman, master. The relations between these sectors were governed by mutual rights and obligations. In cooperation with the authorities, the guilds set prices, wages, hours, and production; settled conflicts; administered charity; and lessened competition. The guild, along with such other corporate groups as the Church, the family, and the local community, set limits on state power. They would check against tyranny and serve also as the representatives of their members to the state. In the modern conception, the corporative agencies were to perform the same functions, thus eliminating the need for divisive political parties and class associations (138).

The fourth main current of thought critical in shaping the Iberic-Latin corporatist tradition was the political philosophy of the Spanish and Portuguese consolidation, from the fourteenth through the sixteenth centuries. During this period, the model of the modern Iberic-Latin state was put together into a coherent whole. It was based on a system of guilds, municipalities, nobles, and other corporate elements and classes fused together under the guidance and authority of the Crown. The Crown became the center of an elaborate nationwide patronage and bureaucratic system. The structure was hierarchical, authoritarian, corporatist. Power was to be exercised paternally and change would take place through the gradual widening of the elite as well as the admission of new corporate units to the system, provided they also gave service and loyalty to the Crown. The cortes was to be subordinate to the Crown. And the economy was similarly organized on a mercantilist, patrimonialist, statist basis in which wealth, position, and special privileges were awarded to the deserving in return for loyalty to the Crown (183).

By the sixteenth century, these ideas had been further refined to provide a sophisticated model of a modern, bureaucratic-authoritarian state. The state system now encompassed the colonies as well as the metropoles. The state was based on an organic and Thomistic conception and its moral and political bases remained fused. The prevailing model was of a unified, Christian, authoritarian, and corporatist system which, in updated form, remains probably the dominant one today. Far more research needs to be done on fifteenth- and sixteenth-century Spanish and Portuguese law and political theory, for it was during this "siglo de oro" that the "ideal type" of Iberic-Latin state and society, to which many nations of the area still hark back, was established (191, 263).

Although this dominant sixteenth-century model was subsequently refined and modified, it continued to serve as the foundation on which Spain, Portugal, and their New World colonies were grounded. In the absence of the profound social revolutions in the Iberic-Latin world that we associate with the modern age, those structures remained unchanged in their essentials until the onslaught of liberalism in the nineteenth century. But even then the underlying social and economic structures remained largely unaltered and liberalism came to represent a thin veneer superimposed upon, but not replacing, an older tradition that was corporatist and patrimonialist to its core (111, 144). A new synthesis and updating were, hence, required, and that is precisely what the corporatist revival of the nineteenth century sought to provide.

THE THREE GREAT "ISMS": LIBERALISM,
SOCIALISM, CORPORATISM

The French Revolution of 1789 had as one of its chief goals the abolition of feudal rights and privilege. The heady concepts of liberty and equality gained prominence, and by decree of March 2, 1791, the guilds of the ancien regime were swept away. These events also affected Spain, Portugal, and their soon-to-be-independent colonies in the New World: new and liberal constitutions were written and corporate privilege was diminished--at least in law. In Iberia and Latin America, however, unlike the situation in France, the liberal laws were not accompanied by social revolution, with the result that the underlying landholding system, Catholic political culture, and sociopolitical relations remained, essentially feudal, hierarchical, elitist, and corporatist. There was no "wipe-out" of ancient corporatism; in many respects, instead, while overlain with a liberal constitutional facade, the system of corporate privilege was strengthened (188).

During the next several decades, roughly 1820-70, in both Iberia and Latin America, conflict between liberal and traditionalist forces was almost continuous. Reactionary thought was strongly present. In Portugal, the traditionalists inveighed against Rousseau and the Encyclopedists, urged restoration of a strong monarchy limited only by the traditional estates, and advocated the unity of Church and state. In Spain a better-known school, Donoso Cortés, Balmes, Menéndez y Pelayo, and Maeztu, sought similarly to resurrect the status quo ante, a system of order, hierarchy, and corporate privilege. A number of these thinkers, anticipating later solutions, were willing to expand the system of corporate elites to include the new bourgeosie (67, 504).

These brief comments on the liberal and traditionalist currents in Iberia and Latin America help place in perspective the corporatist current, which purported to offer a middle way and thus help resolve the almost continuous civil strife between the other two. For if, as the traditionalists argued, liberalism ignored centuries of Iberian history and cultural formation, the traditionalists had ignored the major changes of their own century. Beginning in midcentury, therefore, a body of ideas began to be fashioned, aimed at a new synthesis, seeking politically to ameliorate the old conflicts while also facing up to modern socioeconomic realities. Capitalism, industrialization, and accelerated social change had begun to have their effect, and the trend in ideas was also away from the old medievalism toward the serious study of contemporary problems. French, Spanish, Portuguese, German, and other Catholic writers started to wrestle with the same fundamental issues as Marx or Weber. They sought to fashion a political order consistent with the past but adapted to the new realities, a modernizing framework but distinctive from either liberalism or Marxism. This body of thought came to be called "corporatism," a tradition almost wholly ignored in our theory texts but crucial for comprehending Iberic-Latin development.

The corporatists drew upon familiar ideas: utopian socialism, Proudhon, Comte, Durkheim (especially his analysis of occupational groups). They also read the reformist ideas of Saint Simon and LaFarelle, who elaborated guild schemes more adapted to the new age than to medievalism. In this way, important features of traditional institutions might be retained, while new elements would be accommodated to the system (138). The regard for order and hierarchy would be fused with the need for change. Mass man would be dealt with through agencies of class harmony, not conflict, structured participation rather than rootlessness and alienation. New corporative agencies would be created for the new middle and working classes, instead of their being dealt with through repression.

The crisis posed by "the social question," the challenge of organized labor, in mid-nineteenth-century Europe was primarily responsible for the revival of corporate thought. How to provide for change but without precipitating revolutionary upheaval? Corporatism helped provide an answer. Representation would be determined by function (business, labor, industry, etc.) rather than through individualism and one-man, one-vote. The state would control the admission of new groups to the system (32, 93). Hence, change would come but it would be carefully managed. The new social forces would be recognized without sacrificing past organic-corporatist institutions (c).

By the 1860s and 1870s, these ideas began to be brought together into a coherent social doctrine. Wilhelm Ketteler, Bishop of Mainz, parliamentary deputy and a long-time leader of the German Catholic social movement, was perhaps the first modern corporatist spokesman. In his <u>Liberty, Authority, and Church</u> (1862) and <u>Christianity and the Worker Question</u> (1864), Ketteler spoke of the evil effects of unlimited competition and social atomization, and the need to limit arbitrary power. He talked of the social responsibility of capital, a wider distribution of society's goods, and the need for a corporatist reorganization of society. He supported the new workers' associations, greater wages, and profit-sharing--ideas that went beyond traditional Catholic charity. Drawing upon the long tradition of German organicist and precorporatist thought (Hegel, Fichte, Gierke), he proposed a regenerated guild scheme as a solution. Ketteler's influence on two generations of young prelates, unionists, and social workers was considerable (50, 154).

Another important current was the French corporatist school of the Marques La Tour du Pin, Albert de Mun, and Leon Harmel. They and social-Christians Charles Périn and Emile Keller formulated the idea of a network of organizations combining employers and employees to regulate each industry, trade, and profession. They also emphasized such "natural" corporations as the Church or the family as forming the basis of the state. La Tour and de Mun formed an association of Catholic Workingmen's Circles which, beginning in 1871, had grown to 50,000 members in 400 Circles by 1884. The Circles were directed <u>by</u> their elite leadership <u>for</u> their laboring members. The aim was not to promote independent trade unions but to place workers and employers in Christian "corporations" under the direction of executive committees recruited from the "better" classes. La Tour remained an aristocrat and monarchist, but de Mun came to see the need for independent corporatist associations of workers. Harmel shocked fellow industrialists by instigating profit-sharing and independent labor unions in his factory (138).

Other Catholic social movements, workers' associations, and farm cooperatives began springing up throughout France. Similar corporatist ideas were put forth by Baron Karl von Vogelsang in Austria, Cardinal Henry Manning in Britain, G. M. Bosco in Italy, Kaspar Decurtino in Switzerland, Mgr. Antoine Pottier in Belguim, and James Cardinal Gibbons in the U.S. A body of corporative doctrine, thus, began to emerge that cut across national boundaries and that purported to offer a non-Marxian answer to the ills of capitalism and liberalism. Nor were the Church and Leo XIII unaware of these doctrines. In 1884 La Tour met with the Pope, and there is no doubt Leo himself was strongly influenced by the corporatist ideas. By the 1880s, a considerable body of corporatist writings and movements had emerged; the job remained of bringing unity to these still vague ideas and of strengthening the organizational base.

In 1881 the Pope charged a commission of theologians and Catholic social thinkers to study these issues in relation to Catholic

teachings. They met at Freiburg in 1884. Corporatism was now
clearly defined for the first time as a "system of social organization that has at its base the grouping of men according to the community of their natural interests and social functions, and as true
and proper organs of the state they direct and coordinate labor and
capital in matters of common interest." The Freiburg meeting
brought corporatist thinkers from different nations together for
the first time, gave their movement legitimacy and coherence, and
stimulated the growth of new activities. The theses adopted at
Freiburg also influenced the Vatican representatives and helped
inspire Rerum Novarum. Another gathering in Berlin in 1890 under
Papal auspices adopted a similar corporative program, on the eve of
Leo XIII's promulgation of his "workingman's encyclical."

By today's standards, these early movements were hardly radical, but in the context of the times (Bismarck's Germany, Restoration Spain) they did represent some new departures. And while concerned with social justice, corporatism was also a response to the
perceived Marxian threat. Its conservative nature was reflected in
the makeup of the committee of ten that drafted the Freiburg theses: two barons, five counts, a duke, and a bishop. La Tour continued to speak of a "natural" ruling class, and the workers' associations were generally led by priests and wealthier elements who
sought to provide paternalistic protection to the workers and to
combat socialism. The early Catholic social movement was at most
mildly reformist.

And yet, the 1880s and 1890s marked a real watershed in the
Catholic movement. Aristocratic attitudes toward "the social question" gradually changed. A positive conception of trade unions
began to replace the negative one. The earlier Workers' Circles
had attracted the pious and weak; now real working-class movements
began to be organized, run by the workers themselves. The older
paternalism was proving inadequate. While collaboration between
classes remained the ideal, both labor and capital had to be strong
enough to defend their own interests. The workers could achieve
their just demands by collective action under their own leadership.
The clerical influence was reduced and the workers' associations
were no longer necessarily confessional. Independent action now
included the right to strike. Clearly, these new formulations
still carried heavy Catholic, paternalistic overtones, but the
Catholic social movement also saw the need to update its thinking
to provide a progressive social reformism capable of competing with
socialism. The trend toward independent working-class movements,
however, was far stronger in France and Germany than in Spain and
Portugal, where the older paternalistic conception still dominated
(154, 202, 278).

Rerun Novarum provided a special impetus to the growth of
Catholic social and labor movements. It argued that, like the family, labor organizations were a part of the natural order. The
right of men to organize and engage in trade union activities was
inherent, not to be denied by employers or the state. Property was
given a social function and worker rights considered equal to employers'. Rerum Novarum provided a legitimacy the Catholic movements had not had before and elevated the laboring class into a

position where its rights had to be recognized. The trade unions were given their place alongside other pillars in the corporative system. Though weakly implemented at first, until given stronger expression in Quadragesimo Anno (1931), Rerum Novarum helped inspire a host of Catholic social and worker movements throughout Europe and Latin America (319).

An added impetus to corporatist ideas was provided during this same (pre-World War I) period by the rejection of the liberal and democratic conceptions in the writings of Gumplowicz, Mosca, Pareto, Michels, and Sorel. Antiliberal, antiparliamentary ideas were strong and widespread. All these writers criticized the egalitarian assumptions, saw society as inherently pyramidal, and emphasized the role of elites. Like the Catholic corporatists, they were organicists, emphasized group over individual rights, posited a strong role for the state, took up "integralist" and "solidarist" positions. They saw change as occurring from the top down with the state exercising control over the process. These were all secular conceptions and had a strong impact on Italian Fascism. But many of their ideas dovetailed with the Catholic corporatists and their critiques of democracy, egalitarianism, and parliamentarism were applauded. It is no accident that subsequent corporative institutions in Iberia and Latin America derived from both the secular conceptions of Mussolini's Carta del Lavoro and the Catholic ideas of the encyclicals, and that the tension also continued between their inclination toward bureaucratic authoritarianism and the pull of paternalistic Christian humanism (184, 386).

By the turn of the century, a great variety of Catholic and/or corporatist worker and social movements had sprung up. In 1895 the first national Catholic trade union federation had been founded in Germany; and, by the first decade of the twentieth century, similar federations had been established in a number of other European countries. In Spain and Portugal the Catholic Círculos were flourishing; the Semaines Sociales and other Catholic study groups were spreading; and a general Catholic revival was underway. Associations for youth, women, university students, and professionals were also established, in addition to the sindicatos and gremios for workers and employers. In 1900 the International Association for the Legal Protection of Workers was created; meanwhile, new concepts of social security were being articulated, and a variety of Christian-democratic movements began (340, 426).

Our purpose is not to discuss these movements in detail or their national variations but only to show the context in which corporatism took root and how widespread the new movement was. In most of these associations, heavy stress continued to be placed on family and religion and many existed as mutual benefit societies. But the changes in the Catholic social movement since the aristocratic paternalism of the 1870s were considerable. By 1900 an increasingly modern, progressive, even militant in some cases, series of organizations had been established. They sought to deal with the complex issues of modern mass man and class conflict, but in ways that would also preserve intact those institutions considered valuable from the past (religion, family, authority, community, etc.). Corporatism began to emerge as a "Third Way," an alternative to the other great "isms" of liberalism and Marxism.

In the peaceful, conservative decades before World War I, the Catholic social movement grew gradually. In the chaotic decade following the war, however, it grew rapidly. The social question loomed bigger; violent workers' revolts took place; Bolshevism threatened. To most Latin Americans, socialism remained an unacceptable alternative; and, with the market crash and depression of the early 1930s, it seemed capitalism and liberalism had also collapsed. In those desperate times, with no other available alternatives, corporatism, particularly (but not exclusively) in the Catholic and Southern European countries, appeared to offer the only solution. In Spain under Primo (1923-30) and then Franco (1939-75); Greece under Venizelos (1917-20) and Metaxes (1936-41); Bulgaria and Lithuania (1926-29); Poland under Pilsudski (1926-35); Albania (1928-39); Yugoslavia (1929); Portugal (1926-74); Turkey, Estonia, and Latvia (1934); Austria (1934-38); Ireland (1937); Romania, Vichy France, Italy (1922-45); Germany (1933-45), corporatist regimes came to power or were strongly infused with corporatist ideology (38, 458).

Corporatism also made strong inroads into Latin America. The chief influences were the Catholic-corporative states of Spain and Portugal, although the Italian and French influences were also present. For many Catholic writers, Salazar's Estado Novo was viewed as a model. In the 1930s, a host of regimes, movements, and parties were fashioned, in varying degrees to be sure, on the basis of corporatist influences. The "corporatist" label was not always used and the formal-legal structure of corporatism was nowhere so complete as in Portugal, but the corporatist influence was still strongly present. The regimes and movements which borrowed concepts and institutional arrangements from corporatism include Vargas's Brazil, Trujillo's Dominican Republic, Perón's Argentina, Ubico in Guatemala, Hernández in El Salvador, Benavides in Peru, the Bolivian MNR, Peru's APRA, the Mexican PRI, and numerous others (304, 400). Corporatism seemed the wave of the future.

A number of reasons help explain the popularity of corporatism in Iberia and Latin America during this period. These include the widespread dissemination of European corporatist ideas throughout Latin America in the 1930s, the neo-Thomistic and Catholic revival, the promulgation of <u>Quadragesimo Anno</u> in 1931, Spain's aggressive <u>hispanismo</u> with its strong corporatist overtones (396). The fact that corporatism was strongly congruent with Iberia's and Latin America's patrimonialist, natural-corporatist tradition was also important; corporatism seemed a part of the accustomed landscape. The fact that corporatism was European and seemed the wave of the future provides another reason for its widespread acceptance.

Related to all these factors and perhaps most important is the fact that corporatism provided a way out of the political crisis of the time without tampering overly with Iberia's or Latin America's existing structures. The depression, the collapse of oligarchic rule, and the rise of "the social question" had created both a vacuum and a need for a new formula. Corporatism filled that need without implying revolutionary upheaval. It meant a shift in the locus of power from oligarchic to middle-sector rule without destroying "the system"; it provided a way of absorbing the emerging workers' organizations into the prevailing structure and channeling certain benefits to them but without this signifying much real transfer of wealth and power; it meant a means of accommodating new power contenders in the classic Andersonian pattern but under a system of state control and regulation (21). Corporatism also implied a shift from geographical localism to a comprehensive national political order, a way to fill the historic associational vacuum, to expand state control over the economy, to correct the traditional "falta de organización," and thus to become a modern, developed nation. For all these reasons, corporatism was exceedingly attractive. It is no accident that the new labor ministries created during this period, the regulatory agencies, labor laws, trade unions, farmers' associations, etc.--all showed such strong corporatist influence.

After World War II the labels changed and some of the corporatist institutional arrangements were set aside. But although baptized with new names, other corporatist institutions continued; certainly the historic corporatist political-cultural tradition remained alive, now rediscovered in the wake of the failure of so many of the liberal experiments of the 1960s; and many of the Latin American nations remained corporatist (or mixed) systems de facto, even if not in law or constitution. It is this tradition of thought and sociopolitical organization, long neglected or mistakenly consigned to the ashcans of history, that we have argued is critical for understanding Iberic-Latin development patterns. Prejudices concerning corporatism's alleged affinities to fascism (fascism is one form of corporatism but hardly the only one), a social science that insists corporatism's era has already passed historically, and sometimes willful neglect because we do not always appreciate the values that corporatism enshrines, should not blind us to the importance of corporatism in the Iberic-Latin tradition. It is one of our basic arguments here that such biases should have no place in scholarly analysis, that they have frequently blinded us to the distinctive character of Iberic-Latin development, and that, if we are to comprehend Iberia and Latin America on their own terms rather than through the sometimes ethnocentric conceptions of North American social science, we must come to grips with corporatism as a past--and continuing--influence.

THE CORPORATIST VISION OF STATE AND SOCIETY

Although the corporatist resurgence of the mid-nineteenth century had begun chiefly as a Catholic movement, by the turn of the century there were several major corporatist currents, both religious and secular. In the interwar period, as various corporatist regimes came to power, new permutations and national variations appeared.

Clearly, a wide spectrum of regimes and movements fall under the corporatist umbrella. In Iberia and Latin America initially, the chief influences were the social-Christian and the etatist-authoritarian. Franco Spain, Salazar's Portugal, Vargas's Brazil are the major examples. In the more-developed European countries, with stronger trade unions and socialist traditions, the reformist and Left varieties were also present. However, as Latin America continued its development, the Left and syndicalist varieties emerged there as well: Cárdenas in Mexico, Goulart in Brazil, the military-nationalist regime in Peru.

Although political discourse in Latin America in the post-World War II period was usually couched in terms of the familiar liberal-conservative debate, the real struggle, it may be suggested, was between alternative corporatist conceptions. In Brazil it was the Left-syndicalist position of Goulart as opposed to the authoritarian-gremialist position of the army; and so on. It was not so much a debate between corporatism and something else (although that was present, too) but on the appropriateness of conflicting corporatist solutions. This implies corporatism may be an ongoing characteristic, not confined to a single type of regime or historical period. It also means corporatism is not static but dynamic, that its varied alternative forms are related to processes of social change and modernization. Putting it this way helps illustrate how long-lasting and pervasive the corporatist influence, in its several forms, is in Latin America. It may also show why the "liberal" and "conservative" labels often confuse the issues more than they enlighten.

Given the heterogeneity, it is difficult to define a single set of ideas to which all corporatists subscribe. Corporatism is no longer a single "ism" but encompasses a variety of conceptions. Nevertheless, these are some common threads in these conceptions, particularly as they have been applied in Iberia and Latin America. The "ideal type" of corporatist state and society presented here glosses over some of the differences and national variations in the interest of providing a clear, coherent picture. It emphasizes not the several branches of corporatist thought but the main trunk (11, 32, 38, 50, 65, 66, 68, 94, 138, 175, 312, 340, 401, 443, 447, 449, 451, 497).

Most of the voluminous writings on corporatism begin with a repudiation of its alternatives, liberalism and communism (d). Communism is rejected for its bloody past, its totalitarian impulses, its materialism, its stress on class strife, and so on. Liberalism is rejected for its excessive individualism; its inorganic conceptions of the state; its representational system based on one-man, one-vote; its interest-group pluralism and inattention to the common good; its divisive party politics; its laissez-faire economic structure; its atomistic concepts of man and society. In the Latin American context, the critique of liberalism was often more muted than in Iberia and an attempt made to fuse corporatism with the older republican institutions. Nevertheless, throughout the entire culture area the corporatist ideology found a fertile ground in the 1930s, given the unacceptability of communism and Iberia's and Latin America's often unhappy experiences with liberalism. The critique of liberalism was not necessarily a blanket condemnation but only of its divisive, chaotic tendencies in the Iberic-Latin context. If liberalism worked in Britain or the United States, fine; but in Iberia and Latin America where the traditions were distinct, liberalism was viewed as inappropriate, a set of foreign institutions imposed on a culture and societies where they did not fit (e).

Along with the rejection of liberalism went its institutional accoutrements. The need for unity and authority was at cross purposes with checks and balances and a coequal parliament. Divisive political parties would be replaced by a single movement. Since society's interests were to be represented functionally, competitive elections were no longer necessary. Civil liberties would be respected, but they could also be limited for the common good. While these changes would likely serve to expand the power of the central state, the creation of corporate intermediary structures and the revitalization of society's natural associations (family, community, guilds, etc.) would provide for decentralization and limits on state power.

Corporatist ideology was nationalist in two ways. It implied a rejection of the foreign influences (chiefly U.S.) implanted in Latin America contrary to its own cultural traditions, a repudiation of moral, political, and economic dependency. It meant also a search for what was viable in Iberia's and Latin America's own traditions on which a new nationalist sociopolitical structure could be based. Some corporatists went back to Rome for their ideal, others to a romanticized medievalism, some to the pre-Columbian Indian civilizations, most to a blend of these plus the sixteenth-century Spanish model, the guild tradition, Catholicism, and such strong Iberic-Latin institutions as the family, community, religion. The nationalist argument was thus strengthened by a resurgence of cultural nationalism. In a sense, this effort to build a new order in Iberia and Latin America upon the ruins of the old was comparable to that of the new nations today: rejecting the foreign, colonialist models of the past and seeking to discover in their own histories an indigenous framework for national development.

Repudiating the extremes of liberal individualism, the corporatists sought to reconstruct state and society on an organic basis. Attempts to function under an inorganic form, they argued, had led to chaos and civil conflict. In contrast to contract theory, corporatists saw society as natural, ordained by God and nature, and necessary for man's social and political well-being (f). Their natural law conception implied that political society should be based on such "natural" groups as the family, the clan, the locality, etc., and not on such "unnatural" associations as political parties or interest groups. In the corporatist vision, each man was to be rooted and secure in his natural station in life, whether he was an urban worker, cleric, or professional. Representation would also be based on such natural associations, though in practice most corporatists combined functional with politico-geographic representation. Membership in a corporate group guaranteed representation to all societal elements, as well as enabling them to qualify for the rights due them as members of the group.

Authority would also be required in both social affairs and government. The so-called "black box" concept of liberalism, by which government is merely the filter through which competing interests are channeled, is rejected. The role of government is to

<u>govern</u>, not just serve as a neutral referee. The state was to be a moral leader, authoritative, and integral. Its role was to coordinate, prod, and stimulate national development, also to regulate the relations among corporate groups. Authority, hence, had to be centralized and monistic rather than divided and dispersed (g).

But if the state was to be authoritarian, it was not totalitarian (267). Here is where corporatism's critics have sometimes foundered, for to them it seems inconceivable that a system not based on Montesquieuian checks and balances would not become totalitarian. But the corporatist state would also be limited. It was, for example, to help manage and regulate the economy but not completely run it, a concept that helps explain the emergence of state capitalist economies throughout the area distinct from both laissez-faire and total state ownership. The state would also be limited by the rights and <u>fueros</u> of the corporate groups that constituted society. Finally, in the Catholic conception, the state was to be limited by a higher moral law. By this the corporatists meant not pragmatism or utilitarian ethics but the Eternal Law which laid down immutable norms for human conduct. The state was viewed not as an end in itself but an instrument; it was obliged to recognize moral values with a greater claim to legitimacy than its own. Of course, in some corporative systems (Mussolini's Italy, Franco Spain, Salazar's Portugal, Trujillo's Dominican Republic), the abuses of both corporate group rights and moral restraint became such that they verged on totalitarianism. But in other corporative systems (and even to some degree in those just mentioned), the limits on state power continued to exist. Further, where authoritarianism (permissible and widely accepted) approached totalitarianism (unacceptable), corporatist theory (as well as Saint Thomas) provided legitimacy to the right of rebellion.

The corporatists believed that laissez-faire had failed, but neither could they countenance totalitarian rule. They believed the state was obliged to accept responsibility for the national economic life but not totally direct it. The state's role was to stimulate and adjust the economy to serve the common good. In this the corporatists were not far from Keynes and modern economic theory (242). The state was particularly obliged to encourage cooperation among classes and economic groups, to help raise production, to approve collective contracts, and to veto exploitive economic practices. The state was, thus, given broad regulative powers, though with some limits placed upon them. These broad powers help account for the curious presence in the Iberic-Latin economies, which we assume to be capitalistic, of public sectors roughly twice as large as that of the United States. The Iberian and Latin American economies came increasingly, under the influence of corporatism, to take on an etatist form, with a strong role accorded the state to manage the economy in the public interest. The corporatist influence also helps explain the equally powerful role of the state in labor relations. Indeed, it is the conflict between the concepts of a strong but limited state and the almost irresistable tendency toward complete state power that accounts for much of the early political dynamics of corporatism, of the divergence between the more limited <u>corporatisme d'association</u> and its more fascistic form as corporatisme d'etat (170, 463).

The corporatists sought to respond not just to man's economic needs, however, but also to his moral, cultural, and social needs. This was in keeping with both their critique of Marxism and their hostility to capitalism. The corporatists recognized the alienation of modern mass man, but they argued it was social and cultural as well as economic. Hence, they aimed not just to raise wages and improve benefits but also to organize people's clubs, social centers, libraries, retreats, dances, and sporting events. These represented ways of reintegrating the lower classes into society and of reforging the link between state and society. The corporative agencies were charged with implementing these socialization functions as a way of educating, "civilizing," and incorporating the rising social forces into the system.

The individual has his place in corporatist society chiefly as a member of the groups that make up the system: Church, army, trade unions, employers' groups, farmers, etc. Although the individual enjoys some fundamental human rights, his social and political rights (social security, representation) come via his corporatist association.

The state is obligated to uphold these rights, which serve as a further check on unbridled state power. The separate existence of agencies apart from the state is what corporatists mean when they refer to theirs as a system of corporate pluralism (h). By pluralism they mean a system in which the rights (fueros) of each group are defined in law and the group enjoys both representation in the system and a contractually defined independence from the state. A state is pluralist in the corporate sense insofar as it allows and safeguards associations other than the state: municipal government, corporate associations, and the like. Some agencies, like the Church or the family, are considered prior to the state in both natural law and history. Organic laws or charters of autonomy, such as those governing the university or the army, are designed to promote the interests of their members and protect them against the state's encroachments. The corporatists proposed to extend these rights to labor and, eventually, to rural workers and thus give them legitimacy and a place in the system. A government that abridged these basic rights sacrificed its own right to continued loyalty.

These same groups formed the base on which the corporate order would be fashioned. At the grass-roots level would be the family, municipality, sindicatos, local community centers, and the like. Then there would be provincial, regional, or state associations. At the cupola would stand the higher agencies of the system: functionally representative bodies, regulatory agencies, corporations, etc. The corporations might be organized vertically to encompass all those (workers, managers, employers) involved in the production of a single product, or horizontally in terms of the major branches of production (agriculture, commerce, industry, etc.). The Church, army, or university would be organized into separate corporations. These associations were to evolve naturally, organically, and not be imposed; in the best of situations, the state was only to give legal sanction to already existing corporations. All these groups would be represented in a corporate assembly or council of state, and <u>in</u>corporated into the regulatory agencies and economic bureaus. The councils of state organized in Spain, Portugal, and several of the Latin American countries, for instance, usually included the archbishop, the heads of the armed services, the rector of the university, several ministers (labor, agriculture, commerce), and the presidents of the chief business, agricultural, and patronal groups.

Instead of "artificial" political parties and special interest groups, the corporatist system would be based on society's "natural" groupings. The corporative agencies, furthermore, were not mere agents of their private members but institutions of <u>public interest</u> integrated with the state. Each group was to be "institutionalized" and guaranteed its legitimate place in the system; its voice would be heard in national decision-making without the corrupting influence associated with American-style interest-group lobbying. This structure would serve to unify society and ensure that government and its constituent groups worked harmoniously. The fact the corporative agencies would be autonomous from the state was supposed to guard against totalitarianism.

Within each corporative agency, capital and labor were to work together harmoniously for the common good. Instead of class conflict, corporatism provided for obligatory coexistence and negotiations. Workers and employers would still have their differences but these were to be adjusted and accommodated (under state supervision). Hence, both strikes and lockouts could be prohibited. The rights of workers and employers would be respected, and they would both be represented equally in the highest agencies of the state. Various schemes of co-government and co-participation were elaborated. No one class could or would profit disproportionately; all would share in decision-making and in service for the common good.

Although corporatism shared certain characteristics with fascism, the two should not necessarily be equated. The corporatist writers rejected the extreme nationalistic implications of fascism and its cult of the leader. Corporatists also rejected the antirationalist proclivities of fascism. They repudiated totalitarianism, the Nazi behemoth, and racial persecution. Whereas in Italy and Germany all associations had been subordinated to the state, in the corporatist vision these were to enjoy a separate existence. Corporatism had a long and independent history of its own, and most corporatists quickly disassociated themselves from the real fascists in their country. A condemnation of fascism, therefore, ought not to be extended into a blanket condemnation of all corporatist systems.

The corporative solution evolved from the fundamental guild assumption of the unity of purpose of masters and journeymen. Corporatist historians recognized also the limitations of the guild system and repudiated its monopolistic tendencies. They argued, however, that in the wake of the French revolution both the bad and the good aspects had been abolished, not only the abuses of the guild principle but the principle itself. While favoring freedom of association, they argued men could best realize their rights through a corporative associational life. In a period of conflict, breakdown, and societal disarray, that was an attractive vision.

Underlying the corporative conception was also a strong, though frequently forgotten, social justice motive. The men who articulated the corporatist ideology were genuinely concerned with alleviating poverty and backwardness, throwing off inappropriate foreign models and designing new indigenous ones, and providing for national social, political, and economic development. The corporatist system was not just a means, as some have alleged, of preserving elitist rule and stifling the lower classes. Of course, the corporatist scheme is open to a host of questions and criticisms and one can easily challenge its assumptions, its functionality, the way it was often manipulated in practice to serve not the public good but some narrower interest, whether the praxis of modern corporatism would necessarily be distinct from the medieval, the implications of corporatist-technocratic rule, and so on. But at least in theory and intentions, as well as the class background (middle rather than upper) of those who articulated and fashioned the various national systems, the corporatist conception was by no means wholly reactionary or elitist. Corporatism's powerful urge for social justice, for securing representation for new social groups, for dealing with the great issues of alienation, mass man, and accelerated social change in a way that was less conflict-prone and more in keeping with the Iberic-Latin tradition than either liberalism or communism, cannot be forgotten.

SOME IMPLICATIONS

The corporatist theory and sociology presented here emerged as a full-blown ideology during the same epoch in which Marxist and modern-day liberal ideologies were articulated and out of the same context of rapid industrialization and social change. Because corporatism's roots were strongly grounded in the Catholic tradition, Roman law, and a certain Northern Mediterranean tradition and "ethos," it found particular (but not exclusive) receptivity in the Southern European countries and the colonies they had founded on a similar basis.

A study of corporatism is crucial if we are to understand the responses to modernization of the Iberic-Latin nations. Corporatism and the corporatist tradition are not just ideas and institutional forms of passing interest, reaching their heyday in the interwar period and then disappearing, but instead constitute an on-going tradition, strongly intertwined with the history and culture of the area, and continuing today to influence political behavior and the structure of society and polity in a great variety of systems, both traditional and modernizing, both left and right.

The corporatist influence remains strong despite the fact few Latin American nations used that label or enacted the full gamut of corporatist institutions. Nor was corporatism ever the exclusive pivot of Latin American political society. Nevertheless, all the Iberian and Latin American nations adopted some elements of corporatism and in virtually all cases, though under different names, these continue today. In Latin America corporatist practices and institutions were frequently combined with liberal and republican forms, fusions that still exist at present. At the same time, there were distinct national traditions in all these countries which shaped the varieties of corporatist blends; the particular form corporatism took was also related to levels of development, class structure, and the stage and type of capitalism. None of the Latin American nations was completely corporatized in terms of the ideal-type model here presented, but all felt the corporatist influence at least partially. They were, in Manoilesco's terms, not "pure" corporatist systems but "mixed" or "subordinate" ones.

The mixed nature of these systems means that the corporatist framework is by itself incapable of explaining all of Iberic-Latin social behavior. Other models, for instance the dependency or class approach, must be used in conjunction with the corporatist one to explain a range of activity that does not fall within the corporatist framework. In addition, genuinely liberal and socialist movements have obviously made their presence felt, and some countries, however successfully, have sought to transcend their corporatist pasts. Some of these phenomena call for models of interpretation that the corporatist one does not completely provide; they also imply the utility of a conflict model not given sufficient attention in the "social harmony" conception of corporatist theory.

Corporatism was at the front and center of the sociopolitical systems of Iberia and Latin America in the 1930s, then followed a certain eclipse (perhaps more disguised than real), now it seems again resurgent. Throughout all these periods, corporatism was of critical importance in some (though not all) areas of national life. It seems inconceivable, for example, that one could understand trade unionism in the Iberic-Latin systems, the structure of labor and industrial relations, social security and assistance, the organization of labor, commerce and other ministries, the system of representation, the state's relations with its constituent groups, political economy and numerous areas of public policy without coming to grips with corporatist theory and concepts. And if one uses corporatism in the broad historical and political-cultural sense, viewing the recent, more manifest experiments with "corporatism" as a modern-day extension of an older historic pattern, then the corporatist framework has a utility and explanatory power for studying an even wider range of phenomena: the structure of class relations, the nature of the state system, the particular pattern of economic and social development, patron-client relations, the nature of the change process, the structure of political institutions, etc. For then the form of corporatism presented here seems closely attuned to the prevailing Iberic-Latin value system, a part of the _natural_ political-cultural ambience in which all the Iberic-Latin systems function, to a greater or lesser degree, an historic and indigenous response that often renders inapplicable the liberal model, on the one hand, and the fascist-totalitarian one, on the other (i).

The implications of these arguments are large. Much of the literature on Latin America written in the 1950s and 1960s which pictured the area as either aspiring for or developing inevitably

toward liberalism and democracy on the United States model would
require rewriting. Much of the developmentalist literature and its
unilinear perspectives must be called into question; so must the
presumption of a common, universal social science. For the thrust
of this article has been toward the identification of a distinct
sociopolitical tradition and model that is closely attuned to the
political-cultural tradition of Iberia and Latin America and essential for understanding it, but which is not in accord with the
major existing paradigms in the social sciences and in some
respects represents an alternative to them.

Corporatism and its related sociopolitical institutions and
behavioral patterns are not just "problems to be overcome," as in
so much of the development literature and U.S. aid programs, but
living, operating realities that are intrinsically a part of the
Iberic-Latin sociopolitical order and may well provide a viable
alternative path to national modernization. This understanding may
force us to reexamine the bias and ethnocentrism of so many models
used in the social sciences, to take Iberia and Latin America on
their own terms rather than through our own rose-colored glasses,
to bring area studies (understood as a culture area rather than a
geographic one) back into prominence in place of the often misleading and not very illuminating exercises in grand universal theorizing and cross-national comparison on a global basis, to rethink
some of our commonly accepted notions of the science of man (484,
566). This would be a healthy set of undertakings in any case, and
if the study of corporatism helps stimulate such rethinking, it
will have served a useful purpose.

NOTES

     a. None of the standard English language works on Latin American political thought, such as those by Crawford, Davis, and Jorrín and Martz, devote much attention to corporatism.
     b. The corporatist approach has occasionally been misrepresented all the easier then to "straw-man" it, most notably by Prof.
Schmitter. Seen in the perspective presented here, corporatism is
neither to be considered as belonging to the now-discredited "national character" studies, nor is it to be thought of as a "culturalist" explanation. Rather, corporatism is viewed as an important albeit heretofore neglected feature of Iberic-Latin political
culture and society that merits serious attention; moreover, no
claim is advanced that would elevate a useful but still partial
explanation into a complete, all-encompassing one. We need to be
concerned with corporatism, both as an independent variable <u>and</u> in
terms of how it may be manipulated to become a dependent variable.
     c. Implied in these comments is the fact that, while corporatism was an important aspect of Iberic-Latin political culture, it
could also be used for partisan or class favoritism. Franco, for
example, played upon Spain's historic corporatist and authoritarian
institutions and sought to elevate his particular conception of
what constituted the national tradition into the only permissible
one.

d. Some corporatists condemned not only communism but all forms of socialism.

e. The critique of liberalism and materialism had a long history in Latin America and was not confined just to corporatists.

f. Recent research in sociobiology seems to indicate the group conception of the organicists may be a closer approximation to reality than the individualism of contract theory.

g. These comments imply that criticisms of Iberia and Latin America for not developing a separate and coequal parliament, or judicial review, are beside the point.

h. Schmitter (458) has confused the issue by positing pluralism as the polar opposite of corporatism; in fact, corporatism may also take a pluralist form, although with varying limits on group formation and activity.

i. Some parallel comments are offered in 565. The word "natural" is employed in the same sense that Frances FitzGerald uses it (146) to refer to the habitual, _natural_ mode of political response of the Vietnamese, a mode the Americans no more understood than they apparently do that of Latin America. Newton called this "natural corporatism" (360), and sociologists refer to the tendency of a culture, even in disruption, to favor one solution (in this case, corporatism) over others as "conduciveness."

Part 3
Comparative Studies: Theoretical and Empirical

The materials presented in Part 3 are the result of various comparative, empirical, and cross-national investigations. They begin the process of adding meat and flesh to the theoretical skeleton presented earlier, of testing empirically the general propositions previously offered, of adding substance and concreteness to the discussion, of seeing where the model applies and to what degree.

The first essay wrestles with the issue of what Latin America means and understands by democracy and human rights, as contrasted with the United States conception, and whether it is possible for us to export our view of human rights to a culture area which often sees these in a quite different light. The second study examines comparatively the origins of the Iberian and Latin American labor relations systems and the degree to which these are governed by corporative principles and institutions. The third examines the role of political parties and explores how and why, in the nations of Iberia and Latin America, political parties and elections are often peripheral to the main arenas of politics.

The fourth essay, although written for a volume on Bolivia, actually has a more general purpose: to present a systematic schema of the stages of Latin American corporative development, as contrasted with "stages" and "developmentalist" models of Rostow and others. The last part of this section contains brief statements of research currently in progress: a consideration of Latin American intellectuals and the "myth" of underdevelopment, a study of the political theory and political tradition of Latin America, a research project on state-society relations and public policy, and a paper-in-formulation on the political economy of Latin American development: a "mercantilist model."

8 | The Struggle for Democracy and Human Rights in Latin America: Toward a New Conceptualization

The number of books and articles on Latin America describing the "struggle for democracy" there runs into the legions. And in much current foreign policy discussion, the issues of the protection of human rights and United States relations with authoritarian regimes have received a great deal of attention (a). This paper deals with these issues with special reference to the Iberian and Latin American context and raises the troubling questions of whether democracy and human rights are everywhere the same and universal, whether they are relevant in the same sense to all societies and time frames, and hence whether grounds exist for the hope of exporting democracy and human rights to other lands and culture areas.

The difficulty is that terms like "democracy," "human rights," "representative rule," "pluralism," "freedom," "participation," "social justice," and the like mean different things, convey different connotations, or enjoy differential legitimacy in different societies. Moreover, even in a single society, obviously including the United States, these concepts may change over time, relating generally to broad-scale cultural, socioeconomic, and political transformations. We have long been acutely aware of such differences of meaning with regard to the "peoples' democracies." What this paper suggests is that within the "West" these concepts and terms of reference may also imply, in the distinct societies, some quite different meanings and understandings. Neither adequate grounds for moral judgment, nor the bases for an enlightened and rational foreign policy, can be established until these differences are clearly understood. Although the focus here is on Iberia and Latin America and what democracy and human rights mean in that culture area, the discussion also has relevance with regard to the same or similar issues in Africa, Asia, and perhaps elsewhere.

In offering such a large macro-focus, this essay necessarily at times glosses over the various nuances, national variations, and ambiguities that exist, elements which must be taken into consideration in any final and definitive analysis of the subject. Obviously, the situation of democracy and human rights in present-day

From Orbis 22 (Spring, 1978): 137-160.

Colombia, Costa Rica, and Venezuela is different from that of Argentina, Chile, and Paraguay. Although we must certainly be cognizant of these variations and differentiate carefully between the diverse nations of the area, as well as how they change over time, the emphasis here is more on the common and continuous features. Our purpose is to offer a way of thinking about the meaning and practice of democracy and human rights in Iberia and Latin America as distinguished from the North American conception, to present an ideal-typical construct that stresses the similarities in the Iberic-Latin political culture as compared with that of the United States, rather than emphasizing the distinct national patterns within the area. Sound policy, of course, demands that each country be looked at on an individual basis, but before that an understanding must be achieved of the common context in which such individual variations take place. The present paper is conceived, therefore, not as a set of concrete prescriptions to be applied in individual cases but, perhaps more fundamentally, as an essential prelude before any such policy measures can be intelligently thought about.

DEMOCRACY AND HUMAN RIGHTS IN IBERIA AND LATIN AMERICA:
APPLYING A NORTH AMERICAN PERSPECTIVE

In 1945 the Inter-American Conference on the "Problems of War and Peace," meeting at Chapultepec, Mexico, adopted a resolution calling for the international protection of human rights. At the Bogotá Conference in 1948, in addition to adopting the Charter of the Organization of American States, the Latin American nations also adopted the American Declaration of the Rights and Duties of Man, a document based largely on the United Nations' Declaration of Human Rights, to which the Latin American states are also signatories. And in their own constitutions, the Latin American nations have consistently enshrined the principles of republican government, separation of powers, and human rights (234). Based on such documents, we often assume Latin America means the same things in the use of such terms as in the United States.

A useful starting point for the discussion of just how "democratic" is Latin America and how its interpretations of "human rights" may be different from the North American is the influential, periodic surveys of "democracy" and its "progress" in Latin America by Russell H. Fitzgibbon and his collaborators (b). The following criteria, among others, are included in their definition and measures:
1. The degree to which freedom of the press, speech, assembly exist.
2. Whether there are free elections and honestly counted votes.
3. Whether there exists freedom for political party organization, party opposition in the congress, freedom for opposition groups generally.
4. Whether there is an independent, coequal judiciary and congress.
5. The degree of public awareness of accountability for the

collection and expenditure of public funds.
6. Whether there exists civilian supremacy over the military.
7. Whether there is freedom of political life from ecclesiastical controls.
8. The strength of independent local government.
9. Whether there is representative, participatory, pluralist, democratic government.

Few of us would disagree with these values and institutions. But it may be argued that is so because the concepts and criteria used correspond closely to the liberal, Lockean, Anglo-American tradition and polity. The Fitzgibbon definition, to which most in the United States subscribe, has in it a powerful Montesquieuian, Jeffersonian, Madisonian bias. It is based on contract theory and the civil law tradition. It stems directly from the [sic North] American Constitution and the Bill of Rights. Its model is the independent yeoman and individualist of the New England ideal, grass-roots democracy and popular (electoral) participation, separation of powers and of the military and ecclesiastical realms from the political, a pluralist and egalitarian polity with a hallowed tradition of respect for individual human rights. The question is whether these fundamental characteristics apply equally and in the same sense to Iberia and Latin America, or whether instead they represent a peculiarly United States set of expectations and practices inapplicable in other culture areas.

A second difficulty with the Fitzgibbon formulation, in addition to its ethnocentrism, is that it ignores those features in the Latin American constitutions, at least as prominent as the "liberal" and "democratic" aspects, that enshrine authoritarian rule, corporate privilege, and constitutional and legal restrictions on human rights. Reserving further discussion for later, let us for now emphasize that authoritarian rule in Latin America does not, as much of the literature implies, mean necessarily a usurpation of the laws and constitution but often a new emphasis on those features that the Fitzgibbon criteria ignore (c).

Third, there is no sense in the Fitzgibbon studies that "freedom of the press," "elections," "opposition," etc., may mean something different in Luso-Hispanic civilization and law than they do in the Anglo-American, or that they may exist at distinct levels of popular acceptance and legitimacy. Keeping in mind the ups and downs, vicissitudes within nations as well as variations between them, let us examine the Fitzgibbon criteria individually, both as a way of examining what Iberia and Latin America generally understand by these terms and how these understandings are distinct from the North American.

1. Freedom of the press, speech, assembly. These freedoms are a part of the Latin American legal and constitutional tradition and some countries, to a greater or lesser degree, have striven to uphold them. But even allowing for the formal presence of such freedoms in Iberia and Latin America and their implementation in some countries in ways that parallel that of the United States, it is also clear that the meaning of these terms in the Iberic-Latin culture area implies different understandings and expectations than in the North American one. These liberties do not enjoy the

hallowed place they do in the United States Bill of Rights, nor are they enshrined as inviolable principles. To a far greater degree than in the United States, freedom in Iberia and Latin America also implies obligations and duties, including the obligation to obey those in authority. Liberty carries with it the obligation for self-censorship and the exercise of prior restraint.

The lists of human and social rights contained in the constitutions, or injunctions to democracy and representative rule, constitute aspirations and future goals for the society to achieve. They are not presumed to correspond to actual operating reality, nor is any regime expected to live up to them completely. Frequently, the human rights (<u>derechos</u>) must be subordinated to even more fundamental corporate group rights (<u>fueros</u>), the notion of the "common good" (generally as defined by the state), and the even higher-order requirements of natural, eternal, or, if one wishes, divine law (although even in Catholic Latin America the latter is seldom explicitly invoked). There is, in short, a hierarchy of laws which command differential obedience, and what in the United States are considered fundamental rights in Latin America often occupies a third- or fourth-order priority. Human rights are respected and honored, but they may be subordinated to such perceived higher-order priorities as the unity and integrity of the state. Hence, when the two conflict, it is individual human rights that must most frequently give way (328, 542).

Not only can these freedoms be consigned to a lower rung on the hierarchy but there are other provisions contained in the Iberian and Latin American constitutions (for example, "emergency" clauses and those providing for the declaration of a "state of siege") that make it possible to suspend them altogether, sometimes indefinitely. Freedom of the press or of assembly may legitimately be curbed if the peace and order of the nation are threatened. Of course, there are abuses of these clauses and degrees to which they are practiced. But the point is that historically the rights contained in the U.S. Constitution have in Latin America seldom been considered inalienable. It is the state itself, rather, that is the arbiter and dispenser of both rights and justice. What the state conveys, obviously, it can also revoke. Even in those habeas corpus, writ of personal security, and <u>amparo</u> cases where an individual or group challenges the suspension of human rights, further, it is the state itself, acting in the name of some higher order "common good," that must ultimately decide (234).

2. Elections. Electoral politics and elections have also become both important and imbedded in Latin American law and constitution. In Colombia, Costa Rica, and Venezuela, and in some other countries in other times, competitive elections have become a regular part of the political process. But in most of the countries, even in some of those mentioned, elections do not necessarily convey definitive legitimacy to a regime or individual for a prescribed term. Alternative routes to power, such as the skillfully executed coup d'etat or the heroic guerrilla struggle, remain open and also carry the potential for achieving legitimacy (21). Further, even when the electoral results are accepted in principle, numerous legal and constitutional means exist to nullify their

impact. The election in Brazil in 1960 of João Goulart, who was allowed to assume the presidency only after agreeing--temporarily, as it turned out--to the transfer of most of his authority to the Congress, provided a dramatic case in point.

When elections do occur and they do count, seldom is there a genuine choice between alternatives; rather, it tends to the Bonapartist model that is followed. That is, elections often take a plebiscitary form; they frequently are used to ratify a government in power more than to provide real choice, or party pacts and accords are employed to provide for continuity (and oligopoly) and to exclude other challengers. Of course, genuinely competitive elections do occur, but even in those countries often thought of as "democratic" (Colombia, Venezuela, Costa Rica, perhaps Mexico and the Dominican Republic), one is also struck by the tendency frequently toward accords within and between the major parties and, hence, the shutting off of possible alternatives. In these ways, two potentially conflicting functions may be served at once: the opposition and the ruling groups may have the "democratic" campaign both can agree is necessary, and the government "party" will generally "have" its election (113, 488).

3. Party freedom and loyal opposition. Freedom for opposition groups and parties is generally allowed in principle in Latin America; but, like the others already mentioned, this freedom is often constrained and subject to higher priorities. These constraints derive from both the legal-constitutional framework and the overall political culture.

The law and constitution provide the executive with ample power to limit opposition political party activity or to suspend opposition functions altogether. The more liberal and democratic regimes of Latin America have seldom been inclined to use the full gamut of these powers at their disposal, but the power is there nonetheless. Second, there is often relatively little "party politics" in the Anglo-American sense. One can easily overdo the differences but they remain important nonetheless: in the U.S. system parties are usually viewed as at the center of politics, carrying out many and important functions, and providing about the only legitimized route to power. In Latin America, in contrast, and again with several notable exceptions, parties operate at the margin of the public law, frequently enjoying neither respect nor much legitimacy. The hurly-burly and chaos of party competition are frequently viewed as intolerable; divisive party politics are seen as detracting from the unity and coherence of the state. Hence, a "technocratic" regime devoid of "politics" (and parties) is usually much preferred.

Under the organicist, monistic conceptions that so pervade Iberia and Latin America, thirdly, opposition by definition is often viewed as subversive, traitorous, and to be dealt with harshly. A "loyal opposition" is thus almost a contradiction in terms. Finally, even where parties are organized, the party label is often avoided. One forms a "movement" or "civic action association," but seldom a "party." The parties tend to become official appendages of the regime in power, bureaucratic state machines, or national patronage agencies; rarely do they maintain an independent existence. Terms, like "party freedom" or "opposition freedom," must be understood in this light (76, 120).

4. Independent, coequal congress, and judiciary. Checks and balances a la Montesquieu exist in the formal law and constitutions of Latin America. But in that same law and constitution, as well as hallowed tradition, centralized, unitary control is also enshrined. The extensive power of the executive, in the "Caesarist" or "imperial" traditions, and the weakness and lack of independence of courts and legislatures, are familiar features of Latin America. Though lip service is often paid to "separation of powers," and though in some countries legislatures gained prominence, the prevailing pattern has been presidential predominance (62, 112).

The strong executive is neither a quirk, aberration, or sign of Latin American "underdevelopment." It is the logical outgrowth of the assumptions on which the polity is based. For under the prevailing "organicist" conception, government is "natural" and "good," not "unnatural," "bad," and, therefore, to be distrusted as in the historic U.S. conception. If government is natural and good, there is little need to limit or check-and-balance it. One should not, therefore, look for a coequal congress or courts in a system where that has not been the tradition, in law, constitution, or history (263).

5. Accountability in the collection and expenditure of public funds. A quite sharp distinction is made in the United States between the public and the private weals. Abuses occur, but the fact we are incensed when a congressman or vice president enriches himself in public office is indicative of the strict separation we seek to maintain. Our model of the good public servant is that of the Burkean savant idealized in our civics courses: fair, responsible, serving the public interest, strictly segregating private and public affairs.

In the Iberic-Latin patrimonialist tradition, no such sharp separation exists. The lines between public and private are blurred. Historically, both "private" and "public" wealth were considered a part of the ruler's domain. Land, mines, and trading contracts could be granted in trust to individuals for development, but the Crown always expected to receive a share of the profits and reserved the right to receive back the grants it had made. Moreover, the granting of lands, a charter, virtually any service involved mutual obligations and generally the payment of a fee. For any official document to be expedited required another, often monetary, favor in return. This, of course, is not to imply that North Americans are by nature "honest" and Latin Americas are not. But it is to say that "honesty" may mean different things in different contexts and that in the prevailing patrimonialist conception of Latin America no strict separation is possible between private and public weals. Any scale that purports to measure "accountability" in the collection and expenditure of public funds must take these differences into account (42, 183).

6. Civilian supremacy over the military. The concept of civilian supremacy over the military is a major premise of the Anglo-American polities, but is often circumscribed in Latin America or even nonexistent. One must not overstate the differences,

for the military influence in the U.S. has probably long been stronger than we usually presume, and in Latin America there are usually constitutional injunctions against the military exercising political functions. However, in Latin America, first, no strict separation exists between the military and civilian spheres. What we refer to by the hyphenated term "civil-military relations" implies a dichotomy that in Latin America does not always exist. The military is often the strongest "party," a fact recognized by both civilians and military men, with the result that most political conflicts take the form, not of a civilian versus military struggle, but of competing factions that overlap and crosscut the civilian and military spheres.

Second, the military in Latin America is no mere "interest group" in the U.S. sense but is an integral part of the bureaucratic system and inseparable from it. Stemming perhaps from the role of the military orders in the formation of the Spanish nation, the army is one of the fundamental props and backbone of the state system, with a hallowed and elevated position, special prerogatives and functions. Even in the more democratic countries, the military has consistently acted at or close to the surface of power. The military, additionally, by law and constitution, has certain "higher level" priorities to preserve order and tranquility, maintain domestic peace, and exercise a "moderating" role in national affairs. The military serves almost literally as a "fourth branch of government" with a certain duty and obligation to step into politics under certain circumstances. That the military stepped into power in Argentina, Brazil, Chile, Uruguay should not be entirely surprising; what is shocking and repugnant, especially in Chile, is what the military did <u>after</u> it came to power (179, 411, 477).

7. Freedom of political life from ecclesiastic controls. Much of what was said for the military also applies to the Church: (1) The Church is intimately a part of Iberian and Latin American culture, in terms of both the philosophic base of the political order and the frequent fusion and reinforcing aspects of Catholicism and the legal, educational, and social systems. (2) The Church, like the army, is often a part of the state system and inseparable from it, with special obligations in the administration of schools, orphanages, hospitals, and the defense of public morality and order. (3) The Church is not a mere interest group but bears certain primary responsibilities in the political realm. Despite the sometimes formal separation of Church and state in the Latin American constitutions, the reality is more ambiguous. The principle of "freedom of political life from ecclesiastic controls" is either meaningless or requires further refinement (254, 399).

8. Strong, independent local government. This principle, too, derives from the Anglo-American tradition, particularly the oft-romanticized model of New England's town meetings. But it is not an appropriate measure for Latin American "democracy." (1) Despite difficulties of implementation, the Latin American pattern has been one of centralized, administrative rule-from-the-top rather than much grass-roots participatory democracy from the bottom. (2) As in most nations whose administration is based on

precepts of the Napoleonic Code, little power has ever been devolved upon the local units; rather, most local officials are appointed and power is concentrated in the central state. (3) There is little expectation at either local or national levels that local government can or should be effective. The national regime must usually respect local charters where they exist and has some obligation to listen to local demands. But virtually all decisions are made in the capital city and programs are implemented by the national government through its local agents. Local governments themselves have no power to tax or to devise educational or any other important local programs. Nor by history or law is there much expectation that they should (180).

9. The existence of representative, participatory, pluralist, democratic government. Again, few would argue with these principles. The difficulty is that what Iberic-Latin civilization means by these terms frequently varies from Anglo-American:

a. "Representation" in Iberia and Latin America means not just geographic representation and one-man, one-vote but often implies also representation of society's major functional or corporate groups. Although lip service (and sometimes more than that) is paid to the principles of equal representation, group rights and corporate elites frequently receive preferential treatment. The mere fact of birth does not necessarily carry with it the right to representation; rather, that is "earned" through a "civilizing" process that usually means incorporation into one of society's recognized component groups. Hence, the importance often of functionally representative legislatures, councils of state, or special access for those groups with "juridical personality," or the mixture of corporate and individualistic modes of representation (400, 519).

b. "Participation" also takes place through, generally, officially recognized and sanctioned agencies, not necessarily on the basis of free associability. Hence, the importance often of official parties, trade unions, and the like, and the sanctions often used against unofficial and unrecognized groups (Chapter 9).

c. "Pluralism" may also exist in Latin America, but it is usually a system of limited pluralism rather than the free-wheeling laissez-faire pluralism of Tocqueville and the United States. The plural groups are often structured and controlled; an infinite multiplicity of groups, uncontrolled, "out there" will not do. To be accepted as one of the groups permitted to bargain in the political process requires more than an informal, ad hoc association; often it requires licensing and regulation by the state (267).

d. What "democracy" means in the Iberic-Latin context is treated more fully in the next section. Suffice it here to suggest that, while democracy is honored in Latin America and has been established in some countries in some time periods, it, too, represents more an ideal to strive for than a reflection of actual operating reality. Further, "democratic rule" is not necessarily incompatible with elitist rule and an hierarchical, pyramidal, nonegalitarian structure of society and polity (523).

It is clear from the foregoing that the commonly used measures of "democracy" and "political rights" in Latin America are strongly culture-bound. They derive largely from the Anglo-American constitutional model, which is often far removed from Latin American culture and reality. Indeed, what such indices purport to measure, democracy, is not being measured at all; instead, what is actually gauged is the presence or absence of United States institutional molds in Latin America. Naturally, using such criteria, Latin America shows glaring deficiencies. Hence, to my mind, not only are the measures faulty, but the questions raised are the wrong ones. A set of measures that seeks to assess Latin American democracy on its own terms rather than by United States criteria, and which hopefully does begin to pose the right questions, is offered in the following section.

But before condemning the earlier indices entirely to the ashcans of outdated and ethnocentric models, it should be said that these measures do have some relevance for Latin America. For probably all the Latin American nations, in fact, represent a blend of both the corporatist-organicist-patrimonialist features highlighted here and the liberal, republican, representative ones based on the Anglo-American model. There are, thus, two sets of institutional pillars on which the Iberic-Latin state systems rest. Sometimes fused, sometimes parallel but largely untouching, these two institutional foundations continue to exist side-by-side (34, 192, 344, 521). Any attempt to measure Latin American democracy, therefore, must take both traditions into consideration, and the criteria we use must reflect the composite, sometimes hodgepodge mix of both the historic organicist concepts and the newer liberal-democratic ones.

TOWARD A NEW DEFINITION OF DEMOCRACY AND HUMAN RIGHTS IN LATIN AMERICA

Given the differences of meaning outlined above, let us proceed to a new definition of democracy and human rights in Latin America that takes into account both the distinctive features of the Iberic-Latin political tradition and the newer fusions. This definition has been fashioned in the form of a set of measureable indicators substitutible for the Fitzgibbon indices and based more on indigenous Latin American criteria than those derived from a foreign model (518). They provide not only a gauge for measuring Latin American democracy on its own terms but also a handy checklist to determine when a government oversteps its democratic legitimacy and is, thus, likely to be challenged or overthrown. It must be recalled that the model presented is an ideal-typical construct and that a fuller exposition would be required to account for the considerable variations between countries as well as within countries over time.

1. Strong, personalistic, executive leadership, caudillo or Bonapartist rule, is not only permissible but expected. The president may rule in an authoritarian fashion but not a totalitarian one. He should be strong and paternalistic, but not a tyrant. The president is only partially limited by a separate congress, courts, or constitution; equally important are the corporate group rights or <u>fueros</u> serving to check unbridled authority and the restraints

imposed by moral law. By "moral law" is meant immutable standards derived from Christian doctrine or in somewhat more secularized standards of "right" behavior beyond which strong leaders are constrained not to go. The index we use to measure the limits on presidential power must, therefore, take into account the widespread acceptability of authoritarian, paternalistic rule, as well as the fine line that often distinguishes authoritarianism from the unacceptable forms of tyranny and totalitarianism (267).

2. Although the principle of "separate, coequal" branches of government has not been so firmly established or desired in the Latin American tradition as the United States, it does exist. This provides an example of the "mixed" or "overlapping" nature of the Latin American systems already mentioned. The congress is not coequal, but it does have some important advisory, consultative, and representative roles, corresponding to the historic functions of the ancient <u>cortes</u>. The executive may be dominant, but the congress can still make life difficult for him; and if he rules entirely without a parliament, he runs the risk of alienating public opinion (3).

The same applies to a government that rides roughshod over its own national court system. Any government that comes to power, especially if it is by extraconstitutional means, must immediately resolve its legitimacy problem. No court can entirely frustrate a government determined to pursue a particular action and willing to use force to accomplish it; much less would any court interpose itself to prevent an armed insurrection aimed at overthrowing an existing government. But though circumscribed, judicial review and a functioning court system do often serve as checks on unbridled executive rule; further, the courts have a certain power in their ability to confer legitimacy on de facto regimes. A court may issue accords legitimating a regime in return for guarantees to observe human rights, preserve or restore the constitution, even maintain the independence of the judiciary itself. Governments of doubtful legitimacy may, thus, be nudged toward greater commitment to respect constitutional rights, although, of course, broad political support for such moves is also necessary (436). Hence, while the principle of <u>separate</u> and <u>coequal</u> power among the three branches is not always an established or accepted principle of Latin American government, the courts and congress do have some autonomy and power. An index that measures these relations in terms of the Latin American conception of the role and functions of the courts and congress rather than from the point of view of the United States would be both useful and feasible.

3. Free speech, free press, and freedom of assembly are also principles of Latin American constitutionalism, but they can similarly be limited for the "common good." Freedom is not an absolute but implies, to a far greater degree than in the United States, predeterminate bounds. Nor should one mistake the formal constitutional enactment of such rights, designed as goals and aspirations rather than actual operating realities, for their implementation. In addition, the laws and constitutions of Latin America give the executive broad discretionary power to declare a state of siege in times of emergency and suspend the usual guarantees. These

emergency powers, however, are not intended to extend to violations of the human person. Nonetheless, the centrifugal forces that have torn and continue to tear these societies apart are such that in Latin American constitutional law, the political rights that might otherwise seem inviolable must give way before the need to preserve the state itself.

At the same time, the Latin American nations are signatories to a number of international documents for the protection of human rights. These include the United Nations Charter, the Universal Declaration of Human Rights, the Charter of the Organization of American States, and others. These encompass both political and human rights (fair trial, habeas corpus, freedom of speech, etc.) and social and economic rights (right to work; to food, health care, etc.). Further, although liberalism and republicanism--and the basic liberties usually associated with them--represent probably still a minority strain in Latin America, the force of this tradition cannot be entirely ignored. Finally, if it is inappropriate to judge the human rights credentials of various Latin American governments by U.S. criteria, one may employ their own criteria. A case in point is Paraguay where a state of emergency has been in effect almost continuously since 1947. Clearly, in this case the emergency laws are being abused to maintain in power an unpopular authoritarian regime, take measures that are disproportionate to the actual emergency, and systematically violate the human rights of the opposition to the regime. In this case, it seems particularly appropriate for the Paraguayan Bar Association--and perhaps us as well--to issue a formal condemnation of the continued abuse of the emergency laws (153, 234). For here it is clear that both by North American criteria and Paraguayan, human rights violations have been widespread.

4. Although the Latin American tradition provides for strong centralized rule with little power given over to local government, a history of respect for the rights of local, state, or regional entities also exists. Frequently, such local "rights" are enshrined in long-standing charters, sometimes in the constitution itself, providing for varying degrees of autonomy from the central government. There are numerous "center-periphery" issues that revolve around the autonomy question, perhaps most dramatically expressed in present-day Spain in the conflict over Basque and Catalan aspirations for independence from national policy emanating from Madrid. The centralization of power in Brazil at the expense of state prerogatives involves a related issue; so do the incomplete efforts of the central government in Peru to extend its control over the more isolated interior (192, 234). This conflict between center and periphery constitutes one of the major arenas of Latin American politics, although this is somewhat different from elevating the strength of representative government at the grassroots level into an index of democracy. To the extent a Latin American government respects local or regional "fueros," it is considered "democratic"; when it rides roughshod over local rights and fails to care for those living in the periphery, it risks losing its "democratic" legitimacy.

5. Closely related to the issue of local and/or regional

"rights" is the matter of corporate group rights or "fueros."
While few Latin American executives are strongly restrained by congressional or judicial limits on their power, they are "checked" by the major corporate "power contenders" that are a part of their respective systems. These groups, the "<u>fuerzas vivas</u>" or "<u>intereses creados</u>," include the army, Church, economic elites, organized labor, bureaucracy, university students, and some others. These are not merely "interest groups" in the U.S. sense, but the more fundamental vertebrae or set of corporate pillars on which the entire governmental superstructure rests. The concept is more a traditional Luso-Hispanic conception than it is a reflection of North American interest group pluralism (359).

Any president that comes to power must respect the autonomy, as contained in their charters and organic laws, of the varied corporate pillars on which the government--any government--rests. This implies a certain respect for the Church and the "concordat" (if such exists) signed between the state and the Vatican; for the university and its charter of autonomy; for landed, commercial, and industrial interests; and perhaps, above all, for the armed forces, their organic law and specially privileged position as the ultimate arbiters of national affairs, their special courts and immunities, their direct access to policy through the <u>casa militar</u>. Any civilian president must be wary if he intervenes in the internal affairs of the military, for that is to invite the reverse process. More recently, corporate group rights have been extended to workers, peasants, and women. Obviously, the power of these various groups is unequal, helping to explain the differential treatment of them by the state. But generally, a government is considered democratic to the degree it respects the corporate group "fueros" of society's component units; to the extent it rides roughshod over them, it not only violates basic rights but runs the risk of its own overthrow (557).

6. A government, hence, is viewed as democratic to the degree it is pluralistic and that all elements enjoy autonomy from arbitrary authority and a considerable measure of freedom of action and movement. By "pluralism" we mean not the hurly-burly of the largely unrestricted United States interest group struggle, but a sense of "limited pluralism" in which the various groups, while controlled, restricted, and often elaborately regulated by the state, nonetheless enjoy a certain contractually defined independence from it (84). The charters of these groups are designed to promote the rights and interest of their members and protect them against unwarranted encroachments from the state or other groups. Except in emergencies (and even then there are some safeguards), these are sacrosanct institutions against which no government may move unless it is willing to sacrifice the loyalty and support of the group affected. A government that antagonizes several groups by violating their rights can, and likely will, be overthrown.

7. In addition to these corporate group rights, the government is also obligated to protect the basic human rights of individual citizens. These individual rights are not necessarily conceived in the same way or afforded the same elevated position as in the U.S. Constitution, although through such devices as the writ of

amparo, segurança, habeas corpus, and cassation individual rights receive some protection. Even more fundamental, because it stems from the natural law, is the obligation of government to leave people alone, respect their individuality, protect the inviolability of the human person. While authoritarian rule of a paternalistic sort may be permissible or even desired, a regime or police agency that beats up its own people is not. The use of torture and killings as instruments of state policy; the turning of the police or army loose on hapless trade unions, students, or opposition elements; summary trials and executions; the beating of women, priests, and children--all are clearly outside the bounds of acceptable behavior. The cumulative effect of such violations may undermine the legitimacy of a regime. Batista, Trujillo, Pérez Jiménez, Somoza, the Chilean regime are cases in point; Brazil seems to be skirting on the edge (414).

8. Government must be both "representative" and "participatory," but in the Latin American sense of those terms. It must be representative of "society," meaning those groups (Church, army, labor, elites, etc.) that have been duly recognized by the state and given official sanction as legitimate "power contenders" in the system. These groups are usually represented in the cabinet, congress, or council of state, through the ministries and state agencies, and with special access to the centers of decision-making. The state must also provide for "participation" through a generally officially sanctioned network of associations for workers, farmers, women, and so forth. To the extent it allows such "representation" and "participation," a government may be considered "democratic"; but to the degree it closes off or stifles such legitimate group life, it may lose its democratic standing. Note, however, that not all elements are represented in this scheme (unorganized peasants, Indians, urban marginals), nor is the principle of one-man, one-vote necessarily applicable (519).

9. While government must be "democratic" in this sense, that is not always incompatible with top-down or elitist rule. The pervasive presence of hierarchy and authority often implies that deference is given to those with a perceived "natural" right to rule. The elites, however, are obligated not to abuse their privileged position. They must provide charity and benefices to the poor and, while retaining social distance, respect the rights and individuality of those beneath them in the social scale. They may be patronizing and paternalistic, but they cannot ignore or entirely disdain their workers, peasants, or servants. Transferred to the national level, that means an obligation also to accommodate and absorb the rising social forces, not close them out as in Nicaragua under Somoza and Paraguay. In classic patron-client fashion, now extended from the hacienda to the state agency, the patron enjoys a preponderance of rights but the situation cannot be entirely one way. The clients also have their rights, and a patron or government that ignores or abuses them may face the loss of loyalty usually given in return for various favors. The cumulative loss of his clients' services and loyalty spells trouble for any patron, including the great national patron, the government itself (563).

10. A new criterion for democratic legitimacy in Latin

America involves the requirement that government provide for both economic development and social justice. "Development" and "social justice" have become part of the ideology of the area and closely linked to its concept of democracy. The older conception that people must be poor, live in wretched housing, and see their children diseased and with bloated bellies because "poverty is good for the soul" or the Church has obligated them to accept their station in life is dead or dying. The "revolution of rising expectations" has come to Latin America; any government must deliver in the way of housing, health services, food, jobs, etc.--or else! Democracy in Latin America has, thus, been redefined to encompass social and economic criteria as well as political ones--though the precise nature of the regime that brings social justice and economic growth is left open and the models used (including varying forms of populism and/or syndicalism) may, again, be quite distinct from those of the United States or Western Europe (22).

11. The right of rebellion. A government that oversteps the bounds of permissible behavior outlined above, rides roughshod over natural law and rights, concentrates all power in its own hands, violates the contracts and <u>fueros</u> governing corporate associational life, turns brutal and oppressive, becomes, in short, a tyranny, deserves to fall. The right of rebellion is as much a part of the historic Latin American political tradition as is the obligation to obedience. Against an "unjust tyrant" the citizen has the right, even duty, to resist, go outside the system, and seek to replace it. But even here, certain ground rules apply. Faced with widespread popular opposition, the tyrant has an obligation to resign instead of seeking to stay in office and thus provoking further bloodshed (e.g., Perón, Batista); such barbarism as the napalming of rural villages and the unleashing of a terror campaign against the opposition has consistently been considered illegitimate and self-defeating. But the opposition is also obliged to play by the rules: the right of asylum for officials of the outgoing government must be respected, the right to go into exile should be allowed, reprisals should be avoided. In short, the final measure of democracy in Latin America is the right to rebel against "the system" if that system proves tyrannous, abusive, and ineffective (167, 439).

Nowhere in this listing of characteristics for measuring democracy in Latin America is the notion of a formalized, constitutional "separation of powers" or "checks and balances" given central focus, nor do elections, political parties, and the like constitute the chief criteria. Of course, in some countries presently and others in the past, elections do make a critical difference, but it must be reemphasized that elections are not the only legitimate route to power and certainly do not, by themselves, constitute an adequate measure of "democracy." The criteria developed here seek to go beyond the older, largely U.S.-based procedural gauges of democracy to encompass what Latin America most often means by that term and to develop criteria that derive from the context and tradition of that culture area, instead of being imposed from the outside.

But while the concepts and criteria developed here derive from what is even now probably the dominant tradition in Latin America, it is no longer the only one. For alongside the historic tradition here briefly characterized as organicist, patrimonialist, and corporatist (in the broad, political-cultural sense) has grown up a genuinely liberal and democratic one. These two models (which help give rise to the "two Spains" concept, for instance) may exist side-by-side within a given country, sometimes wholly separate and sometimes overlapping, considerably complicating our measures of "democracy" as applied to Latin America. The situation is complicated further in Peru, Portugal, and Cuba by the superimposition of a third and socialist overlay upon the other two. Any assessment of democracy's presence or absence in Latin America must keep in mind both the distinctively historical and cultural meaning of those terms in the area, and the newer conceptions that have recently emerged.

CONCLUSIONS AND IMPLICATIONS

This study began with the question of whether democracy and human rights are everywhere the same and universal. The answer as applied to Iberia and Latin America is both "yes" and "no." Neither the nations of Latin America nor Spain and Portugal have much trouble agreeing with the human rights principles set forth in various international charters; and there was probably no hypocrisy in King Juan Carlos's message to the American Congress that his goal was to "perfect" Spanish "democracy," or in Ernesto Geisel's labeling Brazil a "relative democracy." At the same time, one must be cognizant of the impact of what Lucian Pye once termed the "world culture" (420), largely Western, which forces dependent countries like those in Latin America to redefine themselves in our terms instead of their own historical ones, to be judged by our criteria of democracy and human rights whether they wish to or not and whether that is even functional, given their own distinct cultural and political traditions.

It is also clear from this discussion that key terms like "representation," "participation," "pluralism," "democracy," and "rights" frequently mean something different in Iberia and Latin America, carry different connotations, or imply distinct expectations than is the case in the Anglo-American context. One must bear in mind the hierarchy and differential importance of distinct bodies of law in Latin America, that human rights ("<u>derechos</u>") may occupy a different level of importance than is true in U.S. law, that individual human rights are often subordinated to corporate group rights ("<u>fueros</u>"), and that both of these may be subordinated to the "common good" or the necessity of maintaining the unity and integrity of the state.

The sweep of the analysis given here is broad and the model presented an ideal-typical one. It is a heuristic device and is not meant to correspond to reality in every instance. However, that should not blind us to the numerous qualifiers and variations that must be recognized. At one level, a macro model such as this is useful as a means of alerting us to the general parameters of a major issue area, but for specific policy recommendations we must also take into account both national variations and within-nation differences over time. We must be alerted to the human rights versus intervention dilemma and must weigh carefully the mechanisms that produce successes in our efforts to promote human rights and those that produce backfires. We must further distinguish among types of human rights: those involving freedom from government violation of the person, social and economic rights, and democratic political freedoms. For the first of these, there exists considerable international consensus and, hence, it may be hypothesized, some possibilities for policy successes in the human rights area; for the second, there is less consensus on the means to achieve these goals and, hence, probably less chance of success; for the third category (the main topic of discussion here), there is still less agreement and, hence, probably even slimmer chances of success.

We conclude with a series of caveats. We must, I think, be skeptical of U.S. journalists, public officials, and others who insist on interpreting Latin American democracy entirely through their own cultural and political concepts. The "liberalizing" and "democratizing" currents and "struggles" of which they frequently speak are often valid up to a point, but they tend frequently to be based on superficial readings derived from North American criteria rather than Latin American ones. The fact political parties exist in Spain, for example, and elections held is insufficient by the criteria developed here to describe Spain as a "democracy." But the reverse also holds. Because the Latin American systems do not always correspond to U.S. notions of democracy, we have frequently been quick to brand them as "failures." The fact is that in many cases they are simply practicing a type of democracy that is reflective more of their own historical and traditional understanding of that term than the Anglo-American conception.

So, too, with human rights. What constitutes a violation of human rights in one context may not be such in another, or is seen in a different light, or may have another meaning. Further, these conceptions may change over time relating to broader developmental changes and giving human rights a different meaning in one epoch or in one group of countries than in another. The "fuero," for instance, will mean something different as the particular group grows in strength or the balance between competing groups is altered. Hence, in the case of both "democracy" and "human rights," a conception is needed that derives from Latin American understandings and not our own culture-biased views. The concepts discussed here represent a first step in that direction. Hence, we must distinguish between what the United States conceives of as human rights violations (and which often become issues reflective primarily of U.S. domestic politics), and those violations that reflect actual Latin American disenchantment with their own governments' actions, which may be on somewhat different grounds. Care, caution, and sensitivity to the cultural and political differences involved are required. That may lead us both to a greater understanding of how the Latin American political systems actually do function, and to less a sense of despair when Latin American politics evolve in directions that do not correspond to our own conception of democracy.

We can and should be in favor of democracy and human rights in Latin America (as well as at home!) while also differentiating between the several categories of human rights, understanding how they apply in different countries at distinct stages of development, and remaining sensitive to the differences of meaning and interpretation of these concepts in societies other than our own. We cannot impose our conceptions on nations where human rights and democracy are conceived in a different light without considerable damage being rendered to them and to us. We must come to grips realistically with the fact that distinct culture areas have different understandings of these concepts and their relative importance (d). At the same time, the criteria of democracy and human rights offered here give us a handle to grasp, a means to support human rights while also being sensitive to the cultural differences existent. Hence, for the policy-maker as well as the scholar, the same caveats apply: prudence, discretion, empathy, and a sophisticated understanding of quite different social and political traditions (e). For if we are to cease being the policeman of the world, we probably cannot, unless with great modesty, circumspection, and sensitivity, presume to be its political and moral superior either.

NOTES

a. Amnesty International has issued numerous reports on human rights violations in Latin America; the New York Times has published several recent accounts on the issue; the Department of State has submitted to the House International Relations Committee some detailed reports on human rights conditions abroad; various congressional hearings have been held; the report of the Commission on United States-Latin American Relations (the "Linowitz Commission") urged a stronger emphasis on human rights; and, of course, the President and his key advisers have referred repeatedly to human rights protection as a cornerstone of United States foreign policy. But see also 61, 464.

b. See 148-52, 226-28. In the more recent formulations, Prof. Johnson usefully distinguishes between Latin American democracy per se and the various nations' reputations for democracy as perceived by the United States scholars surveyed. He has also introduced a number of other qualifications to remove some of the ethnocentrism from the original index.

c. See the comment in 159: "Military governments . . . are an accepted part of the legal system"; they also govern "through laws and acts constrained by custom and constitutional privilege."

d. Fortunately, there are signs that those responsible for policy have begun to grasp these differences; see 80, 489.

e. Both sound policy and adequate grounds for moral judgment in this area must be based on a clear understanding of the broad cultural differences existent. A thorough factual dossier on democracy and human rights in specific countries is also required. The present paper helps provide a theoretical understanding of the issues involved and, hence, serves as a necessary prelude to policy; the reports of the Department of State and growing out of the congressional hearings on human rights in specific countries provide the essential data base. But for those involved in policy who may have already grasped the distinct conceptions involved and who have the factual materials at hand, the dilemma is no longer a lack of understanding but what to do about governments that violate democratic norms and human rights even on their own indigenous terms. What levers can be manipulated, what mechanisms are appropriate, how can human rights and democracy be encouraged without that involving unwarranted interference in another nation's internal affairs. Those issues, however, must constitute the subject matter of a separate paper.

9 | The Corporative Origins of the Iberian and Latin American Labor Relations Systems

Labor relations provide one of the major anvils on which the structure of the modern state and society has been forged. The ways in which distinct societies and nations have dealt with the rise of organized labor as a new aspiring or mass participant in the national life has had a profound, even determining effect on the nature of these systems and their sociopolitical development. The manner in which different systems have tried to react to the rise of capitalism and its accompanying "social question," the "revolt of the masses," the "class struggle," has been the most critical issue of the twentieth century (a).

As the pace of industrialization in Iberia and Latin America accelerated after World War I, the nations of this area also began to grope with, or were forced to face up to, this same "social question." Organized labor emerged in the 1920s and 1930s as a force with which all governments were obligated realistically to deal. The interrelations between labor, employers, and the state continue to be one of the major arenas in which Iberian and Latin American society and the state system are shaped (5, 402).

In trying to sort out both what is unique in the Iberic-Latin development process and labor relations systems, as well as what corresponds to more universal norms, this author's recent research has been concerned particularly with the way these nations have dealt with the new social forces spawned by industrialization and modernization. Although not wedded to the term and recognizing its ambiguities and emotive connotations, the author has termed Iberia's and Latin America's distinctive developmental aspects the "corporative model" or the "corporative tradition." For present purposes, it has been hypothesized that the modern structure of Iberian and Latin American labor relations is still shaped importantly by the peculiarly <u>corporative</u> origins of these systems. That is, that the labor relations systems of the nations of Iberia and Latin America, <u>from the beginning</u>, have been largely cast in a corporative mold, as distinct from the liberal-pluralist or the socialist alternatives, which continues today to influence strongly

---

From <u>Studies in Comparative International Development</u> 13 (Spring, 1978): 3-37.

the nature of class relations, society, the political system, and
the characteristic way these have dealt with change. It is from
this hypothesis that the ideas for the present project emerged,
which involves an exploration of the early literature dealing with
"the social question," the first Iberian and Latin American labor
codes, the social legislation and constitutional clauses relating
to work life and labor, and the earliest government agencies established to deal with the rising labor movements. Our purpose is to
see (1) if, in fact, the early official labor relations systems
were corporative in origins, (2) the impact of this structuring on
the labor relations systems, (3) the dynamics of change within
these systems and the varieties of forms in both theory and practice, and (4) the implications of this in terms of Latin American
society, politics, development, and the state system, as well as
our understanding of these phenomena.

The analysis in this paper represents only the scratching of
the surface of a large, fertile, but heretofore unexplored terrain.
Its purpose is to stimulate discussion and further research and to
present, at this stage, tentative conclusions rather than definitive ones.

THE ORIGINS OF THE IBERIAN AND LATIN
AMERICAN LABOR RELATIONS SYSTEMS

Literature Dealing with the "Social Question"

The earliest literature dealing with the "social question" in
Latin America dates from the 1860s and 1870s; by the 1880s and
1890s, the theme was attracting broader attention. Much of this
literature is derivative, reflecting the ideas and issues then being expressed in Europe. It was strongly influenced by the Catholic social movement, emerging at that time as a major force in
Europe, and was often cast in the mold of Vatican I (1870), the
Freiburg theses of 1884 (one of the earliest documents of an international character in the growing corporatist movement), and the
papal encyclical Rerum Novarum (1891), often referred to as the
"workingman's encyclical"(88, 186, 437). Some of the first labor
associations also emerged during this period, growing from a base
(frequently Church-inspired) of mutual benefit and assistance societies (b).

This early literature often derived from such French corporatists as Albert de Mun and La Tour du Pin, as well as the encyclicals. In an Argentine such as Joaquín Víctor González or the Chilean Juan Enrique Concha emphasis was placed on the need to restore
social peace and promote harmony between workers and employers.
These writers in the Catholic tradition saw the "social question"
as not merely material but moral and religious as well. In part,
their aim was to combat the Marxian appeal by offering an alternative to it, to reconstitute the ordered, stable society of the past
through the incorporation of labor into the official state-bureaucratic system. They would recognize labor's legitimate "rights"
but without undermining or contradicting the requisites of a peaceful, hierarchical universe. The Catholic social movements of this

time (pre-World War I), the mutual benefit societies, the "workers' circles," the social study groups also reflected this corporatist (largely French) influence (345, 375).

While much of this early literature was Catholic-corporatist in general tone and content, it was not exclusively so. Other influences were also drawn upon, and the Latin American writers exercised much initiative in adapting European concepts to distinctive New World and national contexts. As in the Latin American constitutions, liberal and republican influences were strong and were often fused with a corporatist and tutelary-paternalist tradition. González, who drafted probably the first Latin American labor code in 1904, drew upon a great variety of social and labor legislation, including not only the Catholic and Hispanic traditions but also the French Waldeck-Rousseau Act of 1884 (which contained both corporatist and liberal influences), the British tradition as exemplified by Joseph Chamberlain, and the Hungarian Code of 1884. A careful analysis of the works dealing with the "social question" produced during this period demonstrates clearly that they cannot be categorized under just the "corporatist" label or that they fall into but one single tradition.

Robert Alexander (9) and Victor Alba (5) have shown the degree to which the early labor movements in Iberia and Latin America were also shaped by the anarchist, socialist, communist, and anarcho-syndicalist ideas of the time. The difficulty for these emerging labor groups was that up to this point the Iberian and Latin American state systems were dominated by elite and upper-middle-class elements who were not taken with the same ideologies that mobilized the workers. The elite's conception, and frequently that of the labor leaders who served them, was conservative; and it was this more-conservative conception that prevailed in the military, political, and bureaucratic arenas where the "social question" was initially dealt with. While this conception was not always explicitly corporatist, it remained usually Catholic and conservative, with heavy emphasis on order, stability, and carefully structured and controlled change. Thus, while labor ideas were generally radical at the bottom of the social scale, they were most often Catholic-corporatist at the top; and in the early years it was the latter view that predominated. Even in those nations where a liberal and middle-class breakthrough had already occurred (thinking particularly of Chile under Alessandri and Argentina under Irigoyen; we shall have more to say on Mexico and Uruguay later on), the earliest social legislation sought to answer the workers' appeals but largely from an employer's viewpoint and without upsetting the basic structure of society. Thus, even in the liberal and bourgeois conception, to say nothing of the elitist-conservative one, the worker was regarded in some degree as an inferior human being; the labor movement was carefully held in check; and authoritarian, hierarchical, and paternalistic attitudes prevailed (345, 430).

The Constitutions

The constitutions enacted during this period, particularly the articles dealing with labor and social issues, provide a second indicator of these trends. By 1950 seventeen of the twenty Latin American countries, plus Spain and Portugal, had adopted constitutions containing articles dealing with labor's rights and responsibilities. There were constitutions that were manifestly corporatist in character: Vargas's Estado Novo constitution of 1937, the Portuguese constitution of 1933, the Trujillo constitution of 1942, the Ecuadorian constitution of 1946, and Perón's constitution of 1949. But the vast majority of the constitutions enacted during this period (including some of those just listed) were of a mixed sort, reflecting the long influence of liberal and republican forms, now coupled with various corporative features: strengthened central government authority, councils of state, differing formulas for functional representation, and the like. There is, however, no one single or prevailing formula that could be called "corporatist" (c).

Many Latin American constitutions of the 1910s, 1920s, and 1930s incorporated long sections dealing with workers' rights and social justice into the fundamental law. Freedom of association became a basic civil and industrial right; in the majority of the new Latin American constitutions, the right to organize was guaranteed. The newer constitutions included long lists of positive rights: the right to work, a just wage, dignity on the job, freedom to negotiate collective contracts, the right to strike, free trade union associability. The statutory and constitutional establishment of social and working conditions and of these new freedoms had its origins, in part at least, in the historic conception that the state had the obligation to protect the worker as the weaker element in the employment relationship (252, 495).

The restrictions on labor in these new constitutions, however, are often as impressive as the freedoms. Some groups (peasants, government workers) are prohibited from organizing. The executive is often given the constitutional right of recognizing the union or not. The unions are prohibited from involvement in partisan or political affairs. Freedom of association is guaranteed but these same constitutions also regulated--often in great detail--the organizational status, recognition, functioning, and dissolution of both employer and worker organizations. Further, while granting broad and ostensibly liberal rights to the workers, these rights ("fueros") are conceived more in terms of a corporate tradition than a liberal one. Such rights are conceded to the workers as a corporate group rather than, as in the Anglo-American tradition, an individual right. Moreover, while these constitutions grant to labor the right to work, they also embody the older Catholic and Thomistic conception of the obligation to work as a social duty. The paternalistic protection granted by the state to the workers in these constitutions, hence, also includes the responsibility of the workers to serve the state (the "common good"), to give allegiance and loyalty to it and particularly to that government that promulgated these laws. The constitutions of this period, thus, made provision for the formation of unions but then regulated them so closely and tied them so intimately into the state system as to undermine their possibility of an independent existence. Additionally, the right to form unions did not necessarily carry with it the right to strike, and up through 1940 only a handful of countries--Colombia, Cuba, Mexico, Uruguay--had acknowledged this right, without which labor remained ineffective. Freedom and controls, rights coupled with responsibilities, liberties and semifeudal obligations, the new twentieth-century constitutions were hallmarks of a new labor freedom but also of the state's desire to regulate trade union activities tightly. They were liberal- and social justice-oriented in part, but they also exhibited strong continuities with an older corporative, feudal, paternalistic past.

The Mexican Constitution of 1917 provides one of the more revealing examples. It is cited and celebrated as a revolutionary document and, to some degree, it is. But its clauses regarding labor's rights were patterned after a Spanish law of 1900 that was essentially conservative in character. The 1917 Constitution, Marjorie Clark has shown (82), far from being revolutionary, was, in fact, illustrative of Venustiano Carranza's growing conservatism, his hostility toward labor, his fear of any more radical and far-reaching changes in the social structure of the nation. It reflected the growing middle-class dominance of the revolution. The workers received rights and freedoms under this charter, but the fundamental right to form unions was so hedged and "reactionary" (Clark's word) that the Constitution represented several steps backward from the power labor had already gained during the revolution. Moreover, the new rights given the workers were never fully implemented--purposely so, in Clark's analysis. The Constitution sought to reestablish the equilibrium between labor and capital that the revolution had undermined and imposed severe restrictions on the labor movement. It left the unions entirely dependent on official favor and meant that, henceforth, they would be carefully controlled under the hegemony of the state. The labor and social articles included in this and other Latin American constitutions during this period provided the workers with certain corporate group rights and, thus, gave labor a new legitimacy; but these favors came at the price of binding labor into the state bureaucratic system and the elites and middle-sector elements that controlled it, of subordinating labor, structuring it, making it dependent on these same elites, and thus, in the long run, providing often a more conservative labor relations framework than a liberal or liberating one.

The Labor Ministries

The agencies for structuring these relationships were the new labor ministries established during approximately the same interwar period; the nature and functioning of these agencies in their early years form the third set of indicators used here of the corporative origins of the Iberian and Latin American labor relations systems. It was striking in how many cases the first official agencies for dealing with labor were located inside the several ministries of interior. In most Latin American countries, the interior ministry serves also as the administrative agency for the national police, and it is probably no coincidence that the branch of government responsible for labor-management relations was located here. This location makes Brazilian President Washington Luis's oft-quoted statement that "the problem of labor is a problem for the police" ring doubly true.

After 1930 the "problem of labor" could not always be dealt with or dismissed in such a cavalier manner. The Latin American and Iberian nations began establishing separate agencies to deal with labor. While several of these were patterned on the manifestly corporate and semicorporate systems of Italy, Spain, or Portugal, others were not. Once more the Latin Americans were eclectic in their choice of formulae rather than simply borrowing from a single tradition.

The rationale for creating these agencies was cast in much the same conservative and legalistic mold as were the constitutions of the period and the labor codes. Organized labor was a new actor on the Latin American political scene; it would not do to have this new power contender existing "out there" in some laissez-faire arrangement, apart from the central state apparatus, operating independently, potentially a force that might get out of control. Hence, labor's participation would have to be structured through the bureaucratic system and under official auspices. Poblete Troncoso (402), who was influential in drafting and helping establish these early plans, argued that this new social force, organized labor, had to be dealt with by a new and independent state authority. Its ostensible purpose would be to centralize the state's various activities in the social field and give them unity of direction, provide greater efficiency in labor administration, and coordinate the efforts to improve working-class conditions. Hence, the creation of a number of ministries of labor; ministries of industry and labor; and ministries of health, labor, and social welfare (the names varied not only between different countries, but within countries in the 1930s and 1940s the names were also altered and the functions reorganized).

There is a common pattern characteristic of all these agencies: the newly created ministries were designed as much to regulate labor's participation in the political process as to serve labor's interests. Labor was not to be so much "liberated" as domesticated. Its participation was to be structured under the authority of the state. The state apparatus, as well as the labor ministries, was dominated by upper-middle- and middle-class bureaucrats. Their purpose was to tame and "civilize" the labor movement; diffuse its early radicalism by bringing it into the system rather than excluding it; dole out benefits to labor while tightly controlling its organization; give labor its "rights" while at the same time enveloping it in a vast web of administrative restrictions, procedures, and restraints. It is no accident that the new labor ministries, often manned by graduates of the Catholic social movement, came to serve as the final arbiters of most labor disputes, that labor conflict was now taken out of the streets and put in the bureaucratic labyrinths of the labor ministries, that labor was accommodated and, hence, coopted.

A number of the Latin American and Iberian countries provide for compulsory arbitration and/or adjudication by the labor ministry in the settlement of disputes. This usually involves an elaborate hierarchy of investigatory agents and commissions, hearings officers, arbitration panels, and labor courts. In addition to these formalized procedures, it is also the practice for the ministry of labor, the minister, or even the head of government to become involved in labor disputes. In some countries such "intervention" is limited to appeals or conciliation, in others deeper intervention in labor disputes at all stages is an essential part of the everyday activities of the labor ministry. Such intervention frequently brings a political element into the dispute that may ultimately involve the tenure of the labor minister or the stability of the government. But what needs emphasis is the heavy, often paternalistic, day-to-day involvement of the labor minister and the state apparatus in all aspects of labor affairs. There are, of course, variations among these nations, but these are more of degree than of sharply opposed principles. What is impressive is both the constancy and the extent of penetration of the Iberic-Latin state systems into the labor relations field (252).

A careful comparative study of the organization of these labor ministries and how they function in settling wage disputes, establishing minimum wages, administering social services, regulating unions, defining professional categories, overseeing union elections, monitoring internal union affairs, passing on labor charters, etc., is clearly called for. Such an investigation, one suspects, rather than showing the early labor ministries as agencies for progress and democratization, as they are usually depicted, would likely demonstrate that they serve as key instruments to preserve the status quo, to add a new pillar to the almost inherently corporative structures of the Iberian and Latin American state systems, to append a new "power contender" to the prevailing structures but only on the condition that it accept the givens of the system and become reconciled to it (21). Moreover, these results were not unforeseen consequences of "the system"; in fact, the establishment of such labor ministries and the purposes they served were often carefully planned with these ends in view.

The Labor Codes

The Latin American labor codes, formulated during this same interwar period, provide the fourth index for assessing our major hypothesis. These codes are often ignored by commentators who see them as just like the Latin American constitutions: irrelevant to the real issues and whose clauses concerning rights and social benefits for workers are seldom implemented. Such a view is certainly too simple, for by taking the articles dealing with labor's rights and social justice literally and at face value, it misses the purpose these codes were designed to serve and the real significance of their contents. The codes actually provide an important source for understanding the Iberian and Latin American labor relations systems, and there is a considerable body of literature, by now dated and largely ignored, to which to turn (346, 403, 405).

The original expectation of the present research was that the codes would contain a good many corporative features. They were almost all conceived and enacted in the 1920s and 1930s (by 1940 eight of the twenty Latin American countries had adopted comprehensive labor codes; many others had detailed labor laws and regulatory decrees on the books), and it was expected they would contain strong echoes of Mussolini's Carta del Lavoro (1927), the encyclical Quadragesimo Anno (1931), and Salazar's corporative labor law of 1933. There are Latin American labor codes (the Argentine, Bolivian, Brazilian, Dominican, and Paraguayan) that are patterned after these corporative formulae, and others where the corporative influence has been pronounced. Nevertheless, there is far more diversity than had been anticipated; and the codes, like the other indicators here used, reflect a considerable eclecticism (e).

The liberal and social-democratic traditions are reflected in the long lists of labor rights and advanced social programs included in the codes. These derive not so much from Mussolini, the encyclicals, or Salazar but in large part from the model code issued in 1930 by the International Labor Organization. The recommendations and conventions of the ILO stimulated a great deal of labor legislation in Latin America; the ILO also gave technical assistance to various Latin American countries in drafting their codes (f). The codes, like the constitutions, contain detailed articles concerning the right to work and to organize. There are measures dealing with hours, wages, conditions of work, vacations, pensions, social security, working conditions for minors and women. While labor is generally guaranteed certain basic rights within the codes, again these rights are carefully regulated, limited, and circumscribed; and even the fundamental right to work is conditioned by the old Thomistic concept that work is a moral obligation, a social duty that carries the requirement of serving the national common good.

The first two national codes, officially promulgated in 1931, were those of Mexico and Chile. The Mexican code was a product of a reaction against the revolution and the later Cristero revolt, of a desire to restore order and "social peace," of an emerging middle-class order, and of a conservative mood that set in between the 1928 assassination of pro-labor Alvaro Obregón and the emergence of Lázaro Cárdenas in 1934. The code was a restrictive document resented by Mexico's labor leaders; it recognized and confirmed many of labor's earlier gains but it also locked labor in place and helped lead to its secondary position in the Mexican authoritarian-corporatist system (82).

The Chilean code was derived from different sources, but the results were similar. Chile's was the only Latin American code based on the French (Waldeck-Rousseau) model. Largely written by Poblete Troncoso during the middle-class-liberal Alessandri regime, it was promulgated in 1931 by Carlos Ibañez, who had strong corporatist sympathies. The code was thus a mix. It did not establish compulsory unions, but it did not sanction wholly free ones either. Moreover, while it was generally liberal in assumptions, it was conservative in practice--reflecting the values and class structure of Chile at that time. It was in this sense less a "liberating" document than an effort to maintain the structures of a still traditional society in the first spasms of the break up of the old consensus. It helped perpetuate, in James Morris's view, the system of antagonistic class relations and stalemated society that prevails to this day (g). These two codes, the Mexican and the Chilean, both essentially conservative, elitist, paternalistic, bourgeois, served as the models for the other Latin American countries.

It is important to remember that law in Iberia and Latin America, including the labor charters, derives from a Roman and code law tradition. The codes consist of a complete body of written law covering virtually all contingencies and issued by nonjudicial authorities. In this context, the chief aim of the workers' organizations, and the means they use, are ordinarily directed toward inducing the state, particularly the labor ministry, to expand the provisions contained in the codes, effectively implement them, and enact new provisions that can be applied to specific cases at issue through the law and the state machinery. This helps explain why collective bargaining is so weakly institutionalized, why the unions are so "political," and why they ultimately turn to government for satisfaction of demands and not to employers. Unlike labor organizations in the U.S. tradition, with its incremental collective bargaining approach, the Iberian and Latin American unions, governed by the codes, have developed under state supervision where each wage increase and social advance must be sanctioned and ratified by the state (495).

From labor's point of view, the role and indeed duty of the state, or the labor ministry, perhaps the president, depending often on how big the work stoppage is or its implied threat to the government, is to confirm and consolidate any gains obtained by the workers. This is both a legal matter and an eminently political and pragmatic one. In all Iberian and Latin American countries, the state retains the power to intervene in the various stages of the labor bargaining process, a fact reinforced by the state's having in large part defined the nature and parameters of the bargaining beforehand by structuring the legal framework in which they take place. Even the positive "rights" guaranteed in the codes, while in part derived from a "liberal" tradition, owe much to another tradition as well, that of centralized, state, patrimonialist, bureaucratic authority. State intervention in the area of labor relations, which in the case of the early codes stemmed from the "protective" role of the state toward both employers' and workers' associations, the state's position as the chief driving force behind industrialization, as well as the very practical need to structure and control emergent labor's new power and participation, could take a variety of forms. These range from the registration of labor unions, overseeing of collective contracts, and the supervision of union funds and elections to direct patronage and grants-in-aid designed both to encourage the labor movement in its early stages and to tie it closely to the state. What sounds like a list of "liberal" "rights" and "freedoms" found in the codes is, in fact, derived in large measure from an older and almost feudal tradition, implying both code-sanctioned group or corporate "fueros" and a heavy obligation to serve and obey the state in return (h).

It becomes critically important, therefore, to ask who fashioned these codes and why. The codes, like the constitutions and

newly created labor ministries, were formulated and promulgated
from above. They were drafted by elites, not by workers. They
were, thus, hardly the neutral, balanced, and a-political documents
that even their writers often believed. In all but one or two
cases (Mexico is perhaps a partial exception), the role played by
organized labor in the drafting of the codes was practically nil.
Direct pressure from labor was generally low or nonexistent. The
codes were drafted for labor, not by it. It was the educated,
European-influenced elites who shaped these documents, not workers
or even very often their representatives. The purpose of these
codes, thus, was to coopt and assimilate labor, incorporate it into
the state structure, but not to free labor or grant it increased
power. Labor had become potentially dangerous; and, hence, it was
politically useful to patronize it. The labor laws and courts were
given a paternalistic character, and the granting of new benefits
to labor was more an act of charity than of giving genuine independence and bargaining power to the unions. It was a means of keeping the unions from launching radical challenges to the system; it
helped keep them conservative, dependent, and tied to the state--of
necessity since the distribution of real power within the state
system remained elitist, bourgeois, and authoritarian (254, 425).

The rights and obligations listed in the codes, as well as the
decisive role given the state, provide the Iberian and Latin American regimes with a wide range of mechanisms to control and regulate
labor and union activity. For if these nations have given a prominent place in their codes to the "rights" of labor, they have also
been concerned with controlling almost every aspect of labor's activity. Indeed, it seems that the more extensive are the guarantees, the greater is the web of regulatory provisions. While the
"rights" provided labor have received the most celebration from
liberal commentators, the control mechanisms deserve at least equal
attention.

There are six major areas of state regulation of and control
over the trade unions: (1) requirements that must be met to form a
union, (2) prerequisites to obtaining government recognition, (3)
permissible union functions, (4) requirements that make the labor
organizations dependent on government funds, (5) regulations of internal union procedures subsequent to recognition, and (6) labor-
management relations (406). Although a more detailed and comparative analysis is required of each of these aspects, a brief overview of some of the major features may be useful.

The codes generally specify that a certain minimum number of
workers (often set at twenty) must agree to form a union. Union
members must be of a certain age and must work in the same firm or
in related firms. To this end, occupational classifications are
carefully defined. Industrial and professional unions often have
different organizational requirements. Ordinarily, the union members must constitute a majority of workers in a firm. These and a
myriad of other requirements make the organization of unions difficult.

Legal recognition by the state constitutes the <u>sine qua non</u>
for a union's existence. In accord with the code law tradition,
which does not usually admit the right of any group to function

unless it is recognized and granted "juridical personality" (again a semifeudal and corporative conception), workers' organizations are not held to exist legally (i.e., to be able to enter into contracts or exercise their "rights") until they have been officially recognized by administrative authorities. Requirements for recognition are strict. Political unionism is ruled out; foreign ideologies, subsidies, and affiliations are often banned; the objectives of the union must be purely social and economic, or professional. The union's bylaws must be approved by the government; its financial records must be shown; the names and nationalities of all union leaders must be given, along with the minutes of the meeting at which they were selected; a list of <u>all</u> union members (in alphabetical order!) must be presented. There are hundreds of matters, real, imaginary, or technical, on which the state can refuse recognition; appeals and/or resubmission may take years. Unrecognized unions are unable to represent their members before employers or governmental bodies and their activities will not be accepted by law. The police may interfere to suppress any such, by definition, "illegal" activities. And while the state has the power to recognize unions, it also has the power to dissolve them. Uruguay was for a long time the only Latin American country where the unions could operate without prior state recognition.

Once formed and perhaps recognized, the union's activities remain highly circumscribed. Political activities are prohibited. Labor federations and confederations are subject to the same requirements of recognition as individual unions. The creation of union pension funds requires government supervision and approval. The codes allow strikes but then hem that right in by such severe restrictions that it is virtually impossible to organize a legal strike. During one year, 1964, in the Dominican Republic, there were by actual count eighty-three strikes or work stoppages, not one of which was ruled legal by the Ministry of Labor (529). In cases of illegal strikes, as in the case of unrecognized unions, the police may break them up, jail the leaders, etc.

What makes the unions particularly vulnerable is their dependence on the government for financing. Few unions are self-supporting on the basis of membership dues. Dues collection is also closely supervised by the state. But even more importantly, juridical recognition of the union by the state often carries with it a grant of official funds. Without these funds, the union can barely survive; with them, the union becomes a dependent of the government. Unions that support the government and do not ask for much are likely to see their <u>verba</u> remain constant; unions that ask for too much or challenge the government are likely to see their funding taken away. When access to such official funds and favoritism is withdrawn, the union often loses its effectiveness and may well disappear (513).

The fifth major area of state regulation involves the union's internal procedures and organization. There are numerous regulations concerning the membership, leadership, meetings, and internal financing. Detailed provisions govern the selection and activities of union officials. Union elections are supervised and approved by the state (implying nonapproval of unacceptable results as well).

Union finances are subject to numerous regulatory minutiae: dues are set with government approval; who collects them and where they are deposited are supervised; regular accountings are required. Labor inspectors appointed by the ministry can examine the books, and the government may appoint its own "interventor" to manage an unruly union. In some countries each union is assigned an official supervisor, whose power may overshadow that of the union's own leadership.

The final area of regulatory legislation involves labor-management relations. This may include regulation of profit sharing (where that exists), collective bargaining, arbitration and conciliation, and strikes. The state is empowered to intervene at all stages of the collective bargaining process. In labor-management disputes, the state's voice is usually the decisive one. It may even draw up the labor contract and compel both parties to sign. In arbitration proceedings, the state has the strongest vote. All agreements and contracts must be registered with the ministry of labor. There are various levels of official regulation of these matters, and many nations have established labor courts and other machinery to set minimum wages or resolve disputes (214).

The web of regulatory laws, applying to a greater or lesser extent in the several countries, has reduced the effectiveness of the basic rights guaranteed by the constitution and the labor laws. Labor relations have been wrapped in such a tight and all-encompassing network of regulatory mechanisms and controls that it is next to impossible to break out of them. Official recognition of the union's right to exist and bargain in the broader national system is probably the key, but even that by no means guarantees labor a strong voice. At every step, from the earliest formation of the work group through the entire collective bargaining process, the role of the state is overwhelming. For the development and functioning of the Iberian and Latin American labor movements, this carries enormous implications.

THE STRUCTURING OF LABOR RELATIONS:
THE EARLY YEARS

Three points from the previous discussion require emphasis. First, although the constitutions, codes, and literature dealing with the "social question" are often eclectic and contain numerous "liberal" provisions guaranteeing the "rights" of labor, such rights are conceived in a semifeudal and corporative sense and not in the Anglo-American sense of liberalism. Second, although these "rights" receive considerable emphasis, at least equal weight must be given to the regulatory and control mechanisms used by the state in shaping and governing the nascent labor movements. While these restrictions are not all or necessarily manifestly "corporative" in character (in the sense in which that term came to be understood in the interwar period), they _are_ consistent with a longer tradition of centralized control and state patrimonialism that may be considered part of a broader "corporative tradition." Third, it is important to remember that, while the early unions were often Socialist, Communist, or Anarcho-Syndicalist, the elites and rising middle elements who wrote the codes and constitutions of the 1930s, manned the new labor ministries, and dominated the governmental-administrative machinery did not share these revolutionary sentiments. Quite the contrary. The question must be asked, therefore, as to what purpose the codes, social legislation, and new governmental labor agencies were designed to serve. There are at least three sets of explanations that have been offered in answer to this question, and the nature of these respective explanations tells us much about the assumptions of those who have offered them as well as the implications they had for organized labor.

A Political-Cultural Explanation: The
Need to "Educate" the Labor Movement

National attitudes and policies regarding labor are not just determined by considerations of class, economic power, or political expediency; they are also greatly influenced by general legal traditions and history. The code law tradition in Iberia and Latin America has helped lead to the predominance often of legal considerations in the theory and practice of labor relations. This legal tradition finds expression in the tendency to codify all matters relating to labor relations in one comprehensive statute book. Statutory law encompasses all imaginable rights and obligations, working conditions, and benefits. Legislation, hence, plays a far greater part in the determining of labor conditions than does collective bargaining. This is partly due to the low level of development of the Latin American nations, but it is also due to the Roman legal tradition under which legislation must be enacted to regulate the contract of employment and the mutual rights and obligations of workers and employers growing out of it. In Poblete's words, the vast body of codification which governs in such detail the labor relations systems is a manifestation of the "juridical culture" of the area (404).

The desire for legal protection, this argument runs, leads frequently to a situation where the law is in advance of the real social, economic, and political situation. The Iberian and Latin American constitutions and labor codes, with their advanced social provisions, are educational in character and not to be taken wholly literally. These are statements of principles and not of existing reality; they are purposely visionary and abstract, and no one, except perhaps American labor attaches nurtured in a different tradition, expects them to be lived up to (i).

A purely legalistic and political-cultural approach and explanation of this sort is almost inherently conservative. The codes have defined acceptable behavior, and it is up to labor to accept its proper role. Moreover, the codes are unchanging, immutable; they do not make much allowance for accelerated social change or labor's growing strength and demands. The state must exercise a paternalistic and tutelary role as regards labor: as the weaker partner in the economic relationship, labor merits the protection of the state. Labor must be patient, not asking for too much. It must be developed under a form of state supervision, and the labor unions and workers themselves have preferred this relationship (495). So long as the unions agree to the givens of the system, they will be appropriately rewarded; but should they become too big and powerful or their demands too great, they must be disciplined. It is up to the state to do this, to educate employers as to their Christian obligations to their workers, and domesticate organized labor until it, too, reaches its accommodation with the prevailing social order and is coopted in it.

This explanation, with its stress upon Iberia's and Latin America's particular legal tradition and the "learning" process through which the unions must go, serves to lock society in place and keep labor dependent. It implies passive acceptance of the charitable benefits labor receives from government, not active bargaining for more. It means resignation to and acceptance of the status quo, change only within very carefully regulated parameters. Labor cannot challenge the system or it will be suppressed; it must accept the values and assumptions of the elite and can itself achieve success only by subscribing to the same assumptions. In the last analysis, as Poblete once noted approvingly, this means labor is dependent upon the "generous spirit" of those who write the codes, their "noble and high conception of human solidarity," upon the values and assumptions of the elite which have been propagated as the values of the entire national system (404).

A Liberal Interpretation: The Need to
Implement the Labor Laws

A second interpretation, emphasized generally by liberals and middle-sector reformers, both North American and Latin American, stresses the problems of implementing the advanced social legislation found in the codes and constitutions. This viewpoint was shared by many U.S. labor attaches, by numerous American scholars in the 1960s writing on labor's "development" (274) and by Moisés Poblete Troncoso (403), the Chilean who wrote some of the earliest comparative studies of the Latin American labor system. In the liberal perspective due recognition is given to the legal tradition and history, but the emphasis lies with the efforts to effect such growth and reform as to enable the various social justice articles of the codes and constitutions to be better implemented.

Efrén Cordova has identified four major sets of factors which he sees as retarding implementation of these progressive articles (91). The first impediments are "natural," arising from the "ambiente" of the Latin American countries including the vastness of the area and the difficulties of communication and transportation, the low level of industrialization, the high illiteracy rates and low level of comprehension by workers of their rights, and what he calls a "Latin American propensity" to avoid compliance with the law. Second, Cordova points to certain social characteristics of the patronal and working classes. He emphasizes the "lack of receptivity" of the labor laws by employers and states that workers' groups have not always welcomed them either. A third reason suggested for the lack of implementation stems from administrative deficiencies, the inadequacy of the machinery for carrying out such broad and sweeping programs. Finally, Cordova suggests there are problems inherent in the labor laws themselves, that they are sometimes ambiguous or contradictory, that the elaborate regulations sometimes work at cross-purposes.

The set of factors identified by Cordova are a liberal reformer's dream. They are all susceptible to correction and change. By pouring in sufficient funds and well-intentioned technicians, transportation and communication can be improved, industrialization accelerated, illiteracy reduced, labor ministry administration improved, the unions strengthened, employers enlightened, and the inconvenient aspects of the codes rewritten. These suggested prescriptions imply exactly the kind of reforms that aid programs such as the Alliance for Progress could provide. However, they do not speak to the structural factors involved, the system of class and power in Latin America, or the intentions of those who formulated and drafted the labor codes. The one part of Cordova's analysis that does speak to the issue of elite attitudes emphasizes the "lack of receptivity" of patronal interests to the labor laws, a problem that in the full context of Cordova's discussion would also be amenable to change and reform, presumably through "educating" the elites to their proper Christian responsibility. By thus ignoring or glossing over these important structural variables, reform programs such as those suggested by Cordova, or as incorporated in the Alliance for Progress, were bound to fail, prove only marginally successful, or produce some unexpected consequences.

The Structural Critique: The Need to Transform the "Sistema"

Although both the legal-cultural and the liberal-reformist perspectives provide some insight into the nature and functioning of the Iberian and Latin American labor relations systems, they provide only partial explanations. They ignore that the labor laws were drafted by elite and aspiring bourgeois elements, and, in taking the seemingly progressive codes at face value, they ignore the unsaid and often subtler intentions of those who drafted these laws. In addition to the two perspectives discussed, there is a third and often more significant dimension to the Iberian and Latin American labor relations systems, and that involves the structural dimension already alluded to. The structural critique is that, while the codes, legislation, ministries, and constitutions provided certain guarantees to labor on the one hand, they served to control it on the other; that while the new programs for labor represented a recognition of labor's rising strength and legitimate demands, they also provided the conditions on which it could be subjugated along clear class lines.

In Landsberger's perceptive analysis of the Latin American labor elite, one reason suggested for the centralization of the labor relations systems is government desire to <u>control</u> labor by keeping it weak and unable to exert pressure (255). Landsberger states that both highly traditional elites, such as those who drafted the earliest codes in the first two decades of this century, as well as the "modernizing" bourgeois and middle-sector elements who wrote the labor laws of the 1920s, 1930s, and 1940s, have supported this strategy. The codes and labor legislation, he argues, were aimed at forestalling future revolutions from below, capturing labor's awakening political power, enhancing national prestige, and serving the interests and paternalism of the elites. A centrally directed labor movement, closely regulated and under government control, provided the elites and new middle class with a means to stifle or else dominate the growing trade union movement.

A more detailed analysis of how the control mechanisms work is provided by Louis Wolf Goodman (177). He rightly points out that Latin American labor law contains both a carrot and a stick. The carrot takes the form of the progressive provisions already discussed. The stick takes two forms: the blatant regulation of the labor movement, on the one side, and the more subtle manipulation of the workers through advanced social welfare laws, on the other.

We have previously considered the web of regulatory restrictions found in the codes designed to control the unions through the detailed oversight of all their activities. Such regulations, in Goodman's view, have been purposely designed to prevent lower-class organization for revolutionary change. Equally important, however, are the measures to divide the working class so as to keep it weak and isolate its potentially volatile elements. At least four sets of provisions found in the codes help keep the workers weak and divided: (1) those measures which make the process of union organization expensive, time-consuming, and arbitrary and which thus divide the small number of workers who are organized (15-20 percent) from the large number who are not; (2) the provisions in the codes that separate blue-collar workers (obreros) from white-collar (empleados), provide distinctive kinds of wages and benefits for them, and thus serve to perpetuate the class and status differences that separate the two; (3) the regulations that restrict workers' organizations to a single work place, discourage strong national unions by organizing them along geographic, corporatist, craft, or industrial lines, forbid public and private employees from joining the same unions, and prohibit some types of unions (e.g., small farmers and tenants) altogether; and (4) the ever-present possibility that new decree laws may overnight reclassify job categories and thus make the workers affected subject to a whole new set of regulations.

A more subtle technique for controlling labor, Goodman argues, is the progressive labor legislation itself. Such measures tend to prestructure the context in which unions can function. In effect, they subvert the logical class bases for the unions by making them dependent on the givers of these benefits, the government. Since such advanced laws were already on the books, the logic goes, there was no longer any reason to organize to fight for them. Traditional Latin American paternalism, based upon "mutual aid" societies and Church and elite benevolence, was now transformed into state paternalism with the president or labor ministry as the new national patrón. Benefits were given out, but their purpose was to make the workers dependent on the state and the elites who controlled it. Moreover, the benefits were frequently awarded in an arbitrary fashion with the government, for political reasons, deciding when and to whom they should be granted. In this way, both the "carrot" and the "stick" aspects of the Latin American labor laws operate to regulate labor, keep it weak, make it dependent on governmental paternalism, and preserve the existing (elite-dominated) social order.

Schmitter (452), who has been concerned with the more explicitly corporative aspects of the Iberian and Latin American nations, has offered perhaps the most complete analysis of the class biases of these corporatively based systems. In Schmitter's view, derived chiefly from the Portuguese experience but carrying implications for other countries as well, the purpose of the corporative laws and labor codes is not positive and progressive at all but negative. Sponsored or state corporatism is <u>preemptive</u> in setting out agencies of structured associability in anticipation of later and presumably more dangerous (from the elites' viewpoint) spontaneous effort by the affected classes. It is <u>preventive</u> in attempting to mobilize workers along lines favored by the state, thus foreclosing on the opportunities for independent unions to form. It is <u>defensive</u> in encouraging the unions to act to defend their corporate "rights," rather than promoting their active advocacy of newer, positive gains. And it is <u>compartmental</u> in limiting labor disputes within certain narrow confines, thus preventing the creation of broader class alliances and challenges to the ruling regime.

By doing so little positively and so much negatively, Schmitter continues, corporatism as practiced in Portugal and other similar systems prevents the growth of lower-class alliances, discourages polarized class or group confrontations, ties the workers to the state, and at the same time locks in an existing system of state dominance and class relations. Ultimately, in Schmitter's analysis, the structure of corporate controls over the working class is intimately related to the requirements of adjusting an elite-dominated sociopolitical system to the demands of capitalist accumulation, production, and profits.

VARIATIONS IN THEORY AND PRACTICE: THE DEVELOPMENT OF THE LABOR MOVEMENTS

The structuralist critique adds a new and often profound dimension to our understanding of the Iberian and Latin American labor relations systems. It goes beyond the legalistic-culturalist and reformist positions by pointing out the class biases <u>inherent</u> in such systems and the intentions of those elites who formulated and promulgated the codes and established the labor ministries. It is clear from the structuralist analysis that neither a purely cultural interpretation of this labor legislation as being in harmony with a long code law and historical tradition, nor the reformist perspective, is sufficient <u>by itself</u> for understanding how these systems work. A more subtle analysis is required that combines and perhaps reconciles these approaches. Only some of the dimensions of the problem are discussed here.

David Collier and his associates (j) have emphasized that the Latin American systems have provided an opportunity both for the emergence of powerful and autonomous labor organizations <u>and</u> for comprehensive, often coercive, state control. In some countries and in certain periods, labor movements have achieved a considerable degree of independence and become participants in a more broadly pluralist system, with the unions openly competing for the loyalty of the workers and often successfully pressing their demands on employers or the state. In other cases, the pattern of labor relations, although not fully open or genuinely pluralistic, has nonetheless involved a significant amount of independent union bargaining and power. In still others, active state intervention has produced a pattern of interest representation that, in varying degrees, is controlled from above. We need to analyze the dimensions of these variations and the reasons for them.

The Time Dimension

In some Latin American countries—Argentina, Chile, Mexico—the existence of strong unions predated the efforts to regulate and control them through the promulgation of labor codes and the structuring of the unions under the labor ministry. In others—Guatemala, the Dominican Republic, Venezuela, Peru—the emergence of trade unions was approximately concurrent with the 1930s effort to draft new labor legislation. In still others—Honduras—the labor laws predated the organization of the unions and were designed, in part, to encourage certain labor developments. Numerous mixed cases exist. But clearly the time dimension has had an important impact on the relative autonomy of the labor movements, the philosophies incorporated in the codes, the degree of dependence of the unions on the state. The codes and labor legislation promulgated before World War II show a heavily corporative bias; the postwar codes begin to abandon that conception.

State Versus Societal Corporatism

Closely related to the above is the question whether the corporative structures existent throughout the Iberic-Latin world reflect a form of grass-roots or societal corporatism organized from below, or a form of state corporatism derived from above (312, 458). In practice, this distinction is often blurred, since most of the Latin American systems represent blends and mixtures of both forms. Nevertheless, there remains a profound difference between the almost exclusively statist form of a Trujillo, Franco, or Salazar and the more mobilized societal form of a Mexico from 1910-1930 or a Bolivia after 1935. Given these differences, it should be possible to construct a scale ranging from a "pure" (ideal type) societal form to a "pure" statist form, with most of the Iberian and Latin American countries spaced out along such a continuum.

The Degree of Structuring, Control, and Compliance

While all the Iberian and Latin American systems incorporate within their labor laws elaborate mechanisms of regulation and

supervision, there are also considerable variations. Collier and
his associates, focusing on only ten countries, have constructed a
measure consisting of thirty-six different legal provisions involving the regulation, subsidy, and control of the labor movements
(85). These range from a system of almost complete control and
subordination as in Brazil following the 1964 revolution to a more
intermediate range of controls in Colombia, Venezuela, or Chile
before the 1973 coup, to a system of almost complete autonomy and
independence as in Uruguay before the 1973 military intervention.
Within an overall pattern of control and regulation (Uruguay was a
single exception), there remains considerable and often subtle differences in the way the codes are phrased and their regulatory
mechanisms enforced.

The various restrictions contained in the labor laws were
never enforced uniformly. With few exceptions, the more revolutionary labor organizations felt the full force of the law (in the
prohibitions against foreign leadership, foreign ideologies, and
international affiliations, the codes were often aimed directly at
these groups), while with the Catholic and more conservative unions
the law was only irregularly enforced. Some unions were also especially singled out for scrutiny; i.e., the union of bootblacks
(limpiabotas) could be safely ignored while the metal workers, miners, stevedores, meatpackers, sugar workers, and other large unions
that constituted a potential threat were closely supervised.

The reverse side of the enforcement coin involves the degree
to which the codes were obeyed by employers. Many firms disre-
garded or found ways around those provisions calling for labor
rights, sick leave, pensions, and the like. On the other hand and
still in the 1930s context, such disregard for the law was not consistently disastrous for the workers since these were often family
firms whose owners shared the older conception of having a Christian obligation to the poor, and such institutions as the Church or
the family continued to administer charity and welfare where the
state or the employer did not. Foreign firms, in contrast, were
frequently the only ones to obey the law (for various reasons); but
they, and now particularly the corporate multinationals, felt little obligation to Christian charity. In Central America and the
Caribbean particularly, it was often the foreign firms that were
most inclined to obey the labor laws and where, ironically, the
strongest Communist unions were organized.

The Political Context

The differences in the regulatory measures found in the codes,
and particularly in the way they were enforced, stem in large part
from the nature of the regimes that promulgated them or saw to
their subsequent implementation. Although the similarities are
also striking, it obviously makes a major difference that the Chilean labor code was to a large degree the product of the liberal
bourgeois regime of Alessandri and not of the more traditionalist,
Catholic, and conservative prior regimes. The government of López
Contreras in Venezuela was quite different in its concept of labor
relations from that of Juan Vicente Gómez. It clearly is important

that the Colombian labor legislation was promulgated and implemented in a more or less liberal context, while the Dominican labor code was fashioned and implemented by an authoritarian, dictatorial regime. The Mexican labor code, promulgated in 1931 by the conservative Pascual Ortíz Rubio, was quite different from the scheme Obregón had in mind. And though they share a kind of populism, the code in Bolivia which derives in part from the ideology of the Movimiento Nacional Revolucionario (MNR) is quite different from that promulgated by the populist caudilho Vargas of Brazil. Then, too, the differences between the Vargas system and that of Perón are significant.

Political and personalistic variables such as these are perhaps the most difficult for which to construct accurate measures. Still, such an effort must be made since in the final analysis, regardless of the law, it makes a major difference, probably the major difference, if labor has a friend in the national palace or not. For despite their literal similarities, there were vast differences in the ways the codes were applied. We need to sort out carefully, therefore, the relations of labor with the major parties, the interactions with various populist leaders and movements, the functioning of labor under liberal, syndicalist (Bosch, Goulart, perhaps Allende), or revolutionary regimes, as opposed to their functioning under older-style, conservative, and/or corporatist ones. In general, we shall likely find that those nations that have been most receptive to labor's needs, as reflected in their labor and social legislation, have also been the ones most indisposed to enforce fully the laws' minute regulations. It is one thing to have the various controls "on the books"; it is quite another actively and vigorously to enforce them. Political regimes that have wanted to use the coercive powers of government against the labor movement have found this legislation useful. More democratic regimes, while also desirous of having such coercive authority in reserve, have often followed the practice of ignoring the harsher aspects of the labor laws (406).

Economic Development, Industrialization, and the
Growth of the Labor Movement

Whereas the bulk of the labor charters and legislation here under consideration was drafted in the 1920s, 1930s, and 1940s, when the number of industrial workers was small and the power of organized labor limited, much has changed since that time. As economic development, urbanization, and industrialization have gone forward, the number of industrial workers has grown and so has the organized trade union movement. To cite the example of but one Latin American nation, in 1936 the Dominican Republic had an industrial work force of 20,301. By 1942 the figure had risen to 29,475, by 1946 to 48,151, by 1955 to 71,004, and by 1959 (toward the end of the Trujillo era) to 83,625--a fourfold increase in slightly over two decades. By 1970, in the more open climate of the post-Trujillo period, with the economy accelerating, the number had risen to over 250,000, including roughly 100,000 in the public sector. The union movement had grown correspondingly, from a handful

of unions with a combined membership of only 4,000 in the 1930s to
approximately 425 unions with a total membership of about 135,000
just prior to the revolution and United States intervention of
1965. During the same period, the Dominican Republic changed from
being an overwhelmingly agricultural country (85 percent rural in
1920) to one that is now 60 percent rural and 40 percent urban
(531). Similar figures, perhaps not quite so dramatic, show the
same or similar trends in other nations.

In terms of their impact on the labor relations system, these
add up to changes in kind and not just in degree. The figures and
proportions often imply wholesale transformations which have fundamentally altered the balance of national power. Whereas before,
the industrial labor force was small and the organized labor movement weak, now that force is large and the unions strong, or at
least able to bargain with or threaten other major power contenders
in the political arena. The urban population has similarly multiplied, in some cases several times over, putting added pressure on
the state for social services and minimum wages. In addition to
forming a huge urban lumpen-proletariat and a prime recruiting
ground for radical appeals and new recruits to the labor movement,
these urban dwellers are now close to the centers of political
power and thus able at times to make their demands dramatically
felt through work stoppages, sabotage, disruption, marches on the
national palace, etc. Labor is thus a force to be reckoned with
instead of merely one to be ignored, turned over to the police, or
controlled absolutely through an essentially corporative system of
labor regulations. Such controls may still be imposed, but the
point is that the entire context has shifted and that the enforcement of such controls is now more problematical. One may talk,
therefore, of a persistent "corporative tradition" in Iberia and
Latin America, of a distinctive "corporative model" of modern-day,
sociopolitical, and labor relations that bears certain affinities
to the past--and an understanding of this context is important.
But equally important is power, influence, and the ability to mobilize large mass movements; and in this regard in the Iberic-Latin
culture area as elsewhere, there have been immense changes in the
past forty years.

The Dynamics of the Labor Relations Systems

In most of the Iberian and Latin American countries, the corporative and semicorporative codes and labor legislation promulgated in the 1930s and 1940s remain in effect. In some countries--
post-1964 Brazil, Paraguay, more recently Chile--the rigid regulatory and control mechanisms are still being applied, or are being
applied anew, often with a vengeance. In most of the other countries, however, and even in some of those listed, the labor laws
are only irregularly enforced, or they are employed for purposes
other than those originally set forth. It is in these gray areas,
the cracks and crevices of changing Iberian and Latin American
labor relations systems, that some of the most interesting and dynamic aspects of this change process are to be found.

In many countries, for instance, a new generation of

government bureaucrats has grown up and now reached middle-level administrative positions, who do not remember or care about the ideological fights of the 1930s, who themselves may share the social justice values of the 1960s and 1970s, and who are thus more inclined to use the regulatory power of the labor ministries not to side with employers, as was consistently done in the past, but to come down on the side of workers. In labor-management disputes, where government is still the third and decisive voice, such favoritism has won some enormous wage increases for labor (548, 519).

In some countries, also, new ways of dealing with labor disputes have gained strength. Direct bargaining between labor and employers has become an increasingly important feature of labor relations in virtually all the Iberian and Latin American countries--although it is significant that even in collective bargaining the role of the state has remained strong. Moreover, in order to enter into even the negotiations for a collective bargaining agreement, the union must still receive prior recognition from the state. Additionally, new channels exist to further labor-management cooperation, consultation, corepresentation of labor and management on government boards, worker participation in management, and profit-sharing; but these, too, have ordinarily been structured under the hegemony of the organic state system.

In other cases, populist politicians and presidents, themselves recognizing the power and votes of organized labor, have struck new bargains with the labor movements. Some national leaders have sought to use their labor ministries not to preserve the status quo but to effect profound social change. Others have seen in labor a possible counterbalance to the military and have consciously cultivated labor and increased its strength with this end in view, thus providing a skilled labor leader with the leverage he did not previously have. "Democracy" in this context, and in the workers' view, comes to mean not so much the North American conception of elections and government checks and balances but rather still an almost feudal conception, implying intervention by the state on behalf of the workers as a corporate group. The Brazilian case under Goulart remains an especially enlightening one. There, the labor ministry itself came under the control of a radical labor leadership, who then used the traditional methods of patronage and special access not for the benefit of employers, in the usual pattern, but to provide more funds, favors, and bargaining power to the unions (k). There have been numerous modifications and some wholesale turnabouts in the ways government has used the labor ministries, or for whose benefit, and in the ways in which the labor laws are enforced or not enforced.

The use of labor violence provides some fascinating illustrations of how such changes may be effected. James Payne's analysis of the use of such violence--strikes, shutdowns, street demonstrations, provocative acts--as a part of the "political bargaining" (as distinct from "collective bargaining") system of Peru is the most complete study, but similar strategies have been employed in many of the Iberian and Latin American nations (384, 23, 35, 487). These strategies have often been in accord with the more pragmatic interests of individual unions and labor movements rather than

corresponding necessarily to some overarching principle of labor
organization. In Spain and prerevolutionary Portugal, for instance, even though both these regimes maintained networks of officially sanctioned and carefully regulated corporative labor organizations, in both parallel labor associations had sprung up that
operated largely outside the official system. Similarly, while
strikes were prohibited under both these authoritarian regimes, in
fact numerous "work stoppages" took place which frequently had the
same effect as "strikes" (18, 519).

Under the existing labor laws the government could, if it
wished, suppress these extralegal actions and associations. Although in the past it often did just that, by the 1960s and 1970s
it chose increasingly to deal with the parallel unions informally
yet realistically, as if they constituted officially recognized
labor organizations with legitimate bargaining rights and the ability to speak and gain benefits for the workers. Similarly, the
strike. While by their labor laws the regimes in Spain and Portugal had the right and even obligation to declare all strikes illegal, call out the police, and take repressive action against their
leaders, in practice they did so less and less. A "work stoppage"
would be called by labor leaders, and then it would be up to the
government to decide if this violated the prohibition against
"strikes" or not. Oftentimes by the late 1960s, the government or
labor ministry, unwilling to risk slowing economic growth by triggering further disruption, would allow a more limited "work stoppage" to go forward until the dispute was amicably resolved instead
of suppressed by force. Frequently, this meant state pressure being applied to employers to accede to worker demands. Even in
those instances where violence was employed, such as by the miners
in Asturias, and which by definition constituted a "political" and,
hence, illegal "strike," readers of newspapers in Madrid would be
treated to the spectacle of the government denying there was violence even though several people had been killed, denying there was
a strike even though the mines were shut down, and eventually
agreeing to some of the major demands of the workers even though
their bargaining agents had not been officially recognized.

All this is not to say that the corporative labor laws and
codes fashioned in an earlier time are no longer operative or that
the authoritarian-conservative regimes of Franco and Salazar-Caetano, contrary to all earlier indications, had become strong advocates of workers' rights and social justice. Even in the instances
cited, the behavior of the government remained arbitrary and capri-
cious, the laws were enforced selectively, the regime continued to
use repressive tactics as well as to provide new openings for labor,
and the favoritism it showed at times toward workers served to reinforce official paternalism. Still, even in the more authoritarian
of the Iberian and Latin American systems, there is a great deal
more "politics" and bargaining in the area of labor relations than
is often implied in the blanket condemnation of these systems by use
of the "authoritarian," "corporatist," or "Fascist" labels. And in
other more populist, syndicalist, or socialist regimes (Goulart's
Brazil, Bosch's Dominican Republic, Allende's Chile, post-1968 Peru,
revolutionary Portugal), it becomes clear that the older system of

corporative controls and regulations, as well as labor ministry patronage and favoritism, may be employed in favor of workers instead of against them, toward implementing greater social justice rather than frustrating it.

CONCLUSIONS AND IMPLICATIONS

This study began with the hypothesis that most, if not all, of the labor codes and legislation enacted in Spain, Portugal, and Latin America during the interwar period were corporative in origins and essence, and further that these particular origins had important and continuing implications for the structure and character of labor relations throughout the area. This hypothesis has only been partially substantiated. While a close examination of the early literature dealing with the "social question," of the labor codes and constitutions of the period, and of the structure of the early agencies established to deal with labor affairs reveals a great deal of explicitly corporate contents and assumptions, in fact the codes and labor systems were eclectic in inspiration and drawn from diverse sources. While some were manifestly corporatist, the majority were mixed forms, representing interesting, fused, sometimes hodgepodge overlaps of Catholic, corporatist, liberal, positivist, International Labor Office, even socialist influences. But while the majority of these labor charters and the bases of the labor systems were not always manifestly "corporatist" in the 1930s sense (that is, derived directly from Mussolini's Carta del Lavoro or the French, Spanish, Portuguese, and German corporatists), what they did have in common (with Uruguay the major exception) was a set of controls and regulatory provisions that was in keeping with a long Iberian and Latin American tradition of centralized, state-directed, often Catholic-inspired bureaucratic authoritarianism, or "natural corporatism" (360). This web of controls and regulations, and the paternalistic social legislation that went with it, largely defined the parameters and set the mold for the structure and systems of Latin American labor relations for some three decades. In many countries it is still the prevailing pattern.

We then explored the structuring of the Iberian and Latin American labor relations systems during these early years and analyzed why these systems failed to work, or perhaps did work, as intended. The first interpretation we discussed attempted to explain such "failures" and to understand "the system" in terms of legal and historical factors: the code law tradition, the "educational" purposes of the labor laws, and the need to "civilize" workers and employers in these norms, the fact that no one expected these laws, like the constitutions, ever to be implemented fully. The second interpretation, liberal and reformist in nature, sought to explain the lack of implementation of the advanced social legislation in terms of the area's lack of development, which could then presumably be corrected by infusions of economic aid and technical assistance. The third interpretation, structuralist in nature, sought to explain the lack of implementation of the codes, as well as the persistence of relatively weak trade unions throughout the area, in

terms of a conscious and premeditated effort on the part of ruling
elites to organize the unions under strict government control, keep
them dependent on a state system that the elites controlled, and
thus provide the appearance of change and progress while, in fact,
strengthening elitist control and the capitalist structure that
undergirds it. The state, in this interpretation, including its
labor ministry, has served and in most instances continues to serve
as the protector of middle- and upper-class interests, while prag-
matically granting some limited concessions to the workers.

Our discussion of the variations in theory and practice, particularly the analysis of the dynamics of the labor relations systems, was designed to suggest some rough but perhaps useful dimensions for testing these propositions. There can be little doubt
that labor relations throughout the Iberic-Latin world still take
place within a context and tradition that is, broadly speaking,
corporative and authoritarian-patrimonialist in character. This is
not only a continuing and persistent tradition, but it may take a
variety of forms. Hence, the often-noted similarities as between
the more liberal and even syndicalist regimes and the bureaucratic-
authoritarian ones. One must also come to grips with the profound
differences between them, however, particularly as this affects the
area of labor relations, and how differential levels of development, change, urbanization, industrialization, and the growth of
the labor movement itself have altered fundamentally the structure
of labor relations and the place of labor as a major power contender within these systems. At the same time, one must look at the
class and system biases of these structures, at the intentions of
those elites that designed the Iberian and Latin American labor
systems, at the subtle and often effective way the elites provided
more the appearance of change than its substance while simultaneously preserving their own power and status. Finally, we must begin to look now at the on-going efforts, often successful, to go
above, around, or beyond the prevailing "systems," to establish
parallel labor associations outside the corporative confines, to
take over "the system" for the advantage of different beneficiaries, to introduce some genuine structural transformations, to
move from 1930s corporatism to a more advanced form, even to syndicalism or socialism.

To understand these more recent developments, we need to go
beyond the models usually employed to explain Iberian and Latin
American politics. The framework suggested by Anderson (21) is
perhaps the most widely known in this regard. But Anderson's nonrevolutionary "rival power contenders" approach, while still exceedingly useful and particularly valid for most Latin American
and Iberian politics up to the early 1960s and even beyond, is concentrated largely on "systemic" politics and change. It does not
adequately take account of the more recent, often revolutionary,
efforts to go beyond or to transcend this "system," as in Cuba,
Peru, Chile for a time, and Portugal (1). What is needed is an
approach that encompasses the insightful aspects of the Anderson
model along with the newer movements and forces aimed at going
beyond that framework and the "systems" it describes. The realm of
labor relations, particularly in its more recent, often

revolutionary manifestations, provides a critical place to begin that kind of analysis and theory construction.

NOTES

    a. The literature is vast. For an understanding of comparative social change, one can do no better than to reread the classics: Herder, Saint Simon, Proudhon, Comte, Marx, Spencer, Mosca, Pareto, Sombart, Weber, Simmel, Durkheim, Sorel, Schumpeter, Ortega y Gasset.

    b. Ralph Della Cava has undertaken some important recent research in Brazil, Italy, and France exploring these interconnections; based, in part, on conversations with Professor Della Cava.

    c. A compilation of most of these is 147. The constitutions examined for this research were those of Argentina (1949), Bolivia (1945), Brazil (1937), Chile (1925), Colombia (1937), Costa Rica (1949), Cuba (1940), Dominican Republic (1942), Ecuador (1946), Guatemala (1945), Haiti (1946), Honduras (1936), Mexico (1917), Nicaragua (1948), Panama (1946), Paraguay (1940), Peru (1933), Portugal (1933), El Salvador (1950), Uruguay (1934), Venezuela (1936). A useful comparison of those clauses affecting labor is 404.

    d. The influence of the International Labour Organization in providing advice and a model for the organization of a labor ministry was particularly important during the period. A useful comparative compilation of the laws and structures of the early labor systems is 17.

    e. The main decree-laws and codes examined were as follows (based upon the texts contained in the ILO's yearly <u>Legislative Series</u>):

Argentina: Decrees of April 1927, February 1938, July 1943, Industrial Associations of Employees Decree of 1945.
Bolivia: Decree of August 1936, Labor Code of May 1939.
Brazil: Decree of March 1931, Consolidation of Labor Laws of May 1943.
Colombia: Decrees of 1931 and 1936, Labor Code of August 1950.
Costa Rica: Labor Code of August 1943.
Cuba: Decree of November 1933.
Dominican Republic: Decree of 1936, Labor Code of 1951.
Ecuador: Labor Code of August 1938.
Guatemala: Labor Code of February 1947.
Haiti: Industrial Association Act of March 1948.
Honduras: Workers' and Employers' Organizations Law of June 1955.
Mexico: Federal Labor Act of 1931.
Nicaragua: Labor Code of 1945.
Panama: Labor Code of 1941.
Paraguay: Decrees of November 1939 and September 1943.
Peru: Decree of March 1936.
Portugal: Labor Statute of 1933.
El Salvador: Decrees of October 1927, August 1951; Labor Code of March 1963.
Spain: Labor Charter of March 1938.

Uruguay: No general labor law.
Venezuela: Labor Law of July 1936.

For comparative purposes, see the series issued by the Bureau of Labor Statistics, Department of Labor, Labor Law and Practice in - - - - - , for which there is a volume on every Latin American country except Cuba and Paraguay; also useful is the series of the General Secretariat of the Organization of American States, A Statement of the Laws of - - - - - in Matters Affecting Business. Poblete (404) discusses the codes and decrees country by country in Chapter 2; also 17.

f. The extent to which the Latin American nations have ratified ILO conventions, particularly Nos. 87 and 98 dealing with freedom of association and the right to organize, provides one measure of this influence. As of 1952, only Cuba, Guatemala, Mexico, and Uruguay had ratified No. 87; No. 98 had been ratified by Brazil, Cuba, the Dominican Republic, Guatemala, and Uruguay.

g. See 345. It is sometimes amusing, now in retrospect, to read Poblete's comments on his own creation; see 402-406. Louis Wolf Goodman, who had access to Poblete's memoirs housed at the Institute of Organization and Administration (INSORA) at the University of Chile, concluded the drafters of the Chilean labor legislation held very definite purposes in mind: the elimination of the power of both the working class and employers, leaving national economic power in the hands of a presumed neutral party, the state. Based on Goodman's personal communication to the author, October 17, 1975.

h. The language we use helps speak to these differences: whereas North Americans speak of "labor relations" or "labor-management relations," Latin Americans usually think in terms of "derecho del trabajo" or "derecho social" ("labor law"), thus stressing the legal aspects of a relationship which, in their view, is primarily a set of legal rights and obligations.

i. See 403, 495. It should be said that not only do these codes and constitutions establish goals and aspirations for the society to achieve in some distant future, but they are also impressive to outsiders. They are meant, in the Portuguese case, "for the English or French to see," in Latin America for the United States, the ILO, or the Europeans. They make it appear as though these nations are as "advanced," "progressive," or "developed" as their North European or North American counterparts. They impress foreign observers, at least superficially, while at the same time relieving what is often a national inferiority complex by showing that a little Ecuador or Portugal is as advanced as anyone.

j. The material in this section draws heavily from Collier's analysis; see 85.

k. The best study is 140. Implied in this discussion is the point that the traditional dependence on government can mean advantages as well as disadvantages for labor. The disadvantages include labor's sacrifice of its independent bargaining power, the perpetuation of its weak and dependent status, the possibility of an unfriendly, anti-labor regime, the obscuring of labor's economic functions by political ones, and so forth. The advantages include government support in the early establishment and financing of the unions (e.g., Mexico in the 1920s), the enactment of advanced social legislation, the legitimation of labor as a new power contender, and, in certain instances, the possibilities for the "capture" by labor and its allied groups of the labor ministry and/or the state apparatus itself. See 406, 199.

1. For a fuller discussion of one such revolutionary model, as well as of the utility of the Anderson and corporative approaches in that context, see 552.

10 Does Europe Still Stop at the Pyrenees? Politics and the Party Systems of Spain and Portugal

Spain and Portugal have long been considered a part of Europe and yet apart from it. This is true not only in a geographic sense (Lisbon is still a solid four days' driving time from Paris, Madrid three) but in a social, political, economic, psychological, even moral sense as well. A recent European-born secretary of state was not the first to let slip that he didn't really understand very well those nations that lay over the Pyrenees--and in his case, a certain unspecified nation that lay over the Alps as well (a).

At least from the time of Charlemagne and Roland (b), there has existed a certain European prejudice toward Iberia, and a vague hostility. This historic prejudice has complex racial, social, cultural, religious, and political roots. At the same time, the sense of both distance and rejection which the nations of Iberia feel has bred in them a sense of separateness, a national inferiority complex and, frequently, a desire to "go it alone" regardless of the wishes of the Northern countries, to strike off in their own directions and thumb their noses at a Europe that refuses to treat them as equals and cannot appreciate distinctively Iberian ways and institutions.

During the long Franco and Salazar eras, this sense of isolation, distance, and rejection continued--as much for the nature of these regimes as for any historic prejudices. Spain and Portugal remained outcasts of the European community, a position that often strengthened their nationalistic resolve to maintain their separation and the distinctiveness of their sociopolitical structures. But the long-standing authoritarian regimes of these two nations have now been relegated to the past, either by revolution (Portugal since 1974) or a rapid evolution (Spain since 1975). In their place has come the new institutional structures of "democracy," including democracy's various accoutrements: a gamut of political parties, a full-fledged party system, elections, and "party" government. This transition has been accompanied by a new opening toward Europe on the part of the Iberian nations, a sense that they are no longer outcasts but part of the Western democratic

---

From <u>Western European Party Systems</u>, ed. Peter Merkl (New York: Free Press, 1980).

community, as well as a new acceptability and legitimacy for Spain and Portugal in European liberal and social-democratic circles (c).

In this chapter we shall be assessing the role and functions of political parties and the party systems of Spain and Portugal, focusing specifically on the transition from the authoritarian politics of the Franco and Salazar eras to the more open and democratic period of the present. The questions we shall focus on are these: What was the nature of "party" politics under the Franco and Salazar regimes? To what degree was this "distinctive"? How well have the newer parties of the post-Franco and post-Salazar eras been institutionalized? What are the functions of elections in these systems? To what degree have party government, democracy, and representative rule now been established, replacing the corporative systems of the past? Ultimately, the question to which we shall return is the one with which we began, namely, to what extent does Europe still stop at the Pyrenees; how accurate is the assessment that Spain and Portugal are now part of the Western democratic community; and to what degree do parties, party government, and systemic politics in Iberia still diverge from, or correspond to, the broader European and developmental model?

PARTIES AND THE PARTY SYSTEM: THEIR MULTIFACETED DIMENSIONS

The Spanish and Portuguese party systems, like the party systems of other nations, can be approached from a variety of perspectives. One can focus on the ideological spectrum and policy goals presented by the parties, on their organizational structure and the classic distinctions between cadre and mass parties, on their electoral bases in order to formulate theses about voting behavior, or on the role of the parliamentary party, as well as its extraparliamentary organization, in the making and unmaking of governments, the passing of legislation, parliamentary debates, and the like (258, 327, 572).

These approaches may all be utilized in the examination of the Spanish and Portuguese parties and party systems. But the suspicion remains that these may not necessarily be the only or most useful approaches to studying Iberian parties and politics. The question is still open whether parties in Iberia (and by extension in Latin America) stand for or mean the same thing as elsewhere in Europe, whether the "party phenomena" really describe adequately where political power lies and how it is manipulated, whether there are not other more important centers of power and decision-making to which the parties remain peripheral (75, 120, 295).

In Spain and Portugal the fact the parties which have recently burst forth still operate frequently at the periphery rather than the center of national politics may, in part, be explained by the very short history of the parties, their submergence under protracted authoritarian rule, the long-time restrictions on their activities and the downright repression they often felt, the absence of trained cadres, leaders, and the like. These factors help explain the lack of institutionalization, the relative weakness and fragility of the parties--and of democracy itself--in both Spain and Portugal.

But there are other explanations, which provide us with a number of equally provocative approaches for understanding parties and the party systems of Iberia. These have to do with the relations of the parties to a state structure which has historically been far stronger and more important than the parties themselves; the nature of broad, nationwide systems of patron-client relations which frequently render the parties of secondary importance; the tentative nature of elections in both Spain and Portugal and the fact that other legitimized routes to power remain open; the existence of "parties" such as the army which may have more importance in domestic politics than do the parties themselves; and the pervasive presence of corporatist and functionalist influences and modes of representation, based on a structure of group or sectoral privileges and fueros, on hierarchical and inegalitarian assumptions, and, hence, on the denial of some of the fundamental assumptions of democratic rule, such as the principle of one-man, one-vote (109, 112, 519, 545). These areas merit our serious attention as much as do the more conventional approaches to parties and party systems.

INTRAPARTY POLITICS, FACTIONS, AND THE
EMERGENCE OF A PARTY SYSTEM

The origins of the Spanish and Portuguese parties and party systems go back into the nineteenth century. Some would trace their origins even earlier, to the eighteenth century and the emergence of the "two Spains" and "two Portugals" phenomena. The one was Catholic, rural, traditionalist, and inward-looking; the other more secular, urban, rationalist, "enlightened," and European-looking. Although this fundamental schism in the Spanish (and Portuguese) soul still importantly shapes Iberian politics, parties per se did not emerge until later. When they did, they tended to be based on only incompletely digested conceptions of British parliamentarism. From the beginning, the Spanish and Portuguese parties were fundamentally different from their Northern European counterparts (387).

The nineteenth-century Spanish and Portuguese parties were almost exclusively cadre or elitist parties, and they remained so. A bow was made to liberalism and republicanism, then in fashion, but the functions performed were quite different. The parties remained the personal mechanisms of rival elite groups, families, and local notables and were almost totally devoid of ideological or programatic pretensions. They served as the means by which the elites or rival caciques (political "bosses" or "men on horseback") mobilized client support in order to gain power, and to distribute patronage and spoils to the deserving once power was achieved (64, 70, 102, 241, 268, 313).

With social and economic change in Spain and Portugal, principally the development of sizable middle-class and trade-union groups, toward the end of the nineteenth and the beginning of the twentieth centuries, new political associations emerged. These included, in Portugal, not just the liberal, democratic, and republican factions that helped usher in the ill-fated Republic of 1910-26, but a variety of Catholic, monarchist, integralist, corporatist, nationalist, fascist, and socialist groups as well. In Spain many of the same or similar parties were present, along with the Falange, the communists, the anarcho-syndicalists, and various regional groups.

Although we cannot review here the entire history of party politics in Spain and Portugal during this period, carrying us through the establishment of a republic in Spain as well as in Portugal, several features merit attention. First, the new parties were among the chief means to power for the emerging Spanish and Portuguese middle sectors and reflected the gradual transition, itself reflective of broad-scale socioeconomic changes, from aristocratic to middle-sector dominance of the two nations' major institutions: army, government, universities, bureaucracy, etc. Even the socialist, communist, and anarcho-syndicalist groups, while obviously reflecting rising working-class consciousness, were often dominated in their executive committees by aspiring middle-sector politicians and intellectuals (51).

Second, while reflecting a growing middle-class society, that middle class in both Spain and Portugal was severely divided internally. It had no consciousness as a class, tended to ape upper-class ways, while also using an informal alliance with the rising worker elements to wrest control from the old oligarchic groups. Third, reflecting these deep divisions within the middle class, no one party could command a majority; and the distances were so great between the contending factions that lasting coalitions were all but impossible. The party spectrum ranged from communists, anarcho-syndicalists, and socialists on the left to fascists, monarchists, Falangists, and integralists on the right--and all of them dominated by emerging, insecure, aspiring, ambitious, rival middle-sector groups. With a weak or nonexistent center, equally divided, the situation was one of fragmentation and gradual polarization, leading to a condition in both countries of incipient civil war, complicated by rising class consciousness and aspirations (especially in Spain) for regional autonomy (372).

The result, fourth, was a republican form in which parties and parliament seemed incapable of governing. For its frequent coups, cabinet shuffles, corruption, bombs, and sheer instability and seeming incompetence from 1910-26, Portugal's Republic became the butt of the cruelest national-character-based jokes (510). The Spanish Republic, 1931-36, seemed almost equally incapable of concerted, effective government policy-making and implementation; and as the pendulum there swung more violently from left to right and back to a left Popular Front in 1936, with each party faction recruiting large private militias, the Civil War seemed to loom inevitably.

One of the primary characteristics of both the Salazar and Franco regimes involved their efforts to harness and control this emerging pluralism, to control and suppress, if necessary, the perceived looming threat (to the middle sectors now uncertainly established in power) of organized labor. However, this posture must be placed in perspective. Based on their experiences under both the elite-dominated systems of the nineteenth century as well as the chaotic republicanism of the twentieth, Franco and Salazar were not just hostile to the working-class parties but to <u>all</u> parties. Like George Washington and de Gaulle, they saw "party" as diminishing the unity, integrity, and grandeur of the nation. They dissolved, absorbed, or stripped of power both the socialist and communist factions <u>and</u> the integralist, fascist, and monarchist ones. In keeping with an older Spanish and Portuguese conception going back at least as far as the "Golden era" of the sixteenth century, they sought to rule in an authoritative and technocratic fashion, <u>devoid of all party politics</u>. The model was that of an organic and corporate state system in which divisive, political parties were to have no or little role. Rather than one-party regimes, with which we are familiar from the literature and which leads sometimes to mistaken labels being applied, the Spanish and Portuguese systems were essentially no-party states dominated by a technocratic-bureaucratic structure, supported by a number of corporate elites (church, army, landed and industrial wealth), and held together by an overpowering and immensely politically skilled caudillo (Franco and Salazar) at the top (179, 322).

Of course, both these regimes did have official appendages which they called "parties," thus contributing further to our difficulties in categorizing them. But these agencies did not carry out the functions usually thought of as appropriate for political parties. Only incidentally and almost as an afterthought did they present candidates for elections, devise party programs, or exercise parliamentary functions. Their chief purposes were otherwise. They served, in the historic fashion, as giant patronage agencies, helping to put both friends and enemies of the regime, as well as virtually the entire emerging middle class, on the public payroll. They served as agencies of charity and benefices, dolling out bicycles and toys to children, sinecures to veterans and military officials, rocking chairs and sewing machines to old women, jobs to aspiring politicians and university graduates as well as compliant labor officials. The party machinery served as a convenient place to test and bring along rising, politically ambitious persons, as well as to "pension off" older or out-of-favor ones.

The "party" was also a fund-raising mechanism and an agency for securing loyalty and service, since all government bureaucrats had to join and pay to it a portion of their salaries. The party served as an accommodator of various views as well as an agency to suppress some others. It was the eyes and ears of the regime in the countryside, designed both to tap public opinion (though not necessarily by means of elections) and to help administer government policies. The party served both to lock out some groups and to absorb others through its monopolization of political activity. It was thus more a giant bureaucratic apparatus of the regime than a party per se. It liked to be called a "movement," a "union," or a "civic action association" rather than a "party." Hence, while on one level the Franco and Salazar regimes were one-party states, on another they were not. Even the official "parties" themselves were, in fact, antiparty (d).

Since they absorbed a number of groups and parties that had existed under earlier regimes, the official "parties" of Franco and

Salazar were never quite the monolithic organizations they are
often pictured. Rather, the various factions existent within the
"party" always had to be kept in balance. Moreover, as socioeconomic development continued in the postwar period and as Spain and
Portugal became more complex and socially differentiated, the number of factions that had to be juggled also grew. There emerged
left-Falangists, whose ideology was hardly distinct from that of
the socialists or anarcho-syndicalists, as well as rightist ones;
Christian democrats, monarchists, and social democrats also found
something of a home within the official apparatus.

   These factions became, by the 1960s, important in determining
the direction of the regime. By studying the makeup of new cabi-
nets, government appointments, or rotations within the top leadership of the "party" itself, astute observers could determine which
faction was rising or falling in power and, hence, what could be
expected in public policies (179). The Franco and Salazar regimes,
in turn, used the "party" mechanism to raise, check, and balance
off these contending factions. During the last decade, the official "parties," never really monolithic, became the agencies to express and reflect, within limits, the growing societal and political pluralism of these two regimes. Moreover, within the official
"party", differences had to be worked out between the rival factions
in ways that were not entirely undemocratic. The situation was increasingly analagous to the old one-party American South, where
distinct political factions fought it out in the primaries within
the single Democratic Party apparatus and where the subsequent general elections served chiefly to ratify the choices already made
(e).

   The emerging pluralism of the Franco and Salazar regimes, however, remained a limited pluralism (267). Not all groups could be
accommodated in this way, particularly the more militant socialists
and communists. In some instances, these groups continued to be
persecuted. In others they, too, were allowed to function, in a
certain grudging recognition of new realities. In Portugal the socialist opposition was allowed to participate in a series of elections, although its campaign and organizational activities remained
severely hamstrung. Socialist leader Mario Soares was allowed into
the country on an on-again-off-again basis, most notably for the
1969 parliamentary elections which were among the freest Portugal
had ever had. During the period of Salazar's successor, Marcello
Caetano, successive national "congresses of the democratic opposition" were also held; and even though opposition "parties" remained
largely proscribed, opposition "study groups" that were, in fact,
the nuclei of the later parties met regularly (488, 519).

   The communists also remained illegal, but in both countries
they had built up an underground apparatus, most notably in the
workers' commissions organized parallel to the official <u>sindicatos</u>.
As the workers' commissions grew in strength, the two governments,
especially Spain in Franco's last years and Portugal under Caetano,
became increasingly inclined to deal with them realistically.
Though they remained illegal and, hence, though the government
could not admit its dealings with them publicly, it became increasingly inclined to negotiate with the workers' commissions instead

of its own official syndicates as the true representatives of labor. Of course, labor relations, like the situation with the opposition parties, went through various vicissitudes and ups and downs. But this is still a considerable distance from the image we frequently have of a monolithic fascist structure (18, 519).

By the 1960s the bases for a future, more competitive network of parties and a broader party spectrum had been laid. These included: (1) the official "party" with its several major and many minor internal factions; (2) the socialist, communist, and social-democratic opposition, now operating both below and in some areas above ground; (3) the various exile groups, centered in Paris, London, or, in the case of Portuguese Communist Party leader Alvaro Cunhal, Prague. The exile groups tended to be small, personalistic, and highly factionalized, but they would also serve as the nuclei for an even broader party spectrum once Franco and the Salazar-Caetano regime had gone.

Toward the end of the period of authoritarian rule, the dynamics of politics in both Spain and Portugal, and a wrenching internal decision for the opposition groups, revolved around whether to work within or outside "the system." Both the Franco and Caetano regimes were now sufficiently open that it was possible for the opposition, on some levels, to function. This, however, involved considerable costs, for by its willingness to participate, the opposition not only received certain advantages but also gave added legitimacy to a regime in power the opposition had long fought. But continuing to work outside the system was also problematic. It enabled the opposition to maintain the purity of its doctrines, but the costs meant being cut off from an opportunity, in the new climate, for organization and proselytizing. Without going into the details, it can be said that most opposition groups opted for varying degrees of both. They chose to try at one level to work within the system and gain certain advantages from it, while at another they sought to maintain their separate existences as "out" and "persecuted" groups. Generally, it can be said that prior to 1974 in Portugal and to a somewhat lesser degree in Spain before 1975, the more moderate democratic opposition tended to be increasingly incorporated and, hence, coopted by the existing regimes while the more radical opposition, principally the communists, maintained their image of martyrdom. The socialists, especially in Portugal, were a mixed bag, popular at some levels for their heroic opposition but coopted and compromised at others (f).

PARTY ORGANIZATION

The political parties and the "party systems" that have recently emerged in Spain and Portugal are fragile and only weakly institutionalized (g). While many commentators have taken in the past few years to referring to the emerging Spanish and Portuguese "democracies," to a considerable degree, especially as it is based on the presence of parties and a party system, that evaluation represents more wishful thinking than an accurate description of reality. Some other commentators would go so far as to say a "party system" as such, as the dominant means by which political power is mobilized and transferred, does not yet exist in either country.

The weakness, fragility, and lack of institutionalization of the parties and party systems have to do primarily with their short histories and the conditions under which, up till recently, they have been obliged to operate. During the thirty-odd years of the Salazar and Franco dictatorships, the parties were either illegalized, exiled, forced underground, or so hamstrung in their activities that a free and independent existence was impossible. Alternatively, they and their leaders were coopted by the regimes in power, which provided about the only opportunities for employment and/or survival. The parties were never able to build an effective national organization or to develop grass-roots cadres. These organizational weaknesses continue to plague the parties today and make their continued existence precarious. We shall be considering these organizational problems under four major categories: the relations of the parties to the state, the parties and their parliamentary groups, the parties and their relations with extraparliamentary groups and clientela, and internal party organization.

Historically, in Iberia it has been difficult for any party to survive, let alone prosper, without state support and assistance. Indeed, it is precisely because of the importance of official access and favors given the "party" that dominates the state machinery that the competition for control of it has been so intense. Membership dues are usually insufficient to keep an "out" party alive, jobs and patronage flow usually only from control of the state machinery, and elections are at best tentative and irregular and thus there is no automatic rotation of the parties into office. Without access to the great public watering trough, the parties tend to atrophy and disappear (250).

In Portugal the official apparatus of the Salazar-Caetano regime has been disbanded and most of its leading members ousted from official positions, and/or exiled. The period of military rule that came with the Revolution of 1974 meant for a time that no party, except the military "party," had access to the usual spoils and patronage. The formation of a socialist government in 1976 provided that party with some limited special privileges and jobs, but there was not a wholesale reshuffling of the bureaucracy under the Socialists, nor did they use their position in the government to reorganize as a new official party. The precarious nature of the Socialists' mandate was one cause of this, the fact the Socialists shared power with the armed forces another. And none of the other parties has gained much in the way of access to official favors either. The relations of the parties to the state is, hence, still weak and uncertain with none of them able to enjoy the wholesale advantages that control of or special access to the state machinery usually implies (h).

The situation in Spain is different. That is so both because the transition from the Franco regime was not so abrupt and revolutionary as in Portugal, and because the military has not so far stepped overtly into power. Prime Minister Adolfo Suárez inherited most of the governmental machinery, including the largely moribund "party" machinery, from the old dictatorship. Though himself more a technocrat in the "a-political" tradition, in the 1977 election Suárez moved to coopt the center of the Spanish political spectrum by affiliating his name with and, in a sense, taking over the so-called "Union of the Democratic Center," a hastily formed alliance of fifteen other centrist, moderately Catholic, and bureaucratic groups. In keeping with an older tradition, the "Union" is not really a party but a "movement," "alliance," or "rally," and thus far it has remained of secondary importance in the power structure of the evolving new regime. It will be interesting to see, however, if Suárez begins to reconstruct the "Union" as the new official "party" appendage and patronage mechanism of the government, not altogether different from the old regime system but perhaps updated with greater responsibilities and a more broadly based sectoral representation as in the Mexican Revolutionary Institutional Party. It seems likely that the felt need for greater discipline and organization now that the euphoria of the immediate post-Franco celebration is giving way to more sober appraisals may compel Suárez in that direction. The effects of the creation of such a new official appendage on the opposition parties will likely also be serious, and most probably damaging; however, it may, in any case, be that the opposition is too strong and Suárez's UDC mandate so weak that he would not be able to bring off the creation of such a new official, umbrella-like organization (i).

The parties' relations with their parliamentary blocs are also weak and uncertain. That is so, especially in Spain, because the parliament has yet to emerge as a major center of political authority within the broader system. Spain's is simply not a parliamentary government; and even though it is uncertain where exactly power does lie in Spain--king, prime minister, armed forces, economic elites--it is certainly not in the Cortes. In Portugal, too, the parliament must share power with the armed forces under a pact still in effect that allowed elections to be held but reserved for the military a special position as the ultimate arbiters of national affairs. The internal politics of the several armed forces factions are, thus, at least as important as the rivalries of the parliamentary blocs. Within the parliamentary groups, moreover, party discipline and organization have been weak, loyalties have frequently been fleeting, and there have been numerous instances of party splits, indiscipline, and disaffection.

The relations of the parties with their extraparliamentary and clientelist groups are complex. Probably the strongest links have been forged, in both countries, between the communist parties and the trade unions. This is a long-standing alliance going back a considerable period, even during the era of the dictatorships. In both countries the socialists have moved recently and with some success to wrest control of the union structure, or at least some unions and some workers, from the Communists. It is likely, though we lack many monographic studies, that the same kinds of linkages have been fashioned by other parties with distinct clientelist groups. However, each party has sought to establish a tie with like-thinking groups within the military. No doubt Suárez's UDC has begun to develop a network within the governmental bureaucracy; indeed, that is where much of its electoral support in 1977 came from. And in Portugal, the rightist Social Democratic Center (CDS) began to build its support among the conservative, Catholic peasantry in the northern provinces of the country. But the overall impression one has is that all these links are still weak and tenuous, that the parties have been in existence too briefly for any strong or permanent ties to have been forged, and that the parties' relations with extraparliamentary and clientelist groups are still uncertain, shifting, uninstitutionalized, further retarding the strength and growth of the parties themselves (j).

The internal structure of the parties presents a similar picture. It is generally conceded that in both countries, because of long, arduous, underground struggles against the dictatorships, the two Communist parties are strong, disciplined, and well-organized. In Portugal some of that strength has been sapped because of the Communists' failures in 1975 and 1976, but in both countries the nuclear organization remains powerful. The rightist parties have been weak and fragmented, both because they represent the presently discredited old regime and because in the past their other, more informal connections were such they had little need for a strong party organization or a mass following. They can be expected to begin formulating plans for a political comeback.

The two main parties in Portugal are the Socialists (PS) and the Social Democrats (PSD--formerly known as the Popular Democrats, or PPD). Neither is particularly well-organized. Both are led by upper-middle-class elements often more at home in the social-democratic salons of Western Europe than in the harder nuts-and-bolts activities of party organization (k). Both are deeply divided internally and neither has developed the cadres and grass-roots organizations to weld a strong national organization--although with the Socialists in power in Portugal, there were some efforts to use the advantage of control of the state machinery to fashion a stronger organization and to lure the workers and peasants away from the Communists.

In Spain, Felipe González's Socialist Workers Party (PSOE) presents a formidable opposition to the government. The party has been partially successful in wresting some trade union support away from the Communists and, with 29 percent of the vote, it has a sizable mass following. But its organization remains weak; as the principal opposition, it may lose some support by trying to be all things to all men; it has, to some degree, more a regional than a genuinely national base; and there are many who question whether, without its attractive leader, the party would enjoy the same level of popularity.

Prime Minister Suárez's UDC is not really a party at all but a loose collection (some have termed it a "shotgun marriage") of notables, establishmentarians, regime officials, bureaucrats, and others, from a variety of loosely knit centrist, Catholic, and moderately rightist groups, who tend to support the government, no matter which government happens to be in power. It is really a coalition movement or, as its name implies, a "union" of diverse interests and of the Spanish "people," largely devoid of ideology, program, or strong organization. Indeed, it was only after the apolitical Prime Minister determined to affiliate his name with the

UDC and pull it together that it began to flourish and showed signs of becoming the largest "party." That step also marked the end of the UDC as an independent entity and led to considerable initial resentment on the part of some early UDC leaders. But their resentments were lessened by the benefits immediately showered upon the "party" as the chosen agent of the popular prime minister. Although the UDC organization remains weak and though after the election it was consigned to the oblivion that often befalls official machines once their immediate usefulness has expired, there is a potential though now rusting organizational framework "out there" that could form the nucleus of a stronger governmental apparatus. It will be interesting to see if the Prime Minister decides to avail himself of that possibility or whether he will allow the UDC to continue feuding and disintegrating while his government retains its more personalistic orientation.

PARTIES AND THEIR PROGRAMS

The emergence of a broad, European-style party spectrum, with a range of left, center, right parties, is of relatively recent origins in Spain and Portugal. The very newness of the parties and party spectrum contributes to the frequent ambiguity, lack of clarity, and shifting nature of the party ideologies and programs. So does the historic lack of importance afforded parties in the Iberian tradition, as well as the special relationships the parties must maintain vis-a-vis the armed forces or the state machinery. Nevertheless, a party spectrum has emerged and the "party" phenomenon has gained increasing importance.

The party spectrum in Portugal ranges from the right to far left, with no single party able to command a majority, with opinion deeply divided, and with few discernible trends toward a stable, middle-of-the-road politics. These features of the new Portuguese party system were particularly evident in the governmental crisis of late-1977 when the ruling (but minority) Socialists suffered a vote of no-confidence and the government fell; and, hence, the unhappy prospect developed of a government even weaker and more likely to be immobilized and stalemated than the one before.

On the left the most prominent party is the Communist Party led by Alvaro Cunhal and a core of able, long-time leaders whose heroic exploits against the old dictatorship are frequently heralded in party propaganda by the combined years (over 300) these leaders have spent in jail. The PCP is an old-time Moscow-oriented Communist Party which was the only one in Western Europe to applaud the Soviet Union's brutal stifling of liberalism in Czechoslovakia in 1968. The party has so far remained immune to the influences of more liberal Eurocommunism, although in the wake of its debacle in 1975 when the party failed to elbow its way into power and then in 1976 when it did badly at the polls (16 percent), there is now some evidence that Cunhal may have begun to moderate his position (1).

The PCP has problems on both its right and left flanks. The Portuguese Socialists have begun to chip away at its once solid trade union structure. And on the left, there are a variety of Maoist, Trotskyite, Fidelista, and anarcho-syndicalist groups, strong particularly among young people, who argue the party is old, tired, closed to new influences, bureaucratized, Stalinist, and so illiberal as to be unacceptable. A more accurate reading of the situation, however, is that, while the PCP has some problems, it has retained its strength and vigor and, in the current situation of spiraling chaos and economic collapse in Portugal, may well be strengthening its position. Despite the sniping of his numerous critics, whose analysis of the situation is often based on wishful thinking as regards the development of "Eurocommunism" in the Portuguese CP, it may be that Cunhal's harder-line position will prevail and remain the correct one for his party (m).

Because of the special problems Portugal faces, the Socialist Party has not been able to function as a real socialist party, nor is there much prospect that it will. The Socialists were called upon to preside over a policy of economic restraints, wage stabilization, and general belt-tightening which largely eroded its socialist stance and program. Moreover, because it governed only at the suffrance of the army and during a period of widespread popular desire for a return to order and "normalcy," the Socialists were cast in a peculiar position. Their socialist and reformist legitimacy was undermined by the conservative policies they were forced to follow. For example, it was a Socialist government that began to roll back the agrarian reform, strip the trade unions of their independent bargaining power, return some nationalized properties to private hands, impose police controls on the universities, knuckle under to IMF and U.S. Embassy advice, etc. (n). Moreover, there is much doubt as to just how socialist Mario Soares and his fellow well-coiffed and manicured Socialists are. In the nineteenth century, Portuguese liberals were often known as "cafe liberals" or "liberais do chá" because they much preferred the comforts of intellectual discussion in Lisbon's elegant coffeehouses to the difficulties of governing. The suspicion lingers that Soares's party consists of "cafe socialists."

The Portuguese Social Democratic Party (PSD) is similarly somewhat less than meets the eye. Led by *Expresso* editor Francisco Pinto Balsemão and parliamentary opposition leader Francisco Sá Carneiro, the Social Democrats are really the Portuguese equivalents of the American Democratic Party. That is, they are classic but conventional and rather bourgeois liberals who favor some reform but not too much. Similarly well-coiffed and manicured, the Social Democrats want above all else to get to power. They represent a portion of the bourgeoisie who had been excluded from enjoying the benefits and perquisites of governmental position during the Salazar-Caetano era and who desire to make up for these missed opportunities. In 1979, with the increasingly conservative Portuguese electorate, their wish came true.

The more conservative Center Social Democrats (CDS) is, in effect, the Christian Democratic Party of Portugal. It is Catholic (though nonconfessional) and oriented toward the protection of the family, order, stability--although it represents a fairly moderate and mainstream position on these issues, not the extremes. Like some others, it does not consider itself a "party" but a "league" or an "alliance." Led by Diego Freitas do Amaral, the CDS has been gaining in strength, particularly as the support for radical solutions ebbed. It has attracted many government bureaucrats and others associated with the former regime. Whereas in the immediate post-revolutionary period many of the old <u>Salazaristas</u> and <u>Caetanistas</u> called themselves "socialists" because that was politically the thing to do, now they have begun abandoning the Socialists and joining the CDS, seeing perhaps a brighter future there. In 1978, in what many observers saw as an odd coupling, the CDS joined with Soares's Socialists to form a new government.

There is still a monarchist faction alive but not necessarily well in Portugal, and a certain hard core of real fascists (as distinct from those associated with the old regime who were not fascists but have been discredited by the use of that label). In addition, there are a number of prominent individuals who someday might attempt a political comeback basing their support on charisma, their name and stature, and a "following" rather than a "party." These include General Antonio de Spínola, the monocled man on horseback whose book helped destroy the old regime and who still harbors ambitions to be the Portuguese de Gaulle; Marcello Caetano who in exile in Brazil maintains a certain bitterness at the unfair pilloring his well-meaning regime received following the revolution and may still have some hopes for vindication; General Kaula de Arriaga, once Spínola's rival and still with strong ambitions; Franco Nogueira, Caetano's rival, tough and ambitious; Adriano Moreira, a former Caetano protege with ambitions of his own; and perhaps even General Ramalho Eanes, the current president, who may become tired of the present party bickering, abolish them all, and launch a "movement" of his own.

In Spain the Communist Party, in contrast to its Portuguese cousin, is most famous for its moderation, its "Eurocommunism" (o), and its evolving relationship with the center-right government of Adolfo Suárez (if Santiago Carrillo can bow and kiss the hands of the King," say Spanish wags, "perhaps the Pope will be next"). The party's program is temperate and progressive, calling for the defense of democracy, Spain's entry into the Common Market, and some (unspecified) nationalizations. Because it largely owes its aboveground existence and legality to a political decision made by the King and the Prime Minister, it has concentrated its attacks on the far right and not the government. The Spanish CP also has a history of long exile and underground activity directed against the Franco regime, as well as a strong position within the trade unions; but under the wily and genial Carrillo, its position has been moderate indeed. In part, this has to do with the tactical strategy of the party, for unlike the situation in revolutionary Portugal, the Spanish Communists never had a chance to come to power "by fiat" and they thus sought to put their most reasonable and democratic face forward. Then, too, the Spanish Communists made a poor electoral showing in 1977 (9 percent of the vote), in contrast with the strong 29 percent polled by the Socialist Workers Party; and in order to outflank the Socialists and blur their image as the dominant party on the left, the CP has tried to corral the Socialists into a broad popular opposition front (in which the CP would presumably have a stronger voice than its electoral strength showed it merited), while also working in alliance with the government on crucial parliamentary votes. To this end, Carrillo has taken a curiously familiar "above politics" stance and called for a "government of concentration." This has all given the CP an acceptability it lacked before, but many Spaniards are either aghast or bewildered at the party's position and some, who recall its hard-line past, not a little bemused.

With nearly a third of the popular vote, Felipe González's Socialist Workers Party (PSOE) has emerged as the principal opposition group in Spain, to the surprise of the government and even the Socialists themselves. The PSOE has a moderate platform hardly distinguishable from that of the government: a mixed economy, nationalization of "key" but unnamed industries, free unions, entry into the Common Market. It accuses the government of working with the right and the Francoists to defeat the left, and it has been the beneficiary of a widespread desire in Spain for change and a sense of discontent with the existing regime. Since it is the principal opposition, the U.S. Embassy and, to a lesser degree, the Common Market Social Democrats, have moved quickly to try to coopt and capture the Spanish Socialists, as they had the Socialists of Portugal. That may not be quite so easy since the Spanish Socialist Workers Party is probably more militant than the Portuguese Socialists and with a stronger basis in the trade union movement. Nevertheless, the support for the Socialist Workers Party may not be all that firm: its base is often regional and having to do with the autonomy issue; González has proved a charismatic vote-getter who garners considerable support more for his personal attractiveness than the issues he stands for; and the Socialist Workers, and to some degree the Communists, benefitted from a widespread protest vote against the remnants of Francoism and which may prove to be only temporary. Having registered these reservations, however, the point remains that the Socialist Workers Party garnered nearly 30 percent in the 1977 balloting and will be a major, perhaps the major, force to reckon with in any future political consideration(p).

So far as can be determined, the Union of the Democratic Center, the Prime Minister's newly acquired apparatus, has no clearcut program of its own. It has sought to capture the broad center and moderate right of the Spanish political spectrum, and with 166 seats in the Cortes (to the Socialist Workers Party's 118) has largely succeeded in doing so. Its ideology, however, is largely the Prime Minister's ideology, and that means almost no ideology at all. It is pragmatic, vaguely Catholic, technocratic, centrist. As an alliance of some fifteen middle-of-the-road and moderately conservative groups, it is an amalgam of largely middle-class bureaucrats and social and Christian democrats. It favors the drafting of a new and more democratic constitution, economic reform (undefined), a streamlined bureaucracy, free unions, expanded social security, limited regional autonomy, closer relations with Europe. Seeking to avoid the historic polarizations, it advocates a "safe road to democracy." It favors Spain's gradual entry into NATO and the Common Market, but would not be entirely adverse to Spain's going it alone. It favors a gradual dismantling of the outdated control mechanisms of the old regime, but without that implying a

breakdown of law and order. It recognizes the need to deal with
Spain's pressing economic problems, but would do so through a mixture of private and state-capitalist structures, not socialism. In
short, what there is of a "party" here supports the government and
its program and is inseparable from them.

The right in Spain is, for now, discredited and without a popular base. The Popular Alliance (again, an "alliance" rather than
a "party") of Manuel Fraga Iribarne (considered a "liberal" when he
was in the Franco cabinet) polled only 8 percent of the popular
vote (sixteen seats in the Cortes); other rightist groups hardly
even bothered to campaign. The Alliance advocated retaining "the
best of Franco" and drew support from Spain's traditional corporate
elements: big business, Opus Dei, old-time Francoists, Roman Catholic lay groups, some sectors of the armed forces. Its poor showing in the 1977 election should not be taken as the final measure
of the right's influence. First, it recognizes that numbers of
ballots are not the only measure of political influence in Spain,
nor are elections the only route to power. Second, the right feels
the present post-Franco euphoria will probably pass and that, as
reality settles in again, the need for order and discipline will
once more become apparent. Third, the right is betting Suárez's
UDC will eventually split up and that it will receive the support
of many conservatives, moderates, and Catholics who presently support the Prime Minister. Fourth, the right remains strong within
the army, the Church, the economic oligarchy, and some key areas of
the state machinery--all of whose strength is considerably greater
than the individual votes of its members. The right feels that, if
the need arises or a crisis situation develops, it can call on the
support of any of these key groups who can act above and beyond the
electoral arena. Though one might wish otherwise, the right in
Spain, particularly an updated, refashioned, non-Francoist right,
is by no means dead yet (q).

In addition to these national organizations, Spain also has a
number of regional "parties" with some representation in the parliament. The chief of these are the Catalan Democratic Pact
(eleven seats) and the Basque Nationalist Party (eight seats). The
regional autonomy issue is, of course, a volatile one in Spain;
contrary to what Karl Deutsch and others have said, national integration, in Spain and elsewhere, is not a necessary and inevitable
consequence of modernization (119, 106, 270). Sentiment in favor
of regional autonomy remains very much aline, and especially in
Catalonia and the Basque country it is intertwined with complex
class and economic issues (r).

PARTY MEMBERSHIP AND LEADERSHIP

There have been few, if any, studies as yet of either Portuguese or Spanish party membership, and probably it is premature for
such studies to be done. Although there was remarkable continuity
in voting patterns between the 1975 and 1976 elections in Portugal,
party membership in both countries remains highly unstable and
shifting. The tendency to shift party allegiance is strong, and
most Portuguese and Spaniards are not yet inclined to join

definitively any party. This helps explain why party membership
for all the parties in both countries remains small, although the
voting turnout was remarkably heavy. Prudently, most Portuguese
and Spanish voters are still waiting to see which way the political
winds blow before committing themselves. One is inclined to accept
Converse's hypothesis that perhaps several generations of competitive elections and party development are required before fixed
party allegiances emerge--whatever the social bases of the cleavages that do eventually develop (90).

But if the membership remains shifting and the claims of the
parties themselves suspect, so much so in both cases that the figures are all but totally worthless, it is nevertheless possible to
distinguish between "hard" and "soft" voting patterns. The few
opinion surveys and election analyses that have been done in the
two countries show the vote for the Communist Party to be the
"hardest," firmest, and probably most permanent of all the major
parties. In Portugal the vote for the Socialists and in Spain for
the Socialist Workers was considerably "softer," although in both
cases there was an identifiable "hard core" of party loyalists.
These studies and surveys seem to indicate the vote for the Socialist position may be less firm than that for the Communists and,
hence, more fluid, shifting, and susceptible to major changes. The
vote for the conservative and Catholic parties seems to occupy an
intermediary position between these other two, while the vote for
the center parties (Prime Minister Suárez's UDC and Portugal's PSD)
seems to be the "softest" of all (s). Whether this implies the
possibilities for instability in the middle and the potential for
major shifts on the part of the electorate cannot at this time be
finally ascertained. This plus other evidence to be set forth below, however, provides little optimism for the growth of a stable,
happy, bourgeois, middle-of-the-road polity in either Spain or Portugal.

The information on party leadership is much more complete than
that on party membership. Although some bows have been made by the
left parties to the principle of direct worker representation in
their executive committees, in fact _all_ the party leaderships are
dominated by middle-class or middle-sector representatives. Not
only are few workers represented but the old oligarchic elites have
been largely bypassed as well, even in the conservative parties.
This marks a significant class shift in both Spain and Portugal
from the aristocratic era preceeding the 1930s and is a major indicator of the social changes that occurred inexorably under Franco
and Salazar-Caetano, regardless of the generally conservative and
authoritarian nature of these two regimes. From this point on,
politics in Spain and Portugal, at least as defined by the social
makeup of the various parties' executive committees (and probably
also as defined in other important institutions such as the military officer corps and the public service) is essentially middle-
sector politics. The dynamics of political struggle involve no-
longer elite versus bourgeoisie but rival factions within the middle sectors themselves, obviously taking quite disparate ideological positions and looking differentially toward the lower classes
for electoral mass support (168, 315, 330, 355).

VOTING STRENGTH AND BASES OF CLEAVAGE

If the data on party membership are often incomplete and misleading, a useful means for determining the class bases of the polity and the sources of other societal cleavages is provided by the voting itself. The data are incomplete but they nonetheless indicate certain important electoral phenomena characteristics of both countries. Among the most important of these are: (1) the high turnouts and levels of participation; (2) the strongly class and regional bases of the balloting; (3) the weakness and isolation of the extreme left and the extreme right; (4) the relative strength of the center in these early electoral contests, seemingly reflecting a desire on the part of the Spanish and Portuguese electorates to avoid the polarization that had previously torn their countries apart. See Table 10.1.

In both countries the electoral turnout was over 80 percent (90 percent in Portugal in 1975). While some of the high turnout undoubtedly had to do with the practice of compulsory voting begun under the old dictatorships, the chief factor was simply the desire of the people, after so many years of silence, to express themselves and their opinions at the polls. Election day was a major "national holiday" and the campaign itself a long festival of joy and celebration culminating in the vote. For Portugal it was the "first free election in fifty years" (actually the first free election ever)(509), while for Spain it was the first free election in forty years. Both countries experienced a sudden and rapid escalation in participation, what Huntington calls a "burst of explosive energy" when civil freedoms are restored after a long period of repression. The longer-range implications of such a sudden burst of popular participation and high expectations provide some interesting hypotheses for comparative study. Huntington speculates that such sudden expansion typically leads to a conservative reaction and renewed efforts by rightist groups to reduce political participation and restore a more narrowly based political order again (211).

The strongly class and regional bases of the voting are apparent in both countries (see Table 10.2). Both demonstrated a comparatively high articulation of class interest, and in both countries the class and regional bases of the parties overlapped. In Portugal the Communist Party won strongly among rural wage earners in the large estate-dominated provinces of the Alentejo (the southern so-called "red belt") and in the industrial concentrations of the center region, Lisbon, Setúbal, etc. The more conservative parties, the PSD and CDS, were more attractive to rural small-holders of the northern regions, to Catholics, and to the urban bourgeoisie, both north and south. The Socialist Party attracted the votes of workers outside the dominant mode of regional production—that is, industrial workers in the predominantly agricultural north and rural small-holders in the south—and also of workers in the tertiary sector. The PS also attracted the urban bourgeoisie and intellectuals of Lisbon, and many of those associated with the old regime seeking now to establish their "socialist" legitimacy. But note Hammond's conclusion that a Socialist vote appeared often to

TABLE 10.1
Spain and Portugal: Voting Percentages

Spain: 1977

Union of the Democratic Center (UCD)	34.0%
Socialist Workers Party (PSOE)	28.5%
Communists (PCE)	9.0%
Popular Alliance (AP)	8.0%
Others (Christian Democrats, regional parties, independent socialists, etc.)	20.0%

Portugal

1975 Constituent Assembly Elections

Socialists (PSP)	38.0%
Social Democrats (PPD/PSD)	26.0%
Communists (PCP)	12.5%
Center Social Democrats (CDS)	8.0%
Others (chiefly extreme left or null and blank ballots)	16.0%

1976 Elections for the National Assembly*

Socialists (PSP)	35.0%
Social Democrats (PPD/PSD)	24.0%
Center Social Democrats (CDS)	16.0%
Communists	16.0%
Others	9.0%

*The most striking changes from 1975 to 1976 are that the Socialists and Social Democrats lost somewhat, the Communists gained (in large part because other extreme left parties chose not to participate), the number of blank ballots and votes for "others" declined significantly, and the CDS doubled in strength (reflecting both a growing conservatism in Portugal and the influx of many embittered "returnees" from Angola and Mozambique).

TABLE 10.2
Distribution of Votes by Region and Size of Place: Portugal, 1975

	PS	PPD/PSD	PCP	CDS
Rural North	29.9	38.6	3.8	1.2
Urban North	41.7	27.4	7.1	9.5
Rural South	41.8	8.5	28.2	2.3
Urban South	45.1	12.4	22.7	4.3

Source: 193.

have been a vote against the party of the most numerous class, in favor of the alternative nearest on the spectrum in the direction that the affected constituency's interests led it (i.e., to the left for nonproprietors in the north and to the right for agricultural or industrial workers in the south). Thus, it would appear the actual vote supports our earlier conclusion regarding the "softness" of Socialist support. Or, as Hammond put it, "the PS's campaign and the electorate's response appear to have led it to victory by turning it into a residual category" (193, 139).

In Spain in 1977 the patterns were not altogether unlike those in Portugal. First, there was a definite regional split, although not so clear-cut as in Portugal, between the more conservative, rural, and agricultural provinces of the south and west and the more urban and industrial concentrations of the north and northeast. The Union of the Democratic Center, Prime Minister Suárez's electoral alliance, did well in the more rural, conservative, and Catholic regions and among the urban bourgeoisie and government workers (often synonomous). The left did well in the urban, industrial, and more cosmopolitan centers, sweeping such cities as Barcelona, Valencia, Madrid, Seville, and the Basque provinces. A significant correlate of the last was the relative decline of the Basque nationalist party and a sharp move toward the left in these provinces.

The votes show the weaknesses of the extreme left and right in both countries, and the corresponding--and new--strength of the center. It depends on how one counts. In both countries the combined vote for the left (including Socialist, Communist, and some small independent and fringe groups) was over 50 percent. Looked at another way, and given the relative conservativeness and "acceptability" of the Socialists in both countries, as well as the sharp differences between them and the Communists, another and perhaps more valid interpretation is possible. The Communists in Spain polled only 9 percent of the vote and won twenty seats in the Cortes; in Portugal they won only 12-16 percent. Indeed, in Portugal the Communists actively campaigned to force a cancellation of the election, not wishing to have their weak electoral strength clearly demonstrated by the votes.

The Portuguese right was discredited and prohibited from participating in the election, while in Spain Fraga's Popular Alliance polled only 8 percent of the vote and garnered only seventeen seats in the Cortes. Thus, in Spain, if we are correct in assuming the Socialist Workers Party is not outside the mainstreams and is, in fact, rather moderate and middle-of-the-road, then the combined moderate or center vote (PSOE and UDC, plus some small parties) may total 80 percent of the electorate. In Portugal, if the Socialists, liberal-democratic PSD, and Catholic-moderate CDS may similarly be considered all middle-of-the-road and moderate, then the center vote there also surpassed 80 percent. Although the case must not be overstated and one should not underplay the divisions between these parties, as well as the obvious differences that continue to exist, it could be that the lack of support for either extreme and the seeming strength of the center have to do with the increasing "embourgeoisement" of both Spain and Portugal, their increased prosperity, literacy, and overall modernization, and the growth in both of a strong middle class since the 1920s and 1930s, when extremes of wealth and the absence of a middle class tore both countries apart (269, 444).

THE ELECTORAL SYSTEM AND THE OTHER "PARTIES"

While Spain and Portugal have both seen the emergence of new political parties and had democratic elections that can and should be celebrated, we should not forget that there are other "parties" in the system and that elections are not viewed as the only means to power. The case could be made that the parties and elections are really peripheral to the main centers of power in both systems. The elections thus served as useful opinion polls to gauge the relative strength of the various factions, but real power continued to lie elsewhere, little changed as a result of the elections, and the main arenas of politics had little to do with the votes and parties per se.

The Electoral System and the Efforts to Circumvent, Regulate, and Control the Election Results

The Spanish electoral system was fashioned in, and was an integral part of, the struggles involving the post-Franco decompression (323). The principal actors included the king, Juan Carlos; the army; the new-generation "liberals" who supported the king; and the old Franco state apparatus, headed by the Generalissimo's handpicked prime minister, Carlos Arías Navarro.

Arías Navarro was willing to hold parliamentary elections, but he insisted the entire process be tightly controlled and regulated to preserve the continuity of the Franco regime. He proposed a bicameral legislature with the lower house popularly elected by universal suffrage, but the Communists would be excluded from participating and regime loyalists would be the chief candidates. The upper house was to be appointed from among the traditional corporate interests: the army, the Church, central and provincial government authorities, government labor unions, and business associations. Additionally, the upper house could veto any action by the lower house, and all legislation would require approval by the prime minister's cabinet.

But moderates and the left claimed the election and a Cortes would be meaningless if they were not democratically based and open to all political groups, including the Communists. The king and his supporters concurred; and in a series of intricate and politically deft steps that followed in 1976, he moved to legalize the Communist Party, get rid of Arías, diminish the strength of the Francoists (the so-called "bunker"), increase his own standing and popularity, retain control and the support of the army, appoint his own prime minister (Suárez), and promulgate a new electoral law. The Juan Carlos/Suárez Political Reform Act called for a two-house Cortes consisting of a Chamber of Deputies of 350 members elected by universal suffrage, with its membership proportionate to the population of Spain's various provinces and with each province guaranteed a minimum number of seats. The Senate would have 244 members, 204 popularly elected, 40 appointed by the king, and with each province having equal representation. The Senate could still veto legislation of the lower house and the king was to select the prime minister. Juan Carlos and Suárez then moved to gain the approval of the old Cortes for their plan, which would give it democratic legitimacy but required Cortes members to vote for a proposal that put their own positions at severe risk. Passage was assured both by subtle threats and by the promise of at least 150 sinecures to those who voted for the measure and then subsequently might themselves be ousted in the balloting. The Communist Party was also legalized.

Election day brought some surprises, chiefly in terms of the low level of support for the government coalition, the UDC, especially considering <u>all</u> (from its own point of view) it had done for "democracy" in Spain. Even though the Political Reform Act ensured a moderate outcome by favoring rural and conservative provinces at the expense of populous and heavily industrial ones (the fifteen smallest provinces with 3.4 million population had fifty-three seats in the Cortes, while the largest province, Catalonia, with 4.5 million population, had only thirty-three seats) the UDC still did not gain its expected parliamentary majority. It won only 34 percent of the popular vote but, because of the electoral system, garnered 47 percent of the parliamentary seats: 166 of 370 in the Chamber and 107 of 204 in the Senate. The results were apparently so disappointing to Juan Carlos/Suárez that they have been despondent and largely immobilized ever since, slowing considerably the process of Spanish liberalization and reform policy implementation. As another indicator of how the election results were read, the American Embassy began putting some distance between itself and the government while establishing new links with, and thus giving added legitimacy to, Felipe González and the Socialist Workers Party.

In Portugal the situation was different. There was no king or prime minister to provide continuity. Rather, the Salazar-Caetano regime had been destroyed by military coup d'etat, the "Revolution of Flowers." The revolution had been led by the Armed Forces Movement (MFA) and, though elections had been promised by the revolution's leaders, evidence mounted in late 1974 and early 1975 that the MFA enjoyed its leading and heroic position and wished to perpetuate its supervisory role. By this time, it had built an elaborate set of military cum political agencies parallel to and often bypassing the civilian ones, and had also become the nation's strongest "political party," more coordinated, better organized, and, at least in its own eyes, more popular and with a stronger sense of the national will than the perpetually squabbling civilian parties. Its leading officers had come to believe that further institutionalization of the MFA was necessary and that it should continue to play a directing role even after the scheduled elections for a Constituent Assembly (552).

To this end, the MFA began to downgrade the importance of the elections and make efforts to control their results. Although it could not cancel them altogether and thus run the risk of sacrificing its democratic legitimacy, it did postpone them as long as possible (to April 25, 1975, the first anniversary of the revolution). It also hinted it intended to continue playing a primary role in the drafting of the new constitution. It established an institutional structure giving an especially privileged place to the armed forces and enabling them to continue serving as "guarantors" of the revolution. Among other things, the MFA insisted on a system of representation in the Constituent Assembly that would guarantee a dominant voice for the military itself. It demanded the "right" (the traditional military "<u>foro</u>") to reserve to itself the selection of the defense and economic ministers and the right to approve beforehand (and presumably reject) any presidential candidate. The Council of State, which the MFA officers already controlled, was to be converted into a "superior" upper chamber which, as in Spain, would hold veto power and also enable the army to stay in power indefinitely and ensure that its program would be carried out. Some MFA officers flirted with the idea of forming a party of their own which would surely sweep the elections, and Leftist Premier Vasco Gançalves vowed in a nationwide TV speech that the military in control of the government might ignore or discount any election vote which "did not express the will of the people"--presumably as defined by the MFA.

These notions were formalized in an accord, which the civilian parties were forced to sign only two weeks before the election, giving the military the power to choose the president, veto unacceptable legislation, and continue to rule for at least three to five years. This accord considerably diminished the importance of the election by tying the hands of the Constituent Assembly even before its members had been chosen and eliminating the possibility for an effective opposition or alternative to the MFA. However, the civilian parties had no choice but to sign it or risk their own legality and continued ability to function, as well as the possibility the election would be cancelled.

Even after the elections were held (with the Socialists getting 38 percent, the PSD 26 percent, the CDS 8 percent, and the PC 12.5 percent), the MFA, particularly Gonçalves and the Communist Party, continued to disparage their importance. The Constituent Assembly met under a cloud and continuously faced the threat it would be disbanded. The streets remained at least as important a political arena as the ballot box. Only after the turn-around of November 1975, when Gonçalves was forced out and the CP deprived of some of its special access, did the civilian parties and electioneering (new elections for the parliament were scheduled for 1976) begin to emerge as preeminent. But even with the establishment of a civilian, parliamentary system and the formation of a Socialist government, the president remained a military man and the armed forces continued as the ultimate arbiters of national affairs.

Other "Parties within the System

In both countries the party arena, on this and other issues, was not the primary focus and there were clearly other and often more important "parties" operating in the system (t). In Spain this meant the king, the armed forces, the bureaucracy, the Church,

the Francoist element, the economic elites, and the prime minister
(who is appointed by the king and whose position does not derive
necessarily from his electoral strength). In Portugal the principal nonparty "party" was the MFA, but there are other groups and
individuals that also must be taken into account.

In Spain, too, the principal political arenas were not necessarily party-related: the king and his efforts to build his own
popularity, the king's relations with the armed forces, the internal politics of the military institution, the trade union struggle,
the change-over in the prime minister's offices, the relations of
the government to the Cortes, etc. In Portugal the principal
arenas were also the internal politics of the armed forces and the
MFA, the relations of the premier to the Communist Party, the
struggle for control in streets, factories, and government agencies. All these arenas either took precedence over, or were just
as important as, the party arena.

Similarly, as regards elections. They are significant, but
one should not read too many implications into them. They are tentative rather than definitive (21). The elections in Portugal
were, in effect, a referendum on the revolution and the MFA; in
Spain on the king, the prime minister, and their performance. They
were an indication of the current balance of political forces. In
Portugal they did not offer a full range of choices (the right
groups were excluded, as were prominent personalities like Spínola)
and their importance had previously been downgraded by the military. The elections in Spain provided a set of signals, like an
opinion poll, which did not convey definitive legitimacy to any
groups or party. At best, they provided a tentative mandate.
Hence, the elections in both countries may be seen as part of an
ongoing political process which afforded new opportunities for some
groups and a new defensiveness for others. Other routes to power
remain open and are presently being actively explored by a variety
of forces, which again implies that arenas other than the party one
must also command our attention.

THE ROLE OF PARTIES WITHIN THE SPANISH
AND PORTUGUESE SYSTEMS

Political parties, a party system, and party government are
comparatively new phenomena for Spain and Portugal. With the exception of the chaotic and short-lived republics of two generations
ago, neither country has ever had a functioning party system. Some
would say the parties and party systems in Spain and Portugal have
been and remain mere concessions to foreign fads, or else that they
are contrived and rather synthetic creations for satisfying the a
priori conditions for U.S. aid and entry into NATO and the Common
Market. They show the Iberian nations are as "modern" and as "democratic" as the rest of Europe, when a little scratching of the
surface reveals the parties to be ephemeral and not central to the
functioning of the political system.

The findings in this study lend support to these contentions,
in part. With the exception of the Communists and possibly the far
right, the parties and party systems in both countries are

exceedingly weak. They are not well organized; their leadership is thin; funds are scarce; membership is small; party identification is "soft"; loyalties are fleeting; the parties are splintered and fragmented; and party government has not as yet been strongly or irrevocably established. At the same time, the real foci of power in both countries lie oftentimes outside the party arena: with the army, the bureaucracy, the state machinery, the king (in Spain) or a prime minister independent from the parties, the president (in Portugal) who is also an army general, powerful economic groups, and other corporate and institutional interests. Elections, similarly, provide one route to power, but other means are also available.

And yet parties and a party system have emerged and a system of "party government" is evolving. One cannot discount the impressive turnouts at the polls, the new climate of liberty and freedom, and the obvious, often spontaneous outpouring in favor of democratic rule. The parties have been established and party government and respect for the results of the ballot box have gained new-found legitimacy. That legitimacy is now sufficiently strong and democracy sufficiently well-established that no military or civil-military faction, employing some other route to power, could afford to ignore entirely or ride roughshod over these newer expressions of democratic legitimacy.

The result, in both Spain and Portugal, is a dual system of political power and authority. On the one hand, there are the parties and the institutional paraphernalia that go with them: Cortes, elections, campaigns, public opinion, parliamentary maneuvering, and so on. On the other, there is the army, the state structure, and a variety of powerful vested and corporate interests. The political system rests on a complex set of relationships and often an uneasy balance between these two sets of institutional pillars. Hence, the old question of the "two Spains" or the "two Portugals" is still very much alive. What is interesting is to study not only the internal dynamics of each of these clusters of interests but also the involved interactions and potential for conflict between them. Still open to further analysis is the issue of whether Spain's and Portugal's new affluence, their younger generations, and their rising "embourgeoisement" may have transcended these historic differences. Or, alternatively, will the economic crunch, political crises, and general malaise that both countries are experiencing (Portugal far more so than Spain) bring on a new fragmentation and polarization producing stalemate, conflict, breakdown, and the renewed and familiar turning toward an authoritarian solution?

The question, therefore, remains whether Iberia, with its new elections, parties, and party systems, is now a part of Europe or still apart from it. The answer remains: both. There is much survey and other data that point to the conclusion that Spain and Portugal may in some areas be even more authoritarian, conservative, inward-looking, and oriented toward the preservation of historic, traditionalist values and institutions than were their own authoritarian-conservative governments: Franco and Salazar. There are also many indicators of change, movement, even revolutionary upheaval. As Prime Minister Suárez once noted, "Spain will surprise you." Which way the balance will tip is still an open question, and the complex currents, blends, and overlaps that provide possibilities for both clash and reconciliation between them also furnish numerous opportunities for further research.

NOTES

a. As reported on a "not for direct attribution" basis during the course of one of the Secretary's shuttles about Europe.

b. In the legend of Roland, it is only the Moorish armies of Iberia that are able to defeat the forces of Christendom led by Charlemagne, and Roland himself was killed in Spain, apparently in the Basque country by the "Saracens."

c. Portugal, however, continues to flirt with "Third World" ideologies and Spain is not entirely certain it wants to join NATO. At the same time, a number of the European nations have yet to be convinced that they want Spain and Portugal in the Common Market, and by the latter that sense of rejection is often reciprocated. Although the thrust has been mainly toward integration with Europe, the old prejudices are still often strong and the Iberian nations stand ready, yet and again, to "go it alone" if necessary.

d. The Spanish Falange became the "Movimiento"; see 268. In Portugal it was the União Nacional under Salazar, remodeled and rebaptized as the Aliança Nacional Popular by Caetano; see 519.

e. See 19, 519. Actually, while this description of the Franco system holds for the earlier period, by the 1960s the Movimiento had become so limited and restricted that these functions were often carried out through direct bureaucratic manipulation without bothering with the state party as such.

f. For some general comments on the cooptation versus repression strategies, see 557.

g. The materials in this section are based on field work in Portugal and Spain in 1972-73, 1974, 1975, 1977.

h. On the importance and role of the state, see 557.

i. The author was in Spain in the spring of 1977 when there was much public discussion of the possibility of "the Mexican model."

j. For Portugal these events may be best followed in Expresso and Jornal Novo; for Spain see Cuadernos para el Diálogo and Cambio.

k. In office Mario Soares proved an abler and tougher politician than most observers anticipated; nevertheless, the criticism holds.

l. The most devastating portrayal of Cunhal was his celebrated interview with Oriana Fallaci, New York Times Magazine (July 13, 1975); in more recent statements, Cunhal has begun to shed some of his "Stalinist" image.

m. Author's assessment, based upon field research in Portugal in 1977 and 1979.

n. These events may be followed in Expresso and Jornal Novo. During the period preceding the cabinet crisis of December 1977, there was much talk in the Portuguese press about the vacuum of political leadership, the ineffectiveness of the government, and the widespread desire for a "government that really governs." See 553.

o. See Santiago Carrillo's book with this title.

p. Based on interviews with Spanish social scientists and SPOE officials.

q. Based on the field work in 1977 and interviews with elite group representatives.

r. The upheavals and general strike in the Basque country in May 1977 struck many observers as based on class conflict rather than regional aspirations.

s. For Spain see the Fundación FOESSA surveys and the data and studies done for them by DATA S.A. under the direction of Amando de Miguel, as well as the Gallup surveys; for Portugal see 193.

t. For a general discussion of this phenomenon, see 557.

11 Does the Future Still Lie in Bolivia? Politics and the Stages of Corporative Development in Latin America

Back in the 1960s when the Cuban Revolution was still young and trying to export its revolution, when many (chiefly United States policy-makers) took seriously Che Guevara's idea that the fire would soon spread throughout the Andes, and when Guevara himself established a small guerrilla nucleus in the heart of the continent, a new slogan was coined by some of the young: "The Future Lies in Bolivia!" Some observers were skeptical that a guerrilla revolution could succeed in Bolivia; others commented to the effect that "Heaven help us" if Bolivia represents any kind of future; and by the late 1960s that particular guerrilla group had been largely eliminated and Guevara killed. The slogan died with him.

Although it is still difficult to make any strong case that the future does, let alone ought to, lie in Bolivia, it may be that Bolivia is not altogether a-typical. Though Bolivia has experienced one of the stormiest histories in all Latin America, it can be argued that such political violence, coups, and revolutions are an integral part of that nation's--and indeed the general Latin American--political process. The proposition may be advanced that the coup in Latin America may serve many of the same functions as do elections in the United States--and may even be no less "democratic" and probably no more "comic opera" (526). When coups and revolutions occur so frequently, they ought to be considered a regular, normal part of the political process and not necessarily exceptional; in this sense, Latin American--or Bolivian--politics may be every bit as <u>systematic</u> as that of the United States. Finally, it is suggested that there may be a certain logic, order, and sequence to such occurrences over time that enable us to trace the stages of development through which Latin America has gone--stages based not on the Euro-centric analysis of W. W. Rostow (438) whose categories no one relies on any more for studying Third World countries, but based on the actual experience of Latin America and showing some distinctive developmental routes and patterns.

This essay has three major purposes: (1) to offer some general comments about the role of the military, political violence, and coups in Latin America viewed as a regular, rule-conforming, systemic, even functional aspect of the political process; (2) to

---

From <u>Bolivia at the Polls</u> (tent.) (Washington: AEI, forthcoming).

suggest some categories or "stages" of Latin American corporative development derived from the area's own history and tradition, indicating the periods through which the nations of the region have evolved and providing an alternative formulation to Rostow's outdated concepts; and (3) to place the Bolivian developmental experience within this broader Latin American context of change and thereby come to grips seriously with the issue of whether the future does indeed lie in Bolivia. [Because of space considerations and since it is not directly related to the main theme of this collection, the Bolivia section of the chapter has been omitted.]

THE "SYSTEM" OF LATIN AMERICAN POLITICS

Latin American politics is often considered, chiefly by North Americans, to be so violent, "irregular," and coup-prone as to be entirely unsystematic and unpredictable. Indeed, one of the most difficult and onerous tasks of those who study Latin American politics professionally in the United States (and why so many become discouraged and sometimes give up the battle) is constantly to demonstrate to their colleagues in academia or in government that their field of study has some legitimacy, that it is possible to study Latin American politics every bit as systematically as that of the United States. Because it is so irregular, unpredictable, and "chaotic," the argument runs, Latin American politics cannot be systematic; and if it is not systematic, it cannot be dealt with comparatively or scientifically (21).

In fact, coups, political violence, and revolutions are in Latin America among the most regular of phenomena. Let us take Bolivia as an example. As of December 1, 1978, Bolivia had had five successful revolutions in the past fourteen years; it has had no less than seventy (the figures vary somewhat depending on what, precisely, one counts) successful revolutions in its 153 years of life as an independent nation. The qualifier "successful" is used here because we have no data to measure unsuccessful coups; if there were such data historically on other kinds of political violence, pronunciamientos, and lesser uprisings, undoubtedly the number of incidents would be far higher. Based on these numbers alone, I think it is fair to say that coups in Bolivia are not exceptional events; rather, they are a regular, recurring, almost constant feature of the political process (467).

They are also predictable--not necessarily to United States Embassy political sections nor very often to CIA missions. Nor did the ambitious but aborted "Project Camelot" come up with very useful sets of indicators for measuring revolutionary change in Latin America. But other scholars drawing upon new concepts and data have been able to predict, with considerable success, when coups may occur (115, 163, 354, 419, 454, Ch. 8). While these models are far from perfect, the track record of these scholars is probably no worse than that established by the pollsters in the most recent United States elections.

If coups and revolutions are both regular and often predictable, they are also systematic. They are an integral part of the system of Latin American politics. They are not something apart from it, nor do they represent aberrations or deviations from "normal" politics. Rather, the coup d'etat, political violence, and the involvement of the armed forces in national politics are, in the Latin American context, quite normal. There is no way these occurrences can be separated from the practice of everyday Latin American politics; they must be accepted as "givens" of "the system." Hence, it is not that Latin American politics is somehow unsystematic; instead, it is that we, the outside observers, using criteria derived largely from the Anglo-American experience, do not see or refuse to accept coups, political violence, and revolutions as being part and parcel of systemic politics in a culture area based on political foundations and behavioral characteristics other than our own. Several corollaries of this theme merit brief examination.

1. The Place of the Military within the System

The armed forces in Latin America represent more than a mere pressure group; they are one of the fundamental corporate pillars undergirding the state. They have an obligation to maintain public order, moderate among the contending factions, and restore domestic harmony should this be disturbed. It is not necessarily that the armed forces are usurpers of the constitution; instead, their higher order and, frequently, constitutional functions may oblige them, often reluctantly, to step into national affairs. The military is thus much more involved in the national political life than has been the case in the United States. It is a part of the system, not apart from it (557).

2. Civil-military Relations

In Latin America the hyphen in the term "civil-military relations," implying a strict segregation between the two domains, is frequently invisible. Latin American politics revolves not so much around conflicts between the civilian and the military powers but rather between one group of civilians allied with one group of military officers and another group of civilians allied with another group of officers. In such a system, a sharp distinction between the military and the civilian spheres is not possible, for most political factions consist of both civilian and military elements. Students of Latin America have begun to come to grips realistically with these interfacing civilian-cum-military factions and to analyze them on their own terms rather than on the bases of the artificial separation between the two as derived from the United States pattern (145, 455).

3. Elections and Legitimacy

With the possible exception of the Nixon case, Americans consider elections the sole means of choosing, or removing, our highest public officials. In Latin America, too, elections are preferred, which helps explain why many governments that have come to power through extraelectoral means have moved quickly to strengthen their legitimacy by holding plebiscites designed to ratify an exiting government in power.

But two major qualifiers should also be kept in mind: (a) elections carry only a tentative mandate in Latin America; and (b) there are other routes to power (21). A candidate receiving an electoral victory cannot count automatically on completing his term or even beginning it in some cases; rather, the delicate juggling act and coalition building that go into creating an electoral victory must be continued even after the election. If one fails to do so or loses control of the various balls being juggled, they may fall and hit the juggler on the head. Governing Latin America is, in this sense, more difficult than governing the United States because electoral victory carries only a conditional, not final, mandate to rule. New challenges may come at any time.

These challenges to the regime in power--<u>pronunciamientos</u>, marches, plotting, demonstrations, general strikes, <u>golpes</u>--have the potential both of toppling a government and of ushering a new group into power. That group must then move to establish its own broader legitimacy. It may hold mass rallies or even elections to demonstrate its level of popular support. Even with such electoral "ratifications," however, it is clear that a political system providing for a variety of alternative routes to power besides elections is a much more open-ended political system than that of the United States.

4. The Military as a "Party"

In the absence of strong civilian institutions, the army in many Latin American countries or in Portugal, as shown in the previous chapter, may be the strongest "party" in the system, obliged to fill the institutional vacuum. It is not just the army that may feel this way; frequently, the sense that the army constitutes the only bulwark against chaos is widespread among diverse sectors of the population. Further, with its officer corps no longer drawn from the oligarchy but from the middle sectors and its ranks drawn from the lower classes, the armed forces may be as representative of the national society as any other group making a similar claim. In such countries as Brazil and Peru, additionally, the armed forces may possess skills in modern management, economics, finance, engineering, planning, administration, and development superior to any civilian group, or they may be able to draw upon skilled civilian technicians to govern in conjunction with them (134). In these ways the army may constitute, or be recognized by the general population as, a "party," often better organized and equipped to run the country than the civilian parties.

5. A Political Culture of Violence

While we have recently heard that violence may be as [North, sic] American as apple pie, in fact we usually think of Latin America as being a much more violent political society. Latin America legitimizes such violent means as coups, general strikes, and revolutions as ways to power that the United States, historically, has

not. Since it is often the principal agent of violence in a wider
political culture of violence, and since in many countries it seeks
to maintain a monopoly in the use and control of force, the Latin
American military merits special attention in this context.

In a political culture that legitimizes elections only as the
route to power, the ends of public policy, or the capacity of the
elected government to do much to effect change, will also be limited. In a political culture of violence that legitimizes other,
alternative routes to power, the ends are liable to be as open-ended as the means. In short, in a political culture of elections,
the ability of elected officials to carry out major domestic
changes is also, necessarily, circumscribed; whereas in a political
culture in which coups, street action, and revolutions are also
legitimated, the possibilities for effecting major structural
changes may be far greater (248). Those seeking to effect such
fundamental changes in the United States may wish to ponder the
implications of this proposition.

6. The Coup as a Political Process

A skillfully carried out coup in Latin America is not a simple
event; complex processes are involved (27, 354). The planning must
be careful, taking into account both domestic and foreign considerations (which helps explain why many Latin American coups take
place on weekends, when both Embassy officials in the country and
State Department officials in Washington are often out-of-town).
The preparations must be meticulous. The government to be ousted
must be discredited and rationalizations for the coup prepared.
Support must be mobilized, allies recruited, leaders chosen, coalitions built. The coalitions ordinarily must involve persons and
groups representing diverse sectors of the society, not just the
military. In these ways the coup process is not entirely unlike
the election campaign in the United States (526).

The results of coups and violent tactics also generally produce subtle changes, the understanding of which will not be improved by our blanket condemnation of all such activities. Generally, cabinet personnel will be changed or shifted around in the
aftermath of a coup. Policy shifts will generally take place. A
hostile labor minister may be replaced by one more amenable to labor's interests. Or, a new group of "elites" or officials may circulate into power with clientele to be served that are different
from that of the previous groups (385). In this way, Latin American politics may not be quite the succession of "dreary" coups, as
it is usually portrayed in New York Times headlines and other
sources. Rather, some quite dynamic changes and processes, often
reflecting shifts in public opinion or popular demands, may be involved. Sometimes even more dramatic changes may be involved. Our
condemnations of coups as "just another" in a "dreary" history may
reflect more our own lack of background as to why the coup took
place in the first place and our malcomprehension of the political
dynamics involved than it does the realities of the political process in the country affected. In these areas, too, the subtle policy shifts involved, the changing of high-level personnel, the new

clientele being served, and the rotation of elites, the Latin American change process may not be so different from the North American as we sometimes think.

7. Critical Elections and Critical Coups

Students of United States politics are in substantial agreement that the elections of 1800, 1828, 1860, 1896, and 1932 were "critical elections" marking significant turning points in the nation's history. The periods leading up to such elections have been called "critical" or "realigning" periods. But if, as suggested here, coups in Latin America represent something of a functional equivalent to elections in the United States, if coups are complex political events also involving recruitment of support, mobilization of resources, and coalition-building, and if there is such a thing as "critical elections" and "realigning periods" in the United States, then would it not also be appropriate to suggest the possibility of "critical coups" and parallel "realigning periods" in Latin America (526)?

It is not necessary to overstate the parallel or to proceed from the intriguing to the ridiculous. However, it may be useful to suggest that some coups in Latin America, just like some elections in the United States, have achieved greater importance for having involved more significant changes than others. Among the best examples is the wave of coups that swept Latin America in the early 1930s that signified not just the impact of the world depression but also a class shift from oligarchic to middle-sector rule; or the Mexican coup of 1910 that ushered in a ten-year-long revolution, or the Cuban Revolution of 1959, or the Bolivian Revolution of 1952. These were critical or realigning coups comparable to the realigning or critical elections in the United States. In Latin America such more fundamental realignments may come through either coups or elections, or some combination of them.

Keeping in mind these concepts of realigning periods in Latin American history, ushered in through a diversity of means, let us proceed to look at the several epochs or stages of Latin American development. Our purpose will be both to identify these several stages, using criteria developed from Latin America's own developmental experience rather than from Rostow's famous aeronautical metaphors, and to explore some of the dynamics involved. The discussion and ideal-type model that follows provides a means of placing in broader perspective the developmental background and experiences of the Latin American countries, viewed comparatively.

THE STAGES OF CORPORATIVE DEVELOPMENT
IN LATIN AMERICA

W. W. Rostow's once-celebrated "stages" of economic and sociopolitical "growth" are now generally discredited as a guide for patterning the processes of national development, as is much of what has come to be known as the "development" literature. No one really believes anymore that development and modernization lead inevitably or necessarily toward more democratic, participatory,

and socially just societies, nor is it any longer conceived that
development is a unilinear and nonreversible process. The Rostow
"stages" and the literature of the 1960s on "development" are now
widely thought of as Euro-centric and/or based largely on the
Anglo-American experience with development, which may or may not
have relevance for Third World nations. The growing consensus
among academics, if not yet among policy-makers, is that the Third
World nations are not likely to follow and palely imitate the developmental experiences of "the West" but may well follow some distinct paths of their own; that there may be many, not one or two,
alternative routes to modernization; that few of these are likely
to be democratic and based on the particularistic Anglo-American
political tradition; and that if we are to understand development
in the Third World, we must come to grips with it on the bases of
the dominant institutional and behavioral patterns of these nations, not through some wishful images and metaphors derived from
our own history (537).

In the study of Latin America, authoritarian and corporate
models of social and political organization and change have gained
particular prominence in recent years. Two general lines of inquiry have been staked out: one which focuses on authoritarianism
and corporatism as political-cultural constants, inherent within
the Latin American sociopolitico-legal-religious tradition; and the
second which sees authoritarianism and corporatism as elite, or
class-based, responses to the rising pressure of labor and mass
challenges. Authoritarianism and corporatism have both multiple
causes and multiple effects in Latin America, and certainly the two
lines of inquiry noted above are neither incompatible nor mutually
exclusive. Among more sophisticated observers, the political-cultural and socioeconomic determinants of authoritarianism and corporatism have both been employed, or combined, in a more complex
explanatory model of Latin American change (84, 140, 169, 261, 481,
506). But of the fact the change process in Latin America takes
place generally in an authoritarian-corporate context and not a
liberal-democratic one, more and more professional students of the
area are agreed.

Corporatism as here used refers not to the modern joint stock
company and is not necessarily to be equated with Mussolini's corporately organized fascism. In its most general sense, corporatism
is defined as a particular pattern of organizing state-society relations. In contrast to liberalism, which implies a system of pluralism and more-or-less autonomous interest groups, in a corporatist system, it is the state that usually structures and controls
interest representation through the organization of officially
sanctioned, noncompetitive groups and associations established
mainly in terms of legally prescribed functional categories (a).
The strongly authoritarian-corporate base of virtually all of the
Latin American nations calls into question United States favoritism
toward and policy initiatives designed to promote democratic government in Latin America, since it seems to be based more on wishful thinking than on the sociopolitical realities of the area. It
also helps direct us toward two key variables that form an important part of the definition offered above, that lie at the heart of

the Latin American development process, and that provide some crucial indicators for the analysis of the stages of Latin American development that follows. One has to do with the growth and institutionalization of the power of the state and its ability to exercise control over vast territories and often unruly populations. The other has to do with the growth and elaboration of the national associational life and the progressive organization of ever-wider sectors of the population.

Although authoritarianism and corporatism often provide the context and structure in which change in Latin America take place, it should be emphasized that authoritarianism and corporatism represent generally a <u>response to change</u>, not a <u>theory of change</u> per se. The great motor forces of economic modernization, industrialization, and the class restructurings and greater social differentiations to which these give rise are still viewed as the key driving forces of change. Changes in the realm of ideas, religious beliefs, legal constructs, and political culture are also important; indeed, I would prefer to keep open the issue of whether it is economic change that causes political transformations, political and cultural change that causes economic transformation, or, most likely, a complex, multicausal combination of these. But for now at least, I wish to argue that corporatism and authoritarianism represent not some new and overriding explanation of change but rather a form of reaction to it. In Latin America authoritarianism and corporatism seem to constitute the dominant, prevailing response to change, regardless of the immediate issue or historical time period involved (112, 347).

In the pages that follow, I hope to elaborate the stages of Latin American <u>corporate</u> development. At each stage the dominant economic, social, political, and corporative aspects of that particular epoch will be described. The stages serve to indicate the various periods through which the Latin American countries have passed and that they have been not nearly so stagnant and immobilist as is our popular image of the area. In the transition from one stage to the next, the points made in the first part of this essay will have renewed relevance, that such changes in Latin America may come either through "critical coups" or through "critical elections." The changes traced will also serve to demonstrate that development in Latin America has characteristically taken place within a generally authoritarian and corporate, or perhaps "organicist," framework, and not a Lockean-liberal and democratic one. The analysis is summarized in Table 11.1 (b).

I. The Colonial Era

The colonial era in Latin America, from approximately 1492 to 1820, was a period of mercantilism and exploitation in the economic realm, of a two-class and dominantly elitist social structure, and of an authoritarian and absolutist political system. Though we cannot resolve here the question of whether the Latin American economies during this era were "feudal" or "capitalist" (obviously both, albeit with different emphases from region to region), there is no doubt the colonies were viewed from a mercantilist

TABLE 11.1
The Stages of Corporative Development in Latin America

Stage	Designation and Time Period	Economic System	Social Structure	Political Organization	Corporative Features
I	Colonial Era (1492–1820)	Mercantilism, exploitation	Two-class, elitist, hierarchical, steeply pyramidal	Colonial-authoritarian	Transfer of 16th century Spanish model to the New World
II	Independence and After (1820–1850)	Disrupted, stagnation, subsistence	Two-class, elitist, Creole elite replaces peninsular elite	"Republican" on paper; much disruption which Creole elites and caudillos seek to dominate	Disruption, regression, lack of institutionalization, position of Church, army, state defined
III	First Stages of Modernization (1850–1890)	Quickening, consolidation and slow growth, foreign capital	Two-class, elitist, commercial class emerges alongside landed elites	Modicum of stability; "Liberals" challenge "Conservatives"	Greater centralized authority, emerging associational life
IV	Era of National Consolidation (1890–1930)	Population increase, infrastructure building, economic growth and early industrialization, more foreign capital	Wedding of older and newer elites; emergence of middle sectors and nascent labor movement	Order and Progress Caudillos, Consolidating oligarchies, U.S.-imposed order	Growing centralization, mushrooming associational life, "systemic" patterns developed

TABLE 11.1--Continued

State	Designation and Time Period	Economic System	Social Structure	Political Organization	Corporative Features
V	Populism and Middle Sector Dominance (1930-1960)	Growth and industrialization, import substitution and state capitalism	Middle-class consolidation; emergence of labor and entrepreneurial groups	Centralization and statism, populist and middle-sector parties and movements	Corporatist restructurings, manifest corporatist theory and sociopolitical organization; "inclusionary corporatism"
VI	Era of Mass Challenges--and the Authoritarian Response (1960-)	Expansion and stagflation, rising statism	Growing power of labor, organization of peasants, emergence of "new rich"	Middle-class conservativeness, rising popular pressures, and military-authoritarian responses	Three patterns: assimilationist, revolutionary syndicalism, and reactionary reversion or "exclusionary corporatism"

perspective as existing chiefly for the benefit of the mother countries, Spain and Portugal. It was an exploitive system grounded on the "milking" of the mines and resources of the New World. Little of the considerable wealth was used for the internal development of the colonies (73, 164, 195).

The social system was structured on a two-class basis, with a small, white Spanish and Portuguese elite at the top; a hugh Indian and, depending on the area, African mass at the bottom; and only a small, "old" middle class in between. Class, caste, and social lines were tightly drawn with each "estate" and grading in the hierarchy having its own rights and responsibilities, and sometimes its own courts. The predominantly two-class system persisted; many argue it persists even today in Latin America (33, 498).

Politically, Latin America was organized on an authoritarian and absolutist basis, from king to viceroy (literally, "vice-king"), to captain general, to local hacendado. Power flowed from the top, the central state, down rather than from the bottom up; participation was of a structured sort carefully controlled by the Crown. It was a highly rationalized and bureaucratized system among whose most remarkable features was that it lasted for over three hundred years (176, 195).

The corporative features of the colonial system are also interesting, for Spain tried to create in the New World a model based on the "glorious," sixteenth-century model of Spain herself. The state was the preeminent corporation. The king was the highest authority, ruling through a series of royal councils, often functionally organized, of which the Council of the Indies was the most important agency for the administration of the New World. Beneath these existed a number of other "corporations," orders, and "estates." The main corporate groups, which as a sine qua non for their existence had to be duly recognized and, hence, legitimated by the state, included the army, the Church, the public administration, the universities, the guilds, and the local (cabildo) government. While each of these corporate groups was subordinate to the central state, each also enjoyed a certain contractually derived independence from it. Thus, while North American "contract theory" largely involved the relations of the individual to the state, Latin American contract theory emphasized the relations of the corporate group to the state or, more specifically during this time period, to the crown (c).

The several corporations that were part of the Spanish colonial sistema were limited chiefly to Europeans and included few, if any, blacks or Indians. Although the pre-Columbian Indian civilizations in Hispanic America were also organized often on a corporative basis, a subject that has yet to be explored in detail and its implications both for the colonial system and more recent periods spelled out, the major corporate groups for our purposes here remained those dominated by the European elites and organized as a series of pillars under, and helping to prop up, the Spanish crown and its bureaucratic structure.

While the colonial system of corporations was based on the Iberian model of an emerging national sociopolitical organization (183), in the New World the system was far less structured than in the Old. Nor did they emerge as full-blown agencies overnight. The mother countries were thousands of miles away; and the vast distances, small populations, unsettled conditions, immense territories, and generally inhospitable climate and geography of Latin America were not conducive to the growth of a vast network of tightly organized and interconnected guilds, corporations, etc. The prevailing condition, except in the major colonial centers such as Mexico or Lima, was one of a lack of any kind of organizational and institutional infrastructure, not of a strong existing one. One can make a strong case that virtually the entire history of Latin America from the early sixteenth century on involved not a struggle for democracy and liberalism as North Americans usually envision it, but rather an effort to impose order, authority, and organization on a vast unruly continent where all of these have historically been in very short supply. The agency of this long-term "civilization" process would be an expanding network of corporate structures (534).

II. Independence and After

The period of the early 1820s marked a critical turning point in Latin American history, a "realigning period" in my terms, involving a series of wars of independence, separation from Spain and Portugal, and the effort on the part of the new states of the region to find a new basis of legitimacy and of sociopolitical organization. This period, from the early 1820s to approximately 1850, was a period of general anarchy and chaos (Brazil and Chile constitute the major exceptions) and, in some countries, of retrogression to earlier, more primitive forms (189, 216).

Economically, the disruptions occasioned by the wars of independence, the loss of protected colonial markets, the comings and goings of rival men on horseback in and out of the presidential palace, and, in Haiti and the Dominican Republic, slave uprisings and takeovers led to a closing of many mines and industries and the disruption of many plantations. In some countries in what had been flourishing mining or agricultural areas, life reverted to a simpler form of subsistence existence. There was little development, practically no investment, almost no economic growth. The first thirty years or so in most of the Latin American countries were marked by stagnation, a lack of infrastructure building (banks, port facilities, roads, and the like), and unimproved, if not depressed, living standards.

Socially, the system remained two-class, except that now a creole or native-born white elite replaced the peninsulares as the dominant group. Few efforts were made to integrate the lower classes into national life and, in fact, with the vivid example of Haiti's slave revolt before them, many efforts were made by the elites to stamp out the possibility for social revolution even more firmly. Nor were the sizable and growing mestizo and mulatto elements accorded positions of equality.

Politically, the Latin American nations became republican and liberal on paper, but the structure of power remained elitist and the same constitutions that enshrined democracy as an ideal also made elaborate provision for the continuation of authoritarian privilege. The creole elites sought to consolidate their power and in a few instances, as in Chile, were successful; but the more general picture was one of chaos and anarchy alternating with long periods of caudillo rule a la Rosas in Argentina and Santa Anna in Mexico. The political vacuum and the legitimacy crisis occasioned by the withdrawal of royal authority was not quickly or easily resolved (111).

The corporate group life was also disrupted. In the wake of the French Revolution and the separation from the mother countries, some of the older feudal corporations were abolished--at least in law. The guilds all but disappeared. Many of the universities closed or became mere skeletons; local government became the province of local caudillos and hacendados. There was almost no permanence in the public administration and no conception at all of the bureaucracy as a separate, autonomous corporation. Rag-tag unprofessional armed bands replaced the colonial militias; and while the subordinate place of the army was frequently delineated in the new constitutions, this seldom served as a check on the caudillo armies. The army replaced the Crown as the chief "moderating power." The powers of the state were similarly spelled out in these new constitutions, but the actual situation was somewhat more chaotic and irregular than the laws stated. The one corporation whose place in the system and relation to the state were fairly well-defined in these early years was the Church, but that did not prevent the Church-state issue from serving as a divisive one in some countries in future years. The chaos, regression, and general disorder prevailing in the corporate group life reflected the disruption, upheaval, and lack of institutionalization in the economic and political spheres. However, for many the ideal of a strong state with a well-organized corporate group life remained very much alive; and with the failure of republicanism to work effectively, such sentiment became more widespread (188).

III. First Stages of Modernization

The period of the late 1840s and early 1850s also marked a watershed, or "critical realignment," in Latin American history, though probably not so sharp or clear-cut as was that of the 1820s or would be that of the 1930s. Externally, a major stimulus to the changes of this period was the European revolutions of 1848 and their aftermaths, though clearly other factors were also involved. The period of the "first stages of modernization" may be dated from approximately 1850 to approximately 1890 (92).

Economically, this was a period of the enlargement and consolidation of agricultural landholdings and of a growing export market for Latin America's agricultural products. The mining sector expanded and Latin America's first banks and industries were established. It was an era of economic quickening and of the large-scale influx of foreign capital, at this stage chiefly British (181).

Socially, Latin America remained two-class, but by this point a small commercial elite had grown up alongside the older landed elite. In the growing cities a nascent middle class had also begun to emerge.

Politically, this was a period of growing national consolidation and, in some countries, of a semblance of governmental stability. The early post-independence criollos and caudillos had passed from the scene and a new generation of leaders, often better educated and equipped to rule, had come to the fore. To continue the economic expansion and lure foreign capital also required a greater degree of political stability than before. Nevertheless, many countries continued to experience instability and the competition between the landed elites (by now often organized as a Conservative Party) and the newer commercial elites (who often called themselves "Liberals") was often intense. Sometimes "Liberal" and at other times "Conservative" groups and/or caudillos might seize power. As a result of this competition, the suffrage was sometimes extended; but since only 2-4 percent of the population was now included within the "effective nation," politics remained generally elitist (d).

The corporative-organizational-associational developments of the period were significant. To help provide the stimulus for further economic growth, the structure of the state was now more rationalized, bureaucratized, and regularized. Public administration grew and became more routinized; the universities were reopened and reorganized; and the armed forces were restructured on a more professionalized basis, as compared with the caudillo armies of the past. Business groups and guilds, or gremios, practically nonexistent during the preceding three decades, were now revived. In addition, and a subject that to this writer's knowledge has not at all been systematically studied, the national associational life, in terms of the numbers of schools, orders, clubs, brotherhoods, societies, etc., expanded greatly (431). The historic lack of organization ("falta de organización") that had always plagued Latin America and retarded the area's development now began to be filled. This mushrooming associational life was not organized in accord with any coherent national plan, be it "corporative" or otherwise; but clearly the seeds for such a future development were present.

IV. Era of National Consolidation

The late 1880s and early 1890s was another realigning period in Latin America, as important as those that had come earlier or that would come in the future. Although in some senses the changes ushered in during this period represented a continuation and further flowering of the budding that had occurred in the earlier period, there were sufficient fundamental restructurings and reorganizations during this period to warrant designating it a distinct epoch.

Economically, this period from the 1890s to the early 1930s was one of mushrooming trade and commerce and of sharply accelerating growth (170, 208). Vast new lands were opened up to farming and grazing. The import-export business flourished. Vast amounts of capital investment, by now increasingly United States rather than European, flowed in. The national infrastructure for expanded commerce--roads, highways, telephone, telegraph, docks, port facilities--was built or installed. Mining and industry were expanded. The demand for Latin America's products and the terms of trade were such that many nations of the area prospered. Argentina with its vast agricultural resources and expanding exports maintained a standard of living early in the twentieth century not greatly behind that of the United States. But socially and politically, the concomitants that were supposed to follow from the economic takeoff did not follow: Latin America's social structure did not become more pluralistic and its political system did not become more democratic.

Socially, this was a period of urbanization and of rapid population increase. Latin America's vast hinterlands now began to be filled, physically, with people, just as its organizational and associational void had begun to be filled in the preceding period. This was also a period of the wedding of the older (landed) wealth with the newer (commercial) wealth (114). The older elites often acquired banks and businesses, while the business elements frequently acquired _latifundia_. In many instances, old and new wealth became literally intermarried. The result was a perpetuation and extension of the power of the elite groups rather than any kind of discernible trend toward social pluralism. The economic growth and urbanization of the period gave rise to expanded middle-sector groups and to a new labor movement that would eventually make their voices heard, but for the time being these newer social forces were submerged and/or repressed and were seldom given a major role to play in the political life of the nation (222).

The broad-scale changes ushered in during this period came under the auspices of three distinct political formulae, which were not necessarily, however, mutually exclusive. The first, exemplified by Porfirio Díaz in Mexico, Ulises Heureaux in the Dominican Republic, and Juan Vicente Gómez in Venezuela, might be termed the "order-and-progress" dictators. These were enlightened strong men as compared with the cruder men on horseback of the past. They frequently had absorbed the scientific and positivist ideas of the times and they brought peace, order, and progress to their countries, often with a vengeance (208, 568)!

The second pattern involved the consolidation of oligarchic rule and the continuation or rotation of these elites in power. The best examples are the "A, B, C countries"--Argentina, Brazil, and Chile--which during the period were also among the most stable and prosperous in the hemisphere. In each of these a conservative elite largely monopolized power, presiding over an epoch of peace and prosperity unmatched in their previous history, but which would later be supplanted by the very groups (middle class and urban working class) that their policies had helped stimulate (41, 427, 465).

The third pattern, largely limited to the smaller, less-developed nations of Central America and the Caribbean, involved direct United States military intervention and modernization under U.S. auspices. In such areas as Panama, Haiti, Cuba, the Dominican Republic, Nicaragua, and Puerto Rico, the Marines centralized power, both political and military, built modern roads, installed the first telephone and telegraph services, did land surveys, built water and sewer systems, etc. These activities were parallel to those taking place under the "order-and-progress" dictators and consolidating oligarchies patterns. Moreover, they were frequently carried out in conjunction with the interests of the local elites, aimed at securing their positions or strengthening or establishing their hold on power. It is no accident that Marine rule in the Dominican Republic gave way to the rule by oligarchic Horacio Vásquez and then the bloody "order-and-progress" dictatorship of Rafael Trujillo, 1930-1961, and in Nicaragua to rule initially by the elite Sacassa family and then the "order-and-progress" dynasty of the Somozas. The fact these two patterns, oligarchic rule and order-and-progress dictators, came a few years later in Central America and the Caribbean than in South America, and then generally only with the assistance of United States occupation forces, probably relates to the even more retarded development and to the greater lack of institutionalization in these smaller countries than in the larger ones of the area (557).

But note that in none of the three patterns, order-and-progress dictatorship, consolidating oligarchy, or United States dependency, was there much semblance of democratic rule. Contrary to our usual social science models, economic development and industrialization in Latin America seem not to have given rise to a significant tendency toward democratization but to have served chiefly as a means to strengthen the power of the elites.

The corporative developments of the period were equally important. The position and agencies of the central state were, in general, greatly strengthened, so that the state now became, really for the first time, the most important "corporation." Related to this was the centralization and greater professionalization of such groups as the army and the bureaucracy (208, 366). The universities and the system of public education were restructured, and in the middle of the period came the university reform movement emanating from Córdoba, which would lead to some major changes in the relations of the university to the state. The number of gremios, sindicatos, and professional groups continued to expand; associational life flourished. A host of new political parties emerged, sometimes challenging the power of the traditional elites, but usually with the relations of these newer parties to the state also regulated and controlled in a manner not unlike that of the traditional corporate groups (10, 76).

The process by which new groups would be admitted to the system without altering its fundamental structure was now mastered by the elites. It involved extending juridical recognition and a certain legitimized place in the system to a newer group which, in turn, agreed to modify its demands, police and discipline its own members, and support the existing system. For a new group to be admitted to the system, it had both to demonstrate that it constituted a threat to it and that, in return for certain favors and a piece of the national pie, it would not seek to undermine the position of other existing groups (21).

The first group to be assimilated in this fashion, we have seen, was the rising business-commercial-import-export class.

Later on, it would become the turn of the middle sectors, then the labor movement, later the peasantry, to be, from the elites' point of view, coopted in this gradual, peaceful, accommodative fashion that also had the advantage of helping preserve elitist rule. Hence, if Latin American political "society," encompassing what we have termed the "effective nation" (at this stage constituting no more than 10-20 percent of the total, depending on the particular nation of which we are speaking), can be pictured as a system of vertical corporate pillars, centering in the state and encompassing historically the Church, the army, the nobility, the bureaucracy, the university, and perhaps the parishes or municipalities, then to that structure has now been added on and assimilated a new corporate pillar, the business elites (see Figure 11.2). Although in the next period some other new corporate "pillars" will be similarly appended, it will be interesting to see if the basic structure of power and society will be altered in any fundamental ways, or if it will remain concentrated at the top and in a few hands, as it did during this period.

V. Populism and Middle-Sector Dominance

The period of the early 1930s represents the sharpest and most clear-cut realigning period in Latin American history. The "critical realignments" of the 1930s had been anticipated by the Mexican Revolution of 1910, the Argentine election of 1916, and the Chilean election of 1920; but in the years 1930-35 no less than thirteen countries experienced some profound transformations in the structure of social and political power. This was not merely another round in the long and often monotonous history of Latin American coups d'etat but signaled a major economic and class change (421).

Economically, the period from the 1930s on was a period of major transformation from agriculturally and raw materials-exporting economies to more intensified industrial, commercial, and diversified ones. The strategy used was "import substitution"—the replacement of manufactured goods which had to that point been imported by goods produced domestically. During this period the Latin American economies commenced their "drive to maturity"; a kind of rural feudalism was now supplanted by an urban capitalism and industrialism. This was the era when major new national industries, such as iron and petrochemicals, were established and when a host of factories and manufacturing enterprises began to sprout. The capitalism that emerged frequently combined aspects of laissez faire with forms of state-structured development (20, 170).

Socially, some of the most important changes occurred. The older landed elites now lost their monopoly on power and were sometimes eclipsed or supplanted by newer groups. The middle classes that had been emerging for some decades gained power for the first time; the labor movement had also emerged as a force to be reckoned with. The period also gave rise to a new entrepreneurial group, not necessarily dynamic and risk-taking but generally supported by the state and often a creation of it. Protestionist policies, closed markets, and officially sanctioned monopolies were used by the state to create a national bourgeoisie where none had existed

FIGURE 11.2
The Corporative Structure of Latin America, circa 1890-1930

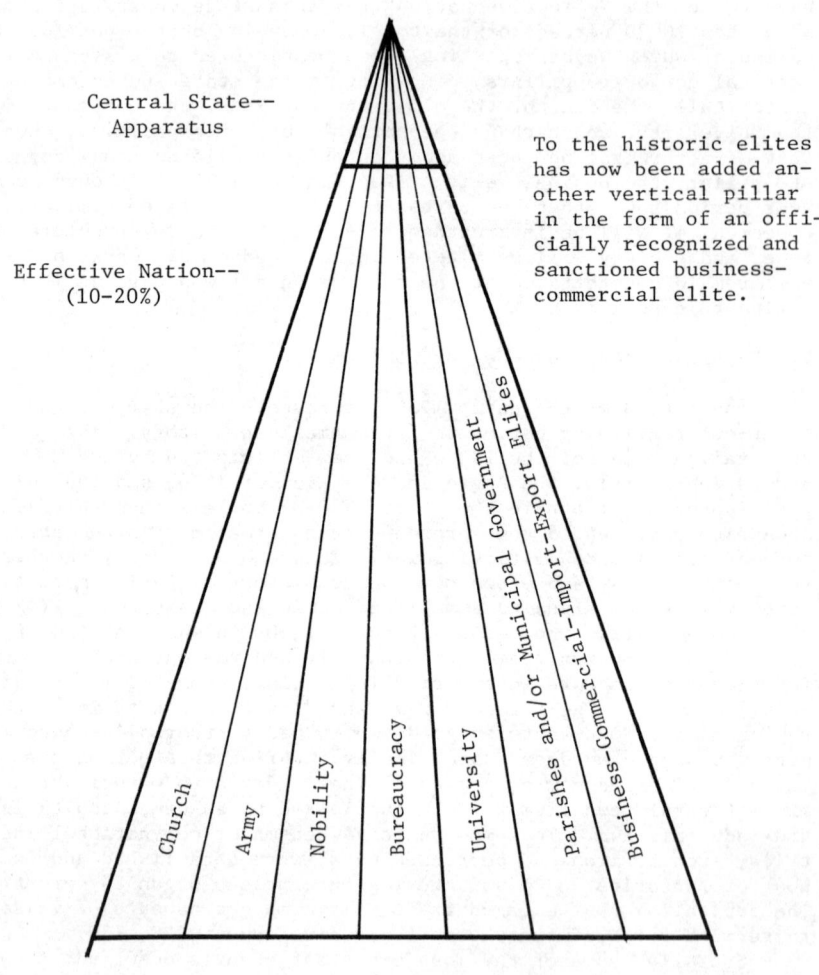

before (452, 519). In addition, the urbanization and population movements that occurred served further to shift power away from the rural latifundistas and toward the burgeoning urban centers.

Politically, the changes were no less profound. A host of new middle-class-dominated political parties vied for power and sometimes seized it, wresting control of the government from the earlier Conservative and Liberal alliances. An equally varied group of populist politicians came to office, some in civilian garb, others as military guardians. The number of political interest groups mushroomed; so did the number of new government agencies designed to control and regulate them. The power of the central state grew, and such manifestly political agencies as the army and the bureaucracy were correspondingly centralized and strengthened (493, 494).

Reflecting these changes, the corporative reorganization of the period was also major. Some nations, such as Brazil, restructured some of the major institutions of national life in accord with the manifestly corporatist ideologies then current. Other nations adopted the new-vogue corporative conceptions only in part, creating functionally representative councils of state or partially functionally representative parliaments. Some nations concocted blends of corporative and liberal features; some allowed corporative principles to govern some areas of national life while retaining liberal-democratic precepts in others. In virtually all the countries, new "organic laws" defining the relations of the group to the state were written for such noneconomic corporative agencies as the armed forces, the universities, or the Church (34, 140, 235, 306, 417).

The 1930s and early 1940s might be characterized as the heyday of corporatism in Latin America, encompassing and seeking to combine both the cultural traditions of "natural corporatism" strongly grounded in Latin American society and history, and the newer conception of corporatism as a manifest ideology and framework for national sociopolitical organization. In many countries the new middle-class groups and parties were granted juridical recognition and thus given their "right" to bargain in the political system, to take their place alongside the other major corporate "pillars." Hence, this period is often referred to as one of "inclusionary corporatism." Through the granting of recognition to them, usually through the host of new labor codes written during the period, organized labor was also coopted in, though for labor the restrictions on its activities most often outweighed its freedoms.

The same laws that governed labor's activities and relations to the state usually also defined the role of employers and capital, though the state's restrictions on the former were generally far greater than those on the latter. In short, this period witnessed the addition of several new "pillars" to the ancient corporate system, but that is not to say all these corporate groups had equal strength or that their position vis-a-vis the state was identical. In the vast web of regulatory agencies, planning commissions, and consultative organs created as part of the growth of state power and designed, at least ostensibly in the corporatist scheme, to guarantee equal representation to labor and capital, employer groups reaped the major advantages, not labor. It should be emphasized that, while these new corporate pillars were added on and absorbed into "the system," the basic structure of Latin American power and society remained hierarchical, steeply pyramidal, elitist. See Figure 11.3.

VI. The Era of Mass Challenges--and the Authoritarian Response

It is more difficult to designate the exact parameters of the realigning period through which Latin America presently seems to be going--just as American historians and political scientists have trouble deciding whether the elections of 1960, 1964, 1968, or 1976 were "critical elections." Surely, the labor-oriented regime of Perón in Argentina, the Bolivian revolution of 1952, the Cuban revolution beginning in 1959, and Allende's election in Chile in 1970 could be considered "critical" turning points; but the precise outcomes of these are difficult to assess and sometimes these more radical restructurings have been followed by authoritarian and repressive responses. Hence, we have termed this new "stage" a period of "mass challenges," often revolutionary in nature, but also one of "authoritarian response" (368).

Economically, this was a period of a gradually expanding economic "pie" for most nations of the area, although for some countries the economy remained stagnant and for some sectors of the population living standards declined. It was also a period of increased foreign assistance, particularly in the 1960s, and of large infusions of private foreign capital. The economic growth of the period came under both private and state auspices, but with the role and dominance of the state gradually increasing until the share of gross national product generated by the state reached 30, 40, 50 percent and more (as compared with approximately 18 percent in the United States and 80-90 percent in the socialist systems of Eastern Europe). The system was often called "neo-mercantilist" or "state capitalist"; and since the degree of state ownership was already so high, the transition from a system of state capitalism to a system of state socialism proved in some countries to be not quite so abrupt and/or wrenching as might otherwise be expected (169-71, 557).

Socially, several major changes were under way. The trade union movement became stronger in most countries, thus forcing governments to deal with it realistically. A large, unorganized "lumpen proletariat" emerged in all the major cities, made up of recent peasant migrants from the countryside and putting severe strains on public facilities. The rural peasants themselves, in varying degrees, were mobilized and organized forcing governments to begin to deal with this group as they had previously sought to handle "the problem of labor." The new-rich plutocracy emerged, often tied in closely with foreign capital. The middle sectors that had largely dominated politics since the 1930s became increasingly factionalized on political and ideological grounds: while some continued to support reformist positions, most aped and imitated what they thought of as aristocratic ways, turned their backs

FIGURE 11.3
The Modern Corporative Structure of Latin America

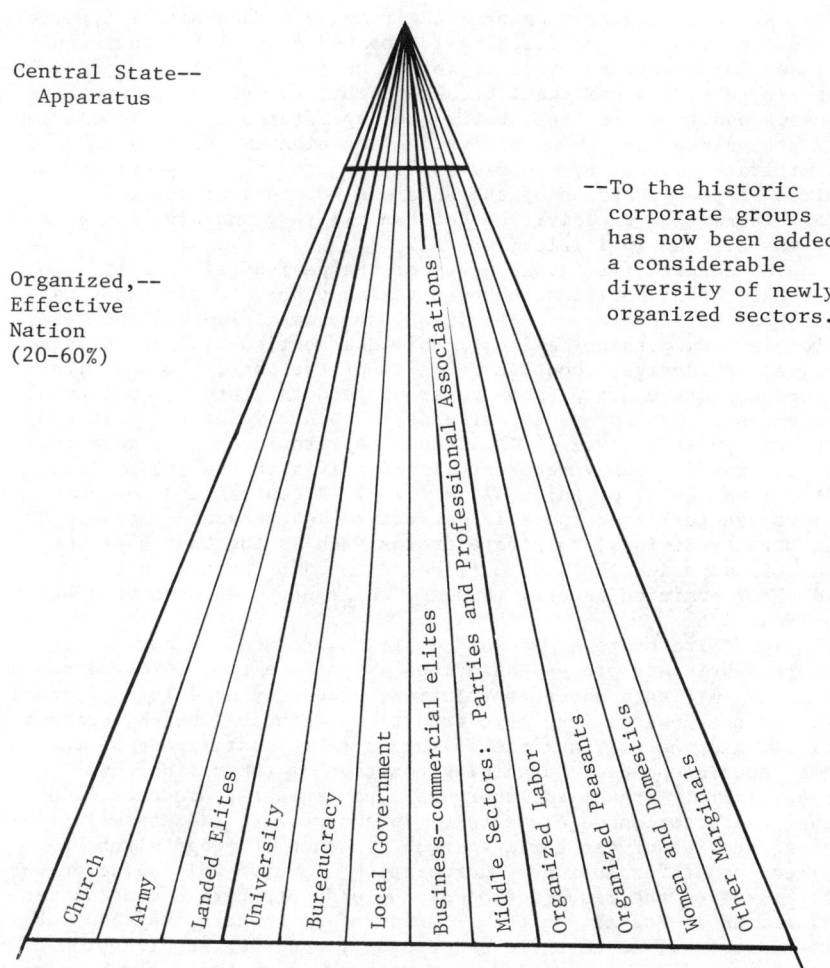

on their former labor allies, and relied often on the military to keep them in power against the rising mass tide (2, 501).

Politically, this was a period in which new mass and middle-class parties and movements were organized, or when some of the earlier groups sought to expand their appeal. New populist politicians rose to the fore, seeking to use and channel the insistent demands for change now boiling to the surface. While in some polities there were significant breakthroughs, in others the new mass demands and threat to the status quo represented by the revolutionary groups produced an authoritarian reaction in the form of a wave of military coups. By the mid-1970s the army was in power in two-thirds of the countries of the area and so close to power in several others that the division between military and civilian authority was all but invisible (365, 518).

The corporative developments of the period reflected the socioeconomic and political changes taking place. Three major patterns may be identified. The first, as exemplified by Venezuela, Colombia, and perhaps Mexico, involved a continuation of the gradual, accommodative, cooptive politics of the past, the assimilation of new corporate groups and "power contenders" into the political system in return for their agreeing to abide by the rules of the historic political game. The second pattern involved a more radical and revolutionary restructuring (Bolivia in the 1950s, Peru after 1968, Cuba, or Portugal in 1974). A centralized, organic, almost syndicalist-corporatist structure was retained but some of the more traditional corporate groups such as the Church or the traditional oligarchy were eliminated as major power contenders or had their position greatly reduced, while new ones were brought to the fore (552).

The third pattern, in many countries produced as a response to the revolutionary process described in pattern two, involved a conservative-military counterrevolution, generally implying a restoration of the power of the more traditional groups (Church, economic elites, and the military itself) and a sharp curtailment of the power and independent bargaining position of the rising newer groups (mainly organized labor but also peasants, students, and other change-oriented elements). In contrast to the assimilationist strategies of the earlier epoch, the new strategy might be called one of "exclusionary corporatism" (305). This solution usually involved the resurrection of the old corporative control mechanisms, as in Brazil, or the creation of such where they had not existed before, as in Chile and Uruguay, and their application to the threatening mass groups. But note again that all three solutions, the cooptive one, the revolutionary one, and the authoritarian-conservative one, had to do more with corporative-organicist type solutions rather than liberal-democratic ones. The choice was usually between one of several rival forms of corporatist-organicist organization.

[The following section on Bolivia has been omitted.]

CONCLUSION AND IMPLICATIONS

In this essay we have set forth some general ideas about Latin American politics, arguing that it is far more rational, systematic, and hence predictable than most observers, particularly North American, are prone to believe. Latin American politics and the change process are played out according to some definite rules and procedures, though these are often quite different from those governing the North American political "game." It is not that Latin American politics is entirely chaotic and unsystematic; it is that North Americans are often ignorant of and unsympathetic to a set of rules and political system grounded on such different presumptions than our own.

We then proceeded to an analysis of the dynamics, patterns, and stages of Latin American development. An ideal-type model of Latin American development was set forth based upon the developmental experience of the majority of the Latin American nations. The model focused on the <u>corporative</u> structuring that occurred generally as a result of major socioeconomic and political shifts. Instead of leading inevitably to liberalism, pluralism, and democratization, which in the schemes of Rostow, Almond, Deutsch, Lipset, and most North American social scientists are supposed to be the concomitants of industrialization and modernization, in Latin America the change process has generally involved the assimilation of new corporate groups into "the system" while its traditional authoritarian, elitist, and pyramidal structures are retained. Corporatism as the historic response to change in Latin America seems sufficiently strong and maleable that it has survived from one stage to the next, with only slight changes in the structure of power being effected, and on into the present as the still-dominant form of sociopolitical organization. In many nations of the area such a corporative-organicist system remains particularly well suited to help fill the organizational and associational void that has always plagued the area, to help preserve elitist rule, and to keep the lower classes in check. In the present era it appears manifest corporative forms are staging a dramatic resurgence.

To say, however, that a regime is corporatist in Latin America is not necessarily to imply any automatic condemnation or approbation or even to give it a "left" or "right" label, since in the analysis presented here corporatism may take left-wing and nationalist forms (the revolutionary governments of Peru or Bolivia in 1952), centrist forms (the accommodative politics of the Dominican Republic, Mexico, Venezuela, Colombia, or Costa Rica), and rightist forms (the authoritarian-corporatist systems of Brazil, Paraguay, or perhaps Chile). Change in Latin America, in short, has produced alterations, even some fundamental, structural ones, in the kind or type of corporative-organicist system; but it has not led inexorably or even inevitably toward liberalism and democratization in the United States sense of those terms.

In Bolivia (8, 26, 123, 244, 306-9, 335-37) what impresses is the almost total lack of institutionalization, in either a liberal, a corporative, or any other way. Politics in Bolivia remains dominated by personalities, cliques, and a shifting kaleidoscope of factions, both civilian and military. But Bolivia, albeit usually a generation behind the larger states of South America, has also gone through its "stages" and is presently in what was here termed the period of "Populism and

Middle Sector Dominance." It is common for this period to begin as one of populism, as illustrated by the early program of the MNR, and to end with increased fragmentation, authoritarian-statism, and national discord, as Bolivia is currently experiencing. In this sense the recent round of coups, scheduled elections, new coups, new scheduled elections, is hardly a-typical.

But to say this represents "politics as usual" in Bolivia is not to say it will be "politics as always." Bolivia has experienced a frustrated and uncompleted revolution, is clearly a nation under stress, class conflict is intensifying, and the traditional cooptive, assimilative mechanisms are no longer adequate. If the stages of Latin American development outlined here have validity, and assuming Bolivia follows this general pattern, it would seem likely that in the not-too-distant future the country may begin to enter Stage VI, the "Era of Mass Challenges--and the Authoritarian Response." Bolivia may be poised on the threshold of an era of revolutionary change that will make the 1952 revolution seem pale by comparison. But while that may lead to a genuinely revolutionary, perhaps syndicalist, regime, not unlike those of Peru or maybe Cuba, it may lead also to another authoritarian response, not the rather mild dictatorships we have seen up to the present but to a much more efficient and likely brutal system, like those of Argentina, Uruguay, or Chile. It is not, therefore, that the future lies in Bolivia but that Bolivia's future may reflect that of its more developed neighbors, however unfortunate that future seems likely to be.

NOTES

    a. The definition follows that of Collier and Collier (84). It is phrased in a way that lends support to the Colliers' assertion of a "growing consensus" among scholars on the subject.

    b. The model presented here may be compared, for example, with the more traditional interpretation of Germani (162).

    c. A corporate group in Latin America is more than a mere pressure group in the United States sense, although some of the same functions may be performed. Implied in the term "corporate group" is a much more formalized and institutionalized structure and organization; as contrasted with the often ad hoc and generally laissez-faire nature of U.S. interest groups, the functions and role of a Latin American corporate group are usually very carefully defined in law and the relations of the group to the state explicitly spelled out in a formal charter. See, for instance, 210, 256, 288, 321.

    d. An excellent study of a key country that has far too long been considered a-typical is 208.

12 | Comparative and Theoretical Research in Progress

The briefer notes presented in this chapter represent research currently in progress and at various stages of completion. Some of the items included derive from research proposals presently being prepared; some involve future research undertakings that are still quite vague in the author's mind.

Taken together, however, these statements serve as useful complements to the materials already presented and as indicators of new research directions. In the studies included to this point, stress has been placed on the historical, theoretical, political-cultural, and sociopolitical aspects of Latin American development, employing--broadly speaking--a corporatist framework. We have also looked at the issue of human rights, the corporative origins of the Iberian and Latin American labor relations systems, the role of political parties in these systems, and the phenomena of political violence, military interventions, and the stages of corporative development in Latin America.

The statements included here help round out the series of comparative, theoretical, and empirical studies relating to the corporatism theme as it applies in Latin America and fill in some gaps in our research and scholarship. Item 1 begins to wrestle with a theme that has long intrigued me: why Latin American intellectuals "bought" the "myth" of their own societies' "underdevelopment" and whether a distinctly Latin American political sociology is possible, feasible, or desirable. Item 2 is a proposal for a full-length study of the political tradition of Latin America as expressed in its major political theory and literature, an attempt to discover the dominant themes of the Latin American tradition analogous to what Louis Hartz did for the United States in his <u>The Liberal Tradition in America</u>.

Item 3 is a proposal for a comparative study of state-society relations and public policy in Latin America, focused particularly on the relations of the major corporate actors to the state system and the implications of these distinct arrangements for policy and policy-making. Item 4 reflects my disaffection with some of the prevailing literature on the political economy of Latin America and proposes as an alternative a "mercantilist model," which is to be differentiated from both liberal-capitalist and Marxian interpretations.

If and when these various studies are completed, I believe I will have said as much as I wish to say on the subject of Latin American corporatism--though, of course, that is not to be taken as an ironclad promise!

ITEM 1
Latin American Intellectuals and the "Myth" of Underdevelopment*

Latin America has frequently been assigned the label of "underdeveloped," not only in terms of various economic indices, where the measures are fairly clear and precise, but in social, political, cultural, psychological, even moral terms as well, where the measures are more ambiguous and culture-bound. It is perhaps not surprising that North American political science and sociology accepted these measures and the labels that went with them; what is more interesting is that so many Latin American intellectuals also accepted the same indices and literature (a la Almond, Lipset, Deutsch, Rostow, etc.) and thus bought the "myth" of their own sociopolitical, cultural, and moral "underdevelopment" and "incapacity."

This paper and the panel on "Latin American Intellectuals" of which it is a part (a) are oriented toward examining these themes. First, they analyze some of the implications of viewing Latin America as "underdeveloped." Second, they examine the reasons why Latin American intellectuals so widely accepted the "myth" of their own nations' "underdevelopment." Third, they explore whether a distinctly Latin American political science and sociology, as distinct from a North American or Northwest European one, is feasible or desirable, what the ingredients of such a new political sociology might be, and some of the implications of this approach.

Most of the development literature assumes that the path of Latin American modernization can be explained by reference to the past or present of the already developed societies (537). Latin America is seen, in Glaucio Ary Dillon Soares's words, as a specific instance of a general course of events already studied and fully comprehended in the experience of the Western European countries and the United States (474). The ethnocentrism of this approach and the absurdity of reducing many distinct histories and social formations to the single matrix of the Western European-North American experience are patent. Moreover, such an approach assumes Latin America can be understood using the same terms and concepts as in the United States. It assumes a unilinear path to development and also the universality of what is, in fact, a far narrower and particular European or "Western" experience and set of institutions. By the same token, it rules out a genuine sociology or political science of Latin America. It has stultified the creation of new concepts, prevented us from understanding Latin America in its own terms, and cast Latin America and those who study it in an "inferior" position vis-a-vis both the more "developed"

---

*Presentation made at the Seventh National Meeting of the Latin American Studies Association, Houston, November 2-5, 1977.

countries and those who study them.

North Americans often accepted this approach, it is suggested, because it conformed to their biases, ethnocentrism, and sense of superiority; it also lent support to the hope for universal principles in the social sciences. Many Latin American intellectuals also accepted the "myth" of their nations' "underdevelopment." Some of the reasons for this include: (1) a strong inferiority complex often widespread in Latin America, the sense that Latin American history has been a "failure" and the area has nothing to contribute; (2) racial stereotypes and prejudices stemming from social Darwinism and other sources; (3) cultural prejudices against Latin and Catholic society, the sense that "Europe stops at the Pyrenees" (or that "civilization" ends at the Rio Grande); (4) the tradition of aping European ways and denigrating Latin America's own society; (5) a form of cultural imperialism practiced by the United States and Western Europe in their dealings with Latin America; (6) manifest political and socioeconomic reasons for keeping Latin America "down" and the United States and Western Europe on top.

At a JOSPOD (Joint Seminar on Political Development) session held at MIT in which the speakers were Jorge Domínguez, Claudio Véliz, and the present author, this question of the existence or not of a distinct Latin American social science was poignantly raised by Tony Smith. Véliz (492) had just held forth concerning the _absence_ in Latin America of the ideologies spawned by the Enlightenment, liberalism, and the industrial revolution, while I had made a presentation on corporatism, organicism, and the "mercantilist model." The question was this: Why is it that a Latin American intellectual should make an analysis denying there was any genuine ideology in Latin America, while a North American scholar should not only assert that there is but presume to identify its chief ingredients.

In mulling over a response to this question, I have reached some definite, though doubtlessly controversial, conclusions. First, any effort to identify the main ingredients of a Latin American ideological and political-philosophical tradition would necessarily have to include authoritarianism, corporatism, elitism, organicism, and patrimonialism in the list. Second, the problem for Latin American intellectuals is that none of these traditions, in a Western world that emphasizes democracy and egalitarianism, is an idea they can be proud of; most Latin American intellectuals would prefer to ignore the bases on which their own societies have been grounded since the rest of the "civilized" world has condemned them as nefarious. It is, therefore, easier, third, for a North American to identify and talk about the ideological traditions of Latin America than it is for a Latin American intellectual to do so. Fourth, unwilling to explore their own societies' underpinnings because of these stigmata, Latin American intellectuals are more comfortable with explanations blaming their "underdevelopment" on exterior forces rather than looking inwardly; this, in part, explains the popularity among them of Marxian explanations, dependency theory, analyses of external and internal colonialism, etc. There is, in short, a "sociology of knowledge" that helps explain the different perspectives that Latin American and North American scholars may take on this issue.

Various concepts must ultimately be fused and analyzed if a genuinely Latin American sociology and political science of development is to be fashioned. Some key concepts and currents in this new political sociology, in part already hinted at, would include patrimonialism and the growth of national patron-clientelistic, or "cartorial," states (215); a tendency toward corporatist forms of sociopolitical organization and toward organic state systems (480); dependency theory and its emphasis on the distinct international context in which Latin American development must take place (b); the new literature on internal colonialism and "center-periphery" relations (c); the particular features of Latin American urbanization (348); the history of mercantilist and state capitalist, "milk-cow" economies (170); the particular role of the Latin American middle class, the armed forces, and so on (2, 292, 501, 562).

The emergence and articulation of such a Latin American sociology and political science of development raises a series of intriguing issues. It means we take Latin America seriously and on its own terms rather than through the condescension and "superiority" of North American or Western European perspectives. It means that the sense of nationalism and independence growing in Latin America is likely to be reflected also in a new assertiveness of indigenous Latin American institutions and models. Fascinating, too, is how the concepts recently developed in Latin American studies, such as corporatism and dependency, are now finding their way into studies of Western Europe, instead of the reverse process by which Latin Americans were always obliged to "learn" from the United States or Western Europe. Finally, what is required is a new assessment of the influences and mixes of the universals and the particulars, how much the Latin American experience does correspond to universal and Western models of change and modernization and the degree to which it is truly unique and requires separate explanatory paradigms. This discussion begins to consider these themes.

NOTES

    a. The other papers presented were 74, 157, 317, 364.
    b. Thinking particularly of the more sophisticated writers on dependency, such as Fernando Henrique Cardoso.
    c. See especially the writings of Pablo González Casanova.

ITEM 2
Political Theory and the Political Tradition of Latin America*

James Reston, the New York Times writer, has said that "the United States will do anything for Latin America except read about

---

*Proposal submitted to the National Endowment for the Humanities.

it."

And further, when we do read about Latin America, we almost always understand it from a United States perspective--that is, from the point of view of why Latin America fails to live up to U.S. concepts of liberalism, republicanism, and pluralism.

I want to undertake a study of the "Political Theory and the Political Tradition of Latin America." As a way of beginning to help overcome the problems of ignorance and ethnocentrism noted above, I plan to approach this project from the perspective of Latin America's own political theory and political culture and not just from a United States viewpoint. The question I want to explore is this: If the prevailing ideology of the United States is Lockean liberalism and interest-group pluralism, what is the prevailing value system and ideological tradition of Latin America?

In this study I hope to do for Latin America what Louis Hartz did for the United States in his The Liberal Tradition in America (192). I hope to analyze the history of Latin American political thought, not comprehensively but interpretively, to identify the main ingredients of a unique, distinctive Latin American tradition. Through an examination of the prevailing social and political theory, I hope to elucidate the basic philosophical premises of a society grounded on principles other than our own, which we only weakly comprehend and often, as Reston implies, do not wish to comprehend. I plan also to contrast those principles with the basic premises of U.S.-style Lockean-liberalism, as set forth by Hartz and others.

What is the prevailing Latin American tradition? It has been variously described as Roman, Thomistic, "feudal" or semifeudal," organicist, corporatist, patrimonialist, Suárezian, positivist, "monist," etc. Although these are often disparate traditions, it is my thesis in this study that there are some common ideas and concepts running through them, irrespective of the labels used. Though other ideologies--for example, the liberal--have at times and among various groups been present in Latin America, these have not been dominant. We should recognize, as Hartz did for Lockean-liberalism in the United States, that, while there may be a single dominant tradition in Latin America, that tradition has undergone various modifications and permutations as different eras and schools of thought have risen and fallen. It has also, like Lockean-liberalism recently, been severely challenged by other quite distinct ideologies, and whether in the present circumstances it can maintain its traditional essence intact or whether it will be swept away by revolutionary change remains an open question. Whatever our final resolution of these issues, the first step in dealing with Latin America is to seek to understand it and what its dominant philosophical premises are--in its own cultural context, on its own terms, and often in its own language.

The discussion in the study, as presently conceived, proceeds as follows: In Chapter I we shall be assessing both the common cultural and political-theoretical currents existent in the New World (North and South America) as well as the differences. The argument will be advanced that, while Lockean-liberalism was the philosophic foundation on which the U.S. polity was founded, Latin

America was founded initially on some quite different premises. Chapter II explores what those premises were and their philosophic origins in Roman law and governance, Thomism, and the Iberian medieval tradition of law and philosophy.

Chapter III explores the sixteenth-century concepts of organicism, patrimonialism, and state-building royal authority in the writings of Suárez, Molina, Dom Pedro, and others, and the transfer of these ideas to the Spanish and Portuguese New World during the colonial era. Chapter IV deals with the restructuring of these ideas in the nineteenth-century independent Latin American states, the thesis being that, while the laws and constitutions of these new nations were in part liberal and republican, in other parts they were continuous with the older and historic Spanish and Portuguese tradition (the writings of Bolívar, the great independence leader and the dominant political writer of the time, are especially revealing in this chapter).

Chapter V deals with the first stages of modernization in Latin America in the late nineteenth century and the grafting on of positivism to the dominant Latin American tradition as a way of securing "order" and achieving "progress." In Chapter VI we shall seek to show how in the interwar period corporatism came to represent a further graft, a means of organizing the society institutionally for national development and resolving the "social question," while also remaining in the mainstreams of the Latin American tradition.

Chapter VII, as presently planned, deals with the contemporary (post-World War II) crisis in Latin America, the conflict and discord that exist, and the challenge of new and competing ideologies that threaten to supersede and in some countries have replaced the traditionally dominant ideas. In Chapter VIII, the conclusion, we return to some of the themes of the introduction; namely, the contrasting philosophical and political-theoretical traditions of the United States and Latin America, the growing challenge to the prevailing ideologies of both systems, and the existence or not of any signs of convergence or congruence toward a newer, better, more humane synthesis. In this way the study seeks to illuminate not only the Latin American tradition but also to speak to our own time and circumstances.

These are, of course, all preliminary ideas. They are subject to change, modification, and further refining as the research proceeds.

ITEM 3
State-Society Relations and Public Policy in Latin America[*]

The study of the state and state-society relations in Latin America has received increasing attention recently, but the existent studies have left some important gaps in our knowledge and they have seldom been explicitly policy-relevant. My own research

---

[*]Proposal submitted to the National Science Foundation.

recently has dealt with the interactions between the Latin American state systems and the corporate and group life that swirls about them, a University of Chicago Workshop has focused on "Historical Perspectives of the State," CLACSO has organized a "Working Group on the State," and several individual researchers have contributed important papers on the contemporary bureaucratic-authoritarian state. While these studies have provided a wealth of theory, background information, and context for the study of the state and state-society relations in Latin America, a number of critical arenas of state-society conflict and interaction have not received the attention they deserve. In addition, these arenas of state-society relations have not yet been integrated into the main theory and the public policy implications of this new focus on state-society relations have not been adequately explored. In the project proposed here, I hope both to say something new about the role of the state and the theory of state-society relations in Latin America, and to explore more explicitly the policy ramifications of these issues.

The first part of the study will be concerned with developing a theoretical model of the Latin American state system and of state-society relations. The formulation builds upon my earlier published research work, as well as the writings of Anderson, Cardoso, Glade, Hirschman, Jaguaribe, Morse, O'Donnell, Schmitter, Stepan, Véliz, and others. The discussion begins with a critique of the existing alternative models, the classical liberal and the classical Marxian. In the classical liberal model, state power was purposely divided and limited and public policy was presumed to be a reflection of "inputs" and interest group struggle, with the government serving as a more-or-less neutral referee. In the classical Marxian model (now refined in important ways), the state was presumed to be a part of the "superstructure," a reflection of underlying class interests. Both these conceptions carry considerable explanatory power in terms of understanding Latin American state-society relations. But they do not provide a complete picture, and other explanatory models must also be employed.

In the model to be presented here, the state in Latin America is viewed as a more-or-less autonomous variable with considerable independence and life of its own. The first part of the discussion deals with the historical and legal role of the state in Latin American culture and tradition, and the relations of the state system to the broader structure of sociopolitical power and the economic and class structure. We shall be concerned with tracing the historical and contemporary functioning of a state system that has been variously described as cartorial, patrimonialist, organicist, mercantilist or neomercantilist, corporatist, and bureaucratic-authoritarian.

A second chapter in this section will deal with the growth and institutionalization of the Latin American state systems from the nineteenth century on, and will also begin to develop a comparative profile and classificatory scheme for the various Latin American countries based on such variables as levels of socioeconomic development, levels of structural differentiation and institutionalization, degrees of public sector ownership, size of the public bureaucracy in relation to the total work force, etc.

A third chapter in this section moves toward the presentation of a model of Latin American state-society relations. The model derives from the historical and theoretical analysis of the state system presented earlier, from the comparative empirical indices presented in Chapter II, and from a preliminary statement regarding the state's relations with socioeconomic and/or institutional groups.

In Part II of the study, entitled "The State and 'The Classes,'" I shall be treating in detail the relations of the state to various societal groups and units. My focus will be on the state's relations both with socioeconomic groups and with nonsocioeconomic ones. My approach will involve empirical work, description, analysis, and systematic comparison.

The first chapter(s) in this section will focus on the state's relations with major socioeconomic groups: landowners, peasants, workers, the middle sectors, and the business-commercial-industrial elites. This section will draw from my own and others' work on the structure of Latin American corporatism as well as the literature on dependency and class analysis. It will seek to show the evolution and varied patterns of state efforts to try to control and regulate the activities of various socioeconomic groups, as well as the efforts of some of these groups themselves to capture or control the state system. One of the key issues to be explored is whether it is the state in Latin America that shapes and determines the class system or if it is the class system that shapes and determines state policies. Implied in the very posing of the question in this way is the idea that these relations are probably more complex than our usual models imply. Obviously, it is the case that class structure shapes if not determines state policy outputs; but evidence is also accumulating of the reverse process as well, of the role of the state in creating and shaping the class system by its selective policies--i.e., the creation and/or fostering in the 1930s in some countries of a national bourgeoisie that had not existed or been strong before. This analysis seeks to explore the complex interrelations between the state and the class system and to sort out the sequences, stages, and causalities involved.

But state-society relations in Latin America encompass not just the relations of the state to socioeconomic groups; they involve the relations of the state to various professional, institutional, and bureaucratic groups as well, sometimes referred to broadly as "the classes." While most of the research on Latin American state-society relations of late has concentrated on the socioeconomic groups, the case can be made that the arenas of conflict and interaction involving the state and these institutional, professional, and bureaucratic groups is equally important. Further, there has been little effort to date to integrate both socioeconomic and nonsocioeconomic groups into a comprehensive theory of Latin American state-society relations.

In this study, successive sections will be devoted to state-military relations, state-church relations, state-university relations, and state-bureaucracy relations. The research will focus on the dynamic and virtually constant tension that exists between a central state system seeking to consolidate and possibly expand its control and regulatory mechanisms, and the various institutional and corporate groups trying to maintain varying degrees of autonomy. Research will be focused on both structural variables (for example, the legal and constitutional position of the armed forces within the state system, the existence of a concordat or other institional charter for governing state-Church relations, the existence of a charter of autonomy for the university) as well as more dynamic socioeconomic and political ones. It is my contention that these arenas of state-society relations are critically important in determining the success and viability of virtually every Latin American government; further, when an analysis of these institutional groups and their relations with the state is combined with a sophisticated class analysis, some powerful explanatory tools may be brought to bear.

Running through the discussion of the relations of the state to "the classes" are several key themes. The first has to do with the issue of whether Latin America is structured primarily along corporate or class lines, or perhaps some combination of these. A second has to do with the issue of whether such key groups as the Church or the army should be considered a part of the state system or apart from it. For in some instances, the army and other institutional groups are not mere pressure groups but almost literally fourth, fifth, and sixth branches of government and inseparable from it. A third major theme involves a comparison of liberal-pluralist as opposed to authoritarian-corporately organized polities. The first involves a more-or-less laissez-faire arrangement where there are multiple groups whose relations are chiefly horizontal--that is, the groups ordinarily deal directly with each other. The authoritarian-corporatist organizational form, in contrast, involves a vertical or "pillared" structure where the state is the central focus and the groups deal with each other generally indirectly through the state system.

A fourth and key concern relates to how and when the relations of the state to its component corporate groups become major issues of policy and political conflict. It is clear that state-military relations, state-labor relations, state-university relations, sometimes state-Church relations constitute critical political arenas on whose successful management, or mismanagement, a government's survival or failure often depends. In this research I hope to explore these issues and develop appropriate indicators for gauging how far an authoritarian regime may go, for instance, in violating corporate group _fueros_ before it faces a withdrawal of support and, conversely, how loosely it may hold the reins before a certain national fragmentation or even disintegration sets in. If the success of any regimes depends in large part on the skillful management of these dynamic and virtually constant tensions, we need to know far more than we do about such arenas of state-society relations.

This research on the state's relations with the major classes and institutional and corporate groups carries important implications. Particularly the arenas of state-military relations, the relations of the central state with the professional bureaucracy, or state relations with major socioeconomic groups are critical, both in terms of assessing a regime's chances for continued viability and its possibilities for successful policy implementation. It also sets the parameters of state power and helps define the boundaries of behavior for both the state and societal groups.

In Part III of the study, building upon the analysis of state-society relations presented earlier, I plan to look explicitly at three policy arenas: economic development, political survivalship, and human rights. This section of the study helps provide the indispensable link between the structure of state-society relations in Latin America and the often distinctive processes of Latin American policy formulation and implementation. It also provides a series of tests for the hypotheses presented earlier and carries important implications for our understanding of public policy-making in Latin America.

In the first chapter of this section, the role of the state in economic development, I hope to focus on the nature and dynamics of what have variously been described as etatist, state-capitalist, or neomercantilist systems. My purpose is to show how the structure of state-society relations described earlier helps shape the nature of economic policy formation and execution. In developing a model of economic policy-making in such etatist systems, I hope to focus on the following key variables: the size of the public sector; the system of state monopolies and charters; the state's role in creating a national entrepreneurial class; the state's regulation of socioeconomic groups; state regulation of wages, prices, and production; state oversight of "private sector" activities; the nexus between the state and certain privileged economic elites; the special position of banks in such a system; and the role and functions of public enterprises as major patronage agencies. Clearly, this discussion of economic policy-making in such an etatist system is related closely to the discussion above of the state's relations with corporate and socioeconomic groups. The discussion also carries important implications for economic development in Latin America and our understanding of the processes involved. For if it is the case that future U.S.-Latin American relations will be dominated more by economic issues than by political ones, then we surely need to know more concerning the structure in which Latin American economic policy-making takes place.

A second chapter in this section focuses on "political survivalship." Following Anderson (21), it is the thesis here that politics in Latin America is somewhat more tentative than in some other countries, that political mandates tend to be indefinite, and that sheer survival in office constitutes an overriding and virtually constant preoccupation. Moreover, it is on its successful management of its relations with the major corporate and socioeconomic groups that the survival of the regime depends. Hence, the research planned here is toward developing a set of indices, based on the <u>givens</u> and <u>system</u> of Latin American state-society relations, that enables us to measure "political survivalship." If such survival is indeed the first order priority of any regime in Latin America, before any other policies can be successfully implemented, then it is important to explore these dynamics in the state-society realm and their policy implications.

The third policy area to be explored concerns the state and human rights. Elsewhere (Chapter 8) I have tried to spell out the differences that often exist between United States and Latin American conceptions of democracy, representation, and human rights. In this study I hope to devise some quite concrete indices for measuring these differences, as well as for determining when a given regime is operating within the bounds of tolerable behavior in the human rights area as opposed to when it exceeds those bounds and thus sacrifices its legitimate "right to rule." Nicaragua in the last years of the Somoza regime provided one dramatic illustration of these tensions, but the research is applicable elsewhere as well. In developing indices of the distinct conceptions involved, the state's capacity to act, as well as the limits on state power, the investigation carries important policy implications.

The research here proposed is comparative, interdisciplinary, and policy-oriented. It carries strong theoretical and policy implications. It provides both a broader view of state-society relations in Latin America and their complex dynamics than has heretofore been attempted in the literature, and it provides an important and explicit connection, also not yet available in the literature, between the structure and political arenas of state-society relations and public policy formulation and implementation in some major policy areas.

ITEM 4
The Political Economy of Latin American Development:
The Mercantilist Model*

Latin American political economy is usually interpreted in the light of one of two models: the liberal-capitalist model and the Marxist one. Neither of these is entirely satisfactory in explaining the processes and functioning of the Latin American systems.

The liberal-capitalist model is unsatisfactory because it rests on the assumptions of a dynamic entrepreneurial class, a participatory and individualistic society, a degree of risk-taking willingness, open competition, private initiative, a generally free and unrestrained marketplace, laissez-faire and minimum state intervention in the economy--all features that have been largely lacking in the Latin American tradition. This is not to say that capitalism or capitalists are entirely absent in Latin America, but it is to say that Latin American capitalism--if it can be called that--is characterized by some special features. Capitalism in Latin America has usually taken the form of _state_ capitalism: a comparatively large public sector (accounting for 30-60 percent of GNP in most countries, as compared with only 18 percent in the United States), government regulation and control of major economic decision-making and of socioeconomic groups (instead of laissez-faire), a system of

---

*Presentation made at the Joint Seminar on Political Development (JOSPOD), MIT, February 27, 1980.

national monopolies that are noncompetitive, an entrepreneurial class often created by the state, a closed marketplace, etc. These features help explain why the advice of U.S. economists to various Latin American governments is usually inappropriate or produces unanticipated consequences, for it is based on the laissez-faire capitalism of the U.S. which generally has little applicability in Latin America. Either the liberal-capitalist model must be scrapped altogether as a means of interpreting Latin American political economy, or it must be radically revised to fit the special features of the Latin American state systems.

The classic Marxist model is no less problematic. It assumes, for example, that the Latin American state systems are merely a reflection of the underlying socioeconomic substructure, when, in fact, the evidence seems to indicate the state may be an independent variable that itself shapes the structure of class relations rather than the other way around (a). It assumes also a model of development and class behavior based largely on European patterns that do not necessarily apply in all cases and in the present context in Latin America. It assumes further the development of a capitalistic marketplace and economy that applies only in part in Latin America. And it does not adequately come to grips with either the continuing conservatism of Latin America's lower classes or the flexibility of its elites who, rather than being swept away under the onslaught of economic change, have proved to be remarkably flexible and accommodative.

The discussion needs to be further elaborated, but the point is that neither the liberal-capitalist nor the Marxian model seems to me adequate by itself to explain the political economy of Latin American development. As an alternative, a "mercantilist model" is here proposed. The "mercantilist model" of political economy may be looked on as the counterpart to the "corporatist model" of political society (actually, some corporatist writers in the 1930s argued that corporatism was a method of organizing both the political society and the economy). Like the "corporatist model," the "mercantilist model" is a shorthand term, an "ideal-typical" construct whose dimensions need to be greatly fleshed out and whose overlaps and fusions with the capitalist and/or Marxist aspects, which do also exist in Latin America, need to be specified. Nevertheless, the "mercantilist model" seems a useful beginning point and would appear to be a more accurate reflection of the realities of Latin American political economy and its development processes than either of the other alternatives discussed.

The paper to be prepared on this theme traces the origins and development, in theory and practice, of the mercantilist systems of Iberia and Latin America. It shows how these systems work, their internal dynamics and functionality, and how and why they were (and remain) distinctive from the liberal-capitalist and Marxist interpretations. "Mercantilism" or "neomercantilism" is here defined provisionally as a system of national economic organization intermediate between that of liberal market capitalism in which private interests dominate, and a full-blown command economy in which statism prevails (169). The defining characteristics of the system of mercantilism or neomercantilism which enable us also to

distinguish it from liberal capitalism or an all-encompassing statism, would include the following:
 1. The size and nature of the public sector, roughly 40-60 percent of GNP--more than that of a laissez-faire economy, less than that of a command system.
 2. The system of monopolies created, controlled, and directed by the state; far greater than in liberal capitalism, less than in a command economy.
 3. The role of the state in creating a national but nonrisk-taking entrepreneurial class through grants, favors, etc., where none had existed before.
 4. The state's involvement as creator, regulator, policeman of all socioeconomic and professional groups (here lies the link with societal and state corporatism). Private groups interact with the state apparatus with neither fully subordinate to the other; hence, the system is neither laissez-faire nor totalitarian.
 5. The state's regulation of prices, wages, and production; a bureaucratic-technical integration of production is substituted for a price system.
 6. State oversight of various private-sector groups and activities, including the infusion of foreign capital. The state has extensive interventionist levers.
 7. The nexus between the state system and certain privileged socioeconomic groups; the interface between state and private economic power.
 8. The special position and power of banks in these systems and their interrelations with the state structure.
 9. The role and functions of public enterprises as gigantic patronage and spoils agencies, and the blurring of the public and private domains.
 10. The dynamics of change and radical transformation: the incorporation of new groups into the privileged system; the relatively easy transformation from state capitalism to state socialism; e.g., Portugal in 1974.

The "mercantilist" or "neomercantilist" model represents a distinct type. It does not derive from only one set of historical circumstances, nor does it stand in some predetermined relationship or evolutionary sequence to other forms of macroeconomic organization. The mercantilist form, contrary to some expectations, will not necessarily be supplanted by liberal capitalism or socialism. It may accommodate to urbanization, a welfare system, industrialization, and other "modern" currents without altering its basic features (169). Neomercantilism may be a permanent feature of the Latin American and Iberian nations.

The reasons for the development and lasting capacity of these "mercantilist" or "neomercantilist" systems are complex. Some of the reasons are (169):
 1. History and tradition; they have always been that way.
 2. A reflection of the political system: bureaucratic monarchism and corporatism in the political sphere imply an economic system of neomercantilism.
 3. Bureaucratization and rationalization of society which have led also to the bureaucratization and rationalization of the

economy.

4. The need to structure and control groups constituting a potential threat to the system.

5. Growing economic complexity, the oil crisis, trade and interdependence which call for greater state direction.

6. The thrust in Latin America as elsewhere toward consultative economic planning based on collaborative state guidance of the economy.

7. Incomes policies, indexing, wage restraints, balance of payments problems, inflation--all call for major continuing state economic management.

8. Regional integration, which calls for industry-based negotiations on a transnational basis, again involving the state.

9. The perceived need to shore up and defend national industries against the onslaught of U.S.-based multinationals.

10. The whole complex of forces of post-industrial society, also calling for a greater statist role.

In the body of the paper, both the ingredients of the "mercantilist" model and its causes will be elaborated. The implications of this way of looking at Iberian and Latin American political economy are also major:

1. For research. Latin American political economy must be interpreted in its own terms of "mercantilism" or "neomercantilism," not through a liberal-capitalist model that does not apply. Nor does the U.S. or Western Europe offer a model pattern by which to interpret Latin American development. The mercantilist and neomercantilist forms may be both rational and permanent, not "traditional" and "dysfunctional." What was earlier said about the distinctiveness and permanence of Iberic-Latin political society is also relevant for the discussion of political economy.

2. For policy. (a) The "mercantilist" or "neomercantilist" model has important implications for AID, World Bank, and other officials who must deal with Latin America; (b) it has implications also for those who would hasten a possible transition from state capitalism to state socialism or state syndicalism; capturing the pinnacles of these pyramidal systems (Portugal, Peru) may be seen as more productive than efforts to stir revolution from below.

NOTE

a. In their discussion of "the relative autonomy of the state," some Marxists have begun to come to grips with this latter phenomenon.

Part 4
Country Studies

Corporatism, we have seen, exists in a variety of forms. There are state and societal forms, backward-looking regimes as well as progressive ones, more-or-less "pure" forms in a formal-legal sense as well as mixed types, "underdeveloped" and "modern" versions, both capitalist varieties and socialist ones. By this point, we have sufficient conceptual and comparative materials both to consider these distinct individual cases as well as to reach some evaluatory conclusions about them.

Part 4 contains a number of country studies and reflects the areas of my principal field research. The first study derives from earlier work in the Dominican Republic, explores that country's mixed traditions of corporative-authoritarian and republican-liberal forms, and discusses the implications for development of such a confused, chaotic, disintegrative history and pattern. The second is part of a larger study of the Brazilian Catholic labor movement, a movement grounded on corporatist principles but nevertheless increasingly dysfunctional in the contemporary context. The third is a summary statement of work on Portuguese corporatism, which for a time was probably the "purest" and most complete corporative system in the world and has since undergone a revolutionary transformation--whether to something else or merely to another form of corporatism is a theme explored in the chapter.

The following brief note, in the form of a book review, raises the issue whether Cuba also may be corporatist and bureaucratic-authoritarian. The issue is raised, but much further study is required to resolve it. The last essay, probably also controversial, deals with corporatism in advanced-industrial societies, or "the Latin Americanization of the United States."

Part A
Country Studies

13 | A Dominican Case Study and the Corporatist Model

A conceptual scheme that more closely reflects and is adapted to the peculiar realities of political change and development in the Hispanic-Latin American tradition is more useful than those based upon foreign and outside models and imported and arbitrarily imposed on a social setting where they do not fit. What for shorthand purposes we have termed the corporative model of Latin American society and polity seems a helpful and relevant framework for understanding the present-day social and political life of the region. In this study we seek to explore the corporative model's usefulness in the context of one nation, the Dominican Republic. Using the changing pattern of elite-mass relationships in the Dominican Republic as the major point of reference, our purpose will be to suggest the utility of the corporative approach.

No claim can be made that the Dominican Republic is representative of Latin America or that the pattern of national development in this Caribbean nation exactly parallels that of the area's other countries. At the same time, there are enough similarities between the Iberic fragments in the New World to make comparisons between them meaningful and fruitful of theory-building; indeed, the fundamental sameness or, at least, the comparability of the Latin American patterns may be more impressive than their particular aspects. The discussion of the Dominican Republic that follows is intended to be analytic, interpretive, conceptually oriented, and suggestive of some of these patterns, not detailed, exhaustive, or comparative (529, 531, 533).

THE TRADITIONAL ORDER

Colonial Era

The island of Hispaniola was one of the first to be discovered by Columbus on his initial voyage in 1492. The first permanent colony in the New World was established here and the earliest experiments in Spanish colonial government were conducted. In Santo Domingo the first agencies of the Spanish administrative hierarchy

---

From Dictatorship, Development, and Disintegration: Politics and Social Change in the Dominican Republic (Ann Arbor: Xerox University Microfilms Monograph Series, 1975).

and the first <u>audiencia</u> were established. Here Spain's policies with regard to the treatment of the Indians, the <u>encomienda</u> system, the importation of African slaves, colonial governance were first tried out and set. The oldest cathedral and oldest university in the Americas were founded on the island; Hispaniola was also the scene of Latin America's first palace revolution. Here, too, the first corporations in the New World were chartered (197).

A rigid hierarchical society was established, both class and corporately based. Fashioning the colony on the model of Spain, Columbus's heirs established themselves as the nobility; artisans, craftsmen, soldiers, merchants, clerics, and a few others formed the small middle class; and the native Indians became serfs and slaves. Soon Africans took the place of the indigenous population, but the basic pattern of rigid class-caste stratification has persisted to the present. The distinctions between the first-ranking citizens ("de primero"--pure-blooded descendents of the Spanish <u>hidalgos</u>), second-ranking citizens ("de segundo"--also of Spanish descent but not of the pure-bloods), and the large amorphous mass of the population, of darker skin and with no social standing, were firmly established from the earliest colonial times. The elites themselves were also organized along sectoral lines (48).

Hispaniola flourished during the first half-century of Spanish rule, for it was the administrative center of Spain's colonizing efforts in the New World. The Church and the Catholic faith accompanied the Spanish conquerors to the Americas, and the Spaniards also brought along their entire cultural-intellectual-attitudinal baggage from the Spain of Isabella and Ferdinand, Charles V, and Philip II. This included concepts of patrimonial authority and the corporatist organization of society. The whole structure of fifteenth- and sixteenth-century Spanish society, revolving around the Crown or the Crown's agent, with an elaborate network of functional and corporate entities, and with the new element added of a large slave population, was established anew in the New World.

After 1550 the more lucrative conquests of Mexico and Peru soon turned Hispaniola into a poor way station. The indigenous population had all but been completely exterminated and the more ambitious Spaniards emigrated to the mainland. There was little readily exploitable natural wealth and the colony was of little value to the Crown. For the better part of three centuries of colonial rule, Hispaniola remained the neglected, poverty-ridden, tail-end of the Spanish empire in the Americas. A social and institutional vacuum developed that still plagues the country today.

Relatively little is known of Hispaniola's history from 1550 to 1795. Historians have begun to realize that this long period of colonial rule, fully two-and-a-half centuries, was of crucial importance in shaping the traditions, practices, and institutions which would later hold sway in an independent Dominican Republic, but detailed information concerning the nature and functioning of Hispaniola's colonial system are still lacking. This was a period of almost continuous alien raids and attempts at foreign occupations. It was also a period when the Spanish colonial system was firmly institutionalized and when the culture, traditions, and behavioral patterns of Spain's "golden century" were indelibly

imprinted on the colonial psyche. The institutional structure
atrophied, but the sixteenth-century ideal continued (352).
   Because of the poverty and neglect, paradoxically, Hispaniola
experienced much of the worst of the Spanish colonial heritage.
The practices and institutional ideal established early in the sixteenth century remained fixed, immune even from the gradual changes
and liberalizing reforms that had begun to affect Spain's other
colonies in the eighteenth century. Thus, the model of the political system was rigidly authoritarian; no glimmer--let alone tradi-
tion--of limited government or popular participation could evolve.
The economy was primitive and based on exploitation; economic life
centered around the self-contained estate or large ranches. The
Church frequently served as an arm of the political authority and
was similarly absolutist. The slave-serf society remained, and the
framework for the system of rigid, hierarchical social stratifications and "estates" that still exists today was thus set. What
representation existed in the councils of government was functionally and corporately organized around and beneath the Crown and its
representatives. The slight increase in prosperity in the eighteenth century and the Bourbon reforms of that same era had no effect whatsoever on the fundamental structure of social and political relationships in isolated Hispaniola, nor did the Enlightenment
have any impact. The colonial era thus bequeathed a legacy of institutions and practices that were authoritarian, corporatist, patrimonial, and semifeudal in character, that had remained largely
intact for the better part of three centuries of Spanish rule, and
that in certain respects persist even today.

Independence

   Commencing in 1795, there began a half century of chaos and
turbulence, most of it under Haitian rule, that temporarily
destroyed and interrupted the system of social relationships and
institutions built up by the Spaniards over the past 300 years and
that left Hispaniola even more ill-prepared for independence than
her sister states. In 1795 the Spanish two-thirds of the island
was ceded to France. France was preoccupied in Europe, however,
and a slave revolt soon began in French Haiti which resulted in the
slaughter or exile of the white ruling class, the destruction of
the plantation system, and a declaration of independence by the
black republic. Shortly thereafter, the Haitians also overran the
Spanish-speaking side of the island. The hidalgos fled. When,
with the aid of the British fleet, the Haitians were driven out and
the colony was reunited with Spain in 1809, many came back (108,
428).
   In 1821 the Spanish colony declared its independence from the
mother country. But within a few months Haitian columns again
overran the entire island. The Haitian occupation, 1822-44, was
cruel and barbarous. The white hidalgo elite, the only group which
could possibly have presided over a relatively smooth and peaceful
transition from colony to independent state, was slaughtered and
persecuted until it again abandoned the island; the large estates
were burned and destroyed. The university was closed and the

Church's ties with Rome were severed. All high public offices were held by Haitians. The whole structure of Spanish colonial society and institutions was set aside. Sumner Welles feels that the basic cause of the unrest and upheaval which would soon characterize Dominican independent history should be attributed to the eclipse of European civilization that occurred during the twenty-two-year Haitian occupation (507, 275).

When Dominican independence was finally achieved, it was from Haiti and not from mother Spain. This, coupled with a long history of foreign occupations, lack of a strong native tradition, and national impotency, contributed to the sense of frustrated nationalism which dominates Dominican independent history. When independence came, the country was ill-prepared. It lacked even the residual, colonial, social, and political institutions possessed by the other newly independent Latin American nations, for these had been largely destroyed by the Haitians. The country's independence heroes, who might have presided over a relatively peaceful transition to nationhood, were quickly exiled. Thereafter, much of Dominican history would involve the attempt to revive and restore Spanish culture and institutions rather than to evolve new ones more in accord with the country's changing needs, to resurrect the authoritarian-corporatist model of the sixteenth century, to reestablish the structure of its glorious but remote Spanish past even in times when the traditional Spanish practices had become obsolete.

National Period

The period of the first republic, 1844-61, was the classic era of Dominican caudilloism. Pedro Santana and Buenaventure Báez emerged as the two most prominent personalities in the new republic, alternating in power for some thirty years and perpetuating chaos and the institutional vacuum. The country was governed--at least formally--by constitutional and legal norms; but "civil, republican, representative democracy," as one constitution after another proclaimed, was inoperative. The Dominican Republic, like its sister republics in the Americas, not only lacked any tradition of democratic rule, but it also lacked the nineteenth-century tripartite centers of power--a dominant and wealthy landowning elite, a strong Church organization, and an organized armed force--that had emerged in the other Latin American nations. The Dominican Republic thus remained almost entirely uninstitutionalized in either a liberal or a corporative form. In this institutional vacuum, chaos and anarchy usually reigned until one or another of the strong men stepped in. Sheer power, based on the personal allegiance of armed camp followers, was the method of articulating political views; and revolutions and civil wars were the means for effecting political change. Not only was it impossible to develop a system of constitutional government, it was also impossible to fashion a stable pattern of oligarchic or military rule either. The chaos plus the threat of Haiti's continuous assaults finally led to the reestablishment of Spanish rule, 1861-65 (219).

The failure of the several protectorate plans put forth in the

1860s left the country again in the hands of rival men on horseback. During the seventeen-year period following Spain's withdrawal, there were sixteen chief executives and seven successful revolutions. A new strong man, Ulises Heureaux, emerged in 1882.

Heureaux ruled as a dictator for the next seventeen years. During his rule, however, a national army and bureaucracy were organized, communications and transportation grids were greatly extended, and the economy began to shift away from subsistence and the semifeudal hacienda toward the capitalized plantation producing for the world market. A landed oligarchy reemerged, a new business-commercial elite rose up, and a small middle class began to form. Heureaux was one of the new breed of "order and progress" caudillos; he began the process of Dominican nation-building. He also presided over the first real efforts by Dominican elites to restore the structures and glories of the Spanish past; and the number of new schools, hospitals, clubs, associations, and other chartered corporations multiplied (207, 431).

Heureaux's legacy also included a corrupt administration, an immense increase in the public debt, the bartering of the national sovereignty to foreign creditors, and the total obliteration of the early stirrings of liberalism that had grown up in the late 1870s. Following Heureaux's assassination in 1899, the country returned to the chaos that had gone before. Four revolutions took place and five presidents gained office in six years. Under the leadership of Ramón Cáceres, the country briefly enjoyed a measure of progress and stability. But he, too, was assassinated and civil war broke out again. The country still lacked an institutional infrastructure on which a stable society could be built. In an effort to avert more upheaval, the Archbishop was elevated to the presidency. He was no more able to stem the disorder than his predecessors and soon resigned. As the political situation degenerated still further, United States military forces occupied the country in 1916. Curiously, despite the continuous chaos and the almost constant revolution, this prewar period was one of unprecedented prosperity in the Dominican Republic, though it would take a while for the social and political effects of these changes to be felt (324).

During the U.S. occupation, 1916-24, the Dominican Congress was suspended, the Supreme Court stripped of its power, and the U.S. military governors granted power to rule by decree. The occupation forces improved the sanitation, communications, and educational facilities; but the Marines assumed arbitrary power, abused their authority, and came to be resented by the increasingly nationalistic Dominicans. The long-range effects of the occupation are also important for our purposes. The extension of the road network opened up the countryside for the first time, helping expand commerce and breaking down localism. Centralization resulted from the assertion of control over the municipalities and the divesting of the provincial governors and caudillos of their independent military authority. The constabulary organized by the Marines to keep order after their departure was the first modern, unified, professionalized armed force in the nation's history (173). In addition, the demand for Dominican products growing out of U.S. war needs stimulated the economy. The economic boom continued in the prosperous postwar decade.

By the late 1920s, the Dominican Republic seemed to be on the threshold of a new era. The U.S. occupation forces had been withdrawn, a new constitution had been promulgated, and Horacio Vásquez had been elected president. A combination of relative freedom and order existed, and the government enjoyed a legitimacy that few governments in Dominican history had enjoyed. The several elite groups appeared to have accommodated their differences. The economy was booming, culture was thriving, and the Church was increasing in strength. The country appeared to have caught up with its Latin American sister republics.

The surface calm, however, was deceptive. The Dominican Republic still lacked a system of viable institutions. Personalistic and family feuds were still divisive. A rivalry existed between the older landowning elements and the newer business-commercial groups. A new middle class, together with a nascent organized labor movement, had grown up, beginning to demand greater participation in national life. Surface tranquility temporarily disguised the increased pluralism of groups and viewpoints and the diffuse discontent existing underneath. By 1929 President Vásquez had lost both his health and his support, and the following year the collapse of the world market began to hurt the all-important Dominican sugar industry. The crash served as catalyst for the rising discontent; and when in 1930 the inevitable revolution was launched against the Vásquez government, it quickly fell. That same year Trujillo gained the presidency.

THE TRUJILLO REGIME: DICTATORSHIP AND DEVELOPMENT

The dictatorship of Generalissimo Rafael Trujillo, 1930-61, was probably the strongest, most pervasive, and most absolute dictatorship ever to be established in Latin America (98, 161, 371, 529). Trujillo did not share power with anyone but maintained all power in his own hands. Trujillo's regime, however, was not just another in the long line of Dominican caudillo dictatorships, for the Trujillo era marked a watershed in the nation's history. During Trujillo's long rule, the process of national development was greatly accelerated. Trujillo dragged, at enormous social and human costs, his country out of the traditional semifeudal, agrarian past and into the modern era. He attempted to fill the historic institutional vacuum through the creation of numerous official, government-run political groups and agencies that disappeared as soon as he did. Trujillo disrupted the old structure of society in the Dominican Republic, but he created little of permanence to replace it. Dominican development was again atrophied (530, 558).

For thirty-one years Trujillo governed his country in an imperious fashion that has seldom been equaled. The personal power of the dictator was nearly absolute; and the vast web of controls established over the armed forces, governmental machinery, national economy, communications, education, intellectual life, and thought processes, together with his long-time harmonious arrangements with the Church and the United States, meant that no group, institution, or individual could function independently of Trujillo's control.

The total system of control was considerably greater than merely the sum of its parts; Trujillo's talents as an organizer and leader enabled him to weld together the various control mechanisms into an interlocking honeycomb of power that was probably as unbreakable as the world had ever seen.

It would not be accurate to label Trujillo's regime Fascist or Nazi, for it was essentially the story of a single individual and his personal power. Nor was it simply a form of traditional Caesarism, for this categorization ignores the dynamics of social and political change occurring in the Dominican Republic during this period and, hence, fails to account for what was "modern" in Trujillo's rule. While Trujillo's regime was not wholly traditional, it was not fully totalitarian either. Coming to power in 1930 in a nation where the first stirrings of modernization were only beginning, Trujillo began his rule in much the same way as had other traditional Latin American dictators. His initial power base was the military, which enabled him to take over the governmental machinery. During the 1930s and early 1940s, the Trujillo regime was not unlike those of similarly based and similarly oriented caudillos.

Trujillo began his lengthy rule as a typical man on horseback, but his regime eventually went far beyond the model of traditional dictatorship. Trujillo employed techniques and a system of control which became increasingly like modern totalitarianism. Control over the armed forces and the governmental machinery enabled him to convert the national economy into a gigantic national corporation owned by the ruling family. Greatly improved communications and transportation systems enabled the regime to build up the power of the central state. These and other technological advances made it possible for Trujillo to control intellectual and educational life and to impose a system of thought control. A single official party was created and the terroristic police apparatus became technologically more proficient. All intermediate organizations, such as the new interest associations, corporate, professional, business, and labor groups, were both creatures of the state and dominated by it.

The major reasons why this transformation from simple caudilloism to a more modern form of dictatorship, from an authoritarian-personalistic regime to one of more elaborate corporate controls, took place center around economic development, industrialization, and overall national modernization and their accompanying social and political effects. In the early years of the Trujillo era, the Dominican Republic remained an agrarian, preindustrial, premodern society. Modern kinds of organizations, such as political parties, a professionalized military and bureaucracy, and associational interest groups, were either nonexistent or still in the nascent stage. In this type of society, totalitarianism was not only technologically impossible but there was no need for it.

Rapid economic growth, particularly during World War II and the postwar years, and overall national modernization sparked the set of interrelated processes that ultimately led the dictatorship itself to modernize its techniques of control (237). New social classes emerged and new ideas concerning the way society should be organized filtered in. The beginning of the widespread use of more totalitarian methods corresponded almost exactly with the beginnings of the transition to a more modern, industrialized society. Industrialization gave rise to new trade unions and other kinds of associational groups whose members became conscious of their diverging interests and of their collective strengths--a development which potentially threatened Trujillo and prompted him to subject these groups to strict official direction. During this same period Trujillo began consciously to formulate an official ideology based on organicist and corporatist ideas (529). Similarly, the rise in mass consciousness prompted Trujillo to establish corporatist-style branch associations for everyone under the rubric of the official party. Trujillo's complex network of controls was necessitated not only by the fact that rapid modernization gave rise to new groups which potentially threatened the regime but also because Trujillo's desire to promote growth and his own aggrandizement made him increasingly dependent on the same skilled labor force, professionals, etc., he sought to control.

The trend toward a more modern kind of dictatorship in the Dominican Republic grew out of Trujillo's attempt to maintain his absolute personal power while also making rapid economic growth and national development compatible with the prevention of the growth of the forces which these processes spawned or their suppression where they had already emerged. The techniques he used served to break up the new groups and corporate units which tend to emerge in a rapidly modernizing society. The postwar Trujillo regime involved one strong man's attempt to harness the great wave of social, economic, political, and ideological changes which were occurring throughout Latin America during this period.

Trujillo was not a conscious revolutionary. He had rejected the antecedent system because it had led to instability and national humiliation; he proposed a new order based on authority, organic order, and material progress. He desired no society-wide upheaval. Trujillo had no desire to overthrow the old order, only to command it. He sought to resurrect the system of Heureaux and use it for his own personal power and national advancement, not to topple the system per se or even to effect fundamental changes in it. In Trujillo's ideology and the writings of his major advisers, the resurrection of a strong, authoritarian, and corporativist state with a strong emphasis on order and hierarchy is a constant, permeating theme. Trujillo wanted a more modern nation, but he wanted it under his absolute hegemony and with none of the social and political side effects (such as increased pluralism) that ordinarily accompany these changes. Trujillo sought to dominate the sociopolitical forces he had unleashed and was thus forced to use more stringent measures of control. He sought to resurrect the old Spanish authoritarian system at a time when the changes that had occurred in his country made it increasingly difficult to do so. He thus used the modern propaganda and control techniques of this century to help maintain his own absolute political power, bottle up popular aspirations, and hold back the tide of revolutionary social and political change. The inevitable explosion of all these forces came only after Trujillo had passed from the scene.

Dictatorships like Trujillo's seem to be products of the transition from tradition to modernity. They tend to appear at a time of breakdown of the old order when no new order has been established. The transitional dictator is a product of the societal cleavages and discontinuities which ordinarily accompany the early stages of industrialization and modernization. He usually rules in a deeply divided society where new demands and conflicts are becoming rampant. The transitional dictator may become an embryonic nation-builder, unifying his country for the first time behind a new ideology or his own person, asserting greater national independence, building communications and transportation systems, constructing new institutions such as the army or the civil service, and centralizing authority (567).

If Trujillo had been only another in the long line of Dominican caudillos, the legacy of his rule would not have been so enormous. But Trujillo's regime signaled a turning point in Dominican history; in many ways his long era, however undemocratic, was part of a transition to modernity. The Trujillo regime represented the end of the country's older semifeudal order. In his effort to promote economic growth and development, Trujillo helped break down the traditional order. Roads were built, radios acquired, and overall transportation and communications improved. Concurrently, previously isolated elements were beginning to be uprooted, organized, and imbued with new ideological and value systems. The entire society became more complex; new institutions were created; associational life became more differentiated. While many of these changes constitute the essence of modernization, they also provided in the Dominican context the basis for the growth of more totalitarian controls (129). Trujillo undermined the old order, but the new groups and organizations which had begun to rise were strictly subordinated to the regime. Trujillo's absolute personal control meant that, upon his death, no group or institution could begin to fill the void.

The legacy Trujillo bequeathed the Dominican Republic was a jumbled mixture of old and new, traditional and modern. The armed forces had been built up, centralized, and to some degree professionalized and modernized; but most of its members knew only the corrupt, oppressive habits of the Trujillo era. The government service had been greatly strengthened, but nepotism and corruption had become deeply ingrained habits. The political and corporative agencies, such as parties and labor organizations, which Trujillo established were largely shams, artificial fronts to disguise the excesses of the regime, and most of them disintegrated once the Trujillo family dictatorship collapsed. The economy had expanded, but much of the wealth had been drained off or wastefully used. What there was of social and political solidarity had been destroyed. Both the Church and the United States were shackled by their long-time close association with and support of the dictatorship.

From 1930-61 Trujillo had exercised absolute control over almost all aspects of Dominican, social, political, economic, military, educational, and intellectual life. Because near-total control had been concentrated in his hands, his death produced a near-total vacuum. Few Dominicans knew anything but life under Trujillo, and the entire nation was inexperienced in any other system. The institutions and traditions which might have made for a peaceful and orderly succession after the dictator's assassination in 1961 were wholly lacking. As the martyred Jesús de Galíndez foresaw in the mid-1950s:

> The future of the country may well be chaotic, because there are neither sociopolitical forces nor democratic institutions to facilitate a normal succession the day the tyrant disappears. . . . The greatest danger in the Dominican Republic is that nothing has been left standing. There are no political parties, there are no leaders with authority, there are no doctrines. Everything must begin again from the beginning (161).

The Trujillo dictatorship rechanneled, but also perverted, the course of Dominican development. He took the country in an authoritarian-corporatist direction. While one could argue this was in accord with the Dominican tradition, the sixteenth-century ideal, and the developmental example of Heureaux, Trujillo's rule was so bloody, so oppressive, and so oriented toward serving the megalomania and bank accounts of one man that it was unacceptable. At the end of his rule, not only had the vestiges of liberalism and republicanism been wiped out, but an authoritarian-corporatist solution had been entirely discredited as well. The result was a vacuum, which led directly to breakdown and national disintegration.

THE CONTEMPORARY PERIOD: ELITES IN CRISIS

While Trujillo's rule had been characterized by monolithic control over all aspects of Dominican life, the period since his death has been marked by the frenetic, tumultuous, frequently chaotic activities of a society emerging from the dark despair of thirty-one years of dictatorship but lacking the requisite institutions to enable a viable political system--be it democratic or any other kind--to develop. The post-Trujillo period may be seen as the emergence from near-total control over all corporate groups to a pattern of free associability and almost complete subsystem autonomy, with no central directing nucleus or agreed-upon principles.

Following the overthrow of the Trujillo regime in 1961, the groups which had formerly been tightly controlled by it became independent, and a variety of new organizations--political parties, labor unions, etc.--were formed. A large number of independent intermediaries or secondary organizations came into existence to vie for political advantage; replacing the dictatorship, a multigroup or pluralist system began to emerge. An interim government was formed, elections held, and a new democratic regime inaugurated. Yet in a very short time, the emerging new system broke down almost completely. Why?

The reasons for the breakdown of the Dominican system were

many, fundamental, and cumulative (538). Many Dominicans assumed
that the overthrow of Trujillo would immediately usher in a better
era of prosperity and social justice. But the restructuring of the
nation could not be achieved overnight. The demand for the benefits of modern life outran the capacity of the government to satisfy those demands; frustration quickly set in. Economic growth
occurred, but few benefits trickled down; the gap between rich and
poor widened; in an era of rising revolutionary aspirations, the
standard of living of the bulk of the population actually went
down. Too many changes were sought in too short a time, and the
fragile Dominican institutions that were hurriedly organized after
the death of the dictator could not be rapidly enough developed to
handle the new demands thrust upon them. Failure, disappointment,
frustration, and disillusionment fanned the flames of revolutionary
sentiment.

Whether a society can bridge the transition from tradition to
modernity hinges to a large extent on the integration of the various elites active in its politics. The process requires the assimilation of new groups and values and the preservation of traditional ones. It requires both change and continuity. If a balance between the contending forces is not maintained, the political system
may become disintegrated and collapse. The success of a modernizing government may in large measure be gauged by its ability to
integrate its various heterogeneous components into a community.
As the society modernizes and becomes more differentiated and complex, the integration process tends to become more problematic
(259).

The concept of integration is an especially useful one to
apply to the Dominican Republic. The majority of the population--
especially lower-class urban workers, rural peasants, and some middle-sector elements--had remained outside national decision-making;
in Anderson's terms (21), the legitimacy of these power contenders
had not as yet been recognized. When the democratic Bosch government inaugurated in 1963 attempted to govern for and in the name of
these previously ignored sectors and to integrate them into the national life, it met with the concerted opposition of the more traditional elements. These latter groups, who desired a return to
the peace and order of the pre-Trujillo period, viewed the Bosch
government as illegitimate and were determined to subvert it. The
speed and methods of Bosch and his party in carrying out changes
with regard to mass education and mobilization antagonized some who
would not otherwise have been so disaffected, but it is difficult
not to conclude that important elements in the Church, military,
and business-commercial-landowning elites were hostile to and plotting against the Bosch government even before its inauguration.
Given the disruptive, increasingly polarized forces existing, they
would undoubtedly have found one pretext or another to mobilize
against the Bosch government. The failure of these same status
quo-oriented groups, once they had reinstituted a government more
in harmony with their own preferences, to more rapidly accept the
assimilation of newer groups, resulted, ultimately, in the popular
upheaval of 1965.

The Dominican Republic is currently facing a participation

crisis of awesome proportions. Because of the long Trujillo era and the exceedingly small base on which the regime rested, the participation crisis there is of greater dimension than elsewhere in Latin America. The wants and demands accumulating for more than three decades spilled over all at once. Because of the Trujillo dictatorship, the Dominican Republic never developed in the 1930s, 1940s, and 1950s the moderately reformist middle-class parties and other middle-sector moderating forces that evolved elsewhere in Latin America; beginning in the 1960s, the emerging Dominican middle groups began to demand all those privileges from which they had so long been deprived. But the 1960s were also an era of greatly increased mass demands. All the Latin American nations are currently facing participation crises in the form of new demands on the part of the middle and popular classes for a greater share in national decision-making and the wealth of their societies; but what makes the Dominican situation unique is that middle-sector and lower-sector demands both found a particularly virulent expression at exactly the same time. This was complicated by the status quo-oriented forces' unwillingness to recognize that any social change at all had occurred during the Trujillo era and their desire to return to the status quo ante. Participation crises--first from the middle and then the lower sectors--have sorely tried even the most highly developed political systems, but taken gradually and in sequence some nations have been able to weather these crises. In the Dominican case, however, the fact that all the pressures piled up at once, plus the fact the country had almost no institutional structures to deal with them, helps explain why politics in the post-Trujillo era was a form of permanent crisis (353).

The modernization process necessarily entails an uneven distribution of political advantage and implies the reordering of society and some form of accommodation among its various elites. Traditional interests are likely to be dislocated, while the modernizing elements receive new opportunities for advancement. The old stratification system may be disrupted while new escalators for the traditionally deprived groups appear. The old equilibrium may be undermined; the emerging new society is liable to be marked by such violence and instability that the traditional concepts of the consensus theorists are likely to be irrelevant and misleading. If change comes too abruptly--the Bosch administration, the 1965 revolution--the "system" may break down and the traditional sectors may rebel. If change is too slow--as under the Council of State, the Triumvirate, the Balaguer administration--new leaders and new coalitions may emerge that see the possibilities for development only through revolutionary means. In either case, the different actors in national affairs may become autonomous centers of power, isolated from each other and with few mechanisms of accommodation between them (333). The failure of interelite communication, to say nothing of accommodation, is likely and, in the Dominican case, did lead to national paralysis and collapse.

The reasons why a transitional nation with a weak intermediate group structure may lead, on the one hand, to monolithic regimes like Trujillo's and, on the other, to chaos and anarchy also helps explain why the strength of such intermediaries characterizes highly developed pluralist democracies. Kornhauser warns that democracy requires the existence of a plurality of groups that are similar enough in strength to generate genuine competition and yet prevent any one group, or any alliance of them, from wholly dominating the society (249). In the Dominican case, the more status quo-oriented groups--the armed forces, the Church, the business-landowning-commercial elites, the U.S. Embassy--were able to exercise more influence in national affairs than the newer, modernizing forces; and when they had an issue on which they could unite--such as opposition to the Bosch government or to the revolutionary movement of 1965--they were able to protect their interests and prevent the radical restructuring of society. And yet, the Dominican Republic is no longer such a traditional "banana republic" that a handful of military officers, clerics, oligarchs, and U.S. Embassy personnel can wholly dominate national life. The middle sectors have emerged as a major influence and the popular sectors have by this time been aroused. The dilemma of Dominican development is that progressive governments cannot survive in the face of the concerted opposition of the traditional groups; that the traditional order has lost its legitimacy and cannot last long; and that the moderate middle way is not only weak and generally unacceptable to either the "parties of order" or the "parties of movement" but it is also virtually nonexistent.

In the Dominican Republic, the traditional corporate elites are more cohesive and better organized than the forces for change. Clearly, the degree of unity a group has and the extent to which it is organized are fundamental in determining its measure of success. Though some differences exist within their ranks, both the military and the Church, perhaps because of their hierarchical and orderly chain of command, perhaps because of some fundamental agreement within the ranks on their institutional and corporate self-interests, are relatively cohesive and well-organized; the business-profession-landowning element, while not as tightly organized, is also cohesive and has the advantage of being a primal or face-to-face group, in which everyone knows everyone else or is interrelated in a vast web of personal, familial, and social connections. The newer modernizing political parties, labor organizations, and peasant associations, in contrast, are fluid and fragmented, weakly organized, and not cohesive. It is precisely this configuration that constituted the lineup of forces arrayed, respectively, in opposition to and in support of the Bosch-led reformist and constitutionalist movement; and it should not be surprising that the relatively strong, well-organized, and cohesive forces of order and the status quo should be able to overcome the relatively weak, disorganized, and disunited forces for change (29, 107, 303).

A basic lack of consensus on the ends or means of political action is another characteristic of the Dominican system. A functioning system does not require a single common orientation of all its members toward the government, but it does require a minimum shared basis of values and acceptance of the "rules of the game" (416). In the Dominican Republic, however, the old values that held the traditional society together are no longer so widely shared; yet no new system of consensus has emerged to fill the ideological vacuum, and there is no one single group that any longer can claim its legitimate "right to rule." Further, the newer middle sectors and the rising urban labor class have less sense of rank and hierarchy than do the older, more traditional elements, and the new groups are thus not necessarily wedded to the absolute legitimacy of the old order. The dissensus is reinforced by the country's feudal tradition and its historic system of class-caste stratifications, which divide society into vertical as well as horizontal sectors with little contact, let alone agreement, between them. The political system is rigid and unyielding with each class and corporate group having its own status, responsibilities, and behavioral patterns. Each sector tends to become autonomous in its own sphere with few shared values and contacts with other groups. The old corporate ideal of social and political organization has been retained, but in its present form it is not very functional. There is also little overlapping membership between the various groups, thus reinforcing the dissensus and preserving the pattern whereby each individual tends to go "all out" for his own single loyalty and to view differences in an absolutist, non-compromisable, either-or light (185, 217). The groups and associations in the national life have become monolithic, insulated from one another--not just socially, psychologically, and economically but geographically as well--and this, too, produces a lack of moderation and perpetuates the fragmented nature of the society.

The emergence of a more pluralist system in the Dominican Republic has not led to a stable and democratic polity on the Western European-North American model; rather, the effect has been just the opposite. In the United States the pluralist system that was institutionalized beginning in the 1930s has proved to be the foundation of a more democratic society; in the Dominican Republic, the emerging pluralist system has acquired neither legitimacy nor institutionalization. In Latin America generally, in fact, increased pluralism has generated increased fragmentation, even sharper differentiations among social groups, and the breakdown of national solidarity. In the absence of a system of overlapping multiple allegiances or of horizontal integration, the result has been societal disintegration. In the corporate fashion, Dominican history, for example, has always been characterized by the strict compartmentalization of vertical groups, a system that was manageable so long as the number of groups remained few and they all shared certain primary values; in the present situation, however, the number of groups has increased and there is no longer any common basis of understanding between them. The old corporativist structure seems no longer workable and is prone to periodic breakdown.

The Dominican Republic's lack of consensus may also be considered a crisis of legitimacy. Consensus and legitimacy are intimately related; indeed, Lipset has defined legitimacy as the degree to which the political system is generally accepted by the population--i.e., consensus (271). Particularly relevant to the Dominican case are Lipset's comments that groups regard the system as legitimate or illegitimate to the extent they share primary values and to the degree the system has been able effectively to satisfy their demands. Important groups in Dominican society no longer share the primary values on which the old order was based; nor have a succession of Dominican governments been able effectively to implement programs designed to meet rising revolutionary aspirations. Important elements of the dominant political party, the labor movement, and the middle class came to reject the interim Council of State that emerged as a caretaker following the ouster of the Trujillos and were opposed to the post-Bosch Triumvirate because both were regarded as illegitimate. For the same reason, the armed forces, Church, and economic oligarchy rejected the Bosch regime and the 1965 "constitutionalist" movement. The prevailing value system of those in office was too much at variance with those out of office. In the absence of sufficient legitimacy to govern effectively, all Dominican governments during this period were forced to devote more and more of their efforts to the politics of survival rather than to sorely needed social reform programs.

The development of new kinds of organizations following the death of Trujillo, the rapid mobilization of the population, and the phenomenal rise in popular expectations contributed to the Dominican Republic's legitimacy crisis. Crises of legitimacy, Lipset writes (271), are primarily a recent historical phenomenon produced by new, sharper cleavages among the groups participating in the political process. These cleavages stem from broad-scale societal modernization and differentiation and increase the possibilities for conflict between the more traditional groups and the newer forces. In the absence of any shared primary values and with few mediating mechanisms, this clash resulted ultimately in revolution and civil war.

"A crisis of legitimacy is a crisis of change," Lipset writes, and is most likely to occur in transitional nations given two conditions. The first condition is that all major groups have not been able to secure access to the political system; the second is that the status of the more traditional groups is threatened. Both these conditions existed in the post-Trujillo Dominican Republic. Groups which have regular access to decision-making need not engage in violence; groups which do not may feel this is the only way of exerting pressure. In the Dominican Republic, the gaps between rich and poor became greater at a time when the poor were increasingly disinclined to accept these "immutable" differences with resignation and when they eventually came to feel they had little to lose by violence. Increasing numbers were frustrated and disillusioned by the failure of the political system to achieve reform by peaceful means and came to see revolution as the only alternative. The status quo-oriented forces saw their traditional privileges increasingly threatened and mobilized in 1963 and 1965 to launch counterrevolutionary movements. The overall result was intermittent systemic breakdowns.

If a rapidly changing nation is to maintain any measure of order and its government remain viable, bargaining and compromise are required. Since a feature of modern society is a growing multiplicity of interests and since modernization brings on new social and political differentiations, the very plurality of interests makes such balance and compromise mandatory (461). In the societies born of Spain, however, the inherently corporativist and vertically structured systems have proved often to be incapable of forging such accommodation. Bargaining and compromise were not often characteristic of post-Trujillo Dominican politics; the gaps by this time were too wide to be reconciled peacefully through negotiation. Soon the several corporate bodies, societal sectors, parties, private associations, and individuals were all flying off in noncommunicating orbits; and eventually the repulsion of some of these forces for others culminated in revolt and civil war.

It is a combination of these basic factors which ultimately caused the revolution and civil war of 1965. Dominican political groups and societal sectors were highly fragmented, and they became increasingly polarized; the society was highly unintegrated; there was a decided imbalance among the several political groups, with government and the national wealth being dominated by the few at the expense of the many; successive governments were considered illegitimate by large blocs of the population; deep fissures stratified and divided the society both horizontally and vertically; there was little consensus on the means and ends of political action; and the political system itself proved unable to cope with the new demands and responsibilities suddenly thrust upon it. Given these conditions, it is not surprising that the system broke down.

In Huntington's terms (212), the Dominican Republic in the post-Trujillo era presented an almost classic case of "praetorian politics"--a system where the rapid expansion of political participation had far outpaced the development of political institutions. Praetorian politics is characterized by the fragility and fleetingness of <u>all</u> forms of authority, by violence and naked power displays, and by the chaotic oscillation between different types of political regimes. It usually is characteristic of the early stages of modernization and is closely associated with the disintegration of an outmoded old order and the rise of a decapitated new one. Praetorian politics occur where there is a low degree of social cohesion, where civic institutions lack legitimacy, where there are fratricidal class and other conflicts, where social polarity has set in and a nonconsolidated middle class exists, where the level of group social action is on the rise but where the political parties and government institutions are weak and ineffective, where there is little sense of community, and where there is a praetorian army. In Latin America, with its pyramidal, class-riven, and sectoral-corporatist structures, praetorian politics may be a long-lived, even permanent characteristic of the political system.

Trujillo paved the way for the emergence of praetorian politics in the Dominican Republic. During his era a proletariat had sprung up, but no strong and independent labor organization was permitted. A new middle class had also emerged, but it lacked cohesion. The various interest and professional associations served only to praise Trujillo and enabled him to control more tightly their members' activities. Expanding educational opportunities and communications networks brought more Dominicans into national life; but other than the official agencies created by the dictatorship, no means had been established to help organize and integrate these new participants. Hence, when Trujillo was assassinated and the entire apparatus of the dictatorship collapsed, the country was left with practically no institutional infrastructure. And in the absence of strong institutions and a functioning political system, Dominican politics tended to be unstable and chaotic. Political life is characterized by the raw and frequently brutal pursuit, display, and exercise of power, unrefined by such moderating intermediaries as a strong party system, an effective congress or bureaucracy, or many well-balanced and reconcilable interest associations. The group norms tend to be violent; by the same token, violence or the threat of violence are consciously used by different groups to achieve their political purposes. The rise of new groups and classes has led not to pluralism on the Northern European-North American model but only to an increase in what seems to be endemic violence. Hence, Dominican politics must be approached from the point of view that turbulence, force, and institutional discontinuity are normal and to be expected, while stability, continuity, and peaceful evolutionary change are abnormal and unlikely (280).

The Dominican Republic is neither a wholly traditional nor a wholly modern system but an unstable blend of both. It is characterized by heterogeneous and overlapping patterns, by the uneasy coexistence of social and political forms stemming from different epochs. The political society has become extremely fragmented and with few ties to hold it together. Fragmented political cultures are usually produced as a result of different and uneven levels of political socialization and recruitment. Different societal sectors and subgroups have **radically** different socialization experiences which lead them to have radically diverging perceptions of the best way to organize society and polity. In the absence of workable accommodating agencies, this leads to almost a jungle system where the strongest use brute force to rule, irrespective of traditional civilizing and humanizing considerations (15).

If Dominican society and politics were highly fragmented, dissensual, fissured, fragmented, imbalanced, unintegrated, and dysfunctional before the April 1965 uprising, they have become even more so since that time. The revolution and the U.S. intervention tore apart and nearly destroyed whatever there was of social and political solidarity. Dominican society had become increasingly polarized before the 1965 upheaval, though it took the revolution to make the extreme degree of this disintegrative process clear. The Bosch administration had accelerated the process of polarization by proposing to govern for the poor and by denying to the traditional elites the place and role to which they had historically been accustomed. Eventually, these latter groups came together and promoted the overthrow of the Bosch government. As power was then returned to the status quo-oriented elements, the forces for change were persecuted and deprived of a share in national decision-making. The polarization process eventually culminated in the revolution when the various sectors were forced to choose sides in a bitter, fratricidal civil war, and it has continued with few discernible trends toward reconciliation to the present.

Tensions that before the revolution had existed only beneath the surface became open and frequently violent conflicts. Almost every group active in Dominican politics has been further fragmented, divided, and polarized; the disintegrative forces have been accelerated. Not only were the divisions increased between labor and employers, peasants and landlords, military and civilian elements, clerical and anticlerical forces, rich and poor, the United States and Dominican nationalists, the powerful and the powerless, the various political parties and student groups, but the tensions and fragmentation within each of these sectors has been aggravated and intensified as well. The various corporate interests and social and political groups have not only grown farther apart from each other but they have been deeply divided internally as well. Even those institutions which had helped provide a measure of continuity despite the disintegration occurring all about them--the family and long-standing personal and social ties--were torn apart by the revolution and the issues it precipitated. Dominican society and its political system broke down entirely (538).

In the language of political science, a variety of terms may be used to describe a political system in which there is virtually no consensus and in which the various centrifugal forces are in such distant orbits that they have almost no contact and communication with each other or attachment to a central nucleus. The type of situation existing in the Dominican Republic may be described as one of political anomie, a situation in which diversity and pluralism have become so complete that it has made for a disintegrated social condition with no apparent common purpose (116). Dahl described a system in which the various interests were so far apart that they resembled "independent sovereignties" (103). Riggs used the phrase "prismatic society" as a shorthand way of describing the distinct "colorations" that are refracted through the prism of transitional systems (423). It matters little what terminology or metaphors are used; what is important is to recognize that the Dominican revolution, civil war, U.S. intervention, and many subsequent events resulted in the almost total disintegration of the national social and political infrastructure. The social and political fabric has torn; the slim threads still barely holding the country together are weak, overextended, and ready to snap at any time.

The stress so far has been almost exclusively on the disintegrative tendencies in the Dominican system because these seem to be paramount; but there are some integrating factors that need to be mentioned. Dominican nationalism is on the rise and may help provide the unity that the country now sorely lacks; similarly, the fact the country was able to stand up to the North Americans during the 1965 revolution has given rise to a new sense of pride in things Dominican and to a cultural flowering that may help provide the indigenous cement to help hold the society together. A variety of new development agencies has since sprung up whose long-term effects on the process of nation-building may be considerable. Similarly, there are a number of groups that have begun to bridge some of the gaps that divide Dominicans. Despite these new linkages and mechanisms for change and accommodation, the disintegrative aspects currently seem to outweigh the integrative features.

All this emphasis on the politics of chaos and turbulence,

furthermore, should not serve to obscure the patterns and regularities that exist. Dominican political coalitions are usually shifting and short-lived with little pretense to ideology or principle, its political leaders more often than not demagogues and opportunists, and its political life disoriented and disordered. Nevertheless, there are some patterns emerging that may well carry more importance for the future than these immediate features. First, it is clear that the old order in the Dominican Republic is giving way--and at an accelerating pace--and that the newer bases of power are expanding. And despite the existence of a fragmented, heterogeneous, polypartite system, the country seems to be more basically divided into two major camps, what Dominicans often refer to as two major "families," each motivated by different sets of assumptions and perceptions of the world. The traditional labels, "left" and "right," "liberal" and "conservative," may not be a wholly appropriate way to designate these two camps; however, it is essential to understand that, despite the disorder and chaos that mark the political system as a whole and despite the frequent contradictions and discord that exist even within these two "families," Dominican politics have come to reflect more and more this fundamental alignment: between those who desire the preservation of order, status, special privileges, and hierarchy and those who desire movement; between those who at all costs seek to preserve the status quo or even return to an earlier, more peaceable era and those who by different means seek to alter it, between the forces for tradition and the forces for change. This basic division of the political system closely parallels the fundamental class and societal divisions discussed in preceding paragraphs. Admittedly, this paradigm oversimplifies what is a more complex phenomenon, but it should serve to alert us that beneath the sheer chaos which is superficially the most obvious characteristic of Dominican politics in the last decade are some newer patterns and emerging regularities that are likely to be of even greater significance (1).

The Dominican political system undoubtedly benefitted from the postrevolution interim regime of Héctor García-Godoy and, initially, from the subsequent elected and constitutional government of Joaquín Balaguer. But the larger issues which the revolution tragically and unmistakably brought to the surface have not so far been solved or even adequately faced up to. They relate to the future role of such corporate and specially privileged entities as the Church and the armed forces, the vast gaps in terms of wealth and status that exist between the several sectors of the population, the attempt on the part of certain elite groups to enhance their positions and on the part of other power contenders to find their legitimate place in the system, the divisive questions centering around the appropriate constitutional and juridical organization of the nation, the desirability and manner of instituting social and economic reforms, the growing desire of the Dominicans for control over their own destinies without foreign influence, and the role of such nonindigenous groups as the United States in Dominican affairs.

García-Godoy weathered a stormy interim period, muted some severe conflicts, and managed to stay in office--no small accomplishments in the rocky Dominican political system. García-Godoy, however, was unable to make more than a minor dent in resolving the fundamental issues listed above. The relatively simple expedients of the withdrawal of foreign troops, the holding of U.S.-supervised elections, the inauguration of the Balaguer government, the promulgation of a new constitution, and the promotion of moderate and conciliatory policies on the part of Balaguer helped relieve some of the immediate pressures, too (472). But these accomplishments should not mask the severe, long-term damage that the social and political system has incurred. Surface tranquility barely hides the disintegration of the nation. The atmosphere of terror and discord persists; those opposed to the government or to the military are frequently beaten and sometimes "disappear" without a trace. None of the scars of the revolution has been healed. Disputes which in other systems may be resolved with a minimum of conflict are still frequently disputed in violent clashes in the Dominican Republic. It must be remembered that the dispatch of U.S. troops and their interposition between the contending Dominican forces represented merely the interruption of the 1965 revolution and not its resolution, the temporary snuffing out of the revolutionary spark but not of the smouldering volcano underneath. The Dominican Republic now appears relatively calm and peaceful on the surface and its people have retained their traditional affability, but this is still a boiling cauldron which is liable to explode again at almost any time. It is unlikely that the full disintegrative effects of the decline of the old order and the fragmentation of the new will shortly or easily permit a new accommodation, a new elite equilibrium, or any kind of functioning, viable system in the Dominican Republic.

CONCLUSION

The evolving pattern of Dominican politics provides ample illustration of the pervasive and continuing corporatist influence that seems intrinsic to the Iberic and Latin American nations. In the Dominican case, we have traced the origins of the peculiarly corporatist, hierarchical, authoritarian, two-class, and semifeudal system back to late-medieval Spain and to the institutions and practices which Spain transferred to the New World during the first half-century of the conquest. Thereafter, we discussed the consolidation and hardening of the system during nearly three centuries of colonial rule, its isolation from the modernizing currents of the modern world, the persistence of the corporatist ideal even in times of colonial neglect, and its perpetuation on into the independence period. We then discussed the rise of the forces and pressures during the late nineteenth and early twentieth centuries that began to undermine the traditional order, its collapse in 1930, the wrenching experience of the transitional Trujillo dictatorship, and the eventual collapse and disintegration of the system in the 1960s. Though in many respects the Dominican experience has been unique, it is likely a number of the patterns and themes discussed here may be relevant to the analysis of other Latin American nations.

Several points from the discussion of corporatism in the Dominican Republic merit special attention and deserve further study. The first has to do with what seems an historic and almost natural proclivity of Dominican elites, from 1492 to the present, for a corporatist form of society, for what we might call "natural corporatism." However, after the first "glorious" fifty years of the colony, a decline set in which led to the atrophy of its social and political institutions and the virtual absence of any kind of organizational structure, corporatist or whatever. The repeated Haitian invasions and occupations of the nineteenth century further retarded Dominican development and led to a situation of an almost complete organizational vacuum in which sheer power, force, and clan politics became the prevailing--and persisting--norms. The Dominican Republic throughout the nineteenth century and on into the twentieth had neither the corporatist institutions of its colonial past nor the newer liberal and representative ones that its constitutions proclaimed. As a result, chaos and disorder reigned.

Nevertheless, the sixteenth-century organicist, corporatist, structured, and authoritarian model remained the ideal to which Dominican governing elites continued to strive. The two leaders who came closest to resurrecting the ancient model were Heureaux and Trujillo; and while both these dictators were often admired for their accomplishments, they were also condemned for their excesses. Particularly interesting in this regard were Trujillo's efforts to construct a manifestly corporatist order to go along with the country's "natural corporatist" tendencies, and how these government-run and -controlled agencies came to be despised and did not long survive the end of the dictatorship.

While Trujillo's growing totalitarianism was unacceptable, inorganic democracy has not worked very well in the Dominican Republic either. In all of Dominican history there have been only three brief experiments with inorganic democracy--one in the 1870s, one in 1963 under Bosch, and one begun in 1978. The first two failed ingloriously; the third has still to prove itself. This is not to say that democracy in the Dominican Republic cannot work. But it is to say the country is still searching for and has not yet found a political formula that accommodates its natural and historic preference for corporatism but without this resulting in Trujillo-style totalitarianism, and also its urge for liberty that does not lead to anarchy, chaos, and national collapse.

14

The Brazilian Catholic Labor Movement

The change and development process in Latin America has ordinarily occurred gradually, through adaptation and assimilation, within a framework that combines and reconciles traditional and modern. Owing to the absence of a revolutionary past in all but a few of the Latin American nations, traditional forms, ideologies, and classes pertaining to an earlier feudal, Catholic, patrimonialist and corporative society persist, coexisting with modern movements and currents. The Latin American political process typically involves the combination of diverse elements originating in quite different eras into a provisional, usually short-lived, working arrangement (21).

The traditional order in Latin America has proved to be remarkably resilient, bending enough to absorb some modernization without in the process altering the fundamental structure of society. Change is possible within this framework, but it has been of a tutelary sort, guided from above in a paternalistic fashion. The elitist elements in Latin America have accepted the features of modernity they could control, but they have sought to keep out the rest. The issue has been to fuse and reconcile the institutions of an older, authoritarian, corporatist, and patrimonialist order with the requirements of a more modern, urban, industrial, and pluralist one, not so much to achieve "development" in the North American or Western European sense. The prevailing elites have modernized their institutional paraphernalia and sought to coopt and absorb the newer social forces, meanwhile retaining their own hegemony (347). Until recently this essentially conservative process of gradual systemic adaptation and of elite integration and social control was managed smoothly without provoking major social conflict or systemic breakdowns. Now, however, under the increasing pressures of the contemporary period, the traditional structure has become more tenuous and the possibilities for breakdown greater. It is within this context that we examine the Brazilian Catholic labor movement.

Since World War II, the pace of social change in Brazil has

From H. J. Rosenbaum and W. G. Tyler (eds.), <u>Contemporary Brazil</u> (New York: Praeger, 1972).

accelerated. During this period, both the Brazilian Catholic
Church and the trade union movement have played crucial roles.
Both have struggled to adapt themselves to the changing social and
political realties of contemporary Brazil and to achieve relevance
and legitimacy in these fast-changing times. But while scholarly
work is beginning to appear on both the Church (57, 58) and the
labor movement (140, 141) in Brazil, there has been virtually no
analysis of the hybrid of the two, the Catholic labor movement
(513). This is unfortunate, for not only does the study of the
Catholic trade union organization help us understand better the
role of both labor and the Church in Brazil, but it also illustrates the blend of and clash between traditional and modern that
is characteristic of the nation as a whole. The Catholic labor
movement is not only interesting in its own right but takes on
greater significance for what it reveals about the Church, the Brazilian trade union movement, the functioning of the broader Brazilian system, and, indeed, the nature of the change process in Latin
America.

ORIGINS AND HISTORY

The origins of the Brazilian Catholic labor movement go back
to the "Catholic revival" of the 1920s and 1930s. Concerned by the
widening separation between the Church and Brazilian society, a
number of clerics and laymen sought to promote a rejuvenated Catholicism that answered the needs of the times (266, 446). Building upon a nucleus of mutual benefit associations that had been
formed previously, the first Workers' Circles (Círculos Operários)
were organized in the early 1930s, grew rapidly, and became a national movement in 1937 (a).

There were three major influences on the early Círculo movement. First was the Church's renewed concern with social problems,
particularly as expressed in the 1931 encyclical, Quadragesimo
Anno. Through its new social doctrine, the Church put emphasis on
the whole man--his material, educational, and social requirements
as well as his religious needs--and sought to present an alternative to communism. The second major influence was the corporate
and "integralist" ideas then current. Society was to be organized
in an organic, corporate fashion, based on class harmony and national unity rather than conflict--the organization of society by
function rather than through divisive interest groups and political
parties, and hence the integration of labor into the national "family" under the tutelage of the hegemonic state (496, 497, 500).
These two influences, the Catholic and the corporative, were neatly
combined in the program of Leopoldo Brentano, an Italian Jesuit
and the chief guiding spirit of the Workers' Circles during the
first two decades (6, 52-4).

The third influence was the regime of Getulio Vargas, which
provided a climate conducive to the growth of a Catholic labor
movement. Unlike his predecessors who had been hostile to labor,
Vargas befriended it and became its patron. He created a new ministry of labor, enacted new social programs for the workers, and
incorporated labor into his corporate state apparatus.

Particularly after the establishment of the Estado Novo in 1937, the whole context of labor relations was radically altered. Vargas declared that class conflict should be replaced by class harmony. To the delight of the Catholics, he purged the Communists, anarcho-syndicalists, and other radical influences from labor's ranks. He stated that it was the government's duty to resolve differences between workers and management; hence, both labor and employer groups were to be harmonized under his regime's aegis into organs of class collaboration. Thus, the labor movement became an official organization of the state and one of the prime institutional pillars of Vargas's corporate system (9).

In this context the Catholic Círculos Operários movement flourished. The climate was ripe for their growth and the government provided official favoritism. The movement received official recognition, its membership increased, and its position within the corporate structure was secured. Vargas's ministers eulogized the movement for its ability to conciliate disputes and asked the assistance of Catholic labor leaders in providing a social-Christian direction to the government's welfare programs. As one of the few grass-roots organizations existing in Brazil, the Workers' Circles helped administer a number of these new experiments. There was a strong two-way flow of ideas and personnel between the Catholic labor organization and the Vargas government. With the radical elements purged from the trade union structure, the Catholic labor organization was a logical choice for performing these functions (459, 422).

One reason why the Círculos were so "successful" during this period was that their aims remained so limited. The Círculo movement sought to work within the system rather than destroy it. This implied an accommodation with both Vargas's government and the traditional patronage system. The Círculos' activities were largely limited to charity, religious orientation, and anti-Communism. The Catholic Workers' Circles posed no threat to the established order and were, therefore, encouraged by it. The Círculos were as much agents of social control as of social change. For even though Vargas was the idol of Brazil's working class, he also kept a tight rein on the trade unions as a guarantee to businessmen that they would not gain too much power. He was particularly successful in "the art of getting money from the rich and support from the poor on the pretext of protecting each from the other" (222).

Upon the ouster of Vargas in 1945, the Catholic labor movement went into a decline. It no longer enjoyed the protection it had under Vargas. It was now forced to compete with more dynamic labor organizations. During Brazil's leap forward in the postwar period, the Catholic labor movement failed to keep pace. It was shackled by an outmoded world view, compromised by its close affiliation with government and employers, and inadequately organized to cope with the new and more "modern" society emerging in Brazil.

In the mid-1950s the Catholic labor movement attempted to reform itself. A new leadership replaced the aging clericals who had long dominated the Círculos. New programs were devised to give it a more labor-oriented direction. Catholic labor leaders gained influential positions in the trade union structure, associations for rural peasants were organized, and the Workers' Circles acquired a new dynamism. Catholic labor still represented a minority voice in organized labor, but with its new activities it had come a considerable distance from its earlier catechism classes and paternalistic charity activities (389, 483).

The 1960s were a crisis period for the Catholic labor movement as for all of Brazil. The Workers' Circles, now renamed the Confederação Brasileira de Trabalhadores Cristãos (CBTC), had significantly expanded their activities; but their leaders, particularly the clerical advisers, were apprehensive that this process would proceed too fast and get out-of-hand. During João Goulart's presidency, the pressures for greater labor militancy and a united labor front intensified; and while many of the rank-and-file leaders within the CBTC and radical Catholic peasant organizers in the Northeast favored such a move, the Church hierarchy was suspicious of Goulart's "leftism" and fearful that a united labor front would mean the submersion of Catholic labor into the Communist-dominated Comando Geral dos Trabalhadores (CBT). Because the Círculos failed to cooperate in this solidarity movement, however, many union leaders began to look on them as fundamentally antilabor. These disputes came to a head when the Catholic labor leadership supported the 1964 military-conservative coup against Goulart (b).

The support by Catholic leaders of the coup provoked a split in CBTC ranks. Some CBTC leaders felt that the coup would be beneficial, since the anticipated purge of the CBT, they reasoned, would leave the field open to the Catholic labor movement. They reported many Communists and leftists to the government and helped nominate "interventors" to "clean up" union leaderships. For these activities the CBTC lost much of its support among the labor leadership, youth, workers, and reform-oriented elements generally. The CBTC was also expelled from the Latin American regional organization of Christian-democratic trade unions, CLASC; and within Brazil a reformist rump group split off. Though this faction never gained much influence, the split illustrated the unhappy state of the Catholic labor movement. That the CBTC was the only labor organization in Brazil not to feel the full weight of military suppression following the 1964 takeover may be the most telling evidence of the weakness of the Catholic labor movement, its conservatism when the Church's own self-interests are at stake, and the fact that in an increasingly change-oriented national society, its identification is still with the defenders of an older and more traditional order.

In recent years a new effort has been made to modernize the Catholic labor movement. A new leadership has emerged, impatient with the paternalism of the past. New activities have been initiated, a new program is being articulated, and a new militancy is evident. The new leaders would like to dynamize the Catholic labor movement. They want a Church that speaks to the needs of these times, directed toward answering present-day demands, and genuinely working to alleviate the workers' plight. However, the question of whether the Church and its Catholic labor arm can succeed in making themselves more relevant to the aspirations of the Brazilian lower classes, and can reintegrate themselves into the mainstreams of

Brazilian national life, must remain open.

PROGRAMS, IDEOLOGY, OBJECTIVES

The fundamental tenets upon which the program of the Brazilian Catholic labor movement are based were contained in the papal encyclicals Rerum Novarum and Quadragesimo Anno. Rerum Novarum established three forces as essential for resolving the "labor problem" --Church, state, and the interested parties, employers and workers --and also made it a natural right for the workers to organize. Quadragesimo Anno extended this logic, providing an impetus to Christian-democratic movements and stating that the Christian trade unions ought to further the cultural, social, and religious, as well as the material, needs of the workers (565). These ideas provided the justification for, and could easily be accommodated with, the corporatist, integralist, and organicist theories of the state and society then current. In Vargas's Estado Novo this meant social justice for the workers achieved through close harmony between capital and labor and under the paternalistic guidance of the functionally representative, well-ordered, harmonized, and organic state (140).

The CBTC has been defined as a movement for the workers based upon the Church's social doctrines. Its purpose is to defend the Catholic faith and the welfare of the workers. It repudiated communism and class struggle, defends the sanctity of private property, recognizes the need for state intervention in the social question, and calls for collaboration between workers and employers. The movement derives its inspiration from social-Christian principles, provides the workers with Christian truths as well as material assistance, protects the hearth and home. Its functions include providing Christian education and social assistance, ennobling the working class, combating atheistic and materialistic doctrines, and coordinating the well-being of the workers (52-4).

Other manifestos provide similar statements of the CBTC's purposes. Its ideology was unabashedly Thomistic, Catholic, confessional, and corporatist. It sought to offer an alternative to communism, promote class solidarity rather than antagonism, provide a broad range of activities that would enable the Church to reintegrate itself into Brazilian national life, and adapt itself to such features of the era as urbanization and industrialization but, at the same time, to preserve the essence of a Catholic, patrimonialist order (485).

The Catholic labor movement's program received official sanction almost immediately. The Catholic-corporatist ideas on which it was based found a receptive soil in the Brazil of the 1930s. Many of the ideological aims of Catholic labor were incorporated into the Vargas constitutions of 1934 and 1937, helped provide the basis for the Estado Novo, and found their way into the government's social programs. Similarly, the nationalistic, anticommunist, and paternalistic orientation of the movement corresponded closely to that of the government and the patrões. A nonmilitant Catholic labor movement that was linked both to the state and to employers, that at least partially bridged the gap to a more modern society without in the process undermining the old, could not but be accepted in the Brazil of those times.

The overthrow of Vargas and the defeat of the Axis powers in World War II led to a general discrediting of fascism and the corporative ideology that had earlier been so prominent. The Catholic labor movement lost the official favors it had enjoyed before; in competition with more change-oriented labor groups, it was at a disadvantage. Despite the changed context, the Círculo movement failed to redefine its program, even in the face of dwindling membership; it clung steadfastly to the tenets of the past and looked for a new "savior"--like Vargas--who might rescue it from oblivion. It continued to espouse the traditional Catholic and corporatist philosophy, in spite of the fact that, in the increasingly modern Brazilian system, this no longer seemed appropriate (6, 7, 71, 231).

The reformist mood that swept some sectors of the Brazilian clergy in the early 1960s had little effect upon the Catholic labor movement. A number of labor leadership schools were founded, but little was done to modernize the movement's ideology. It took the revolution of 1964 to demonstrate to the Church and to Catholic labor leaders just how outmoded its program was and how great the need was for fundamental reorientation.

In the wake of the 1964 coup, a number of steps were taken to reexamine the underlying philosophy of the Círculo movement. Particularly since the promulgation of Pope John's Mater et Magistra (1961) and Pacem in Terris (1963) and Pope Paul's Populorum Progressio (1967), there has been considerable ferment within the movement as to how its goals ought to be redefined. The original principles have not been repudiated, but they no longer guide the movement--at least so far as the progressive leadership is concerned. These leaders have been influenced by Pope John's insistence on the dignity of labor and its primacy over capital, and by his and Pope Paul's concern with underdevelopment. The movement's statements now call for greater community action, an end to paternalism, increased leadership training, raising working-class consciousness, organization of a youth movement, and liberation of the masses. Gone are the pious exhortations to Christianity and anti-Communism, the call for class solidarity, the emphasis on gradualism and working within the system, and the older corporative and organicist conception of state and society. Instead, the emphasis is on man, the rights of labor, and the worldly needs of the workers (89, 125).

At present, however, there is no clear-cut program for the movement as a whole. The traditional philosophy has been superseded, but no new set of principles on which all factions can agree has been articulated. Thus, while some of the leaders have acquired a new militancy, the traditional forces in the Church and the Workers' Circles remain paramount. Paternalism, authoritarianism, and the corporate ideal have by no means disappeared in Brazil, either from the Church or from the entire national system, and certainly not from the Círculos Operários. The conservatives fear the opening to the left, identification with radical groups, the unanticipated consequences of social revolution, and the

abandonment of a program of limited objectives that carries some
certainty in favor of an uncertain but total program. They still
want to work within the system. At present, the ideology of the
Catholic labor movement is unclear and uncertain, reflecting the
diversity of viewpoints within its ranks--and in Brazil itself.
Some leaders have absorbed the new social justice doctrines, but
little of this has filtered down into the ranks, where traditional-
istic attitudes still predominate. Nor has the progressive ideology as yet been translated into realistic programs. As one prominent Catholic layman and intellectual has written, the social
action movement of the Church in Brazil still consists chiefly of
"nice words, noble sentiments, and the absence of concrete solutions" (485).

Many Catholic labor leaders are still torn between the conservative and liberal wings of the Church and between the progressive and status quo-oriented forces within Brazilian society. As
the cleavages and pressures in Brazil have intensified, however,
such neutrality has become increasingly difficult to maintain.
There is also a widening gap between the lay leaders of the movement, many of whom have become militant, and the clerics, who tend
to be more cautious. This ambiguity, the pluralism of perspectives
found in the CBTC, reflects the growing pluralism of the Brazilian
Church and nation. No one world view is wholly dominant any more.
Both Church and nation have become increasingly divided, both are
being challenged by forces from within and without, and neither has
been able to cope adequately with the newer challenges or with increased factionalism within its own ranks. The fragmentation of
the Brazilian Church and nation makes prospects for the adoption of
a single, unified program and ideology for the Catholic labor movement unlikely.

FORMAL ORGANIZATION AND INFORMAL DECISION MAKING

The present organizational structure of the Círculo movement
dates back to the 1930s and the conceptions of its founders.
Though some changes have been effected, the organization remains
authoritarian, hierarchical, corporate, and paternalistic. The
structure of the CBTC is in many ways as outmoded, as unresponsive
to the needs of its members, and as ill equipped to cope with
present-day Brazilian realities as is its ideology.

Though the CBTC is organized on the state and national levels,
the focal point of its activities is the local Círculo Operário.
It claims to have 380 Círculos functioning in Brazil, with a total
membership put at 500,000. Each Círculo is run on a largely self-
sufficient basis (7, 351). This decentralized structure reflects
the largely localized nature of Brazilian life in the 1930s, when
the Círculo movement was first organized; but as Brazil has developed a more centralized administration and interest group structure, the capacity of the still locally concentrated Círculo movement to compete in the Brazilian political arena has been circumscribed.

The movement is very weakly organized at all levels. Many
Círculos continue to exist chiefly on paper; the membership rolls

are also inflated. Funds have dried up, forcing the CBTC and the individual Círculos to curtail their activities. Once the initial flurry of activities during the Vargas period had ended, much of the organization was idled and has since become rusted.

While the Círculos' limited activities are focused at the local level, policy is set only at the national level, and ultimately by the Church itself, centered in Rome. It would be wrong to say that the rank-and-file have no influence at all in making policy, but the fact is a virtual monopoly power over decision-making is concentrated in the hands of high Church authorities.

Elections are held periodically at all levels, but the candidates are ordinarily prepicked by Church authorities. The final authority in the movement is not the elected officials but the Church-appointed clerical advisers. Discussion may be initiated at the lower levels, but goals and strategies are determined by the Church hierarchy. The elected officials are important as counselors, but the real centers of power lie elsewhere, and these power holders continue to exercise influence in a traditionalist, authoritarian fashion. Popular participation at the grass-roots level is more apparent than real.

The lay leadership has consistently been white and middle-class, not from the ranks of labor. Originally, in keeping with the corporatist character of the Brazilian labor movement, the Círculos were "interprofessional"--that is, they were for employers as well as employees. Particularly in the early years, and to a considerable extent today, the Círculo movement has served principally as an escalator for Brazil's emerging middle sectors.

The key men in the Círculo organization are the clerical advisers. A clerical adviser is assigned to each Círculo and state federation and to the national confederation. The clerical adviser's duties include attending organizational meetings, preserving the spiritual goals of the movement and vetoing all contrary proposals, examining the slate of candidates for lay offices and eliminating unacceptables, taking charge of the moral and educational aspects of the Círculo program, serving as "adviser" to the lay leadership, censoring materials not in accord with the Catholic faith, and functioning as the general overseer of the movement's entire range of activities (53, 126). The clerical adviser is appointed by the local diocesan authority, on whom the duration of his mandate depends. These charges give the clerical adviser virtually unlimited authority within the Círculo movement and over its lay leadership. The principle of absolute Church control over the entire movement has remained unchanged.

The CBTC is linked with a number of other groups. These ties reflect the paternalistic and authoritarian internal organization of the movement. The Círculos are still as dependent upon the paternalism of the government as they were during the Vargas era; indeed, in many ways the corporate structure, with labor assimilated into the administrative machinery of a benevolent state, remains the operating ideal of most Círculo leaders. Further, the movement is still intimately linked to patrões and employer groups through a variety of informal ties as well as through certain business-sponsored social assistance agencies. While its more militant leaders have rejected this association, the operating ideal of the old corporate system--that is, of class harmony rather than class conflict between workers and employers--remains strong (351). At the same time, although there has been some effort to deemphasize its Catholic-confessional nature, the CBTC remains intimately tied to the Church and its doctrines. The fact that the Círculo movement is still bound up closely with this traditional triumvirate--the paternalistic state, the Church, and the wealthy elites--provides another indication of its fundamentally conservative nature.

The CBTC has never maintained close ties with other labor groups; in fact, its energies have frequently been dedicated to rooting out more radical rival trade union blocs. Its relations with the Catholic left have also been far from harmonious. In part at least, the new Catholic left organizations, such as Ação Popular, the Movimento de Educação de Base, and the youth sectors of Catholic Action, came into existence because their leaders felt the Círculos' old-fashioned program and ideology were inadequate for Brazil's present needs; thus, they organized themselves outside the regular Círculo movement and independent of it. The Círculo leaders, in turn, considered the organization of these groups an encroachment on their domain and condemned them as subversive. They could hardly conceal their glee when the new-left Catholic groups were purged following the 1964 coup, leaving the way clear for the Círculos, which collaborated with the military regime and whose conservative position and limited program were considered harmless by the authorities. The Círculos were thereby enabled to resume their place of leadership within the Catholic social movement (or so they thought) without fear of challenge and with the sanction of both the Church hierarchy and the government. As a result of this pyrrhic victory, however, the CBTC lost support among the youth and the workers, was expelled from CLASC, and seemed to have become increasingly divorced from the newer Brazilian society coming into existence. The Catholic labor movement's organizational ties to other groups, particularly the modernizing ones, seemed to have been irreparably weakened (231, 296, 446).

RANGE OF ACTIVITIES AND INFLUENCE

From the time of its founding, the Círculo movement has proclaimed its goals to be all-encompassing, aimed at satisfying all the needs of Brazilian workers, in a way that leads to a bettering of the whole, integral man--rather than being piecemeal or dealing with only one aspect of man's existence (e.g., in contrast with Marxian materialism). The CBTC considers itself not just a trade union organization, but a movement of religious, social, cultural, educational, moral, spiritual, physical, and material dimensions. Its range of activities has correspondingly been wide (6, 565).

Historically, the Círculos' social assistance mission has been among their most important activities. This usually meant the administration of Christian charity in a paternalistic fashion. Arrangements were made for Círculo members to receive reduced rates at barber shops, drugstores, food markets, even funeral parlors. Under Vargas, CBTC officials worked closely with the government in

the administration of a variety of new social assistance programs--
also administered paternalistically. The CBTC was also given the
task of serving as the social assistance arm of the Brazilian Catholic Church. These activities are more a reflection of the early
mutual benefit associations and of a movement oriented toward
Christian beneficence than of a modern trade union organization.
Hence, in recent years the social assistance mission has been increasingly questioned. Moreover, without government assistance,
the capacity of the Círculos to continue supplying these alms has
declined drastically. In the rural areas the emphasis is still on
the paternalistic administration of charity, but in the industrial
centers other concerns have begun to acquire greater importance(c).

The development of the Christianizing mission of the Círculo
movement has paralleled that of the social assistance mission. The
Christian mission--at least in the eyes of the clerical leadership
--has been the Círculos' most fundamental function. In their early
years, along with the alms-giving, activities of the Círculos consisted chiefly of providing Christian instruction for the workers
and their families. Now, the emphasis has begun to shift away from
the Christianizing mission and toward more worldly concerns, but
the Church has a delicate balancing act to perform here. Its dilemma is how to achieve relevance in the increasingly secular Brazilian society and at the same time maintain the fundamentally
Catholic essence of its labor branch. This dilemma has driven a
sharp wedge between its clerical and lay leadership.

The CBTC has long placed great emphasis on social activities--
parties, festivals, dances, excursions, even cocktail parties and
beauty contests. Círculo leaders argue that these activities provide its members with a sense of participation; they serve to ameliorate the working-class rootlessness and alienation that Marxists
argue is inherent in capitalist society. More recently, the value
of these social activities has been questioned within the movement.
Its lay leadership has argued that the focus should be shifted to
more essential activities, such as organizing the workers, exerting
pressure on the political authorities to raise the minimum wage,
and so on. There is increasing disagreement as to the importance
that should be placed upon social activities; their scope has declined but they still form an important part of the movement's
ideal of providing for the "whole man."

The educational program of the Círculos has long focused on
religious instruction. Little has been done toward tackling the
problems of mass illiteracy or of providing technical training. It
would not be inaccurate to label the Círculo movement's educational
program as essentially catechism classes for the emerging new
groups in Brazil (the middle sectors and now the workers) and as a
means of socializing them into the prevailing system (486).

By now, the educational focus has shifted to the leadership
schools. These schools aim to train lower- and middle-sector people for leadership positions, not only in the CBTC but also in factory, office, and government agency. The leadership schools have
given the CBTC an influential corps of leaders in many areas of
Brazilian private and public life. They are about the only activity that carries any appeal to the youth. Even in the leadership

schools, however, Catholic doctrine has a major place in the curriculum. Further, these schools are confined to the major cities; in the interior towns, the old catechism classes still prevail (513).

The organizational activities of the Círculo movement have been circumscribed, because both its leaders and the government on which it is dependent have wished to avoid the uncontrolled infusion of lower-class elements into the political arena. The attempt has been at incorporating the rising social groups gradually into national life and controlling the entire process to ensure systemic stability and the maintenance of the traditional order, while also providing for some accommodations to change. Debate now rages within the Círculos as to whether more should be done to raise the level of conscientizaçao of the workers and thereby to expand the opportunities for the creation of a large mass movement. Thus far, the clerical leadership has rejected this strategy because it fears that a class-conscious workers' movement may snowball beyond the Church's ability to control it and may become dominated by the communists. Pressures are rising for the Workers' Circles to do more in this area, but so far conscientizaçao has been largely the work of the Catholic Left; and under present military rule, activities aimed at mobilizing the lower classes have all but ceased (231, 490).

The political activities of the Círculos are hindered by the fact that traditionally they have proclaimed themselves outside of partisan politics. In the past decade, however, the CBTC has been drawn inexorably into political affairs, thus producing a widening gap between its traditional ideology and the exigencies of the Brazilian present.

During the early years of their existence, it was fairly easy for the Círculos to avoid partisan politics. Politics was still dominated by the state and local machines, by the coroneis, chefes políticos, and patrões. At the national level, Vargas ruled as a personalistic, nonpartisan caudilho. Ideology was less important than patronage and personalities; politics remained patrimonial, and the fledgling parties had little importance. The Círculos could easily avoid partisan politics, for the centers of power lay elsewhere, in the traditional foci of influence, which is precisely where the Círculos were best connected.

This is not to say the Círculos were apolitical in a sense of the word more modern students of politics would understand. Their primary goal, after all, was to combat communist influences; they were also intimately linked to the national government and to state and local influentials. But this was looked upon as something "natural" that had nothing to do with partisan politics. The Círculo movement saw no contradiction between its apolitical stance and its crusade against communism, on the one hand, or its close ties with the government and the local and state machines, on the other.

As Brazil has modernized, it has become increasingly difficult for the CBTC to maintain its apolitical position. Political power has gradually shifted away from the traditional elements, political ideologies have become increasingly important, and politics has become more class- and interest-oriented. The Círculos have felt these pressures (422). Particularly in the crisis years of the 1960s, their ecclesiastical leaders mobilized opinion against Goulart, publicly applauded the military coup that overthrew him, and worked closely with the conservative-military regime that came to power in 1964.

Yet the political activities of the Círculo movement even now are circumscribed. The military government proved hostile to organized labor. The CBTC is not powerful enough to impose its interests on the national leadership, and the realities of military power make it very cautious in its relations with the government. The Círculos are in a precarious position--their old benefactors have largely been deprived of influence, and whatever new access has been established is still tenuous, uncertain, and characterized by considerable wariness. As a result, the Círculos' political influence at present is extremely limited, confined chiefly to the moral suasion that their pronouncements carry and to issues that are not sensitive. While this has enabled them to escape the governmental crackdown that their more militant counterparts have experienced, it has cost them the allegiance of the workers, who have been tightly squeezed by the government's austerity program at precisely the time they have acquired new demands. The Círculos cannot buck the government's wage policies for fear of reprisals, yet they cannot continue to lose their following.

The Círculos are caught in the dilemma of being an "apolitical" movement in an increasingly politicized society. Traditionally they have sought modest economic gains for the workers and eschewed partisan politics as well as the politicization of the Círculo movement itself. Now, however, the movement has been left with almost no means to make even its limited influence felt. The CBTC must enter the political arena if it wishes to have any say at all in the decision-making process, for such questions as raising the minimum wage are as much political as economic. Some Círculo leaders now recognize this fact and have begun to move toward greater political involvement. A full-fledged plunge into national politics, especially under conditions of dictatorial rule, also carries severe risks, however, and it is not certain that the movement's leaders are willing to take that risk. It seems more likely that the involvement of the Círculos in political affairs will be cautious.

The range of activities of the Círculo movement is broad but shallow. Its aims remain comprehensive, but its activities are limited. One cannot escape the conclusion that many of the 380 Workers' Circles claimed by the national organization operate on a part-time basis or have ceased operations altogether. They represent an extensive but decaying grass-roots organization that has not kept up with the times and that is fading away for lack of much to do and of sufficient resources to do more. The amount of influence the Círculos can bring to bear on any issue is negligible, for it lacks the human, organizational, financial, political, even moral strength to be anything more than a minor influence in present-day Brazilian affairs. It has survived intact thus far and achieved its limited successes because its goals were so limited and so modestly proffered within the prevailing system that they

constituted no threat to anyone. But surely, within the present
Brazilian context, it is no longer possible for any group that
wishes to succeed to cling so steadfastly to the authoritarianism
and easy-going paternalism of the past.

POLITICAL LIFE: PROBLEMS AND CONFLICTS

Whether they wish it or not, the Catholic Workers' Circles are
tied to the social and political life of contemporary Brazil and
are inexorably bound up with the processes of change that have been
occurring in that country over the past four decades. In this section, the focus is on the problems and conflicts facing the Círculo
movement as it seeks to cope with the rapidly changing social and
political situation of present-day Brazil.

It is essential to recall the context in which the movement
was founded. Brazil in the 1930s was just beginning its great leap
into the modern, twentieth-century, industrial world; the dominant
authoritarian and patrimonialist structures that had governed social and political relations for some four centuries were largely
intact. In addition, this was a time when notions of the corporate-organic state and society were most influential in the Latin
countries. The Catholic labor movement--similarly paternalistic,
authoritarian, and corporatist--was closely attuned to the ambiente
in which it found itself. Some of the chief dilemmas of the CBTC
today are in no small part due to the peculiar social, ideological,
religious, and political context in which it was founded and which
still shapes its orientation. For as Brazil has modernized, the
Círculo movement has in many respects become an anachronism.

The dilemmas confronting the CBTC are implicit in much of our
earlier discussion. It is saddled with a negative image--originally anti-communist, but now, given its support of the movement
that overthrew Goulart, antilabor and antinationalist as well.
There is little agreement on its goals or on what priorities should
be established among its activities. The younger clergy are in
disagreement with the older clericais who still dominate the movement, the lay and clerical leaderships have similarly become divided, and the rank-and-file remain amorphous and fragmented. The
CBTC is today a complex, heterogeneous mixture of traditional and
modern, change and continuity, with no clear sense of direction,
and with its foundations resting precariously upon a past that no
longer exists and a present that, because of the increasingly complex and contradictory pressures at work, is shaky and likely to
crumble.

The organizational structure is similarly weak. There has
been little attempt to modernize the organization, boost lay leaders into decision-making positions, reduce the gap between leadership and membership, divorce itself from the traditional authority
structures, expand into rural areas or even urban favelas, overcome its localized focus and be able to bargain effectively at the
national level. It clings unrealistically to the ideal of class
harmony in an era when Brazilian politics has become increasingly
torn by class conflict; it seeks to maintain the myth that it is
apolitical when it is not and in an era in which the entire

Brazilian society has become more politicized. An apolitical
stance may be appropriate in times of peace and harmony when there
are no deeply rooted partisan or ideological issues, as in the Vargas era. But as real issues and real ideological and class interests have become more important, it has become increasingly difficult to remain aloof from politics. Because the CBTC has failed to
take a progressive stand on the great political issues that have
torn Brazil apart in the last decade, the Círculos have lost a
large share of their followers and alienated themselves from such
groups as the youth, the reform-oriented clergy, and the change-oriented trade unions, who probably represent the future of Brazil.

The Círculo movement is also beset by severe financial difficulties that not only force it to limit its activities but also
cast it in a continued dependency relationship vis-a-vis employers,
patrões, and the government. Furthermore, as it has begun to
assert greater independence, even these traditional sources of support have dried up. These limitations on its activities force us
to question whether the Círculos are much more than a moral force,
whether their functions go beyond serving as Christian examples to
their fellow workers. The answer to this question is "yes," but it
is a qualified one. For the impact of the Workers' Circles has
been limited: their efforts on behalf of the workers have been
circumscribed, except, perhaps, in a moral or religious sense; they
have not made a dent in such crucial problem areas as Brazil's
widespread illiteracy and hard-core poverty; their influence as
agents of national modernization has been almost nonexistent; and
they have remained largely neutral as regards the major issues of
national development, except for an occasional "anticommunist"
foray into the political arena. These negative comments must be
tempered by a realization of the complexity and immensity of the
problems faced, the severe limitations placed upon the Círculo
movement by time and circumstances, and the wrenching nature of
the transitional process through which the country--and the
CBTC--is going.

CONCLUSION

The Círculo movement was organized at a time in the early
stages of transition when the Brazilian society and polity were
still largely authoritarian, paternalistic, hierarchical, and corporate. The Círculos both reflected and reinforced the society in
which they were nurtured and grew up. But whereas Brazilian society has changed enormously in recent decades, the Círculos have
not adapted readily to the new environment or kept up with the transformations that have begun to restructure Brazilian society.

Though it has responded tardily to change, the Círculo movement has begun to modernize, and at present it, too, is caught up
in the trauma of transition. It represents an increasingly complex, frequently hodgepodge, pattern of old and new--partly traditional in its emphasis on the family, social activities, religious
orientation, and such--and partly modern (for instance, in its new
militancy and emphasis on man's material needs). It still clings
to the ideals from its past of Christian harmony and order, but it

is now seeking to reorient itself in accord with the contemporary context. The Círculo movement is in a state of flux, where the pull of the past is still powerful but where new programs and a changed societal environment have all had their impact. For the CBTC the present is a period of reassessment and of internal divisionism; the future would seem to be no less cloudy.

Much of what we have just said is characteristic not just of the Catholic Workers' Ĉircles but of the entire Brazilian labor movement, the Church, the Brazilian system as a whole, and, ultimately, the nature of the Latin American development process as well. Though one hesitates to go beyond the data presented and though what follows must necessarily be abbreviated, it may be suggested that the rise of the Brazilian labor movement as a whole parallels that of the Catholic CBTC; that it, too, has traditionally been dependent upon the government and the patrões; that its emergence as a powerful political force for change in the 1960s proved to be an extremely wrenching experience; and that it also is torn by both traditional and modern influences (140). Similarly, the Catholic Church in Brazil has been paternalistic, hierarchical, and authoritarian for centuries, adapting to change rather than leading it, seeking to stake out a "safe" position on both sides of many issues, but now beginning to be affected by the pressures of populism, reformism, and modernization (230, 559).

Brazil has changed drastically. The older semifeudal structure has been increasingly undermined; the transition from agrarian to industrial has gone forward; an archaic, parochial, and highly traditional way of life has tended to give way to one that is more modern and secular. But this process has been sporadic, uneven, and incomplete, marked by the continued coexistence of both traditional and modern forms. The more traditional aspects and institutions seem to be in decline but have by no means disappeared; likewise, a more modern order is on the rise but has by no means been consolidated. It is likely that this hodgepodge mixture of traditional and modernity, of change and continuity, will continue as a more or less permanent feature of the Brazilian sociopolitical system. Meanwhile, as a result of these changes, of the increased intensity of political sentiment, and of the repeated and intensified clash of opposed interests, the Brazilian nation has become increasingly polarized and fragmented, a mosaic of conflict and discord, a praetorian society caught in a seemingly permanent state of crisis (224, 433, 467).

The agony of the Catholic labor movement in Brazil reflects the agony of the labor movement more generally, of the Church, and of the nation as a whole. The Círculos Operários do not exist in a vacuum but interact with—and in a sense are a microcosm of—the larger systems of which they are a part. If the CBTC is in the process of an uncertain transition, then so are these other groups, and the Brazilian nation as well. Given these conditions, it is unlikely that modernization of the Círculo movement will occur outside of or divorced from the modernization of the entire system. Neither in the CBTC nor in the Brazilian nation, however, is dramatic or revolutionary change likely, at least in the foreseeable future; rather, what change occurs—barring a major collapse and assuming the maintenance of the present system--will more likely come gradually and incrementally, by fits and starts rather than dramatically, and as likely as not without much planned and purposeful action.

The Catholic labor movement, thus, provides an interesting example of the way the general development process in Latin America has typically proceeded. Development has occurred within a corporative framework that accommodates traditional and modern rather than implying the transcendence of the one over the other; that implies the persistence of traditional institutions and modes of behavior and their coexistence with more modern ones; that provides for the gradual absorption of more modern elements and ideas without in the process destroying the traditional essence. As the case of the Brazilian Catholic Workers' Circles illustrates, this process often involves delicate political juggling and runs the risk of alienating both the most traditional and the most modern elements within the movement. Change comes about, but it is usually carefully controlled, directed from above, and channeled in the "right" directions. The changes that come about in this fashion-- gradually, through shifting emphases and personnel, on a low-level basis and by means of day-to-day decisions and nondecisions, through new alignments and the assimilation of new corporate groups and ideas, through repeated crises and ad hoc rebuilding--may well be significant, nonetheless, and may be cumulative to the point where they imply a structural transformation (21, 75, 206, 564). That is not only the kind of change that seems most in accord with the realities of power and society within Brazil and the Brazilian Church and labor movement, but also that has been most characteristic of, and corresponds most closely to, the nature of the change process in Latin America. This manner of accommodating to and managing change has been increasingly challenged, however, and it remains to be seen whether, with the rising tensions and stresses of the present, the traditional institutions and mechanisms are any longer capable of handling the new pressures and demands that have been thrust upon them.

NOTES

a. See the various albums and official histories put out by the Círculos, as well as 351. Though no publisher or date is given in a number of the items herein cited, the overwhelming majority were privately printed by various Church-related presses and reflect the orientations of the 1950s and early 1960s. For the more recent orientation, I have relied more extensively on interview data.

b. See the Catholic newspaper O Diario during this period. Based also on extensive interviews with Catholic labor leaders and members, chiefly in Rio de Janeiro, where the CBTC has its national headquarters, and in Belo Horizonte, where the Minas Gerais state federation is centered and where one of the nation's more important Workers' Circles is located.

c. The materials in this and subsequent sections are based largely on interviewing and participant observation.

15 | The Corporatist Tradition and the Corporative System in Portugal: Structured, Evolving, Transcended, Persistent

The term "corporatism" is often used loosely and ambiguously. Enjoying a resurgence and new-found popularity (304, 400, 545), both among political analysts and some political elites, it nonetheless remains a frequently confusing and misleading term and framework. It is often a highly emotive term, conjuring up images of Nazi atrocities and Fascist dictatorships. At one time so-called "corporatist regimes," with Portugal the major exception, seemed to be safely confined to the ashcans of history, but now not only has the term gained a new credence but regimes calling themselves "corporatist" have reemerged in such distinct, from a policy and ideological perspective, nations as Chile and Peru. We are also discovering that regimes we are used to thinking of as liberal and social-democratic often exhibit numerous, though frequently disguised, corporative features (204, 380). Moreover, even those long-term, manifestly "corporatist" regimes, such as the Portuguese, remained almost wholly unstudied and shrouded in myths and misunderstandings. The time to begin clarifying both the meaning of the term "corporatism" and our understanding of how such "corporatist regimes" as the Portuguese actually function is long overdue (a).

CORPORATISM AS TRADITION

> The model for "the system" implemented during his regency (1439-1447) . . . and which was to become the standard system in the Portuguese kingdom for several centuries, was that developed by Dom Pedro in his <u>Livro da Virtuosa Bemfeitoria</u>. Moreover the model developed by this Portuguges prince in the early fifteenth century is almost a prototype of what political scientists and others refer to as the corporate, patrimonial state (183).

Iberic-Latin history, in this chapter specifically Portuguese history, is often analyzed in terms of a presumed unilinear and universal evolution toward liberalism and democracy. This

---

From L. Graham and H. Makler (eds.), <u>Contemporary Portugal</u> (Austin: University of Texas Press, 1978).

viewpoint is not surprising when it emanates from British or North American writers, with their ethnocentrism and culture-bound biases; occasionally, it finds its way into Portuguese writers as well (313).

This perspective uses the British Parliament for its model of the Portuguese cortes, the Bill of Rights as its model of civil liberties, the New England town meeting as its model of participatory democracy, and the liberal-Lockean tradition, updated a la Churchill ("Democracy is the worst form of government except for all others") as the model of the political system. However, the process of development in Portugal has proved to be far from unilinear in terms of this model, and what is frequently presented as a universal framework is, in fact, quite particularistic. The liberal model may thus be appropriate in tracing the patterns of development of the Anglo-American democracies, but it has less relevance for the Hispanic and Portuguese traditions. In Portugal the cortes never had, nor was it ever intended to have, the independent, coequal, or even supremacist position enjoyed by the British Parliament. While a list of civil rights was usually included in various Portuguese constitutions, these rights, in law and in practice, have consistently been subordinated to a higher end. Participatory rule has also come to be a principle of Portuguese governance, but what the Portuguese mean by participation is different from the unstructured individualism of Lockean liberalism. As regards democracy, (1) the Portuguese have not historically been convinced of its efficacy or ultimate legitimacy; and (2) even when they have, their meaning has implied some understandings that are different from the Anglo-American conception (518, 553).

A narrow and ethnocentric view of Portuguese history, which sees liberal democracy Anglo-American style as the inevitable outcome of a long-term societal evolution, not only clouds our understanding but distorts our comprehension of key Portuguese institutions. It not only paints the presumed enemies of democracy, such as the Church, the monarchy, Pombal, Salazar, in the vilest terms, but it also exaggerates the accomplishments of "liberal" regimes (from 1822 to 1926) so as better to discredit as wholly "reactionary" and "Fascistic" the one that followed (313).

A focus on Portugal's "corporative tradition" helps avoid these distortions. Rather than seeing Portugal's history in terms of some presumed, hoped-for, foreign, and nonindigenous model, this perspective seeks to examine Portugal on its own terms and in its own context. Because corporatism seems to be an integral part of the Portuguese tradition and seems so deeply imbedded historically in the Porguguese psyche and institutions, the newer approach has been termed the "corporative model" or the "corporative framework."

It is at this juncture that some conceptual confusion arises, for "corporatism" is now being used in two different senses. One definition is that used by Schmitter (458):

> Corporatism can be defined as a system of interest representation in which the constituent units are organized into a limited number of singular, compulsory, noncompetitive, hierarchically ordered and functionally differentiated categories

recognized or licensed (if not created) by the state and
granted a deliberate representational monopoly within their
respective categories in exchange for observing certain controls on their selection of leaders and articulation of demands and supports.

Professor Schmitter goes on to contrast this kind of corporatism with pluralism, which he defines largely in terms of laissez-faire "free" associability that is the reverse of his corporatism definition, with a "monist" model a la the Soviet Union, and with "syndicalism," which implies an autonomous and less-structured pattern of interest aggregation.

Although the definition of corporatism offered above is neat, terse, and probably useful as a description of the Salazar regime at one point in time, it provides more a static than dynamic model, offers a very biased perspective, gives a too restrictive meaning to the term "corporatism," and thus is not altogether useful for purposes of this analysis. Let us, therefore, acknowledge the utility of this approach with regard to some aspects of the Portuguese corporative system, while also recognizing the following limitations, biases, and reservations with regard to the Schmitter definition and the analysis following from it (b).

1. The definition is put in such negative, loaded terms as to be all but useless as a scientific or value-free formulation. Unless the scholar is willing to admit a preference for or even neutrality toward "compulsion," "monopoly," "noncompetitive," "hierarchically ordered," "singular," "controls," etc., he must perforce condemn the concept. Using this definition obliges him to reject corporatism a priori as necessarily evil, venal, and bad without further investigation. The definition prejudices research on corporatism before it begins and predetermines the conclusions that must be reached.

2. The formulation points to a particular research agenda--the changing nature of industrial capitalism, the relations of dependency to underdevelopment, the "structural" (i.e., class) determinants of public policy--to the exclusion of other interesting subject areas. No one would deny these are important issues, that corporatism frequently has class biases, and so on. But these are not the only aspects of corporatism that are interesting; they may not even be the most important ones. Other features have an at least equal claim to examination.

3. The definition quoted and the analyses based upon it provide a kind of neo-Marxian, economic-determinist view of corporatism and are tied closely to a rigid class explanation of politics. In this formulation, corporatism is necessarily reactionary, nondemocratic, repressive, and fascistic. Of course, corporatism may take this form, but it may take other forms also. And while the Marxian perspective is useful, in its overly deterministic forms it renders a disservice to our understanding of corporatism, the relative autonomy of state and societal actors, etc.

It provides an approach valid to a point, but it should not be viewed as the exclusive pivot on which Latin American politics turns or as the sole explanation of corporatism. What is a helpful explanation (and employed here) should not be reified, nor should an insightful but partial explanation be elevated to the position of a single and exclusionary one. The Schmitter definition is useful, but it is not the only perspective on corporatism; other approaches also shed light on this phenomenon.

4. The definition not only condemns corporatism but it lauds pluralism (defined in equally value-laden terms as "voluntary," "competitive," etc.) and also poses a rigid dichotomy between the two. Pluralism may be as ethically desirable as corporatism is venal, but one would prefer more value-neutral terms to describe them. The definition also ignores that pluralism means something different in Latin America from the U.S. understanding; that pluralism may exist in corporately organized societies as well as liberal ones; that corporatism itself may take both authoritarian and pluralist forms (c).

5. The focus in the Schmitter definition is exclusively on the preemptive, preventive, defensive, compartmentalizing (again, all with negative connotations) functions of corporatism (452). But corporatism also performs numerous nation-building, institutionalizing, social justice- and development-related functions that should command our attention as much as do the "negating" ones.

6. The definition ignores the infinite varieties of corporatism (85). It derives largely from the authoritarian-bureaucratic systems of Brazil and Portugal (where Schmitter's research was concentrated) and ignores the often progressive, reformist, and modernizing forms of a Mexico or Peru.

7. The definition is too rigidly tied to the practice of corporatism during one particular time period--the interwar years--thus ignoring both the newer and quite distinctive forms as well as its longer historical and political-cultural tradition, what Newton has called "natural corporatism" (360). A broader definition is thus needed to help us analyze these newer as well as the historical forms. Such a definition will, unfortunately, lose something in rigor and precision while it gains in comprehensiveness, but that is a price that will have to be paid to achieve a less-time-bound, more-inclusive conception of corporatism.

8. In the Schmitter definition and analysis, too many corporative agencies have been left out. His formulation is useful for studying some socioeconomic groups and their corporative relations, but it is entirely silent on such key corporative institutions as the Church, the armed forces, the university, the bureaucracy, municipalities, and others. The interrelations among these groups and their relations to the state constitute among the crucial arenas of Latin American politics; yet they are completely

ignored in the definition quoted above and cannot be entirely subsumed under the economic-determinist analysis it puts forth. There is even considerable doubt among scholars as to how useful this design is for the analysis of the very socioeconomic group relations that are at the heart of its analysis; e.g., labor and industrial relations (525).
9. The definition makes no provision for the dynamics of change within a corporative regime; i.e., from the innovative, often social justice-oriented corporatism in Portugal in the early Salazar years, to the repressive, statist system that followed, to the rejuvenated system of Caetano. Corporatism is fixed as an archtype when, in fact, it evolves, changes, has numerous forms and shadings.
10. Equally relevant for our study of Portuguese corporatism is the fact the Schmitter definition contains no possibility for an even more fundamental transformation from corporatism to syndicalism, nor does it entertain the possibility the latter may be a more-developed and socially differentiated progression from the former. In Schmitter's detailed formulations (452, 457), he plainly saw the particular form of corporatism he had studied and defined as a <u>permanent</u> modern form of sociopolitical organization. But in 1974 Portugal had a revolution that overthrew that form of corporatism and substituted something else. While there were many structural changes that accompanied the revolution, there were numerous continuities also. Portugal went from a conservative form of corporatism to a socialist or syndicalist system, meanwhile retaining many of its vertical, hierarchical, organicist, "pillared" features. In the wake of the 1974 revolution (or <u>regeneração</u>, in Portuguese terms), Portugal underwent a major reordering, as we shall see, that could also be interpreted in the light of that nation's historic corporatist tradition, now updated with syndicalist/socialist features (552).

What then is meant by the "corporative model" or the "corporative tradition" in Portugal? First, let us recognize that to pin a single all-encompassing label on a varied national and, more broadly, cultural tradition represents a series of oversimplifications. Second, let us recognize that other "key words"--"organicist," "patrimonialist"--should also be employed along with the "corporatist" one to describe this system and tradition. Third, let us accept the fact that, in speaking of the "corporatist model," we are employing a streamlined, paradigmatic, ideal type, only the main parameters of which are spelled out. The "corporative tradition" has been used here to describe only some of the more salient features of Iberic-Latin development, particularly as that model stands in contrast to the liberal-Lockean tradition and to other social science paradigms with which we are more familiar.

Space constraints rule out a detailed treatment of the emergence and gradual institutionalization of the particular Portuguese variant of the "corporative tradition." In other writings (519,

520), I have traced the beginnings of the model to the origins of Portuguese civil society in the clan and patriarchal order; the Roman concepts and system of law, citizenship, governance, and functionally representative colegios; the Catholic-Thomistic emphasis on hierarchy and organicism; the particular pattern of emergent feudalism in Iberia during the Reconquest; and the theory and practice of Portuguese society and the state system from the thirteenth century through the fifteenth. The corporative tradition implied a value system based upon hierarchy, elitism, organicism, and authority; it meant a pattern of corporate sectoral and functional representation with authority vested in the crown or central state apparatus and with the various corporate units (nobility, Church, military orders, university, municipalities) incorporated into a single, organic whole for purposes of integral national development; it implied a system of bureaucratic-patrimonialist state authority and a social order based similarly on patron-client interdependence; it meant a predominantly Catholic society and political culture based upon Thomistic principles; it implied an etatist and mercantilist economic system; and it implied a political order grounded on patrimonialism, a bureaucratic state, controlled and regulated participation, with a centralized, vertical, pyramidal structure of power and decision-making.

The terms "corporatist tradition" or "corporatist model" are shorthand terms used to describe some fairly distinctive features or combinations of features of Portuguese history, political culture, and the development process. For example, in keeping with the Catholic conception, the Portuguese state has historically been based on the reciprocity of a patron-client system, a state that was natural, moral, and just and, therefore, did not have to be limited by institutional checks and balances. Stratification and differentiation in the social and political sphere not only exist but are presumed to be right, necessary, and not to be challenged. Society consisted of functionally diverse corporate groups, each of which made its distinct contribution to the political society and was guaranteed representation in it. The nobility, the Church, and the fighting knights stood near the apex, directly below the Crown, in this vertically segmented, hierarchically ordered scheme. They constituted the higher order "corporations"; their function was to govern, to harmonize the human social order with a higher responsibility, to be responsible not just for themselves but for the good of all. The king (or, later, prime minister or president) remained unfettered by a coequal parliament or judiciary, as in the Anglo-American conception; but he, too, was obligated to rule in accord with a higher natural law, to govern for the common good, to respect the foros of the constituent corporate groups, and he could not overstep the bounds which separated authoritarianism (legitimate) from tyranny (which justified rebellion). Politics usually centered on the competition among rival elites and corporate groups to capture the patrimonialist state apparatus, from which wealth and position flowed, and on the dynamic, changing relations between these constituent units and the central authority (37, 144, 183, 326).

Although this brief description does not begin to do justice to the complexities and subtleties of the workings of the Portuguese corporative system historically, it does provide a hint as to some of the main directions. It makes clear how far removed this dominant Portuguese tradition is from the dominant liberal-Lockean one of the Anglo-American nations. Although no claim is made that all of Portuguese history can be interpreted in this light, and though as with all ideal-type constructs a greater understanding of the Portuguese weltanschauung is obtained at the cost of a certain definitional preciseness, still an understanding of the "corporative tradition" or of "natural corporatism" helps illuminate some areas of Portuguese development that were unexamined before or examined only in the light of Anglo-American referents. It provides a needed, valuable corrective to this other approach. Moreover, this model applies not just to the centuries of national organization and then consolidation in premodern times but also, in reconstructed and updated form, on into the "liberal" and "republican" periods of the nineteenth and early twentieth centuries. Despite the constitutional façade, Portugal remained more a corporatist than a republican regime; the power of the major corporate units (Church, army, bureaucracy, nobility) remained undiminished and even enhanced; and the parliamentary regime worked best when it was least parliamentary; i.e., when it had a strong monarch or president and when the organic-corporatist conceptions prevailed. The corporative pattern of sociopolitical relations was, thus, not only deeply imbedded, but it also proved to be remarkably long-lasting. It remains as a major, persistent tradition even today. "Corporatism" as a shorthand term to describe this Portuguese tradition is comparable to the use of "liberalism" to describe the dominant American tradition, and also serves further to distinguish these two national and political-cultural traditions (197, 347).

Some Portuguese corporatist theorists would go even further and dismiss all of nineteenth-century republicanism as mere façade, a temporary interruption in an otherwise dominant corporatist tradition (68, 443). This perspective, however, seems as inaccurate as the earlier interpretation from the liberal perspective. The "liberal" and "liberalizing" perspective of Portuguese history produced one set of distortions, but an equally unrefined corporatist perspective implies a distortion of another kind. Beginning in the eighteenth century, a fissure began to appear in Portuguese culture and society. On the one hand stood the dominant inward-looking Catholic-corporatist-traditionalist-patrimonialist conception; on the other, a European-oriented, nascently liberal-rationalist-urban-middle-class-secular one. From the nineteenth century on, these two perspectives and world views, and their accompanying institutional arrangements, stood side-by-side in Portugal, parallel but generally untouching. No one viewpoint would enjoy absolute legitimacy any more, no one dominated entirely, and much of Portuguese history during the period 1822-1926 can be interpreted in terms of the conflict and virtually constant civil war between the two. As in Spain during this same period, two distinct Portugals had evolved and there was little basis for compromise between them.

This development had two major implications for our study. First, in terms of Portuguese history, it implies that neither

the liberal nor the corporatist interpretation can any longer be
used exclusively to the neglect of the other, that from this point
Portuguese politics and society can be understood only in the light
of both models and what each tells us about the two distinct, separate Portugals, and that perhaps some of the most fruitful areas of
research lie in the creases where these two models and the parallel
structures they represent meet and overlap. Second, on the practical political level, it implies that no regime that comes to power
in Portugal can any longer afford to govern wholly for and in the
name of one tradition and its attendant sociopolitical forces while
entirely ignoring the other. When the monarchy tried in the late
nineteenth century, it faced a series of republican revolts that
eventually toppled the monarchy itself; when the Republicans disfranchised the Church and sought to rule without the traditionalist
elements, they faced a series of revolts that eventually succeeded
in toppling the Republic in 1926; and when Salazar sought subsequently to reestablish the corporatist tradition as the sole national tradition, he found he could do so only with the use of
widespread repression and police-state methods, and his regime and
system were repudiated in 1974. Whether the new regime that came
to power in the wake of the revolution can transcend or overcome
these historic divisions, or whether the revolution marks the
superimposition of a third layer, Marxist and socialist, onto the
already-existing corporatist and liberal ones and, thus, introduces
a further source of discord and fragmentation and, hence, makes the
forging of a truly national regime even more complex and problematic than before, are questions we shall have to weigh. But of the
existence historically of a powerful, perhaps dominant, corporative
tradition and model of sociopolitical organization, there can be
little doubt.

CORPORATISM AS MANIFEST SYSTEM

> In seeking to avoid imitation of United States liberalism and
> of Marxian approaches in finding models for government, social
> relations, and economic development, much of the Iberian World
> has been turning increasingly to . . . corporatism (400).

The 1926 revolution that toppled the Portuguese Republic was
carried out by the armed forces with strong backing from a variety
of civilian parties and movements. The chaos, disorder, and corruption of the Republic, the apparent bankruptcy of liberalism as
practiced in Portugal, had led to their general discrediting; and
when the coup finally came, it was warmly welcomed. It had the
support of a variety of monarchist, integralist, nationalist, Catholic, and center elements, together with the bulk of the middle
class and many <u>políticos</u> and republicans who sought to break the
patronage and sinecure monopoly of the Democratic Party. Although
the military was itself vaguely integralist, corporatist, and nationalist in character, it lacked a clear-cut program. Once it had
restored order, banished some of the Republican political groups
and politicians, rooted out corruption, and restored a degree of
economic solvency--the usual practices of military regimes--it

floundered for several years in search of a new national formula. It was precisely such a formula that Salazar and the corporatists provided and which helps explain their ascendance to power within the context of a military regime (d).

The corporatist system gradually institutionalized in Portugal in the course of the 1930s can be explained in terms of at least seven dimensions.

1. The corporatist regime represented a reaction against the chaos and disorder of liberalism and the Republic. By restoring order, stability, and national solvency, Salazar enjoyed widespread initial support. The early strength and popularity of the corporatist regime can only be understood in the light of the disorder and national humiliation that went before.

2. The corporatist regime was a strongly nationalist regime. It was nationalist in three senses. First, it was the heir of the Catholic and conservative Nationalist Party. Second, it represented a nationalistic repudiation of the influence of foreign institutions, chiefly British parliamentarism, which had governed the country often with ruinous results intermittently from 1822 to 1926. Third, it was nationalist in its efforts to fashion a new political model based upon indigenous Portuguese sources: the family, the local community, the fishermen's centers, such "natural" corporations as the Church, the army, the gremios, university, and so forth.

3. The corporatist regime was a middle-class regime. It marked the replacement of the older elitist and oligarchic order with a new middle-class one. That process was begun under the Republic and completed under the Estado Novo. Obscured by our attention to the political aspects of the Salazar regime is the gradual class shift that occurred; by the end of the Salazar-Caetano era, virtually every institution in the country had become middle-class dominated: army officer corps, Church hierarchy, bureaucracy, universities, high civil service, political parties, even the trade union structure.

4. The original corporatist scheme was a close reflection of the kind of society Portugal was still in the 1930s: predominantly rural and small-town, Catholic, traditionalist, hierarchically structured, governed by a nationwide system of patron-client relations, largely static. To the extent that Portugal had urbanized, modernized, and industrialized by the 1960s, become secular and change-oriented, and with its historic hierarchies breaking down, corporatism in the original Salazarista sense became less and less viable with wrenching social and political consequences.

5. The corporatist regime had a strong, initial, social justice orientation. This concern was genuine and real. It can, I think, be explained along two dimensions. First, it seems clear that the strongly Catholic orientation of Salazar and his collaborators led them to be concerned with the welfare of the poor, to feel a powerful

obligation to Catholic charity, and to initiate a series of social programs, paternalistic to be sure and undoubtedly insufficient but still no less genuine, to relieve the miserable plight of the poor, and to speak to the problem of alienation in the emerging mass society that Portugal was in the early process of becoming. Second, the social justice measures were related to the efforts of the emerging middle-class system to consolidate its power, to forge an alliance with some working-class elements so as better to wrest control away from the oligarchy and the historic governing elites. Once middle-class domination had been consolidated, the old alliance with the working class could be--and was--conveniently forgotten; but for a time, the middle class needed labor support and that was accomplished by instigating a large number of programs of social justice (e).

6. The corporatist system was designed, in Schmitter's words (452), to fill organizational space. The early 1930s was not only a period of economic depression in Portugal but of potentially threatening revolutionary movements from below. The corporative system was designed, therefore, not, as is often alleged, as a reactionary throwback to some status quo ante, but as a way of structuring, channeling, and, hence, controlling the emergence of new groups, principally labor, who might otherwise threaten the entire edifice. Corporative principles of social solidarity and class harmony were emphasized as a way of discouraging class conflict, and corporative <u>sindicatos</u> and structures of participation were introduced and made obligatory, filling the organizational space once occupied by the now-illegalized socialist, communist, and anarcho-syndicalist groups. Through the corporative restructuring, a middle-class-dominated change process was initiated from the top down as a way of holding in check and heading off in advance the possibility of more mass-based revolutionary solutions.

7. The corporatist regime must also be understood in the light of the foreign inspirations and influences of the time. The Portuguese corporatists built not only on their own indigenous history and institutions but also drew heavily upon Mussolini's <u>Carta del Lavoro</u> (1927) and the encyclical <u>Quadragesimo Anno</u> (1931). Corporatist regimes or corporatist institutions seemed to be the wave of the future, not just in Fascist Italy and Nazi Germany but seemingly everywhere. Manoïlesco (312) was about to proclaim that, whereas the nineteenth century had been the century of liberalism, the twentieth would be the century of corporatism. Corporatism's impact on Portugal must be understood in the context of a period when in the Western world corporatist solutions seemed to be becoming universal.

Once the corporatist formula had been decided upon, Salazar and the regime sought rapidly to institutionalize it. Although some of the first corporative decrees had been promulgated earlier, 1933 marked the real beginning of the corporative restructuring. That year a new constitution was adopted proclaiming Portugal a "unitary and corporative republic" and establishing both a superior Corporative Council and a functionally representative Corporative Chamber; a new labor law was handed down that detailed the new benefits the workers were to receive as well as restructuring their participation in the political process under strong state control; and a series of decree laws was promulgated governing virtually all areas of Portuguese associational life. These encompassed the creation of a nationwide system of casas do povo (people's centers) for rural workers, casas dos pescadores (fishermen's centers) for fishing communities, sindicatos (syndicates) for industrial workers, and gremios (guilds) for business, commercial, and industrial employer interests. A Subsecretariat of State (subministry) of Corporations and Social Welfare and the Instituto Nacional do Trabalho e Previdencia were established to administer the corporative system.

The flurry of corporative legislation in Portugal in 1933 was comparable to the changes ushered in by Roosevelt in his first ninety days, and probably just as far-reaching in its implications. By 1937, with the designation of the casas do povo as the representative agents of rural workers and, hence, the creation of separate gremios da lavoura for landed interests, the corporative restructuring had been all but completed. The creation of the corporations themselves, nominally the capstones of the entire system, had been scheduled for late 1939, but the outbreak of the war that year forced a postponement and it was not until 1956 that the regime got around to creating the first six corporations. For twenty-three years Portugal remained a corporative state without corporations.

From 1933-35 the regime moved quickly toward implementation. The trade unions were reorganized under the sindicato system; by 1935, 191 had been duly recognized by the state and 141 casas do povo were granted charters. The first gremios and fishermen's centers were also organized. A nationwide system of caixas de previdência was in the process of being established; the first elections under the corporative Constitution of 1933 were scheduled; the organizational scheme for the Corporative Chamber was promulgated; and the detailed provisions concerning workers' rights and obligations contained in the Labor Statute of 1933 began to be fleshed out. The period 1933-35 was a heady, exciting period for Portuguese corporativists; the corporative revolution was en marche; the system was being implemented. But it was precisely at this point in the mid-1930s that the first biases began to appear in the corporative structure and that the main lines of corporative development were fundamentally altered. Rather than a corporatism of free associability and social justice, the Portuguese system became a corporatism of the state, of controls and repression, and of favoritism toward one social group at the expense of others.

CORPORATISM AS CONTROLS

Traditionally corporatism has been a means of providing social solidarity, avoiding class conflict, and discouraging individualism among the masses, while at the same time providing opportunities for participation by the masses in local, regional, and functional groups. In its new guise in the Iberian world, corporatism also aims at replacing an entrenched oligarchy with a more nationalistic elite whose members hope to mobilize popular support for development and greater economic independence. <u>Above all, it is the objective of the new corporatism to prevent a revolution from below by initiating one from above</u> (400). (Emphasis added.)

Corporatism as originally conceived had been posited on the coequal representation of capital and labor; the corporatist solution had been proffered as a "third way," which repudiated both capitalism and socialism. In practice, however, corporatism in Portugal became one of the most oppressively monopolistic of state capitalist systems, favoring employer interests at the expense of labor to the point where industrialization was achieved by imposing its costs primarily on the industrial working class (which thus corresponds to Organski's definition (f) of "fascism").

The promulgation of the corporative decrees had been greeted in early 1934 by one of the most massive strikes Portugal had ever experienced. The brutal repression of the strike made it clear that, if the <u>sindicatos</u> refused to accept corporatization peacefully, it would be forced upon them. No such repression was ever practiced against employer groups, although over a long period the regime used strong leverage to subordinate capital as well as labor to state direction. The business and fledgling industrial elements were long able to make the case to Salazar that, if corporatization was to be enforced upon them as it was upon labor, it would lead to a lack of investment and the ruination of the economy. Particularly in the depression years of the 1930s, and then as the regime moved to stimulate economic development, these arguments were persuasive.

A second bias may be found in the decree laws themselves. For workers, membership in a sindicato was made obligatory; furthermore, the sindicatos could gain no benefits for their members until their charters had been granted by the state and they had been reorganized in terms of corporative principles. Business groups, however, had two major "outs." First, the government had allowed the old "class associations" (chambers of commerce, merchants' associations) to continue without forcing them to reorganize along corporative lines. Second, the regime provided for voluntary employer gremios as well as compulsory ones, while on the labor side this possibility had been ruled out.

A third bias had to do with the enforcement of the corporatist decrees. The government was enforcing the corporative legislation more on labor than on employers. The corporative system increasingly meant a web of controls for those on the bottom while providing for little accountability for those on top. In urban areas, this implied favoritism to business and commercial interests and industrialists at the expense of labor; in the countryside it implied a perpetuation of the traditional patron-client system

through both benign governmental neglect and the domination by
wealthy landed elements of both the gremios da lavoura and the
casas do povo.

A fourth bias had to do with the growing security and consolidation of the Salazar regime itself by the mid-1930s, to the absence by now of major internal threats. Hence, the regime and the
broader middle class on which it rested no longer felt the need for
coddling labor. The social justice orientation and legislation of
the early corporative regime was increasingly shunted aside.

Biases in the regime were one thing, but the next step involved the development of a full-fledged system of authoritarian
state corporatism, replacing the "corporatism of association" of
the original conception. The move toward an authoritarian, state-
directed corporatism was dictated by the fact that corporative consciousness in Portugal was still inchoate, the corporative agencies
that had been created enjoyed meager support, and Salazar became
convinced that something else had to be created to fill the institutional void. The continued depressed economic conditions, the
perceived need for a stronger set of economic controls, the outbreak of civil war in Spain, a new series of internal conspiracies
and assassination efforts launched against Salazar and the regime
in 1936-37, and the publication of Manoïlesco's book and its dissemination in Portugal--all contributed to the growth of an increasingly centralized and bureaucratic system of state corporatism
(8).

In 1936 the regime created a variety of "Organizations of Economic Coordination"--commissions, juntas, and institutes--which
were to serve as "precorporative" intermediaries between the state
and the still-nascent corporative complex. These agencies served
as the Portuguese equivalents for the plethora of regulatory bureaus that have grown up in other modernizing systems for the coordination and regulation of national economic life. But in Portugal
the process went further. The Organizations of Economic Coordination helped set wages, fix prices, and regulate production, imports, and exports. They served as the means by which state power
was extended to virtually all areas of the national economy, including control over those elusive business groups that had to this
point evaded full corporatization. The Organizations of Economic
Coordination were the prime instruments for the growth of etatism
and state corporatism (519).

The relations between the Organizations of Economic Coordination and the business community were more subtle than this, however, for while, on the one hand, these agencies were used to subordinate business to state control, on the other the same business
elements were moving to infiltrate and eventually capture the entire regulatory complex. Makler (302) has documented the interrelations between the Portuguese corporative state system and the industrial elite, and particularly how individual career patterns
showed an almost constant coming and going between private firms
and the government regulatory agencies--including the frequent
holding of private and public positions simultaneously. Salazar
had brought some of the major economic satrapies--the wine industry, fishing, canning, cork--under state direction, but they had

also learned to manipulate him, chiefly through the argument that his hopes for continued stability and prosperity would be ruined if he really moved to divest this powerful, emerging bourgeoisie of its power and wealth. These arguments were even more persuasive because of the constant crises the regime faced: depression, opposition, the Spanish conflict, then World War II. The result was a sellout to private economic interests, a vast expansion of state power, and the end of the vision of a free system of corporative associability and social justice. The process in Portugal was not altogether unlike the takeover, as described by Ralph Nader, Lowi, and others, of the American regulatory agencies by the very groups they were designed to regulate (282). It was at this point that the Portuguese system corresponded most closely to the definition of corporatism propounded by Schmitter.

To the system of corporate structures and controls, Salazar now added a series of economic laws and regulations which served both to reinforce the corporative structures and, eventually, to supplant them. These laws have generally been ignored by students of the Salazar regime, but they are essential to an understanding of it and the evolution of the Estado Novo toward an increasingly state capitalist or "mercantilist" form. Briefly, what these laws did was to prohibit the creation of a new economic enterprise, or the expansion of an old one, without government permission, and to give the government virtually all power to set wages, prices, production quotas, exports, and imports. The laws vested enormous, heretofore unprecedented economic power in the state (political and associational life had already been concentrated in the state through the new constitution and the corporative system) and gave it the power to regulate and command virtually all of national economic life (96, 293, 316).

Though these laws were "neutral," that is, adaptable to virtually any economic goal, under Salazar the purpose was concentration and consolidation of the economy under state direction. Where monopolies already existed, they were protected; in industries where they did not, new monopolies and oligopolies were created through the use of these laws. By the time World War II broke out, the nation's major economic sectors had all been reorganized on the basis of a great, interconnected complex of conglomerate monopolies, intimately tied to and inseparable from the government structure, linking both continental Portugal and its colonies through the same monopolistic companies, and protected against competition from local businesses or abroad. The result was enormous economic power concentrated in the hands of the state (in this sense, Portugal came ironically, given the regime's anti-communist ideology, to resemble more the centralized, state-run economies of Eastern Europe than the largely laissez-faire systems of the West) and extraordinary wealth concentrated in the hands of a new plutocracy--precisely the same elements who had come to dominate the state regulatory agencies.

A system of state capitalism thus grew up alongside, and eventually supplanting, the corporative structure as one of the main institutional pillars of the regime. As corporatism's original principles were abandoned and as the role of the corporative complex was increasingly circumscribed, confined to limited representational functions, the regulation of labor relations, and the administration of woefully inadequate social security, still other agencies began growing up to fill the vacuum. A police state apparatus, whose controls previously had been sporadic and unsystematic, became increasingly brutal, total, and systematic, another of the prime pillars on which the Estado Novo rested. The power of the state regulatory agencies grew even more. During the war, the corporative agencies were given the unpopular tasks of administering wartime austerity measures, including rationing, price fixing, and wage freezes and decreases, and their popularity declined to a new low. With the end of the war and the general discrediting of all such "fascistic" schemes, the corporative system was still further shunted aside, circumvented, and ignored. The moribund, "dinosauric" character of the system was reflected in the regime itself, which seemed to have lost all purpose and direction. Meanwhile, as the liberal and social-democratic opposition mounted in the postwar period, the police state apparatus grew and repressive, dictatorial measures were increasingly employed (519).

In the 1950s and 1960s, efforts at a corporate revival were undertaken. The old Subsecretariat of Corporations was now made a full ministry. The first corporations were established and a "Plan for Social and Corporative Formation" was initiated. Some new functions were found for the corporative agencies and new concepts of social welfare were articulated. These developments were related to the new economic prosperity in which Portugal shared from the mid-1950s on and to the regime's conviction that, since its first-order priorities of maintaining political stability and providing economic solvency were now accomplished, it could again move ahead with further corporative implementation. But by now it had become clear that corporatism and the corporative complex were no longer (if, indeed, they had ever been) at the base of the system, constituting, as the early ideology had proclaimed, the focus of national life. The gaps between corporative theory and corporative practice were distressingly vast, plain for all to see; and even the new social security legislation existed more on the paper of the Diario de Governo than in actual fact. Corporatism as a manifest system and ideology was, hence, increasingly ignored, both by the regime and by the Portuguese people. It had ceased to have meaning; the entire national system functioned almost as though corporatism and the corporative complex were not there.

By the late 1960s, it was not just the corporative system that had increasingly gone to sleep but the entire national system. Salazar was old and tired, some say senile. The fighting in Africa dragged on, by now on three fronts. The ship of state seemed rudderless, directionless. Needed decisions were not being made. Corruption had become widespread. The secret police constituted almost a separate state-within-a-state. The opposition grew and so did the terror tactics used to repress it. Both the regime and the corporative system seemed to be locked in a deep freeze. In the historic way, demands began to mount that something be done, not only because the regime had become "dinosauric" but also because it seemed to have overstepped the bounds between permissible authoritarianism, which was at the heart both of the historic Portuguese tradition and its most recent manifestation in the corporative regime, and outright tyranny, which seemed now to be characteristic of the Salazar system and, therefore, legitimated the right to rebellion. By the late 1960s, the demand was clear: either renovação from within or revolução from without (h).

CORPORATISM REVITALIZED

> The corporative spirit lives and is practiced . . . . The Government, in remaining faithful to the Political Constitution, of necessity remains faithful to corporative ideals.
>
> Marcello Caetano

The regime of Marcello Caetano was quite different from that of his predecessor, Salazar, but it did not correspond to the picture of it portrayed in the foreign press. Those accounts described Caetano as a would-be but frustrated "liberal," seeking to preside over a process of "democratization" and constantly thwarted in his efforts by powerful rightist, Salazarista forces. The evidence, however, points to the conclusion that, while Caetano sought to update, loosen, and modernize the main pillars of authoritarian-corporate rule, he remained an authoritarian and a corporatist. His rule must be judged in that context and not in the context of some supposed desires for "liberalization" and "democratization" (519).

Caetano had inherited a sluggish government. Government, administration, decision-making, public policy, the corporative structure, the entire national system had all but come to a standstill during the last years of the Salazar regime. It would be Caetano's job to invigorate and revitalize it. Note that nowhere among these purposes do the words "liberalize" or "democratize" appear. Caetano aimed to broaden the directing elites somewhat but not at democratization; he tried to widen the base and appeal of the official party but not real choice between parties; he sought to rein in the secret police but not by sacrificing authoritarian control; he aimed at better implementation of corporatism, not liberalism. Caetano changed the style of the regime more than its essence, presided over a more open, pluralist, socially just system than his predecessor; but that was done within the parameters of the corporative system. Caetano's goal was to adjust the system to new realities, recognize and accommodate the new social forces that had grown up, restore confidence in the economy and the public service, wake up and invigorate a nation and system that had gone to sleep under Salazar, revive a slumbering, almost stagnant set of corporative institutions. It is on these criteria, not according to some imagined "liberal" ones, that his regime must be judged. Both the revolution of 1974 and the judgment of history indicate that by these criteria the regime failed.

While Caetano remained a corporatist and authoritarian, as a leader he proved weak, vacillating, unable to manage the complex divisive currents that modernization had set loose. Although the pattern was similar in other policy areas--educational reform,

governmental remodeling, African affairs--for our purposes the
arena of labor relations is central. Caetano's strategies may be
summarized as follows: first, a tenuous opening up, then a crackdown, followed by uncertainty, vacillation, new openings, more indecision, and an ultimately disastrous temporizing. The breakthrough for labor came in June 1969 in a decree that gave the sindicatos the right to select their own leadership without government
approval. Under Salazar the labor leadership had ordinarily been
imposed by the regime. Another decree provided that, on the threeman arbitration commissions used for settling wage disputes, one
member would be chosen by the sindicato, one by the gremio, and the
third by the other two. Under the old system the third member had
been selected by the government and had invariably sided with employer interests in enforcing austerity and wage controls. Another
provision shortened the time limits given the gremios to respond to
sindicato demands and made it impossible for the gremios, as in the
past, simply to ignore labor demands (429).

Within months the sindicatos, which for decades had been trade
unions in name only, began to be transformed from amorphous government agencies into genuine instruments of the workers. For the
first time, opposition elements, including Communists in the case
of some sindicatos, swept the union elections, and the elections
were allowed to stand. Under the old regime, whenever an oppositionist had managed to win a union election, the election was immediately canceled and new leaders were found more amenable to government direction. At the same time, the new arbitration commissions were in numerous cases deciding in labor's favor. This was
due both to a general political and generational shift that had begun to take place within the state ministries (in this case the
Corporations Ministry) and to explicit directions given out by Caetano's office. As the trade unions gathered strength and some independent bargaining power, the government began enforcing the corporative laws obligating the gremios to respond and calling for coequal power between workers and employers. Strikes, slowdowns, and
protest demonstrations, although legally banned, increased with
government acquiescence. A number of new collective bargaining
agreements were signed between 1969 and 1971 that provided for major wage increases. With government approval, the sindicatos had
begun to acquire some teeth. Meanwhile, under Caetano's Estado
Social, a vast range of new social programs was introduced, no
longer just "para inglês ver" but actually being implemented. The
corporative system was revitalized and for perhaps the first time
started to live up to some of its original ideals (519).

These changes were related to broader Portuguese social and
political developments. Accelerating industrialization had created
a larger and more militant work force and a real laboring class in
such centers as Lisbon and Setúbal, as distinct from the earlier,
deferential workers on whom Salazar's Rerum Novarum-based conception of corporatism had been based. Large-scale emigration and declining population produced severe labor shortages, thereby
strengthening the sindicatos' bargaining position; the commitment
of the government to expanded production and economic growth also
gave it a strong interest in avoiding ruinous strikes by acceding

to labor's demands. Expanded tourism and contact with the outside
world, the push for entry into the Common Market, the emigration of
Portuguese workers to other industrialized nations also helped
break down the Salazar walls of isolation. The freer climate, in
turn, and the 1969 legislative elections gave the opposition a new
impetus, stimulating it to greater organizational efforts among the
workers.

Then came the clamp-down. In the fall of 1970 the metallurgists, one of the most politicized of the sindicatos, had rejected
a proffered labor contract, demanded higher wages, and called a
meeting to rally support. The government banned the rally and ac-
cused the metallurgists of "fomenting class struggle." Other militant unions followed the metallurgists' lead. Employers appealed
to the government to do something to halt the ferment; and it responded with two decrees, the first giving the right to appoint the
third member of the arbitration commissions back to the government
and the second restoring the government's right to suspend elected
sindicato officials for activities "contrary to social discipline."
The decrees opened the way to renewed state control of the sindicatos and, armed with this power, the government moved against the
metallurgists and the other militant oppositionists.

These actions failed to restore labor peace. Once the door
had been opened, it proved difficult to slam it shut. Other unions
increased their demands. Since strikes had been outlawed in corporative Portugal, it was left to the government to decide whether
a work "slowdown" or "stoppage" was really a "strike" or not. A
whole new politics grew up around the question of when a "work
stoppage" was a "strike" and, therefore, required suppression and
when it was not and could, therefore, be allowed to go forward.
The government vacillated: it broke up with police brutality a
demonstration by the clerks, but it acceded to other union demands.
New restrictions were enforced, but new openings were allowed also.
The government gave local authorities the right to approve candidates for sindicato elections and, according to local labor leaders, "these petty bureaucrats use their powers unmercifully." Candidates for union elections had to meet endless qualifications, and
local authorities--if they wished--could always find one that would
disqualify a particular candidate. Whether the labor laws and restrictions were enforced or not depended on the play of forces at
particular moments and frequently on whim. One week the government
would approve an important wage increase for one sector, the next
it would reject it for another. The sindicatos were bitter about
the indecision and uncertainty, but they kept up the pressure. The
regime, too, continued to face in two directions at once, sometimes
paternal, at others brutal.

As the challenges from inside the regime's own sindicato system mounted, a new and equally ominous threat loomed from without,
as workers in sizable numbers began reorganizing in unsanctioned
factory committees. These clandestine, nongovernment unions were
organized into a broad umbrella organization called the "<u>Intersin-
dical</u>" and had appeared in all the nation's major industrial firms.
As part of its strategy to keep labor in check, the Salazar regime
had consistently disallowed the creation of a strong, independent

national labor confederation, but now Caetano, believing he could
contain it, tolerated precisely such an interunion group which came
to represent some fifteen to twenty of the largest sindicatos with
a membership variously put at between 150,000 and 200,000. Intersindical, however, was not content with the wage increases Caetano
had secured and began making stronger demands for full freedom of
association and the right to strike. In mid-1971 Caetano moved to
outlaw the organization and to purge its affiliated unions (293).

But now the union movement could not be suppressed so easily
and Intersindical, having gained a foothold, moved underground
where it provided a ready vehicle for infiltration by the clandestine Portuguese Communist Party. The government now had to deal
with both a restless official sindicato structure and the subsur-
face Intersindical. Intersindical moved to organize "unity committees" in industries and offices where it could convert worker dis-
satisfaction into crippling strikes. The government responded by
arranging wage increases which it hoped would increase its popularity and undercut Intersindical's appeal, but it was unwilling to
give the unions independent bargaining power. It sought to preserve the essential paternalistic, authoritarian structure of the
system while, at the same time, staving off discontent. When that
tactic failed, it used riot police to break up demonstrations, ar-
rest strike leaders, and curb the clandestine unity committees.
But these tactics seemed only to lead to still larger strikes. The
tendency of foreign and domestic firms to respond differentially to
worker demands and pay different wage scales (the foreign firms
paid more and were more responsive; domestic firms sought to resist
negotiations and rely on the state for support against the unions)
added to the inequalities and the bitterness.

By 1973, while the government continued to provide for some
wage increases, industrial unrest had become so rampant that forty
major strikes occurred, almost literally closing down the economy
in some cases, undermining both the African war effort and Caetano's plans for social reform, leading to paralysis, and thus
stimulating increased rumblings of discontent against the vacillating, uncertain Caetano government on the part of center and rightist elements who now began to plot in earnest to overthrow the regime. As the pressures from labor, center, and _Salazarista_ forces
increased, and as the question was more frequently asked whether
the regime could continue to cope with these conflicting currents,
the government lost all _confiança_, the plotting grew more intense,
and several aborted coup attempts were launched before the final
one succeeded in April 1974. Caetano had proved incapable of managing the divergent forces now loose, the regime fell, and the effort to preside over a revitalized corporatism failed.

CORPORATION DISMANTLED, TRANSCENDED, PERSISTENT?

> Corporatism is far from dead. Many continuities exist in the
> present regime. Corporatism may reassert itself, not just in
> a Fascist form but in more subtle manifestations (285).

The 1961 _Programa para a democratização da república_ (415),

drafted by the Portuguese opposition movement, urged that the following action be taken with regard to the corporative structure:
1. The corporations were to be abolished and replaced by institutions of a "democratic nature."
2. The various agencies and institutions of the corporative state were to be dissolved, transformed, or integrated into a new democratic order.
3. The functions of the Organizations of Economic Coordination would be integrated into the normal services of public administration.
4. The casas, ordens, and sindicatos connected with the corporate structure would be converted into genuine class associations; complete sovereignty would be granted their general assemblies.
5. The gremios would be converted into class associations whose leaders would be elected by the membership.
6. The casas do povo and casas dos pescadores might continue as reorganized agencies without prejudice against the rights of labor associations also to organize their members.

In the wake of the 1974 revolution, this program became the basis for the dismantling of the Portuguese corporative system. Not only were the control mechanisms of the Salazar regime--secret police, censorship, etc.--quickly overturned, but the entire web of corporative agencies, the corporations, and the corporative complex were also eliminated. The dismantling of the corporative system took place initially at the street level and then was ratified by official decree. The initial April coup had been followed by hundreds of "mini-coups" in industrial plants, professional associations, and government offices. There were innumerable confrontations between workers and employers, servants and patrons, students and faculties. In scores of offices and agencies, signs appeared in the windows announcing "liberation" from the "fascists." The old official sindicato system broke down as the underground factory unity committees emerged and workers seized factories; plant managers and directors were driven out, strikes multiplied, and direct action became the means for solving disputes. The Corporations Ministry became the Labor Ministry; it was given over initially to the Communists who used their control of the pinnacles of the labor pyramid to gain advantages for themselves while keeping the basic structure intact. The Labor Statute of 1933 was declared inoperative before a new one had been drawn up to replace it. The whole panoply of Labor Tribunals, Arbitration Commissions, collective contracts was abolished; also overturned were the networks of economic regulatory commissions, institutes, and juntas. The leadership of the ordens and gremios was soon replaced, and the Communist-dominated Intersindical gained an overwhelmingly preponderant position in the trade union movement. The social services, also administered through the corporative system, were severely disrupted (552).

Direct action in the streets was followed quickly (and occasionally anticipated) by action at the official level. On May 2, 1974, it was decreed that harbormasters (generally state appointees or the servants of employer interests) would no longer serve as the presidents of the casas dos pescadores. On May 9 the Junta of National Salvation (the Spínola government) gave itself the power to suspend all employees of the corporative agencies and Organizations of Economic Coordination and to name all replacements. On May 27 a decree overturned the old sindicato structure. On June 3 the Junta Central of the casas dos pescadores was relieved of its duties. On August 17 the corporations were dissolved. On September 9 the Junta da Acção Social of the Ministry of Corporations was "extinguished." On September 12 all corporative agencies "dependent" upon the old Corporations Ministry were dissolved and their responsibilities transferred to the Organizations of Economic Coordination. On September 25 the gremios da lavoura were abolished; on October 23 the Fundação Nacional para a Alegría no Trabalho was "restructured." On December 23 the Federations of Casas do povo were scuttled; in January 1975 some gremios were eliminated, others were to be "investigated." The "obligatory gremios" were replaced by a new confederation of industry, while the "voluntary gremios" were reorganized as private interest associations. By the end of the first year of the revolution, virtually the entire formal structure of the corporative state had been dismantled or restructured (i).

But the process was nowhere near so thorough and the changeovers not so complete as the analysis of the "street" action and the formal decrees implies. There was no "180° turnabout," as some accounts have alleged. While many agencies of the corporative system were abolished, many others (gremios, sindicatos, casas do povo, casas dos pescadores) remained in existence. They were reorganized, often renamed, and their leaders changed; but a good part of the structure continued intact and, while the leadership often was turned over at the top, at lower levels the same personnel often continued in their same jobs. We saw this particularly in the sindicato structure and the Labor Ministry, and at the local and municipal government levels, where a new leadership moved in but where the hierarchical, top-down, pyramidal, and sectoral structure was often preserved. The new private associations continued to act in most respects as had the old gremios; the casas do povo and casas dos pescadores remained almost identical to what they had been under the old regime. This is not to discount the revolutionary transformations that occurred in some agencies and some policy areas, but it is to say there were important continuities as well. Some of the corporative agencies continued largely intact; in others, the names and faces changed but the same functions continued to be performed. A close examination of the unfolding of the revolution indicates that it may have been less abrupt, less disruptive of basic institutions, than the United States press accounts conveyed. While no one would deny the fundamental transformations and <u>regeneração</u> that the revolution implied, it is also important to understand the sheer persistence of some earlier forms and practices.

Not only were some of the older corporative agencies and practices often slow in being confined to the ashcans of history, but then the new regime moved to resurrect a new set of corporative institutions. They were called by other names but their character was essentially corporative. Lucena (285) has analyzed the post-revolutionary thrust toward an ideology and structure of class collaboration rather than conflict, a feature which he correctly identifies as one of the essential features of corporatism. The movement toward an increasingly strong and authoritarian state structure, an increasingly state-directed economy, a carefully structured and state-directed system of interest associations and representational bodies is similarly characteristic of corporate state systems. The Portuguese government and its constituent agencies are still heavily military dominated, infused with hierarchical and authoritarian structures. The regime presumes to govern for and in the name of the "common good"; it has shown little enthusiasm for democracy and genuine grass-roots participation on the liberal model; and elections carry but tentative, not definitive, legitimacy. The Portuguese state is still largely the administrative and technocratic state that it was before, heavily bureaucratic, still carefully regulated and controlled, with elaborate legal-administrative procedures left over from the old regime, still organized from the top down and governed by decree-law. Increasingly, the control mechanisms of the historic tradition have been resurrected as a way of preventing the spontaneity and joy of the early street demonstrations from getting out-of-hand and of channeling them, again, in preferred directions. Finally, our attention must be called to the new institutional arrangements inaugurated by the MFA and then reorganized by succeeding regimes, with their functionally representative bodies, their corporative and syndicalist tendencies, and the special place within the system given the military and other corporate groups. As Lucena concluded, the present regime shows some "unexpected similarities" with the regime of Marcello Caetano.

A third consideration in weighing the corporative system and the corporative tradition in Portugal has to do with the models we have used to interpret the changes underway both before and after 1974. Many of these models, implicit in the popular accounts but finding their way into more scholarly analyses as well, paint the older corporative system in rigid and entirely static terms, hence portray the post-1974 regime in generously liberal and liberating terms, and see the entire political process in Portugal in the light of a dichotomous struggle between dictatorship and democracy. It is fair to call the later Salazar regime rigid and static, there were some liberalizing and liberating aspects to the 1974 revolution, and there is clearly something of a struggle between dictatorship and democracy. But that is not the entire picture. For from this analysis as well as Lucena's, it is clear there are various dynamic aspects to corporatism and not just static ones, that the corporatism of Caetano was quite different from that of Salazar, that corporatism is not entirely impermeable but may evolve depending on societal conditions and developmental transformations, and that instead of being perceived wholly through "liberal" or "liberating" frameworks the postrevolutionary regime might also be examined in the light of revolutionary, more complex, perhaps "higher" forms of corporatism. The dictatorship-democracy dichotomy is too confining, too restrictive, too culture-bound to provide a very useful model; it represents a false choice, a too-limited set of possibilities. It fails to recognize that corporatism may take populist, leftist, and revolutionary directions, as in Peru, as well as conservative and rightist ones; or that even within a single country various corporative forms may be related to broader societal transformations. Where the dictatorship vs. democracy framework is useful and bears some relation to actual Portuguese events, let us use it; but let us keep open the possibility that from Salazar through Caetano to the present regime we have witnessed both some remarkable changes in--as well as the persistence of--an essentially corporative system, from the conservative, rigid, unyielding Rerum Novarum-Quadragesimo Anno form of Salazar, to the more open, pluralist, and socially just form of Caetano, to the more populist, revolutionary, socialist, and/or syndicalist forms of the present. That is a paradigm that also carries considerable explanatory power (552).

We return to the two meanings of the term "corporatism" with which we began. Corporatism has been discussed here in two ways: a political-cultural sense that implies a long tradition of what was called "natural corporatism," and a more manifest and explicit ideology and structure of "corporatism" that found expression in the Estado Novo of the 1930s. It has proved rather easy to dismantle the corporative institutions associated with the Salazar regime since they were often ephemeral agencies that lacked deep roots, were weakly institutionalized, and enjoyed but limited legitimacy. Whether Portugal can as easily transcend its corporatist tradition and culture may be quite a different matter. The continuities with and persistent features of that historic tradition remain strong even in the wake of the revolution of 1974. Portugal may evolve toward a more "developed," more pluralist, socialist, or syndicalist form, but of the fact that those forms will continue to exhibit important corporatist characteristics there would seem to be little doubt. For Portugal to depart from this broader corporatist tradition would involve shucking off some 800 years of history, and that seems more problematic than simply ridding itself of the corporative institutions fashioned by Salazar.

FINAL CONSIDERATIONS

The formal corporative system in Portugal from 1933 to 1974 was a mixed bag of successes and failures. Corporatism was successful in the 1930s in providing Portugal with a new national mythos badly needed after the chaos and failure of republicanism, with a new sense of national purpose, with restoring order and stability and a set of institutions based upon indigenous sources, with helping to restore rationality to the national accounts, with providing for economic growth and development, and with helping to fill the organizational void of a country whose historic, long-term problems had always included a vacuum in its associational life. The reestablishment of a stable, functioning regime and the strengthening of the economy, closely related to the creation of the corporative system from 1933 on, were among the more notable and fundamental accomplishments of the regime. But after 1945, as the regime became more brutal, repressive, and fascistic, as corporatism in the earlier 1930s sense was discredited and became increasingly dysfunctional, serving more to retard national growth than stimulate it, the failures of the system came to outweigh its earlier successes. The efforts of Caetano to revitalize the corporative system were again a mixture of successes and, ultimately, failure (519).

But perhaps "success" or "failure" is the wrong way to answer the question. Perhaps we should simply take the Portuguese regime on its own terms and in its own context. In that sense, the regime neither "succeeded" nor "failed"; it was rather the product of an historical period whose time had simply passed. The 1930s were probably the high point of corporatism in the global context and when the conservative <u>Rerum Novarum</u> form of corporatism as propounded by Salazar still fitted fairly well the rural, conservative structure of Portuguese society. By the postwar period, this was no longer the case. Portugal had changed and so had the international content. What was required was no longer a corporatism of control, demobilization, and selective repression but a corporatism of change and development. Corporatism in the earlier 1930s (or 1890s?) form was an idea and mode of organization whose epoch had been superseded. Time had passed the Portuguese regime by, while Salazar continued to uphold a system that had become anachronistic, even on its own corporative terms.

Here, then, lay the real difficulty for the Portuguese regime. It was not that it refused to go toward liberalism or socialism (neither at that time strongly favored nor enjoying the support of a majority of the Portuguese population) but that it failed to modernize even the corporative structures that it did have. The regime instead stagnated, became dinosauric. While other countries--Spain, Argentina, Brazil, Mexico, Peru--gradually evolved away from the older forms of corporatism toward more dynamic, participatory, change-and-development-oriented forms, Portugal remained locked in the older conception, in the outdated bourgeois ideal of an ordered, hierarchical, Catholic, paternalistic state and society. It failed to take account of the new social forces emerging, or sought simply to repress them. Caetano made some frantic, feeble efforts to rescue and dynamize the system at the last minute, but these came too late. Portugal's chief problem was that it failed to update and restructure its institutions and programs even within the prevailing corporative framework.

By the same token--at least until the revolution of 1974--it was not necessarily corporatism per se that was increasingly rejected by the Portuguese population in the postwar period but the particular direction it had taken under Salazar. If Salazar had been adaptable, if he had modernized the nation instead of letting it drift, if his had not become a repressive dictatorship, and if he had been willing to recognize the changing nature of Portuguese society and the just demands of the middle and lower classes (all big <u>ifs</u> obviously but <u>ifs</u> that in considerable measure came to pass in the warp and woof of postwar change in other Iberian and Latin nations similarly cast in the earlier corporative mold), the corporative system might well have lasted. It became instead a symbol to be despised of dictatorship and backwardness. The outdated, discredited, Salazarista corporative conception was thus repudiated, as it deserved to be. Had that conception and its accompanying institutional arrangements proved more accommodative and adaptable, it is likely that Portugal would still be a corporative system, not in the old-fashioned, now thoroughly discredited sense, but in a newer, more modern sense, providing for the development of the Portuguese nation and people. That is how development has usually gone forward elsewhere in the Iberic-Latin world; unfortunately, it did not take place in Portugal.

All this augurs ill for the future of the Portuguese system and for the possibilities of establishing any stable, functioning, development-oriented regime. If it is, in fact, the case that corporatism in its natural, historic forms lies at the heart of Portuguese political culture and may even today be still a dominant tradition, then we should recognize the possibility that the particular Salazar system may have so thoroughly discredited corporatism that no new government will be able to build upon that heritage. We must also recognize that corporatism is no longer the only tradition in Portugal, that alongside it have grown up a liberal-republican tradition and a nascent socialist one. But these latter traditions are still so new and weakly institutionalized that they may not have sufficient support or legitimacy to serve as the basis for the establishment of a new regime either. With these three concepts and world views continuing to coexist uneasily side-by-side, representing wholly different ways of life and modes of organizing society and polity, with little connection between them, and with no one enjoying absolute legitimacy or even majority support, it may well be that Portugal will remain, like Argentina, ineffective and inefficient, chaotic, fragmented, and disintegrated, subject to recurrent breakdowns, a kind of permanently crippled nation unable to establish any functioning system, be it liberalism, an updated form of corporate pluralism, or a newer variant of socialism or syndicalism, to replace the older form of corporatism that has since been dismantled.

NOTES

    a. The longer, more detailed case study from which some of the present analysis derives is 519.
    b. The critique that follows combines elements from two papers, 524 and 526. Interested readers may wish to consult the originals for the full context of these remarks. Another devastating critique is 203.
    c. "Pluralism" is another of those terms, like "democracy" or "representation," that means something different in the Portuguese context than in the Anglo-American one; see Chapter 13. Nor should the possibilities for corporate pluralism be ruled out or defined away. In the absence of a strong liberal-democratic tradition in Portugal, a degree of corporate pluralism may be about all that the political liberal may hope for.

d. Salazar was also very clever in his relations with the military. Although he had incorporated many of the integralist, monarchist, nationalist, and Catholic principles into his own corporatist formula, he had not accepted one of their chief goals--the restoration of the monarchy. Instead, Salazar elevated the armed forces into the role of the "moderating power" historically reserved for the crown, thereby securing the loyalty and support of the military while at the same time retaining the backing of all but the most fervent of the monarchists, integralists, and Catholic traditionalists.

e. This analysis is related to the question of the Latin American middle class and whether it is progressive or reactionary. The answer is: a bit of both, depending on the pragmatic circumstances. For the debate, see 222, 391.

f. Fascism, according to Organski (369), is a model of development based on a partnership between agricultural and industrial elements to carry out industrialization but to impose its costs primarily on the industrial working class.

g. Manoïlesco's book, published in 1934, was soon being widely read by Caetano, Salazar, and other leading Portuguese corporativists. Manoïlesco provided a subtle, secular, and materialist corporatist conception. He presented corporatism as a permanent institutional arrangement which could be employed to subordinate particular interests to broader national goals and to provide for the growth of a development-oriented, state-capitalist system. I am convinced his book had a profound impact on Portuguese corporative developments, since the correspondence between what he advocated and what Salazar, in fact, did is too close to be circumstantial.

h. Implied in these paragraphs are two ideas that need to be developed at greater length. First, it seems clear that the biases that developed in the Estado Novo and the particular directions that the regime took were not necessarily inherent in corporatism per se but had to do more with the nature of power and influence in the broader Portuguese system, the priorities that Salazar and the army had established, which relegated corporative implementation to a third-order priority, and the particular choices that Salazar opted for at especially critical junctures. Corporatism in Portugal might just as well have taken a more populist, developmentalist, and pluralist direction, as it did in other nations organized initially on some similar corporatist bases. Corporatism per se seems not to be the independent villain variable on which Portugal's retarded growth could be blamed; a more likely candidate is Salazar himself. For further discussion, see 519.

Second, it seems worth considering that the regime was eventually repudiated and overthrown, not because it was corporatist and authoritarian, or because it refused to go toward liberalism or social-democracy, but because it had become oppressive, ridden roughshod over corporate group foros, violated the natural rights of its people, and become a full-fledged tyranny--all of which constitute grounds for revolt, both in Portuguese practice and in legal theory. The regime both developed and was eventually repudiated, not in terms of the liberal-democratic paradigm, but in terms of the very Portuguese institutions and practices on which it was based. For some orienting concepts, see 439.

i. Based on the field work and interviews in Portugal in May-June 1975. The decree laws are published in the Boletim do Instituto Nacional do Trabalho e Previdência for this period.

16 | Cuba: Is It Also Corporatist and Bureaucratic-Authoritarian?

> The Cuban government rules from an authoritarian center because it is Cuban rather than because it is communist.
>
> Claudio Véliz

In Latin American and Iberian studies of late, much attention --and a large body of ground-breaking recent literature--has been devoted to the phenomena of corporatism and bureaucratic-authoritarianism. Specifically, the issue has been raised as to whether corporatism and bureaucratic-authoritarianism may not, despite frequent regime changes, periodic circulations of elites, "modernization," and the comings and goings of rival civilian and military governments, represent more-or-less permanent, ubiquitous, and lasting aspects of Iberic-Latin political culture. The debate has been lent particular poignancy by the growing realization that corporatism and bureaucratic-authoritarianism may take left-wing directions, as in Peru or Portugal, as well as rightist ones. Obviously, Cuba and its revolutionary regime constitute the acid test for the cultural continuity argument.

Related to this is the growing popular disaffection with authoritarian and state-bureaucratic systems, whether they take the form of state capitalism or state socialism. The Soviet Union seldom provides today's radicals and revolutionaries with a model to seek to emulate, and we have become disillusioned with the New Class of self-interested and self-perpetuating bureaucrats--be they in Western, Communist, or Third World countries. In an era of new concern for the decentralization of existing structures and of renewed emphasis upon freedom and human rights, we must be concerned when these trends are reversed, or when freedom and human rights are seen as negotiable rather than self-evident, to be granted or withheld at the pleasure of the all-embracing state. These themes, too, have begun to come together in the study of contemporary Cuba.

The argument that Cuba was governed autocratically and constituted a Communist dictatorship has long been made by the right and the exiles. But now that criticism comes from a new and unexpected

---

Part of a larger study of Cuban institutionalization; originally based on a book review of S. Dolgoff, The Cuban Revolution (Montreal: Black Rose, 1976).

source, the left, in the form of Sam Dolgoff's The Cuban Revolution: A Critical Perspective. Dolgoff's criticism is especially devastating because he is himself an anarcho-syndicalist, anti-imperialist, and revolutionary.

Dolgoff begins with a history of the Cuban anarcho-syndicalist movement. He argues, apropos of the cultural continuity thesis, that anarcho-syndicalism is closer to the Cuban tradition than is Marxism-Leninism; and he emphasizes that there can be no affinity between the authoritarian socialism of present-day Cuba and the libertarianism and defense of civil liberties and workers' rights of the anarcho-syndicalists.

Dolgoff advocates a decentralized, voluntaristic society based on genuine popular participation and worker self-management. He finds all these features sadly lacking in Fidel's Cuba. Instead, what he sees there is the growing role of the armed forces in the economy and the militarization of Cuban society, the growth of bureaucratic rule and the omnipotence of the state and its leader, an autocratic and dictatorial regime that has no respect for human rights, a people who are no longer the masters but the servants of the leadership, a university and trade union structure completely subordinated to the power of the state. The absolute power of the state, he says, dominates all other institutions. Dolgoff calls it a "totalitarian dictatorship."

It seems in some ways ironic to find support for the cultural continuity thesis coming from an anarcho-syndicalist and an avowed revolutionary. Dolgoff argues that the anarcho-syndicalist ideas correspond to both the historic experiences and the true aspirations of the Cuban people. But instead, he states, the Cuban revolution has resurrected another and contrary model, which is militaristic, pyramidal, authoritarian, hierarchical, patrimonial (in terms of the personalization of power and of the revolution itself, and the favoritism shown the friends and relatives of leading members of the Communist Party or of Fidel himself), and corporatist (in the structuring of a set of official, monopolistic, government-sponsored and -sanctioned interest associations and institutionalized bodies, with all major sectors guaranteed representation along functional lines: army, bureaucracy, local entities, workers, peasants, women, etc.). He draws parallels with Perón and Mussolini, arguing the Cuban revolution is paternalistic and in the tradition of Latin revolutionary caudilloism and a militarized society.

Dolgoff prefers workers' control of major industries rather than the all-pervasive power of the central state or its national planning agency. He wants cooperatives, not state farms. He insists on effective mass participation instead of top-down rule. He argues the Cuban form of a hierarchical and authoritarian state is incompatible with true socialism. The Cuban revolution, he says, has become a counterrevolution carried out by the state against the people. Without its bloody terror but in terms of its authoritarian statism, Dolgoff argues, Cuba is the Latin American version of Stalinism.

Dolgoff tells how the anarcho-syndicalists fought both Batista and the present regime to help preserve their liberties, in contrast to the Communists who worked out mutually beneficial arrangements with both. He criticizes the deification of Fidel as comparable to the megalomania of Stalin. He recognizes some of the social accomplishments of the regime but argues it is a dictatorship with which the population is gradually becoming discontented. Cuba, rather than at the forefront of change, is instead retrogressive by the criteria of genuine popular participation, workers' control, individual rights, and its centralized control and etatism.

Some of Dolgoff's criticisms are especially telling. The Cuban labor movement, as he analyzes it, has been placed in a straitjacket, subordinated to the state, consolidated into a single official institutional pillar, and its right to strike withdrawn. Cuban education has also been "militarized" and regimented, with an official curriculum, indoctrination substituting for learning, and the autonomy of the university destroyed. The press has been made similarly subservient and dissenting intellectuals continue to be muzzled. He notes that the key posts in the government have been increasingly given to military officers, that a barracks discipline and authoritarianism now prevail. The bureaucratic maze is choking the economy. Power concentrated in the army, the bureaucracy, and the state, he argues, adds up inevitably to oligarchy, dictatorship, and lack of freedom.

The new Cuban constitution was supposed to help decentralize the system and expand local initiative and self-management in field and factory, but in reality, Dolgoff finds, it will lead to even greater concentrated power. "Institutionalization" of the Cuban revolution implies stricter centralized authority exercised at the top, by the leadership of the Communist Party and Fidel Castro. All organs of state power are now concentrated under one-man control. The Communist Party governs Cuba, says Dolgoff, and Fidel rules the CP. There is no union democracy, the Committees for the Defense of the Revolution have lost all vestiges of democracy and been subordinated to the Party, workers' self-management nowhere exists. Instead, the unions serve as transmission belts for the administration and greater implementation of production, under the CP. Real corporate or sectoral power rests not with the unions and the grass-roots associations but with the military, the bureaucracy, the CP, and the "líder máximo."

Dolgoff argues that the 1970s institutionalization of the revolution, in the long run, is bound to undermine the structure of a personalized dictatorship. The various power blocks and corporate-bureaucratic groups tied into the regime are certain to expand their power in the future, and Fidel will be forced to share power with them. Personal rule must inevitably give way to collective rule; although under the present power arrangement, tyranny (Dolgoff's term) will nonetheless be perpetuated. So far, however, institutionalization is only in its initial stages, reinforcing for now the personal authority of Fidel Castro.

Dolgoff's book is marred by several factual inaccuracies, a number of dubious interpretations, and considerable verbal overkill that apologists for the Cuban regime are certain to pounce upon. At the same time, the conservative exile community is sure to use it as confirmation, in an "I told-you-so" fashion, of beliefs it has long held a priori. Regardless of these political uses to which the book will be put, it still will stand as a massive and devastating criticism and indictment of the Cuban system, particularly so for having come from a source himself on the revolutionary left. It also raises some intriguing and bigger questions concerning the authoritarian-bureaucratic and corporatist nature of revolutionary Cuba, regardless of the language of Marxism-Leninism which is its own idiom, that merit further consideration.

Cuba, unlike many other Latin American nations, never developed a strong tradition of institutionalized corporatist-authoritarian structures in its past. As a colony without abundant gold or silver or a large-scale Indian civilization to be enslaved, it never felt the full weight of the Spanish colonial system as did Mexico or Peru: an authoritarian-hierarchical political structure, a strong Church, a feudal economy, or a rigid two-class society. And in the nineteenth-century Cuba, in contrast with its neighbors, remained a Spanish colony, both shaping its history of frustrated nationalism and preventing the growth of such powerful corporate groups as a dominant national landholding oligarchy or military.

The pervasive North American presence in the twentieth century served to retard further Cuban institutionalization. Its economic elites were new-rich and so closely enmeshed with U.S. capital that they never developed a corporate elan and self-identity of their own; the Church remained similarly weak. The army developed something of a corporate self-identity, but it was never so strongly institutionalized as in other nations and was discredited under Batista. Nor did a manifestly corporatist movement emerge in the 1920s and 1930s, as in Argentina, Brazil, and almost everywhere else in Latin America, patterned on the European model. Its political parties were similarly weak, fragile, and all but completely discredited by the corrupt "party" regimes of Grau San Martín and Carlos Prío Socarrás. Cuba was such a remote part of the Spanish empire and so close to the United States that it never developed a dominant corporatist tradition and institutions; at the same time, it was sufficiently "Latin" and its resentment toward North American colonialism such that liberalism never took firm root either. Indeed, what strikes one most about prerevolutionary Cuba is not the strength of its traditional corporate or other institutions but the almost complete organizational and institutional void and the corresponding disorder of its politics.

That is one reason Fidel was able to make such a sharp break with the past. With the collapse of the Batista army, there were no other strong institutions to overcome. Nor were there really any viable, established alternatives to Fidel's 26th of July Movement and the Communist Party. The sheer absence of any kind of institutional infrastructure--of whatever political orientation--also helps explain why the Cuban revolution for so long remained so highly personalized and dominated by the forceful personality of Fidel Castro. In the absence of any working, organized institutions, charismatic authority, along with the emerging authority of the Communist Party and the Revolutionary Armed Forces, are about all that did--or could--hold the Revolution together.

But now with the recent movement toward the institutionalization of the Revolution, Cuba is, perhaps for the first time, becoming organized, bureaucratized, hierarchically ordered, and corporatized, in Dolgoff's meaning of these terms. The family has been declared the "basic cell" of the society. A series of organizations has been created reaching from the grass roots to the top levels that give Cuba an institutional base it entirely lacked before. New officially sanctioned and hierarchically ordered associations have been created for virtually everyone: workers, peasants, intellectuals, women, students, youth, etc. In an effort to build a labor movement supportive of the revolution, Cuba introduced a series of new corporative provisions in its labor legislation that, in a recent study by David Collier and Ruth Berins Collier (84), produced some of the highest scores on a "corporatism and labor law" index of all the Latin American countries. A degree of <u>functional representation</u> has also been introduced by the new constitution into both the People's Assembly and the Council of State. In addition, some groups have been assigned the responsibilities for certain functions in coordination with corresponding state agencies (e.g., INRA, the agrarian reform agency, now has incorporated some peasant representatives into its own organization, who are assigned by the official peasant association) in ways that are reminiscent of other corporate systems.

In short, the organizational void that has long plagued Cuba has begun to be filled. And the model being used is a bureaucratic-authoritarian and, to some degree, corporatist one, albeit obviously a left and socialist variant of that model (comparable perhaps to Peru or Portugal for a time or perhaps Yugoslavia or the Soviet Union) rather than a rightist one.

A series of provocative questions follow, which cannot be answered finally here but should serve to stimulate further thinking and discussion about Cuba and the nature of its revolution. Given the absence and fragility of Cuban institutions historically--both corporatist and liberal--were there realistically any genuine alternatives to Fidel's charismatic authority and the organizational nuclei of the 26th of July Movement and the Communist Party? Could the Castro revolution, and the recent moves toward institutionalization, be understood not just in terms of Marxism-Leninism but also in terms of Cuba's historic quest to fill her long-standing organizational void, to correct the traditional "<u>falta de organización</u>" that has always plagued Cuba? And in the absence of many effective and standing institutions of its own, does the Cuban revolution represent, in part at least, a reaction to the strong inferiority complex vis-a-vis Europe and the United States, and to its profound sense of frustrated nationalism, that Cuba has always felt? Is the revolution, in other words, an effort to "show the world" that by its new socialist institutions Cuba is just as "advanced," just as "modern," just as "progressive" as anyone else? Was the revolution, therefore, a way of leapfrogging to the forefront among nations and for Cuba to thumb her nose at those who treated her always with contempt? And once institutionalization began, did those institutions almost inevitably begin to reflect both the Hispanic and particularly Cuban past as well as the

Marxist-Leninist model on which they were ostensibly based?

So is Cuba corporatist? The answer is both yes and no. No historically and during the early, charismatic years of the revolution. But in its recent efforts at bureaucratizing and institutionalizing the revolution, clearly the tendencies and possibilities are present, and perhaps in the aspirations of its present leadership as well. Certainly Dolgoff, in his discussion of the parallels with Mussolini and Perón, has concluded that Cuba is both corporatist and bureaucratic-authoritarian; and in this connection, and recalling the left wing and syndicalist intellectual origins of corporatism as well as its rightist variants, it might be noted that Trotsky considered Stalin a corporatist. One is reminded again of Claudio Véliz's comment that Cuba, with all its revolutionary changes, remains both Cuban and socialist, with all the inclinations toward centralism, caudilloism, organicism, authoritarianism, and perhaps institutionalized corporatism and vertical sectoralism that implies. To understand Cuba, we must, of course, understand Marxism-Leninism, but we would likely do well to come to grips with Saint-Simon, Sorel, Gramsci, and the Southern European traditions of corporatism and syndicalism as well.

17 | The Latin Americanization of the United States

Recent commentaries on the American malaise and the decline of the American condition have focused on some remarkably parallel themes. Whether it is Schlesinger's "Imperial Presidency," Goodwin on "The American Condition" and "The Sources of the Public Unhappiness," Galbraith's "New Industrial State" and more recently "The Planning System," Robert Lekachman on "liberal" government and the new capitalism, Bernard Nossiter on "The Myth of Countervailing Power," David T. Bazelon on "The Overriding Issue of Organization," Lowi's "The End of Liberalism," Glazer or Moynihan on the limits of social policy, or Bell's "Technocracy" (a), there are numerous common currents of thought. These include the degree to which bigness, bureaucracy, impersonalism, hierarchy, authority, and concentrated power have come to dominate our lives; gigantic corporations, multinationals, and governments pursuing irresponsible policies but beyond our capacities of control; a stagnant economy and, hence, a zero-sum economics game where everyone is out only for himself; the decline of our sense of moral purpose and mutual tolerance; a similar decline in the individual's or the local community's ability to influence decisions or even mold his or its own life; the incorporation and cooptation of labor, business, and farm groups into the bureaucratic structure of the modern, highly centralized state; the preponderance of administration and technocracy rather than genuine popular choice and participation; corruption and public immorality; fragmentation and national disintegration; and the "decline," "crisis," "demise," or "death" of American liberalism. Serious questions are being asked as to whether these broad-scale social, economic, value, and political changes are any longer compatible with the liberal tradition, with conventional party politics, with separation of powers, with the Constitution as written for an older and agrarian society now rendered outmoded by the march of industrialism and large-scale capitalism, and with the fundamental tenets of the Bill of Rights and democratic rule.

I wish to suggest that these currents and changes in the American condition add up to an almost inevitable "Latin Americanization of the United States." By this I do not have in mind Time

---

From The New Scholar 7 (1978): 51-86.

writer Hugh Sidey's Watergate-inspired comment that we have become something of a "banana republic" with an almost weekly upheaval. The fact is the so-called banana republics have been doing quite well lately, and without American aid; "banana republics" exist now only in New Yorker cartoons and residual popular stereotypes. The spectre of a helicopter gunship firing away as it lands on the White House grounds, of a vice president and then president removed from office by means not altogether different from the classic coup d'etat, of private militias like "the Plumbers" formed for political purposes, of a power failure in the middle of a nationally televised presidential campaign debate, and of a whole host of other banana-republic-like occurrences is not what I mean by "the Latin Americanization of the United States." Nor do I wish to imply the false and misleading parallel drawn often by politicians and university administrators that our institutions of higher learning are becoming like their image of the Latin American university. No, what I mean by "the Latin Americanization of the United States" implies far profounder and deeper changes than these. It has to do specifically with the increasing bureaucratization, centralization, and corporatization of the United States, with our developing structure of bureaucratic-patrimonialist authority, with the growth of bigness, impersonalism, large-scale organization, and of a technocratic-administrative state apparatus that, in considerable measure, runs contrary to the whole liberal-democratic tradition. It is precisely these emerging features of the American system that have been at the heart of the Iberian and Latin American political tradition for centuries. It is a system and organizational form from which we, in our present condition, can now learn.

THE MODEL OF CORPORATIST-PATRIMONIALIST STATE AND SOCIETY

The United States did not have a feudal nor a strongly imperial past. This helps explain why corporatist forms of societal organization and/or political authority have historically enjoyed but limited popularity. John Quincy Adams and, in his notion of "the concurrent majority," John C. Calhoun were early corporatists, but in the history of American thought their ideas are usually viewed as curiosities, outside the mainstreams, without relevance in the dominant American liberal tradition. Such agencies as the National Labor Relations Board (NLRB), the National Recovery Association (NRA), the Works Projects Administration (WPA), to say nothing of the other depression-years regulatory boards and the mechanisms set up to administer wartime controls, constituted early, nascent, semicorporative organizations; but these have usually been considered emergency and, hence, temporary agencies, destined to disappear once the existing crisis had passed. Nowhere in the Mayflower Compact or the Constitution, nor in the ideas of Locke, Madison, or Jefferson, are there to be found the seeds and philosophical basis for corporatism and an all-pervasive statism.

In contrast, the nations of Iberia and Latin America have always been based upon a tradition that is authoritarian-bureaucratic, hierarchical, elitist, patrimonialist, and corporatist to its core. Theirs is an imperial and a mercantilist (or state capitalist) tradition, and it is no accident that, in contrast to North America, the nations of Latin America are consistently referred to as being "feudal" or "semifeudal" in character. This characterization has to do not only with their historic economic retardation, in a Rostowian "Stages of Growth" sense, but also with a distinct, alternative set of philosophical assumptions and institutional arrangements on which society and polity are based. "Distinct" rather than "backward," an "alternative" corporatist path to national modernization rather than any earlier phase on some unilinear liberal-democratic route, the "corporative model" would seem to be the structure and form of organization toward which the United States has recently evolved.

As here used, corporatism refers not to the modern joint stock company nor to the structure of what is called "corporate capitalism," although we shall in this essay explore some of the relations between corporatism and capitalism. Rather, corporatism implies an organic-unified view of society and polity, a theory derived originally from Catholic and Latin sources (though later secularized), a system based upon a strong hierarchical and state structure, organized on bureaucratic and patrimonialist lines, grounded in functional representation and corporate elites, a structure of authority and interest associations predicated upon central state control and regulation and including the integration of all major social and economic groups into a vast organization of monopolistic official and semiofficial agencies, guided, directed, formed, and controlled by the state. This description of a corporatist state system may be summarized in terms of the following major characteristics:

1. A strong, authoritarian state structure.
2. A society and polity grounded on an organicist conception and where ideas of community and social good take precedence over individualism.
3. A system based on official or semiofficial interest groups and the enforced (if necessary) harmonization of classes.
4. Government direction and control of the economy, generally implying a structure of state capitalism or etatism.
5. Vastly increased government control and direction of the entire social order, the bureaucratization of society.
6. A system of technocratic rule and control which administers away class conflict and traditional "politics" (parties and the like).

"Corporatism" in this sense can be contrasted with liberalism which implies limited state power and checks and balances, an inorganic and contractual theory of the state, a system based on unfettered pluralist interest groups independent of the state, on laissez-faire or limited state economic control, one which stresses freedom and individualism above bureaucratization, and where conflict, competition, and "politics" are a normal part of the political process. Let us proceed to examine these models in the light of the historic Latin American, and the more recent United States, experiences.

[The essay then proceeds to a discussion of the Iberic-Latin

corporative model as set forth earlier in this book; for brevity
and to avoid repetition, these pages are omitted here.]

THE CORPORATIZATION OF THE UNITED STATES

The model of corporate state and society set forth here was
fashioned originally in an attempt to come to grips with what appeared to be a distinctive Iberic-Latin mode of national development, a unique way of managing and coping with the great issues and
pressures that accompany the modernization process, a framework of
change that seemed to be inadequately explained by Marxian analysis,
on the one hand, or the inevitability-of-pluralism-liberalism interpretation, on the other. This reinterpretation came after a tumultuous decade in which Latin America not only developed a great deal
but where neither the Marxian categories and their various convolutions nor Eastonian-Rostowian-Almondian "systems theory" and the
"development" literature proved fully satisfactory in explaining
the changes taking place. In short, the Iberic-Latin nations required special treatment as a "4th world of development" which was
ill-served by interpretation through the prisms of the great systems theories most commonly used in the social sciences. In various writings the term "corporative framework" was used to account
for the distinctiveness of this developmental model, and its origins
traced in Iberic-Latin history, society, and political culture.

More recent scholarship has made it clear that corporatism and
its associated traits are not unique to the Iberic-Latin nations,
however. It may be that the particularly Catholic, Roman, and
Thomistic-Suárezian forms of corporatism are unique to that culture
area, but not corporatism or patrimonialism per se. FitzGerald
(146) has a fascinating passage in which she reports how Ngo Dinh
Diem's ideology of "Personalism" in Vietnam derived from his brother Ngo Dinh Nhu's attraction to corporative ideas during his years
in Paris in the 1930s, when corporatism seemed to represent the
wave of the future. Other nations touched or shaped by the Hispanic or Portuguese influence (the Philippines, for instance) share
a common corporatist political-cultural influence. In nations as
diverse as Yugoslavia and Ghana, India and Tanzania, natural corporatism in its varied bureaucratic-authoritarian, communalist and
integralist forms also appears strong.

But it is not just the developing nations that exhibit corporatist traits; it is the developed, advanced-industrial ones as
well. Denoon (117) has reported on the pervasive, perhaps permanent influence of corporatist institutional forms and behavioral
patterns in modern Japan and other Asian nations. Beer (39) emphasizes similar corporatist influences in Britain; and if the research of Rokkan (435), Dahrendorf (105), Heisler (204), and other
European experts has validity, the corporative tradition remains
powerful and now apparently reemergent in Holland, Belgium, Germany, and the Scandinavian countries. The Soviet bureaucratic-
authoritarian state and its sectoral and often functionally representative group arrangement may also be looked at in terms of the
corporative model, and by now, with the "death" or "demise" of liberalism and the concurrent growth of immense bureaucratic

structures and a more authoritarian state system in the United States, it would appear that this country, too, may be seen in the light of the corporative model. In reconsidering the model of Iberic-Latin political structure and behavior, it is striking just how many of the institutions and practices described apply to the United States. The web of nations encompassed within the corporatist framework spreads wide; corporatism now seems almost ubiquitous.

Spain and Portugal especially, even before the recent changes, and the nations of Latin America as well, have long claimed that their northern neighbors do not understand them, that their ostracism from the European or Western community for their supposed "fascistic" forms was wrong and misleading. They have argued that their polities have consistently been more open, pluralist, progressive, and free (although still within the corporatist context) than they are given credit for, that the sanctions and isolation practiced against them are really the result of Northern European or North American prejudices toward Iberic-Latin and Catholic society and culture, which are woefully misunderstood and toward which intellectuals, politicians, and opinion-molders continue to exhibit an ill-defined hostility.

While claiming with much reason to be more "liberal" than they are often pictured, the Iberic-Latin nations also argue that the Northern European nations and the United States have since World War II been themselves practicing a disguised form of corporatism passed off erroneously as the continuation of a liberal-pluralist tradition. They point correctly to the rise of state-sponsored and protected capitalism in all the modern "mixed" economies; the growth of public corporations, utilities, and services; the emergence of immense bureaucratic and etatist forms for controlling and policing virtually all areas of social and economic life; the tremendous growth of regulatory agencies and commissions designed to coordinate and regulate every sector of production; the disappearance of the strike (except in exceptional cases) or the lock-out in our "complex" and "interdependent" economies in favor of obligatory collective bargaining and arbitration through a state agency; the existence of numerous commissions and other high decision-making bodies based in part on functional representation; the cooptation and absorption of both labor and business into the state system through their inclusion in planning agencies, hearings on proposed legislation, and even the agencies designed to regulate them; the growth of "managerial" and, hence, often arbitrary and authoritarian state systems; the decline of ideology, politics, and even laissez-faire in favor of administration and technocracy. Few would deny that these trends have been occurring in the more developed nations at an accelerating pace in the past thirty years; what we have not faced is the fact that, taken together, they all point to a <u>corporatization</u> of the modern state and society in a form not altogether different from that historically characteristic of the Iberian and Latin American authoritarian-bureaucratic systems.

In the modernization and "liberalization" of Iberia and Latin America and the concurrent "Latin Americanization" of the already industrialized and northern nations, there is a new kind of convergence that we have not thought very much about before. For while in the past two decades the Iberic-Latin model has been greatly modernized and made more pluralistic to account for the greater complexity and diversity of these nations and their societies, the developed countries have also undergone a process of increased corporatization. In the by-now vast literature showing (and often lamenting) how far we have diverged from the liberal model, we have ignored how closely we now correspond to the corporative one. In 1934, in a volume that was one of the classics of the period and of a whole genre of corporatist literature (but now almost completely unknown), Manoïlesco (312) proclaimed that the twentieth century would be the century of corporatism just as the nineteenth had been the century of liberalism. In the immediate aftermath of World War II and the extinction of many of the interwar corporatist experiments and regimes, Manoïlesco's prediction appeared wrong, if not ludicrous. But in a recent essay building on the Manoïlesco theme, Schmitter (458) has suggested in a vein parallel to this one that Manoïlesco may have been right after all.

The evidence for the on-going corporatization of the United States, as well as of the developed European nations, is enormous. Only some of the currents can be noted here. When Arthur Schlesinger talks of the "Imperial Presidency," for example, that implies something more than a historical trend toward increased presidential power often at the expense of the people or the other branches of government. To a Latin Americanist, it also conjures up images of an organic and authoritarian state, the impossibility of separating the president as a person from the institutional office he fills, "royal" mandates emanating not from free elections but from some higher end and purpose like "the national interest," a blurred line between the public domain and private profiteering on the part of elected or administrative officials or their friends, cronies, families, or favorites, a highly personalized presidency in which the wealth of the realm as well as its subjects is all a part of and inseparable from the ruler's private domain. Max Weber called this form of authority patrimonialist; it has been characteristic of Iberia and Latin America for centuries, and sociologists Lloyd Rudolph, S. N. Eisenstadt, and others are now arguing that, contrary to Weber, who implied the patrimonialist form was a type of traditional authority bound to give way to more legal-rational standards as society modernized, it may be an enduring, permanent feature of even the most developed nations (137, 434, 440). Although not always recognizing the full sociological implications, students and popular commentators may have been right in referring to former President Nixon as "King Richard."

Imperial presidents tend to emerge in floundering, divided, fragmented societies. It is not just that our recent presidents have reached for excessive power or that they have been the beneficiaries of a worldwide series of trends and circumstances enhancing executive authority, but that in a context of fragmentation and centrifugal pluralism carried to a point where there is little underlying consensus any more or attachment to a central nucleus, the presidency becomes the one point of unity and cohesiveness in the system, the single core to which all groups may relate. If he works well, the system works well; if he fails, the system may also break down. Such a system is almost inherently unstable and the tenure of the government--any government--is bound to be uncertain and probably short. Argentina, Uruguay, and Chile (or perhaps Italy) are cases in point. These are by no means "banana republics" but the most literate, most mobilized, most modern nations in Latin America or Southern Europe. It is precisely because they are so modern that they are so unstable and prone to periodic breakdowns and/or authoritarian-corporatist rule: societal and political modernization has produced not a happy democratic pluralism but a conflict society marked, in a time of economic stagnation and, hence, of a fixed total social product, by a zero-sum economic and political game that becomes a virtually permanent (at least since the 1930s in the Argentina example) war of all against all. In this case, <u>contrary</u> to what the students used to say, the future lies not in Bolivia, and maybe not in Cuba, nor in any of the other "model" societies sometimes mentioned, but far more likely in Argentina with its spiraling discord and disintegration. Those who ponder these same trends in the United States would do well to read Ortega y Gasset's classic with its suggestive title, <u>Invertebrate Spain</u> (372).

The difficulty with the United States's evolution from liberalism toward corporatism is that in the process it may well have taken on some of the worst aspects of both systems. While we have gravitated increasingly toward a bureaucratic state and an imperial presidency, we seem to have preserved few of the moral restraints and natural law traditions that still undergird the Iberian and Latin American nations. In the Iberic-Latin systems, strong efforts (and efforts well worth our attention) have been made to adapt to modernity and stimulate development while at the same time preserving those institutions considered valuable from the past: strong human and interpersonal relations even in the largest-scale organizations, a sense of family and community, ethical and moral values, an integrated associational life based on mutual assistance and harmony rather than conflict and alienation, and, of course, a similarly unified-organic view of state and society. These are all features whose passing we now often lament and wish we could recapture, but they are features which this society has perhaps irrevocably shunted aside, reinforced by the belief that modernization, secularism, and impersonality were inevitable and went hand-in-hand. It is more than sheer coincidence that such an a-moral, materialistic, and managerial society should give rise to a-moral leadership, that in such an organizational and administrative system perhaps the epitome of organization men (thinking particularly of the Nixon White House staff) should emerge dominant. Iberia and Latin America have had their share (perhaps more than their share) of tyrants, but at least these were real persons and, however undemocratic by North American lights, most often immensely popular (e.g., Vargas and Perón both later returned to office by overwhelming electoral mandates), cast in the role of paternalistic father-figures to their large national "families." The tyrants we get have few of these redeeming qualities; they are plastic men, organizational men, and PR men, men without a sense of history, tradition, community, or moral sense. To such the ends necessarily justify the means, manipulation takes precedence over human values, the absence of moral conviction or natural law eliminates all restraints. The United States is a system of greatly expanded and centralized authority in the corporatist mold, but it may well lack the moral underpinnings that in Iberia and Latin America have often tempered such rule.

It is not just the imperial presidency that commands our attention, however, but the bigness, impersonality, and bureaucracy of the modern state itself. The modern state is a regulatory state, a managerial state, an administrative state. The origins of this system in the United States may be traced to the 1930s and the New Deal (perhaps earlier) when big government began to become a fact of life, when the government became the omnipresent referee of the interest group struggle and the regulator (not the owner) of the economy and of the nation's major economic forces. It is interesting that modern-day liberals in America accepted and welcomed these early trends toward the modern corporatized state, largely abandoning the older concept that government is best which governs least in favor of one that accepted strong governmental action designed to give the individual a positive material foundation upon which freedom would not be destroyed but enhanced. By now, the more abhorrent fruits of that concept have become all too apparent: a government that has run amuck with bigness, bureaucracy (in the "bad" sense) and impersonality; administrations wholly out of touch with the people their agencies were designed to serve; a "revolution of rising expectations" among blacks and poor whites which when frustrated or not satisfied leads to violence and widespread alienation; inadequate and demeaning governmental paternalism toward these same sectors; a public service that has become a vast patronage and social security agency chiefly for the benefit of those employed in it; those "pointy heads" in Washington who have no sense whatever of what the grass roots are thinking; bureaucrats who with the unthinking stroke of a penned regulation can literally wipe out an entire class of small businessmen, farmers, individual storeowners and entrepreneurs, universities, builders and carpenters, tradesmen, and others. Bureaucratization, "rationalization," and centralization have led inexorably and perhaps inevitably to bigness, technocracy, hierarchy, and concentrated power; it is directly related to the rise of alienation among all classes and to our national malaise. It is almost universally agreed that our existing institutions are inadequate for the new and rising demands being placed upon them, that we are ill-equipped to deal with our present problems and, worse, do not even know where to begin to solve them. Hence, as Mills and others have insisted, our liberalism has become divorced from social and economic realities and the "liberal" (now increasingly corporate) state inadequate to the tasks it is called upon to perform. If this language sounds familiar to Latin Americanists, it is because almost the exact same criticisms of the existing structures in Latin America were formulated by "knowing" North Americans in those earlier, headier, Alliance for Progress years of the early 1960s.

Bigness and bureaucracy are characteristic not just in the

public sphere, but in the private one as well--and in the interconnections forged between the public and the private. Galbraith (160) has shown the increasing role of government in the American economy, the absence of adequate controls over the nation's largest private enterprises, paradoxically, the degree to which these industries have become dependent on government for official contracts and handouts, the ways in which these major concerns, whether in agriculture, commerce, or industry, dominate the agencies set up to regulate them, the interchange of personnel between these industries and the agencies which give them contracts (the aerospace industry is the usual example cited, but the practice is widespread), how America remains a free enterprise, laissez-faire economic system for the poor and the small entrepreneur but a system of state capitalism and subsidies for the bigger concerns. The bailing out with public funds of such "private" enterprises as the Penn Central, Grumman, Lockheed, the Franklin Bank, and numerous others still to come, the increased subsidization of all groups from universities to local governments, the concept of government itself as a great public watering trough at which all elements may have their turn through employment, pensions, sinecure programs or outright grants, the giving of monopolies or oligopolies to select industries are all practices or habits with which we have become familiar. Galbraith has recognized and lamented many of these trends, but he has not come to grips with the fact that he is describing the operations of an almost classic form of corporatist, neo-patrimonialist, neo-mercantilist, or state-capitalist economy. His prescriptions, too, tend to reflect his liberal, optimistic North American background; and he has not fully seen that the aberrations and wrong choices we have made may no longer be reversible or that they may be inherent in the kind of society and nation we have become.

What Galbraith has done for the analysis of the American economy, Shonfield (463) has accomplished on a comparative basis. Focusing particularly on the European experience, Shonfield demonstrates the dramatic shift from the old concept of private laissez-faire capitalism to the newer phenomenon of etatism, or state capitalism. He analyzes the growth of the mixed enterprise, describes the growth of planning and public technical-advisory and now managerial offices, treats the experience of wage and price controls, shows how the state has become the chief entrepreneur in Italy, France, and Austria and how the systems of state capitalism and managerial "democracy" have evolved, describes the manpower planning of Sweden, the public enterprises of Britain, the control of wages and income in Holland, the role of banks as governmental "prefects" in Germany, the state-controlled economies of Spain and Portugal. Unlike Galbraith, however, Shonfield recognized that he is dealing with a kind of neo-corporatism and he ponders the limits of planning techniques and public power. He also discusses the same disturbing questions raised here: are bigness, bureaucracy, and the new form of corporatism and state capitalism compatible with the ideal and traditions of parliamentary democracy; does separation of powers make sense any more in a context where centralized planning, direction and technocratic control are both inevitable and necessary; how can elected and presumably nonexpert representatives play a meaningful role in the business of government; how does one protect the rights of the individual citizen against the arbitrary exercise of an ever-more-extensive public power; what of responsibility and accountability? These are questions that Americans have also pondered of late; what Shonfield shows is that such issues are not unique to American society and that bigness, bureaucracy, and etatism may be permanent characteristic features of all the modern economies, societies, and polities.

Corporatism has also come to dominate our system of socioeconomic group interactions. Although we pride ourselves on our interest-group pluralism, which according to Lowi (283) and others has become our official ideology, in fact power has been increasingly concentrated in this sphere as well as others. While the largest groups, such as the NAM or the AFL-CIO, enjoy official legitimacy, direct access to the White House, and virtual coparticipation with government in numerous decision-making arenas, other groups are excluded and many social elements remain unorganized and with only a weak voice in national affairs. The roots of this system of officially sanctioned and coopted interest groups also lie in the 1930s. In reviewing the literature of that period in the light of the present discussion, one is struck by the parallels in the way Roosevelt helped bring organized labor and other groups into the mainstreams of politics and the state system (while excluding less-favored groups like the IWW) and the policies of, let us say, Vargas in Brazil. Bring it in, coopt and absorb its more moderate leaders, put them on the official payroll or in a position to enjoy other perquisites, treat labor paternalistically, give it recognition, meanwhile defuse its potential threat by incorporating it as an official appendage of the state. Other groups have likewise been the recipients of official favors in return for controlling their rank-and-file and agreeing to accept the system's givens. This is not a system of laissez-faire and free-wheeling pluralism but a government-sanctioned and officially approved structure of corporate and functionally representative associational life. Each of the major groups, with government blessing, tends increasingly toward monopoly in its respective sphere; it comes to represent the voice of that group on national issues and it is given a certain prescribed, if still often informal, number of seats in the bureaucratic organs and regulatory agencies of the state. These arrangements lie at the heart of a corporatist system.

The United States has evolved gradually toward corporatism and without calling it by that name, rather than legislating a manifest corporative set of institutions as many European and Latin American nations did in the 1930s. The one institution that was manifestly corporatist, the National Recovery Administration of 1933-35, was unanimously struck down by the Supreme Court. Conservatives on the Court felt the NRA represented unconstitutional interference by the government in private business; liberals objected on the grounds of unwarranted delegation of power by the congress to the president. It is interesting also that at the time both big business and big labor were hostile to what they perceived as government efforts to so tightly regulate the economy as well as the internal structure of both groups in the (presumably) public interest. In addition, the highly laissez-f_aire and individualistic nature of the American system helped rule out this early legislated effort at what would have been a de jure corporative system. But if corporatism could not be legislated in America, it could grow up de facto, and that is precisely what occurred over the next four decades (b).

Although the United States refused to accept a formal structure of etatism in its sociopolitical affairs, it did come to accept the principle of government regulation of the national economic life. This is what the Keynesian revolution was all about. But one wonders if the two were separable. Keynes himself was a corporatist; moreover, he saw the intimate relations between etatism in the economic sphere and the need for a corporatist reorganization of society and polity. He called for a form of corporatism that would compliment his economic theories and serve to help preserve a balance between the state and its component groups:

> Progress lies in the growth and the recognition of semi-autonomous bodies within the state--bodies whose criterion of action within their own field is solely the public good as they understand it, and from whose deliberations motives of private advantage are excluded, though some places it may still be necessary to leave, until the ambit of man's altruism grows wider, to the separate advantage of particular groups, classes, or faculties--bodies which in the ordinary course of affairs are mainly autonomous within their prescribed limitations, but are subject in the last resort to the sovereignty of democracy expressed through Parliament. I propose a return toward medieval conceptions of separate autonomies (242).

Given Keynes's favoritism toward corporatism, one may speculate why the United States came to adopt Keynesian economics but not his politics. Is it really possible to separate the two? Or does our present gravitation toward corporatism represent the "catching up" of our sociopolitical structures with our already existent Keynesian economic ones, a marriage that the court and other forces in American society had ruled out in the 1930s but which incrementally, under different labels and in a different climate, they are more ready to accept now?

The number of areas of life that have passed out of the private and individual realm and into the social or statist sphere is broad. Although many would applaud the policy measures implied, the tendencies toward increased bureaucratization and corporatization should also be recognized. Group or social rights (quotas and ascriptive group criteria in hiring or university admissions, for example; de facto functional representation in the major political parties and in policy making) now routinely take precedence over individual rights and merit. Regulation, licensing, and state control and directives have hamstrung individual choices and initiatives in a broad range of activities, from small businesses to universities, among farmers and tradesmen, in education and commerce.

The concept of property having a social function is laudable in some respects, but it also represents a long step from the Lockean concepts of "life, liberty, and estate." Under a "good" president who has the "right" concern for the common interest, policies based on these concepts may be useful and beneficial; but under a bad one the programs may be disastrous, society may be torn apart, and resistance to an "unjust tyrant" (Johnson, Nixon) will escalate. Recognition of the possibility for such abuse is why the American Constitution writers stressed checks and balances so heavily and the procedural aspects of representative rule; they shied away from the notion of a comprehensive national goal or plan, cognizant of its dangers and preferring to allow individual initiative and the play of political forces to define the public interest in specific circumstances.

Labor relations have also in large measure passed out of the arena of direct bargaining between employees and employers to encompass a vast array of labor courts, government-appointed arbitrators, and compulsory negotiations and collective bargaining laws. Government has become the third partner—often the dominant one—in the labor relations system. Strikes and lockouts are both too costly and too disruptive in our modern and interdependent economy; they, as well as class conflict, have been largely administered away. Further, the idea that wages, prices, and production quotas should be set not in a free market but by governmental fiat and through an official agency is precisely what the various European and Latin American corporative agencies set up in the depression years of the 1930s were also designed to do. Then, as now, the inevitable result of these experiments established ostensibly to institutionalize coequal representation of capital and labor was that those with money, wealth, and good political connections dominated, while the poorer elements and the middle class bore the brunt of austerity and restrictive wage policies. Rather than a neutral referee in the group process, the state became in a newer and more sophisticated way the guarantor of state capitalism, the executor of a state corporative system designed <u>both</u> to benefit <u>and</u> to harness the rising trade unions, and ultimately the protector of the status quo. It is not without historical precedent that, when Nixon froze prices and wages and created the Cost of Living Council and the Wage and Price Board, George Meany immediately called it "Fascism."

It is ironic that the corporatization of American life should have proceeded so far so rapidly at precisely the time we have begun to realize that more money and a bureaucratic program emanating from Washington are in themselves inadequate for solving the immense ills that confront us. It matters not whether we are talking of race relations, cities, education, hard-core unemployment, inflation, health care, hard-core poverty, or other major issue areas, we know that the old liberal solutions do not work very well any more and we are at a loss for what to do. But we are solidly agreed (I think) that another agency, another program, more money and more bureaucrats emanating from the nation's capital are unlikely to solve the problem and may well exacerbate it. Our institutions, as the literature on the developing nations used to say, have become inadequate for the new demands and the revolution of rising expectations now being thrust upon them.

The attempts to reverse the trends toward bigness, bureaucracy, centralization, and a corporatized society have seldom worked and some of the solutions offered would seem to increase the possibilities for an even stronger authoritarian order. The "New Federalism" and "Revenue Sharing" have not been howling successes, just as the corporative attempts in the 1930s to reverse the historical trends, decentralize power, and found society on its most elemental corporate units, the family, the village, and the local community, not only failed but led to the further subordination of these units to absolutist centralized government. Nor have Mr. Carter's attempts to reduce the size of government or its meddling in private matters shown many positive results; indeed, with a new energy "czar" and other programs, the trend seems to be in the opposite direction. Some of the more radical critics have been urging that the concept of government as the neutral referee in the interest-group-liberalism theory be replaced by a concept of a government that really governs, that uses moral authority (not just an interest group balancing act) to serve the public interest. That may be a laudible goal, but quite a bit depends on whose moral precepts are being enforced, and it may well be that, in the kind of pluralist and fragmented society we have become, there is no public interest any more, only diverse and increasing uncompromisable private ones (again Argentina or Italy may serve as models). Further, the call for authoritative rule designed to serve the "common good" or the "public interest" sounds remarkably similar to the Thomistic-Suárezian-monistic-corporatist order laid out centuries ago, with all the possibilities for abuse and tendencies toward absolutism that conception implies.

The Latin Americanization of North American life has proceeded on a variety of other fronts as well. A striking example is provided by the recent trends toward both the politicization of the United States Armed Forces and the militarization of civilian life and, hence, the emergence of an increasingly violent, conflict-prone, and praetorian political society. The weakening of party loyalties, the greater independence of the voter, and other evidence of party "disaggregation" so apparent in the 1960s have led many to question also whether political parties as institutions have any meaningful future in this country, whether administration, bureaucracy, and personalism have not replaced or supplemented the party phenomenon. Do elections any longer provide real choices among alternative programs or do they serve merely as devices for giving rival factions periodic access to the great public watering trough, on the one hand, or merely plebiscitary-like ratifications of the regime in power (Nixon in 1972), on the other? In contrast to the old laissez-faire interest group theory, can any group now hope to succeed or even survive without recognition and legitimization by the central state and absorption into its system of spoils and benefits? What areas of social and economic affairs are there that have not been taken out of the individual and private domain and placed in the public? This essay argues that a serious consideration (as distinct from the jaded popular stereotypes and the

New Yorker cartoons) of the Iberic-Latin state and society and its corporate-authoritarian-patrimonialist forms and functions not only helps answer these questions but affords much insight into our own current condition.

CONCLUSION AND ASSESSMENT

Is the United States, therefore, a corporate system? The question is like asking whether the United States is experiencing a recession, for it depends on what one means by the term and what measures are used. Manoïlesco helps us in this regard by his distinction between "pure" corporatism (a genuinely pluralist and self-regulating form that is probably nonexistent in the real world), "mixed" corporatism (that is, where corporative forms and structures co-mingle and overlap with a system of partial pluralism, liberalism, and free associability), and "subordinate" corporatism (that is, where society's various corporate units—labor, business, religion, university, etc.—have been subordinated to the bureaucratic-administration of the state). Clearly, by the measures I have used (and they are frequently "soft" and impressionistic ones and the examples and illustrations, though pivotal, need to be greatly fleshed out), the United States is a "mixed" corporative system, perhaps tending now toward a "subordinate" form. There are even now many aspects of our national society and politics that lie outside the corporatist mold, still cast in the older liberal and individualistic framework or representing overlapping patterns of both. But of the fact that the tendencies are clearly toward corporatism in its statist forms and that many areas of our national life are already unambiguously and probably irreversibly locked in the corporatist matrix, there can be no doubt.

There remains a significant difference between the corporatism of the developing nations aimed at controlling and regulating the admission of new groups into the system so as to secure integral national development, <u>and</u> the corporatism of the already developed, "postindustrial" and perhaps "postpluralist" nations. Here again the insightful Manoïlesco and, more recently, Schmitter provide a major key. Though the theme cannot be elaborated at length here, Manoïlesco (and Schmitter) has distinguished between the form of <u>state</u> corporatism which many of the developing nations have adapted and the kind of <u>societal</u> corporatism toward which the already developed systems have evolved. The former generally emerged out of a situation of immediate or impending national collapse (Spain and Portugal in the 1920s and 1930s, the postcolonial nations today), of the breakdown of older forms of traditional authority before the consolidation of any newer modern ones, of a condition of national weakness economically and politically, and of a nascent pluralist form that threatened to get out-of-hand or produce national disintegration. State corporatism, hence, required strong leadership and frequently repressive action as a means of keeping the nation together and protecting it from outside enemies and internal civil war.

<u>Societal</u> corporatism, on the other hand, emerges from the slow decline of a more complex and socially differentiated pluralism.

It is not the result of crisis so much as of drift. There may be some triggering causes (the Vietnam imbroglio, economic downturn, mass protests) but, in general, societal corporatism has been the result of a gradual slide and evolution. The decay of pluralism and its gradual replacement by a system of societal corporatism has to do, in Schmitter's view, with the imperatives of the modern state, society, and economy; the need to preserve stable, bourgeois rule; the increasing concentration of capital and ownership; the rise of centralized planning and the requirement that scarce resources like oil, steel, water, power be carefully allocated; interdependence and, hence, with the need to regulate closely the internal economy and the international one; the vast expansion of the public policy arena and the need to rationalize and bureaucratize decision making under state control; the need also to "coordinate" classes and interest groups more closely within the political process. There are, in other words, dynamic and development-related factors in the transition from state to societal corporatism, or from liberalism to corporatism, that are closely bound up with both the international economic environment and the kinds of broader internal societal changes characteristic of the highly industrialized modern nations. An intriguing question is how at this stage a developed or "postindustrial" nation begins to shift its concerns from economic expansion to economic security and how different groups then maneuver to protect their respective income shares, as well as how government seeks concurrently to get a handle on and increasingly manage more and more of national economic and sociopolitical life. These transformations may imply, as in the United States in recent years, a tendency toward the fusion of the state and the societal corporatist forms.

There is nothing necessarily or inherently wrong or evil about corporatism. Some scholars (55, 121) have denounced it as a new form of fascism, a label that to my mind is misleading and inaccurate. Others (239) have seen it as a new and hopeful synthesis of pluralism and statism fusing together the valid components of each, marking out spheres for positive government action while simultaneously leaving other areas open to private initiative. That view is a strongly romantic one that ignores the earlier national experiences with corporatism, its assumptions and biases, and what such classic critiques of the corporative-technocratic state as those by Orwell, Burnham, Hemingway, and Ortega y Gasset, among others, had to say.

Clearly, we must avoid both a knee-jerk rejection of corporatism or an automatic condemnation because of its supposed affinities with fascism; we must avoid also romanticizing corporatist solutions and an elevation of them to a position of constituting the answer for the modern nation-state. Corporatism has both its useful and its not-so-useful, its good and its bad, points, and these must be carefully weighed and evaluated. Moreover, we must recognize the diversity of corporatist formulae and its many national variations. The United States, after all, is neither a Brazil, with its full-fledged state corporatism, nor a Sweden with its societal form. There are both the older Catholic form of Rerum Novarum and the newer version of modern Christian democracy; secular, nationalist, bureaucratic-authoritarian forms; a parliamentary form; a modern societal form in Scandinavia as well as a radical-nationalist and modernizing form as in Peru or Tanzania; a syndicalist form; modern socialist forms as in Yugoslavia and the Soviet Union and modern capitalist forms in France, West Germany, Japan, and the United States. The "corporatist framework," thus, encompasses a considerable range of ideological and political approaches, and there are a great variety of regimes that fall under this rubric. Clearly, within the corporatist tradition there is room for progressive leftist regimes as well as for regressive rightist ones, and many variations in between.

If this approach is a valid one, if Manoïlesco is correct, after all, in proclaiming this the century of corporatism, then much of the recent literature on our own national malaise and the great debate between capitalism and socialism or between the liberals and their critics is irrelevant and fundamentally misses the point. The issue is no longer liberalism or something else but rather what form corporatism will take. The Salazar regime, we have seen, was properly condemned and overthrown not so much because it was corporatist but because it failed to modernize even within the corporatist framework it had set for itself. Similarly, it does us little good to argue whether liberalism is dead or alive or sick or well because that is no longer the context in which we are operating. Centralism, bureaucracy, bigness, the all-encompassing state and its satellite interest associations, corporatism and patrimonialism--these are the conditions and constants under which our polity and society now exist and in which debate should be conducted and public policies proposed. Whether we choose to call what has, in fact, become increasingly a condition of societal and state corporatism "liberalism" or something else may be more a matter of semantics than of substance. By the assumption of Gerald Form and then Jimmy Carter to the presidency, we would seem to have been spared some of the "banana republic" features that had multiplied in past years, but whether this means we will be able to deal with the deeper and more profound sense in which we have become corporatized and "Latin Americanized" seems doubtful.

The ironies in all this are many and cutting. In a significant recent essay, Pike (397) has noted that for years and even centuries members of the developed Western World (and also the handfuls of liberally inclined Spaniards and Latin Americans) have been smugly and ethnocentrically predicting that perhaps one day Spain, Brazil, and other Latin American states, with their seemingly old-fashioned corporate forms, would become modern and "liberal" enough to earn the right to closer association with and inclusion in the society of "acceptable," democratic states. Today, the situation may have been reversed. Many prescient Spaniards and Latin Americans are recognizing that they are not so different after all, that their social and political forms are not so much "underdeveloped" as distinctive, that their long-ago predictions that liberalism would not work may have been right after all, and that, with the corporatization and "Latin Americanization of the United States" and much of the rest of the developed world, their experience may offer lessons from which we may learn. At the least, it is time for Americans and Americanists to begin putting away their narrow and ethnocentric biases, to terminate the literature and thinking that sees the United States as superior and more "developed" not only in the economic sense (also now questionable in a way it wasn't a decade ago) but politically, socially, and morally as well, and to begin comprehending our own condition in the light not of some ancient and now largely imaginary or mythical liberal model but from a truly comparative perspective and in the light of the European-Iberic-Latin corporatist model which socially and politically we now also approximate.

NOTES

a. The names and books cited are familiar; a particularly useful and recent collection with an excellent introduction and summary statements is 331.
b. The flirtation with corporatism on the part of some Americans in the 1920s and 1930s would make an interesting subject for further study.

Part 5
Conclusion

The theory and political sociology of corporatism have now been studied from diverse vantage points, and its implementation and actual structural forms in several countries have been examined. A number of conclusions have already been offered, both as regards corporatist theory and the practice of corporatist regimes as well as the often considerable gaps between the two.

In this concluding essay, hence, we again focus on the use of corporatism or "the corporatist model" as a conceptual framework, a tool of research and analysis. Returning to some of the themes of the introduction, we explore further corporatism's "sociology of knowledge," the background and context of the concept, its powerful reverberations through several fields and disciplines, and the criticisms directed against it. The final part of the discussion suggests new and future avenues of research and points toward an emerging consensus in some of the recent literature on corporatism.

18 | Corporatism in Iberian and Latin American Political Analysis: Criticisms, Qualifications, and the Context and "Whys" of the Debate

"Corporatism" and "the corporative model" have become widely used frameworks or conceptual paradigms for the analysis of state-society relations and public policy processes, both in Iberian and Latin American political and sociological analysis and in comparative politics and development studies more generally. The concept and phenomenon of corporatism have reverberated widely, and the literature on the subject has mushroomed.

While most scholars working in these areas have seen the utility of employing a corporative approach, by itself or in combination with other approaches, corporatism's resurgence has also provoked some serious, at times almost visceral, reactions. Indeed, the fact "corporatism" is both a conceptual model and a manifest ideology and system of sociopolitical relations is part of the reason the reaction to it has been so strong, for as scholars we may be willing to use the former but politically and ideologically we most often disapprove of the latter. The model has also, in part because of the reactions it engendered, been subjected to some searching commentaries at both the general-theoretical and case study levels (34, 110, 192, 344).

The purpose of this concluding statement is to suggest some explanations as to why the reaction to corporatism has been so strong, respond to the criticisms that have been leveled, seek to restore perspective and provide a better understanding of the context and background of the debate, offer some suggestions for further study, and explore the emerging consensus that seems to be developing out of the corporatism debate.

THE "CORPORATIVE MODEL": WHY SO CONTROVERSIAL

The "corporative model" or "corporative framework" was initially put forward in the late 1960s as a way of analyzing and coming to grips with a developmental pattern and complex of institutional arrangements that seemed to be inadequately explained by either the classic Marxian or the liberal-developmentalist categories. It advocated a <u>verstehen</u> approach to understanding Iberian

---

Revised from a briefer note in Comparative Politics 10 (January 1978): 307-12.

and Latin American society and politics, an approach derived from
the indigenous traditions and historical experience of that culture
area, rather than one based upon the narrow, particularistic, ethnocentric perspective of United States or Western European social
science. Emphasis was placed on Iberia's and Latin America's organicist, patrimonialist, hierarchical, elitist, and corporatist
features; the theory, origins, and sociopolitical traditions of
these characteristics; and, hence, the often "distinctive" nature
of the Iberic-Latin change and/or development process. The "corporatist" label was employed as a shorthand way of describing and
summarizing some of the more salient features of a set of social
and political systems that were obviously more complex and varied.
The "corporative model" was always conceived as an "ideal type," a
heuristic device useful for suggesting new areas and lines of research; it was not supposed to be an exact reflection of reality at
all times and in all countries. It, thus, had both the advantages
and the disadvantages that all such ideal-type constructs have
(545).

The "corporative model" attracted widespread attention and became one of the most oft-cited and -used frameworks for conceptualizing Iberic-Latin political society. In most of these studies,
the concept was employed as it had been intended: as a device to
help scholars and policy-makers think about and explore research
areas and sociopolitical relationships which the paradigms with
which we were more familiar only weakly or incompletely illuminated. No claim was made that the corporatist approach offered a
full and complete explanation of Iberic-Latin development, only
that it provided a useful perspective. It was not designed to replace a class explanation of Latin American politics, for instance,
but to complement this and other approaches and to help us get at
questions which the prevailing models ignored or only partially
touched upon.

The corporative model elicited from most the response anticipated and that is usually accorded new conceptual approaches: yes,
let us recognize its utility for illuminating some areas of Iberic-
Latin politics, test its relevance and appropriateness in specific
cases, and employ it where it is useful meanwhile also using other
approaches to explore issues the corporative one does not. That
response was fair and all that any proponent of a new approach
could expect. But there were also some mixed reactions and, occasionally, downright hostility. Although some of the problems derived from a certain definitional ambiguity and lack of clarity in
the earliest presentation of the model, some deeper emotional and
ideological passions were also stirred. Because the model provoked
such an emotional response and, in some of the commentaries, has
been taken out of context and misrepresented--in one notable case,
I feel, purposely so--it is worth speculating why the response was
so strong and seeking to set the record straight.

    1. To some, the term "corporatism" itself was too emotionally
charged. Given the close association for some between
corporatism and fascism, use of this term stirred memories
of Nazi bestiality, totalitarianisms, and racial persecution or even genocide. The distinction between

corporatism and fascism is clear in the literature (the latter being one form, perhaps, of the former, but by no means the only one), but for some persons the term itself carried such negative connotations as to be unacceptable.
2. Related to this was the strong sense among social scientists that corporatism had been superseded, a thing of the past now relegated to the ashcans of history. To find corporatist systems both persistent and resurgent in so many nations and the term itself resurrected from the interwar period ran counter to a number of social science assumptions concerning the inevitability of democratic pluralism and how such "traditional" structures as corporatism are doomed to fade or be washed away.
3. Corporatism historically has been based on a set of assumptions that are grounded in Catholicism, organicism, elitism, nonegalitarianism. North Americans and North Europeans tend to be uncomfortable with and hostile toward societies organized on such frankly nondemocratic bases. Part of the hostility to the corporatism concept stems from antipathy to the nonliberal values it enshrines and because in the corporative model these were analyzed neutrally rather than from the point-of-view of automatic, a priori condemnation.
4. The model represented a challenge to alternative social science explanations by disputing their claims to universality and to all-encompassing verities. To "true believers" in either the liberal-developmentalist model or the orthodox Marxian one, the corporatist approach raised issues that did not seem to fit their preconceived notions and thus were viewed as threats to their own explanations, necessarily to be opposed. By emphasizing the culture-bound biases of the other major models; by its implied claim that Iberia and Latin America were not just "less developed" versions of "the West" fated inevitably to imitate it but were illustrative of a viable, alternative, corporatist route to development; and by its argument there was a functional, distinctive, Iberic-Latin social process "out there" all but entirely ignored in the literature but with a rich and vigorous tradition and worthy of attention in its own right, the corporative approach challenged a variety of deep-rooted assumptions and prejudices in the social sciences.
5. The model analyzed the Iberic-Latin systems on their own terms and demonstrated their functional aspects. By explaining and "rationalizing" these systems, the model seemed also to justify them in an ethical sense. For those convinced a priori of the perverseness of the existing Iberic-Latin systems and committed to sweeping them away, any model that rationalized them and showed their functionality had to be opposed (552).
6. The model disturbed reformers as well as revolutionaries. By stressing the continuity and persistence of Iberic-Latin authoritarianism, statism, corporatism, elitism and

the like, the model seemed to democrats both despairing and deterministic. If Iberia's and Latin America's prevailing political culture was constant, why work for democratic change? In fact, the model was dynamic in showing how change in that culture area occurred but argued such changes would not necessarily be in the direction of "liberalization" or "democratization." For AID officials, reform democrats, and those with a Peace Corps mentality seeking to bring the presumed benefits of U.S.-style democracy to "less-developed" lands, the corporative model sat quite uncomfortably.

7. But conservatives were not content either. Some applauded the emphasis on elitism, hierarchy, and Catholicism and the implied criticism of the liberal and Marxian approaches, but they did not welcome the revelations of the vast gaps between theory and practice emphasized in the comparative and case studies or the analyses of the inadequacies of the traditional institutions. Nor did they find congenial the treatment of syndicalism and left-socialist forms of corporatism or of how easy it was to go from a system of state capitalism to one of state socialism. That implied the possibilities for revolutionary transformation not contained in official U.S. government thinking by the late 1960s or in books such as Mander's which proclaimed Latin America an "unrevolutionary society" (310).

In short, all points on the political spectrum, if they wished, could find in the corporatist approach some reason to oppose it. And the challenge to numerous cherished social science assumptions implied in the model provoked further antipathy.

RESPONDING TO THE CRITICISMS

Let us turn from these general speculations concerning the reception given the corporatist model to some specific criticisms of it. First, several introductory observations.

The corporative model has, as indicated, occasionally been set up as a straw man, misrepresented, and had some of its chief arguments torn from their context. That is perhaps to be expected when any new and controversial approach is put forward. The problem was complicated by the fact the model was presented in bits-and-pieces and published in diverse places over a considerable period of time; indeed, the need to pull these diverse essays and studies together serves as a major reason for this volume. One should probably learn to live with the fact that, for those opposed to an argument or conceptual design on political or ideological grounds, misrepresentation of it will likely continue. However, one may still express the hope that the argument and model should be dealt with fairly, in its entirety rather than piecemeal or out of context, taking into account its reservations and qualifications as well as its claims, in the light of what its author has actually said and not what others have falsely attributed to it. This last comment applies particularly to the mistaken claim the corporatist approach implies a "culturalist" explanation.

Second, the criticism has been leveled at a model and set of concepts as if they were fixed and frozen for all time instead of changing and evolving. Or else, based on a reading of one of the earliest statements of the model, qualifications were called for or criticism made that had already been answered in another place. The fact is that, since its earliest expression, a good number of the suggestions made and reservations offered have been incorporated in the model; and the collection here demonstrates how a statement in one place is qualified in another. It is legitimate to criticize a single essay in isolation or an extant but still incomplete body of literature, but recognition should also be given to nuances and qualifications introduced at other points, efforts to reformulate the model taking into account the suggestions offered, more precise definitions and sharper distinctions introduced in the course of an evolving ouvre, even the right of an author to modify or change his views!

Third, the fact the model is an ideal type has not always been acknowledged. It was designed to be suggestive of new avenues of inquiry, new subject areas and relationships, new ways of thinking; to be provocative in its challenge to various established social science "truths"; to raise questions without presuming to answer them fully. By these criteria and judging from the growing literature and controversy that swirls about it, the model has achieved its major purposes. It was not designed to cover all contingencies, provide a complete and all-inclusive framework for understanding Latin American politics, or account for all national variations. Its more limited purposes were those above, and the providing of a partial explanation for a limited range of phenomena not adequately explained by other models. As a heuristic device, the corporative model was offered not as a final set of "truths" but as a set of propositions and hypotheses to be tested in various national settings and on various research issues, and then to be modified as the evidence came in. It was intended not to brush aside other general paradigms but to supplement them, fill in the gaps they left blank, and explore the overlaps and fusions of both liberal, corporatist, and other tendencies in Latin American politics. It sought a means to explore the dynamic tensions and evolving relations between the central state and its corporate group life, not to fix these in some final arrangement. Many of the suggestions and criticisms offered with regard to the model are hence to be welcomed because, as an ideal-type construct, it needs to be qualified, the limits of the general pattern should be recognized, the national variations should be accounted for, and the places where the model applies, or does not apply, require specification.

The specific criticisms of the model are as follows:
1. It is tautological. Insofar as tautology implies the repetition of the same idea in different words, I plead guilty, having used repetition purposely as a means of giving emphasis and stress to key concepts in the model. Insofar as the charge implies the use in the definition of corporatism of terms that fail to define because they imply the same thing (e.g., "organicist," "patrimonialist,"

even "Catholic"), I suppose there is some validity to the charge. However, (a) that is the case only in the first (and perhaps unfortunately best-known) expression of the model; later expressions contained more precise formulations; (b) the corporatism concept was meant initially to suggest merely an approach, a new way of thinking about Latin American politics, not a rigorous set of propositions or necessarily empirically verifiable hypotheses; (c) the corporatism idea was intended as a heuristic or "teaching" device, not a full-blown or formal MODEL! (d) the corporative framework was, as shown in this volume, later operationalized, put in terms of more rigorous hypotheses, tested in various contexts. Whatever there was of tautology in the earliest expression has since been corrected.

2. It is ill-defined. The first statement of the corporative model (551) defined it largely in terms of an Iberic-Latin historical, cultural, and sociopolitical tradition, a general pattern of cognition in which corporative forms seemed to be a persistent feature. Later expressions (520) saw the utility of distinguishing this form of corporatism from the more manifest "corporatist" ideology and regimes of the late-nineteenth and twentieth centuries, as well as the distinct forms these modern corporatist regimes could take. I think corporatism has been sufficiently well-defined in the course of this book to demonstrate adequately its utility as a social science concept.

3. It provides a "culturalist" explanation. Nonsense! The model did emphasize certain key political-cultural variables often neglected in the past. But it never was claimed that these were the only variables or that the corporative model should replace entirely other explanations. As stated, the corporative model was designed to complement other explanations, not replace them; to shed light on areas not encompassed by these other paradigms; to be a useful device but not a reified one elevated to the level of a sole and exclusive explanation. Since Iberia and Latin America are obviously organized along both class and corporative lines, it seems to me obvious that both class-based <u>and</u> corporatist explanations must be used. No more is claimed for the model, and no less. In their eagerness to discredit the corporative approach for often obscure political or ideological motives or to apply a quick label to it, some scholars have used "culturalist" as a brand, a means to tar and feather. Such labels and misrepresentation--especially if done deliberately--need emphatically to be rejected.

4. Iberia and Latin America are not entirely corporatist. Of course! It has always been my argument that these are mixed systems, with overlapping corporatist, liberal, now socialist and other features. Each aspect merits study, as well as the overlaps and fusions between them. Nor should the grand designs of the corporatist ideologues be

mistaken for how these systems actually operate. But to my recollection, no recent writer has missed the discrepancy between theory and practice in Latin America, nor the fact that the area is organized according to conflicting political and organizational principles. Resting purely on straw men, this is not a valid criticism.

5. The Latin American tradition has not been continuous since colonial times but disjointed, interrupted. Yes and no. The early nineteenth century did represent a break from the past, some aspects of corporative privilege were eliminated, the era of republicanism and liberalism did imply new departures. But as demonstrated in several essays here, there was much continuity from the period before 1810 to that which followed, in some areas corporative privilege was strengthened and new corporative agencies created (e.g., the armed forces), and republicanism represented more an overlap on the older corporatist tradition than a replacement of it. One must, therefore, consider both the changes and the continuities, as well as the remarkable persistence over time of the organicist-corporatist pattern.

6. Corporatism is merely an organizational form of capitalism. Much too simple. Of course, capitalism and corporatism are related. But corporatism is also attractive to other, including socialist, ruling groups seeking to keep society in "harmony" during times of transition. Corporatism is not just a product of capitalism but of the bigness, bureaucracy, complexity, structural differentiation, large-scale organization, centralized planning, and interdependence of all modern nations. The effort to tie corporatism exclusively to capitalism may represent as much an ideological position as it does an analytic approach.

7. Corporatism is not "unique" to Latin America. Agreed! No claim was ever made that it was. Obviously, corporatism may exist in other societies--although it is likely that the traditions of Roman law, Catholicism and Thomism, Iberian feudalism, and the New World setting gave it certain special characteristics in Latin America. When I used the terms "unique" or the "distinct tradition" in some early writings, I did not mean to imply corporatism was to be found only in Latin America but only that its practice there and the path of Latin American development were distinctive from that of the United States and did not conform to the ethnocentric developmentalist models based on the U.S. experience.

8. Corporatism is more an elite response to change than part of a cultural tradition (480). Yes, of course, it is an elite response to change, a point that was made repeatedly in my own writings. But that is not sufficient to explain why it has consistently and almost invariably been an elite response to change in Latin America since the sixteenth century, or why it is the preferred response of all shades on the political spectrum, right, center, and

frequently left.
9. Corporatism generally assumes a strong central state, when in fact in Latin America the state has difficulty making its policies felt. Yes and no. I am not prepared to say that in Latin America, with its centralized, organic, bureaucratic-authoritarian and imperial traditions, the state has been weak! Yet it does frequently have problems of policy implementation, and a number of major groups maintain varying degrees of autonomy from it. That is why in the corporative model emphasis was placed on the <u>interrelations</u> between the state and the major corporate groups, the former often seeking to consolidate and expand its power and the latter seeking to preserve some contractually defined independence. The sixteenth-century concept of an organic and unified system, with both a strong state <u>and</u> strong autonomous corporate groups, has not always been operating reality in Latin America, but it has generally provided the ideal to strive for. Indeed, it is precisely in these arenas of state-corporate group relations that some of the more interesting and dynamic aspects of Latin American politics and development take place.

CAVEATS AND SUGGESTIONS

Given the importance of the corporatism approach and phenomena, and yet the confusions and misunderstandings sometimes still present in the literature, what suggestions and/or caveats can be offered?
1. There must still be greater rigor and precision in the concepts used. Emotive and politically loaded definitions of corporatism must be avoided. The distinctions should be clarified among the various types of corporatist regimes, between secular types and those inspired by Catholic precepts, between Western and non-Western variants, between manifestly fascist regimes and those grounded on authoritarianism and/or paternalism, between corporatism as a facade or smoke screen for other often-nefarious purposes and corporatism as a genuinely alternative and often-social-justice-oriented response to alienation, mass man, and the ills of modern society. We must study the evolution of corporatism over time and in distinct national settings, corporatism in the developing world and its quite different configuration in advanced industrial societies, state vs. societal corporatism and the mixes and overlaps between. We must distinguish between the "corporatist tradition" as it is used to describe certain historic patterns of Iberic-Latin sociopolitical organization, and "corporatism" as a twentieth-century ideology and set of institutions that is both a reflection and extension of that earlier tradition <u>and</u> a response, oftentimes, to a new distinctive set of problems, specifically as a means by which the state or ruling groups (of widely

varying political orientations) may seek to regulate and control the participation of emerging elements in the political system.
2. More case studies are called for which test the model systematically in varied contexts. The corporative approach has been employed in examining such diverse nations as Spain (386), Portugal (519), Mexico (417, 481), the Dominican Republic (534), Honduras (344), Colombia (34), Peru (379), Chile (236), Argentina (466), Uruguay (506), and Brazil (140). Now required are case studies on other countries, systematic comparisons between them, and then a careful assessment of the utility and limits of the model.
3. Greater care must be taken to sort out the corporatist features in the Latin American tradition from the liberal-republican and newer socialist ones, to show the blends that may exist as well as where these may be parallel but untouching traditions. Where the corporative model sheds new light on new phenomena, let us use it; where not, other approaches must be employed.
4. The context in which the corporative model was formulated might usefully be examined. It came at a time when the liberal-developmentalist approach seemed no longer wholly satisfactory, when the Marxian model and/or dependency analysis provided a useful but still incomplete substitute, and when the Latin Americans themselves had begun the search for models based on their own indigenous experiences rather than imported from the outside. The corporatist model was, hence, offered as an approach which helped us analyze issues that neither the liberal nor the Marxian models fully explained, and also seemed to correspond more closely to the actual Latin American experience. Doubtless, in some expressions, the case for the corporative model was overstated in order more forcefully to make it. These comments are not meant to detract from the utility of the approach but only to help put it in perspective, enable us better to understand the context in which it was offered, and serve to remind us of its more modest explanatory claims. The corporative model remains a useful one for understanding and coming to grips with Latin American society, politics, and development, but a fuller understanding of its context and "sociology of knowledge" may also be helpful.
5. The corporative model helped point the way to some features of the Latin American development process that were not adequately encompassed in other major models, a corrective that was long overdue. But that was not to deny entirely the usefulness of the general development literature or to negate the claims of a more comprehensive social science of development. Surely, some greater modesty is called for by social scientists in asserting, based on a narrow "Western" experience, the universality of certain development processes; and there is room also for a distinctive, regional or culture-area-based Iberic-Latin

sociology and political science of development (537). A careful sorting out of what is both unique and what corresponds to universal patterns in Iberia and Latin America is called for.

6. A related point has to do with the way we perceive Latin American politics and change. Most of our nomenclature is "superior" and condescending, condemning Latin America as "backward," "underdeveloped," etc. Or else, as in the Schmitter formulation of corporatism, the definitions we use of some of the area's major institutions are so negative as to lead to a condemnatory stance toward the entire continent. The essays and studies collected here, however, posit corporatism not as a less-developed system or a "backward" step on some unilinear and inevitable road to liberalism or a society that looks just like us, but as a complex, quite rational, alternative paradigm and model for achieving national development. Nor am I convinced that corporatism is necessarily to be condemned in knee-jerk fashion as more nefarious, venal, or "fascistic" than some other systems with which we are familiar. In this and other volumes, we have arrived at some quite definite conclusions regarding corporatism's practice, but as social scientists, especially given the strong prejudices many still hold with regard to corporatism, I believe we must strive to keep an open mind in our moral and ethical evaluations of the corporatism phenomena.

7. Finally, it may be suggested that we again face up to the fact that corporatism is not necessarily regressive or static but may be progressive and change-oriented, that it may take left and syndicalist directions as well as rightist ones and several shades in between. Rather than simply condemning corporatism, we might more appropriately study:

    a. How change goes forward within corporatist systems (551).
    b. How change is frequently accelerated by putting pressure on the system, through the use of structured violence, strikes, coups, threats, guerrilla challenges, etc. (385).
    c. How fundamental structural change, albeit falling short of full-scale revolution, may occur by toppling a government, replacing an unacceptable minister, and so on (525).
    d. How an even more radical transformation may be effected, but still within corporative parameters, by the "capture" of one of the major pinnacles of the system (the labor ministry in Brazil under Goulart) and the rechanneling of its resources to favor labor groups instead of employers (140).
    e. How revolutionary transformations may occur, as in Bolivia, Mexico, Peru, Portugal, which imply the destruction of some traditional corporate

elites (Church, economic oligarchy and the elevation of new ones (labor, peasants) to positions of unprecedented influence. However, even in these revolutionary circumstances, corporatism and organicism may remain the prevailing framework (552).

It may be suggested that these possibilities make corporative systems open to far more changes, renewal, even fundamental transformations than we had imagined, perhaps as flexible and maleable as other systems. Both these dynamic features of corporatism as well as its stand-pat tendencies merit our close attention.

TOWARD CONSENSUS IN THE STUDY OF CORPORATISM?

Charles W. Anderson, as usual, has put the matter especially well (a). The rediscovery and resurrection of the corporatism concept, he states, has given a new elan to the study of Iberian and Latin American politics. It has provoked much and heated debate and stimulated new programs of research that have by now spread into other areas of comparative politics. No longer identified necessarily with fascism, embedded in a context of important theoretical concerns, defined and operationalized, the concept of corporatism and corporative models of sociopolitical organization have important implications for the study of politics, society, the change process, and public policy in the broadest sense.

But corporatism, again following Anderson, has meant different things to different people and can be understood at a number of different levels. From this stems the lively debate. Corporatism in one sense, he says, connotes the political world view of the Aristotelian-Thomistic synthesis, now updated and modernized to deal with the newer contingencies reflecting an industrialized, socially differentiated world. Corporatism in this sense is a general pattern of political cognition like liberalism and Marxism. Because of its history and traditions, the Iberic-Latin culture area has been particularly heavily impacted by this particular political cognition. Hence, a proper interpretation of Iberia and Latin America must start by examining these constructs and societal assumptions rather than from a point of view reflecting the political cognitions of the Anglo-American experience. This point of view was argued in my original World Politics essay (Chapter 4).

A second view takes corporatism as a general model of the political system with no particular cultural, regional, or ideological links. In subsequent writings on corporatism, I employed this definition as well as the earlier one and also explored the relations between the two (Chapter 6). In this formulation, corporate practices and institutions may exist in the advanced industrial nations of Western Europe and the United States as well as developing ones, in both Catholic and non-Catholic societies. Corporatism in this view is a model like liberalism or totalitarianism, part of the taxonomy of political analysis, whose character needs to be clarified and incidence accounted for.

While one group of scholars--Collier (85), Erickson (140), Glade (169), Kaufman (235), Malloy (400), Purcell (417), Stevens

(481), Weinstein (506)--has employed this second definition flexibly and undogmatically; another group--O'Donnell (367), Schmitter (458)--has associated corporatism rigidly with a certain kind of authoritarian-bureaucratic regime and with a particularly dogmatic form of neo-Marxian class analysis. In Schmitter's formulation, corporatism is merely the result of "delayed dependent capitalist development and non-hegemonic class relations" (458). This interpretation seems to me far too easy and too simple; but enough criticism (Chapter 15) has been offered of this formulation previously as to not warrant repetition here.

Aside from both die-hard proponents (492) of a strictly cultural-determinist view (from which I disassociate myself) and a rigidly economic-determinist one (ditto), there has by now emerged a considerable consensus among students of corporatism. There is, again following Anderson, a rough agreement that corporatism signifies a special pattern of relations between the state and other sociopolitical institutions and associations, one in which the government plays the role of architect of political order, defining, structuring, and delimiting the scope of class and interest group activity, coordinating the activities of private and professional associations, and creating explicit mechanisms of direct, sectoral interest representation in public policy-making. Unlike orthodox liberal theory, the state is not seen as refereeing or merely responding to interest group pressures but is an active force itself imposing design and structure on the political system. But unlike totalitarianism, corporatism (except in its fascist variant) does not entail "total" mobilization and politicization of society.

David Collier and Ruth Berins Collier have come to many of the same conclusions, emphasizing both the wide variety of forms corporatism may take (85) and arriving at a definition, less politically or ideologically loaded than some others, with which many of us can agree. The Colliers write:

> One promising focus is suggested by recent writing on interest representation in Latin America that emphasizes the concept of "corporatism." Though this term has been applied to a wide variety of different phenomena, there appears to be a growing consensus regarding its meaning when it is used to describe systems of interest representation. Philippe Schmitter, Howard Wiarda, Kenneth Mericle, Guillermo O'Donnell, Robert Kaufman, James Malloy, and Alfred Stepan have all presented essentially structural definitions that treat corporatism as an approach to <u>organizing</u> state-society relations. While using different vocabulary and phrasing, they all treat corporatism as a type of interest representation based on noncompeting, officially sanctioned, state-supervised groups (84).

In a similar vein Daniel Levy has written:

> Although many social scientists have by now proffered their own definitions of corporatism, there is substantial overlap.

> Among the oft-stated characteristics of corporatist groups
> are: controlled access to a limited number of entities,
> official sanction if not creation, monopoly representation,
> hierarchical ordering, functional differentiation, nonterri-
> toriality, non-competitiveness, subjection to government con-
> trol over leadership selection, subsidization, internal gov-
> ernance and the articulation of demands and supports, and in-
> tended maximization of the values of authority, order and
> harmony (261).

Levy goes on to say that his purpose is not to refine the general definitions already offered but to apply their useful, relevant elements to a new policy field. This consensus both on the essential ingredients of a definition of corporatism and on the need to get on with our research seems to be growing.

That is my own orientation as well. I recognize that there are differences of emphasis with regard to the corporatism phenomenon which have important, continuing implications for our understanding and evaluation of it, and for policy. While the debate between these alternative viewpoints has been spirited and to some degree constructive, it is now time to build upon this emerging consensus, to go forward with our studies of corporatism, to use this new and exciting research framework but also remember its limits.

NOTES

a. See his review in American Political Science Review, December 1978, p. 1478, from which I am paraphrasing.

References and Bibliography

The following works, listed alphabetically by author, constitute the references employed in the studies collected here, the important scholarly influences shaping the author's study of "Corporatism and National Development in Latin America," and a listing of the author's own writings relating to this theme.

1. Adams, R. N. The Second Sowing: Power and Secondary Development in Latin America. San Francisco: Chandler, 1967.
2. _____ et al. Social Change in Latin America Today. New York: Vintage, 1960.
3. Agor, W. Latin American Legislatures. New York: Praeger, 1971.
4. Alba, V. The Latin Americans. New York: Praeger, 1969.
5. _____. Politics and the Labor Movement in Latin America. Stanford: University Press, 1968.
6. Alberto, J. "O Circulismo," Rio de Janeiro, 1966. (Mimeographed.)
7. Album dos Circulos Operários no Brasil. Rio de Janeiro: 1955.
8. Alexander, R. J. The Bolivian National Revolution. New Brunswick: Rutgers, 1958.
9. _____. Organized Labor in Latin America. New York: Free Press, 1965.
10. _____. Political Parties in Latin America. New York: Praeger, 1973.
11. Almeida, J. de. O Estado Novo. Lisbon: Pereira, 1932.
12. Almeida e Oliveira, A. C. de. Principios Fundamentais do Estado Novo Corporativo. Coimbra: Grafica, 1937.
13. Almond, G. A. Political Development: Essays in Heuristic Theory. Boston: Little, Brown, 1970.
14. Almond, G. A., and Coleman, J. S., eds. The Politics of the Developing Areas. Princeton: University Press, 1960.
15. Almond, G. A., and Powell, G. B. Comparative Politics. Boston: Little, Brown, 1966.
16. Altamira, R. A History of Spain. New York: Van Nostrand, 1949.
17. Alvarado Smith, M., and Ruz Duran, A. El derecho del trabajo en las legislaciones latinoamericanas. Santiago: Jurídica, 1950.

18. Amsden, J. _Collective Bargaining and Class Conflict in Spain_. London: Weidenfeld & Nicolson, 1972.
19. Anderson, C. W. _The Political Economy of Modern Spain: Policy-making in an Authoritarian System_. Madison: Wisconsin, 1970.
20. _____. _Politics and Economic Change in Latin America_. Princeton: Van Nostrand, 1967.
21. _____. "Toward a Theory of Latin American Politics," in 545.
22. _____ et al. _Issues of Political Development_. Englewood Cliffs: Prentice-Hall, 1974.
23. Angell, A. _Politics and the Labor Movement in Chile_. London: Oxford, 1972.
24. Arciniegas, G. _Latin America: A Cultural History_. New York: Knopf, 1967.
25. Arguedas, A. _Pueblo Infermo_. Barcelona: Tasso, 1910.
26. Arnade, C. W. _The Emergence of the Republic of Bolivia_. Gainesville: Florida, 1957.
27. Arnade, K. C. "The Technique of the Coup d'Etat in Latin America." _United Nations World_ 4 (Feb., 1950): 21-25.
28. Ashford, D. "Patterns of Consensus in Developing Countries." _American Behavioral Scientist_ 4 (April 1961): 7-10.
29. _____. "Patterns of Group Development in a New Nation: Morocco." _American Political Science Review_ 55 (June 1961): 321-32.
30. Astiz, C. "The Armed Forces as a Political Elite: Can They Develop a New Developmental Model?" Paper presented at the 1969 Round Table of the International Political Science Association, Rio de Janeiro, Oct. 27-31, 1969.
31. _____. "Bureaucracy, Technocracy and Democracy: The Peruvian Military in Power." Paper presented at the Annual Meeting of the Northeastern Political Science Association, Nov. 8-10, 1973.
32. Azpiazu, J. _The Corporative State_. London: Herder, 1951.
33. Bagú, S. _Estructura social de la colonia_. Buenos Aires, 1952.
34. Bailey, J. J. "Pluralist and Corporatist Dimensions of Interest Representation in Colombia," in 304.
35. Bailey, S. _Labor, Nationalism and Politics in Argentina_. New Brunswick: Rutgers, 1967.
36. Baran, P. _The Political Economy of Growth_. New York: Monthly Review, 1957.
37. Barros, H. de G. _Historia da Administração Pública em Portugal no Séculos XII-XV_ (Lisbon: Sa da Costa, 1945.
38. Baudin, L. _Le Corporatisme: Italie, Portugal, Allemagne, Espagne, France_. Paris, 1942.
39. Beer, S. H. _Modern British Politics_. London: Faber & Faber, 1965.
40. Beezley, W. H. "Caudillismo: An Interpetive Note." _Journal of Inter-American Studies_ 11 (July 1969).
41. Belo, J. M. _History of Modern Brazil, 1889-1964_. Stanford: University Press, 1966.
42. Bendix, R. _Max Weber: An Intellectual Portrait_. Garden City: Anchor, 1960.
43. Berle, A. A. _Latin America--Diplomacy and Reality_. New York: Harper & Row, 1962.

44. Bill, J. A. "Class Analysis and the Challenge of Change." Comparative Political Studies 2 (Oct. 1969): 389-400.
45. Bishko, C. J. "The Iberian Background of Latin American History." Hispanic American Historical Review 36 (Feb. 1956): 50-80.
46. Black, C. E. The Dynamics of Modernization. New York: Harper & Row, 1966.
47. Bodenheimer, S. J. The Ideology of Developmentalism: The American Paradigm Surrogate for Latin American Studies. Beverly Hills: Sage, 1971.
48. Bosch, J. Trujillo. Caracas: Nacionales, 1959.
49. Bouviere-Ajam, M. La doctrine corporative. Paris: 1941.
50. Bowen, R. German Theories of the Corporative State. New York: Whittlesey, 1947.
51. Brennan, G. The Spanish Labyrinth. Cambridge: University Press, 1971.
52. Brentano, L. O Clero e a Ação Popular. Rio de Janeiro: n.p., n.d.
53. _____. Guía do Assistente Eclesiástico do Círculo Operário. Rio de Janeiro: n.p., n.d.
54. _____. Manual do Círculo Operário. Rio de Janeiro: 1947.
55. Brittan, S. "Toward a Corporate State." Encounter 44 (June 1975): 58-63.
56. Bronner, F. "Class and Corporate Elements in Hapsburg Lima's Elite Circulation." Paper presented at the VIII National Meeting of the Latin American Studies Association, Pittsburgh, April 5-7, 1979.
57. Bruneau, T. C. "The Changing Political Role of the Catholic Church," in 514.
58. _____. The Political Transformation of the Brazilian Catholic Church. London: Oxford, 1974.
59. Buckland, W. W., and McNair, A. D. Roman Law and Common Law: A Comparison. Cambridge: University Press, 1965.
60. Bugarola, M. Entidades Intermedias y Representación Política. Madrid: Populares, 1970.
61. Bundy, W. P. "Dictatorships and American Foreign Policy." Foreign Affairs 54 (Oct. 1975): 51-60.
62. Busey, J. "Observations on Latin American Constitutionalism." The Americas 24 (July 1967): 46-66.
63. Cabral, F. S. Uma Perspectiva sobre Portugal. Lisbon: Morães, 1973.
64. Caetano, M. Constituções portuguesas. Braga: 1958.
65. _____. O Sistema Corporativa. Lisbon: Jornal do Comercio, 1938.
66. Camp, R. L. The Papal Ideology of Social Reform. Leiden: 1969.
67. Campos, F. O Pensamento contrarevolutionario em Portugal. Lisbon: Fernandes, 1931.
68. _____. O principio da Organização corporativa atraves da historia. Lisbon: Nação Portuguesa, 1936.
69. _____. A Solução Corporativa. Lisbon: Imperio, 1939.
70. Carr, R. Spain, 1808-1939. Oxford: Clarendon, 1966.
71. Cavalcante, E. Orientador do Circulismo. Rio de Janeiro: 1963.

72. Cayer, N. J. "Political Development in Latin America: The Consensus Model, the Conflict Model, and an Alternative Approach." Ph.D. dissertation, University of Massachusetts, 1971.
73. Cespedes, G. Latin America. New York: Knopf, 1974.
74. Chacon, V. "State Capitalism and Bureaucracy in Brazil." Paper presented at the VII National Meeting of the Latin American Studies Association, Houston, Nov. 2-5, 1977.
75. Chalmers, D. A. "Crisis and Change in Latin America." Journal of International Affairs 23 (1969): 76-88.
76. _____. "Parties and Society in Latin America." Studies in Comparative International Development 7 (Summer, 1972): 102-30.
77. Chaplin, D., ed. Peruvian Nationalism: A Corporatist Revolution. New Brunswick: Transaction, 1976.
78. Chapman, B. The Profession of Government. London: Allen & Unwin, 1959.
79. Chevalier, F. Land and Society in Colonial Mexico. Berkeley: California, 1963.
80. Christopher, W. "Human Rights: Principle and Realism." Washington: Dept. of State, Bureau of Public Affairs, Office of Media Service, 1977.
81. Chroust, A.-H. "The Corporate Idea and the Body Politic in the Middle Ages." Review of Politics 9 (Oct. 1947): 423-52.
82. Clark, M. Organized Labor in Mexico. Chapel Hill: North Carolina, 1934.
83. Cole, G. D. H. Guild Socialism. New York: Stokes, 1921.
84. Collier, D., and Collier, R. B. "Who Does What, to Whom, and How: Toward a Comparative Analysis of Latin American Corporatism," in 304.
85. _____ et al. "Varieties of Latin American 'Corporatism.'" Paper presented at the 1975 Annual Meeting of the American Political Science Association, San Francisco, Sept. 2-5.
86. Collier, R. B., and Collier, D. "Inducements versus Constraints: Disaggregating 'Corporatism.'" American Political Science Review 73 (Dec. 1979): 967-86.
87. "Colonial Institutions and Contemporary Latin America." Hispanic American Historical Review 43 (Aug. 1963).
88. Concha, L. M. Sobre la dictación de un código del trabajo y de la provisión social. Santiago: Cervantes, 1907.
89. Confederação Brasileira de Trabalhadores Cristãos, Dinâmica Sindical. Rio de Janeiro: 1956.
90. Converse, P. "Of Time and Partisan Stability." Comparative Political Studies 2 (July 1969).
91. Cordova, E. "Sobre la implementación del derecho laboral en la America Latina." Journal of Inter-American Studies 8 (July 1966): 453-70.
92. Cortes Conde, R. The First Stages of Modernization in Spanish America (New York: Harper & Row, 1974.
93. Costa, J. M. P. da. Capitalismo, Socialismo, Corporatismo. Lisbon: 1958.
94. Costa Leite, J. P. da. A Doutrina Corporativa em Portugal. Lisbon: Classica, 1966.

95. Cotler, J. "El Populismo Militar como Modelo de Desarrollo Nacional: El Caso Peruano." Paper presented at the 1969 Round Table of the International Political Science Association, Rio de Janeiro, Oct. 27-31, 1969.
96. Cotta, F. Economic Planning in Corporative Portugal. Westminster: King & Staples, 1937.
97. Coulter, P. B. Social Mobilization and Liberal Democracy. Lexington: Heath, 1975.
98. Crassweller, R. D. Trujillo. New York: Macmillan, 1966.
99. Crawford, W. R. A Century of Latin American Thought. New York: Praeger, 1966.
100. _____. "The Pathology of Democracy in Latin America: A Sociologist's Point of View." American Political Science Review 44 (March 1950).
101. Crozier, M. The Bureaucratic Phenomenon. Chicago: Univ. Press, 1964.
102. Cuadrado, M. M. Elecciones y partidos politícos de España, 1868-1931. Madrid: 1931.
103. Dahl, R. Who Governs? New Haven: Yale, 1961.
104. Dahrendorf, R. Class and Class Conflict in Industrial Society. Stanford: Univ. Press, 1959.
105. _____. Society and Democracy in Germany. London: 1968.
106. DaSilva, M. "The Basque Nationalist Movement." Ph.D. dissertation, University of Massachusetts, 1972.
107. Davies, J. C. Human Nature in Politics. New York: Wiley, 1963.
108. Davis, H. P. Black Democracy: The Story of Haiti. New York: Dodge, 1936.
109. Dealy, G. Latin America--Ex Unibus Unum. Corvallis: Oregon State Univ., Dept. of Political Science, 1977.
110. _____. "Latin America: Pluralist, Corporatist, or Monist?" Paper presented at the VI Meeting of the Latin American Studies Association, Atlanta, March 25-28, 1976.
111. _____. "Prolegomena on the Spanish American Political Tradition." Hispanic American Historical Review 48 (1968): 37-58.
112. _____. The Public Man: An Interpretation of Latin American and Other Catholic Countries. Amherst: Mass., 1977.
113. _____. "The Tradition of Monistic Democracy in Latin America," in 545.
114. Dean, W. The Industrialization of São Paulo. Austin: Texas, 1969.
115. _____. "Latin American Golpes and Economic Fluctuations, 1823-1966." Social Science Quarterly 51 (June 1970): 70-80.
116. DeGrazia, S. The Political Community. Chicago: Univ. Press, 1948.
117. Denoon, D. B. H. "The Corporative Model: How Relevant and for Which Countries?" Cambridge: MIT, Dept. of Political Science, 1973.
118. Deutsch, K. "The Growth of Nations: Some Recurrent Patterns of Political and Social Integration." World Politics 5 (Jan. 1953): 168-95.
119. _____. Nationalism and Social Communication. Cambridge: MIT, 1966.

120. Dix, R. "Latin America: Opposition and Development." In *Regimes and Opposition*. Edited by R. Dahl. New Haven: Yale, 1973.
121. Dolbeare, K. M. "Alternatives to the New Fascism." *Massachusetts Review* 17 (Spring, 1976).
122. Dolgoff, S. *The Cuban Revolution*. Montreal: Black Rose, 1976.
123. Domínguez, J. I., and Mitchell, C. "The Roads Not Taken: Institutionalization and Political Parties in Cuba and Bolivia." *Comparative Politics* 9 (Jan. 1977): 173-95.
124. Durkheim, E. "The Solidarity of Occupational Groups." In *Theories of Society*, pp. 356-63. Edited by Talcott Parsons et al. New York: Free Press, 1965.
125. Dutra, P. *Materias do Curso de Base e Psicologia Moral do Dirigente*. Rio de Janeiro: n.p., n.d.
126. _____. *Diretrizes Sindicais*. Rio de Janeiro: n.d.
127. Duvignaud, J. *Change at Shebika: Report from a North African Village*. New York: Pantheon, 1970.
128. Easton, D. *A Systems Analysis of Political Life*. New York: Wiley, 1965.
129. Eckstein, H., and Apter, D. E. "Totalitarianism and Autocracy." In *Comparative Politics*, pp. 433-40. Edited by H. Eckstein and D. E. Apter. New York: Free Press, 1963.
130. Economic Commission for Latin America. *Economic Survey of Latin America*. New York: United Nations, 1969.
131. _____. *Social Development of Latin America in the Post-War Period*. New York: United Nations, 1964.
132. Einaudi, L. *The Peruvian Military*. Santa Monica: RAND, 1969.
133. _____. "Revolution from Within? Military Rule in Peru since 1968." Paper presented at the 1971 Annual Meeting of the American Political Science Association, Chicago, Sept. 7-11.
134. Einaudi, L., and Stepan, A. *Latin American Institutional Development: Changing Military Perspectives in Peru and Brazil*. Santo Monica: RAND, 1971.
135. Eisenstadt, S. N. *Modernization: Protest and Change*. Englewood Cliffs: Prentice-Hall, 1966.
136. _____. "Breakdowns of Modernization." *Economic Development and Cultural Change* 12 (July 1964): 345-67.
137. _____. "Post-Traditional Societies and the Continuity and Reconstruction of Tradition." *Daedalus* 102 (Winter, 1973): 1-27.
138. Elbow, M. H. *French Corporative Theory, 1789-1948*. New York: Columbia, 1953.
139. *Eleição para a Assembleia Constituinte 1975*. Lisbon: INE, 1975.
140. Erickson, K. P. *The Brazilian Corporative State and Working Class Politics*. Berkeley: California, 1977.
141. _____. "Corporatism and Labor in Brazilian Development," in 514.
142. Fagen, R. *The Transformation of Political Culture in Cuba*. Stanford: Univ. Press, 1969.

143. Fals Borda, O. "Marginality and Revolution in Latin America, 1809-1969." Studies in Comparative International Development 6 (1970-71): 63-89.
144. Faoro, R. Os Donos do Poder: Formação do Patronato Político Brasileiro (Pôrto Alegre: Globo, 1976.
145. Fitch, J. S. The Military Coup as a Political Process. Baltimore: Johns Hopkins, 1977.
146. FitzGerald, F. Fire in the Lake. New York: Random, 1972.
147. Fitzgibbon, R. H., ed. Constitutions of the Americas. Chicago: Univ. Press, 1948.
148. _____. "Measurement of Latin American Political Phenomena: A Statistical Experiment." American Political Science Review 45 (June 1951): 517-23.
149. _____. "Measuring Democratic Change in Latin America." Journal of Politics 29 (Feb. 1967): 129-66.
150. _____. "A Statistical Evaluation of Latin American Democracy." Western Political Quarterly 9 (Sept. 1956): 607-19.
151. Fitzgibbon, R. H., and Johnson, K. "Measurement of Latin American Political Change." American Political Science Review 54 (Sept. 1961): 515-26.
152. Fitzgibbon, R. H., and Johnson, K. "Measuring Democratic Change in Latin America." Journal of Politics 29 (Feb. 1967): 129-55.
153. Fix Zamudio, H. "Latin American Procedures for the Protection of the Individual." Journal of the International Commission of Jurists 9 (Dec. 1968): 60-95.
154. Fogarty, M. Christian Democracy in Western Europe. London: Routledge & Kegan Paul, 1957.
155. Foster, G. M. Culture and Conquest: America's Spanish Heritage. Chicago: Quadrange, 1960.
156. Frank, A. G. Capitalism and Underdevelopment in Latin America. New York: Monthly Review, 1969.
157. Franco, J. "The Specter of Anachronism and the Latin American Writer." Paper presented at the VII National Meeting of the Latin American Studies Association, Houston, Nov. 2-5, 1977.
158. Freund, E. The Legal Nature of Corporations. Chicago: Univ. Press, 1897.
159. Furnish, D. "The Hierarchy of Peruvian Laws: Context for Law and Development." American Journal of Comparative Law 50 (Winter, 1971): 91-120.
160. Galbraith, J. K. The New Industrial State. Boston: Houghton-Mifflin, 1968.
161. Galíndez, J. de. La era de Trujillo. Santiago: Pacífico, 1956.
162. Germani, G. "Stages of Modernization." International Journal 24 (Summer, 1969): 463-85.
163. Germani, G., and Silvert, K. "Politics, Social Structure, and Military Intervention in Latin America." European Journal of Sociology 2 (1961): 62-81.
164. Gibson, C. Spain in America. New York: Harper, 1966.
165. Gibson, C., ed. The Black Legend: Anti-Spanish Attitudes in the Old World and the New. New York: Knopf, 1971.

166. Gierke, O. von. "The Idea of Corporation." In <u>Theories of Society</u>, pp. 611-26. Edited by T. Parsons. New York: 1961.
167. Giménez Fernández, M. <u>Las Doctrinas populistas en la independencia de Hispanoamerica</u>. Seville: 1947.
168. Giner, S. "Spain." In <u>Contemporary Europe</u>. Edited by M. Archer and S. Giner. London: Weidenfeld & Nicolson, 1971.
169. Glade, W. P. "Economic Policy-Making and the Structure of Corporatism in Latin America." Paper presented at the VI National Meeting of the Latin American Studies Association, Atlanta, March 1976.
170. _____. <u>The Latin American Economies</u>. New York: American, 1969.
171. _____. "The State and Economic Development in Mediterranean Politics." Paper presented at the 1973 Annual Meeting of the American Political Science Association, New Orleans, Sept. 4-8.
172. Glassman, R. <u>Political History of Latin America</u>. New York: Funk & Wagnalls, 1969.
173. Goldwert, M. <u>The Constabulary in the Dominican Republic and Nicaragua</u>. Gainesville: Florida, 1962.
174. _____. <u>Democracy, Militarism, and Nationalism in Argentina</u>. Austin: Texas, 1972.
175. Gonçalves, L. da C. <u>Causes e efeitos do corporatismo Portugues</u>. Lisbon: ISCEF, 1936.
176. Góngora, M. <u>El estado en el derecho indiano</u>. Santiago: 1951.
177. Goodman, L. W. "Legal Controls on Union Activity in Latin America." In <u>Workers and Managers in Latin America</u>, pp. 231-34. Edited by S. M. Davis and L. M. Goodman. Lexington: Heath, 1972.
178. Graham, L. S. <u>Civil Service Reform in Brazil: Principles versus Practice</u>. Austin: Texas, 1968.
179. _____. "Portugal: The Bureaucracy of Empire." Paper presented at the Workshop on Modern Portugal, Univ. of New Hampshire, Durham, Oct. 10-14, 1973.
180. _____. "Latin America, Illusion or Reality: A Case for a New Analytic Framework for the Region," in 545.
181. Graham, R. <u>Britain and the Onset of Modernization in Brazil</u>. Cambridge: Univ. Press, 1972.
182. Green, O. H. <u>Spain and the Western Tradition</u>. Madison and Milwaukee: 1963-66.
183. Greenfield, S. M. "The Patrimonial State and Patron-Client Relations in Iberia and Latin America: Sources of 'The System' in the Fifteenth-Century Writings of the Infante D. Pedro of Portugal." Amherst: Univ. of Massachusetts, Program in Latin American Studies, Occasional Papers Series, No. 1, 1976.
184. Gregor, A. J. <u>The Ideology of Fascism</u>. New York: Free Press, 1969.
185. Grullón, R. "Antecedentes y perspectivas del momento político dominicano." <u>Cuadernos Americanos</u> 120 (Jan.-Feb. 1962): 221-52.
186. Gutiérrez, M. <u>La custión obrera</u>. Santiago: Barcelona, 1904.

187. Hah, C. D., and Schneider, J. "A Critique of Current Studies of Political Development and Modernization." *Social Research* 35 (Spring, 1968): 130-58.
188. Hale, C. A. *Mexican Liberalism in the Age of Mora, 1821-1853*. New Haven: Yale, 1968.
189. Halperin-Donghi, T. *The Aftermath of Revolution in Latin America*. New York: Harper & Row, 1973.
190. Hamill, H. M., ed. *Dictatorship in Spanish America*. New York: Knopf, 1965.
191. Hamilton, B. *Political Thought in Sixteenth-Century Spain*. Oxford: Univ. Press, 1963.
192. Hammergren, L. A. "Corporatism in Latin American Politics: A Reexamination of the Unique Tradition." *Comparative Politics*, July 1977.
193. Hammond, J. L. "Das Urnas as Ruas: Electoral Behavior and Noninstitutional Political Militancy--Portugal, 1975." Paper presented at the conference on "Crisis in Portugal," Toronto, April 15-17, 1976.
194. Hanke, L. *The First Social Experiments in America*. Cambridge: Harvard, 1935.
195. Haring, C. H. *The Spanish Empire in America*. New York: Harcourt, Brace & World, 1947.
196. Harris, N. *Competition and the Corporate Society*. London: Methuen, 1972.
197. Hartz, L. *The Liberal Tradition in America*. New York: Harcourt, Brace & World, 1955.
198. _____ et al. *The Founding of New Societies*. New York: Harcourt, Brace & World, 1964.
199. Hawkins, C. "Reflections on Labor's Relations to Government and Politics in Latin America." *Western Political Quarterly* 20 (Dec. 1967): 930-40.
200. Hayter, T. *Aid as Imperialism*. Baltimore: Penguin, 1971.
201. Hegel, G. W. E. *The Philosophy of History*. New York: Dover, 1956.
202. Heidenheimer, A. *Adenauer and the CDU*. The Hague: Nijoff, 1960.
203. Heisler, M. O. "Corporate Pluralism Revisited: Where Is the Theory?" *Scandinavian Political Studies* 2 (1979): 277-97.
204. _____. *Politics in Europe*. New York: McKay, 1974.
205. Herring, H. *A History of Latin America*. New York: Knopf, 1968.
206. Hirschman, A. O. *Journeys toward Progress: Studies of Economic Policy-Making in Latin America*. New York: Anchor, 1965.
207. Hoetink, H. "Materiales para el estudio de la República Dominicana en la segunda mitad del siglo XIX." *Caribbean Studies*, 1965-69.
208. _____. *El pueblo dominicano, 1850-1900*. Santiago: Univ. Catolica, 1971.
209. Horowitz, I. L., et al., eds. *Latin American Radicalism*. New York: Vintage, 1969.
210. Howe, W. *The Mining Guild of New Spain*. New York: Greenwood, 1968.

211. Huntington, S. P. *Political Order in Changing Societies*. New Haven: Yale, 1968.
212. _____. *The Soldier and the State*. Cambridge: Harvard, 1957.
213. Hyman, E. "Soldiers in Politics." *Political Science Quarterly* 87 (Sept. 1972): 401-18.
214. International Labour Organization. *Labour Courts in Latin America*. Geneva: 1949.
215. Jaguaribe, H. *Political Development*. New York: Harper & Row, 1978.
216. Jane, C. *Liberty and Despotism in Latin America*. Oxford: Clarendon, 1929.
217. Janowitz, M. *The Professional Soldier*. Glencoe: Free Press, 1960.
218. _____. "Social Stratification and the Comparative Study of Elites." *Social Forces* 25 (Oct. 1956).
219. Jiménes-Grullón, J. I. *La República Dominicana*. Mérida: Graf. Universitarios, 1965.
220. Johnson, H. B., Jr., ed. *From Reconquest to Empire: The Iberian Background to Latin American History*. New York: Knopf, 1970.
221. Johnson, J. J. *The Military and Society in Latin America*. Stanford: Univ. Press, 1964.
222. _____. *Political Change in Latin America*. Stanford: Univ. Press, 1958.
223. _____, ed. *Continuity and Change in Latin America*. Stanford: Univ. Press, 1964.
224. Johnson, K. F. *Argentina's Mosaic of Discord, 1966-1968*. Washington: Institute for the Comparative Study of Political Systems, 1969.
225. _____. "Causal Factors in Latin American Instability." *Western Political Quarterly* 17 (Sept. 1964).
226. _____. "Measuring the Scholarly Image of Latin American Democracy, 1945-1970." In *Statistical Abstract of Latin America*, XVII. Los Angeles: UCLA Latin American Center, 1976.
227. _____. "Research Perspectives on the Revised Fitzgibbon-Johnson Index of the Image of Political Democracy in Latin America, 1945-75." In *Quantitative Latin American Studies*, pp. 87-91. Edited by J. W. Wilkie and K. Ruddle. Los Angeles: UCLA Latin American Center, 1977.
228. _____. "Scholarly Images of Latin American Political Democracy in 1975." *Latin American Research Review* 11 (Summer, 1976): 127-38.
229. *Journal of Economic Issues* 6 (March 1972). Special issue on the corporate state in America.
230. Kadt, E. de. "Paternalism and Populism: Catholicism in Latin America." *Journal of Contemporary History* 2 (Oct. 1967): 89-106.
231. _____. "Religion, the Church, and Social Change in Brazil" in 494.
232. Kantor, H. *The Ideology and Program of the Peruvian Aprista Movement*. Berkeley: California, 1953.

233. Kaplan, A. "Systems Theory and Political Science." *Social Research* 35 (July 1968): 30-47.
234. Karst, K., and Rosenn, K. S. *Law and Development in Latin America*. Berkeley: California, 1975.
235. Kaufman, R. R. "Corporatism, Clientelism, and Partisan Conflict," in 304.
236. ──────. *Transitions to Stable Authoritarian-Corporate Regimes*. Beverly Hills: Sage, 1976.
237. Kautsky, J. H. "An Essay in the Politics of Development." In *Change in Underdeveloped Countries*. Edited by J. H. Kautsky. New York: Wiley, 1962.
238. Kearns, D. *Lyndon Johnson and the American Dream*. New York: Harper & Row, 1976.
239. Keehn, N. H. "A World of Becoming: From Pluralism to Corporatism." *Polity* 9 (Fall, 1976): 19-39.
240. Keith, H. "Point-Counterpoint in Portuguese Educational Reform." Paper presented at the Workshop on Modern Portugal, Univ. of New Hampshire, Durham, Oct. 10-14, 1973.
241. Kern, R., ed. *The Caciques*. Albuquerque: Univ. of New Mexico Press, 1973.
242. Keynes, J. M. *The End of Laissez-Faire*. London: Hogarth, 1926.
243. King, D. Y. "Authoritarian Rule and State Corporatism in Indonesia." Paper presented at the 1977 Annual Meeting of the American Political Science Association, Washington, Sept. 1-4, 1977.
244. Klein, H. *Parties and Political Change in Bolivia*. Cambridge: Univ. Press, 1952.
245. Klein, J. *The Mesta*. Port Washington: Kennikat, 1964.
246. Kling, M. "The State of Research on Latin America," in 502.
247. ──────. "Toward a Theory of Power and Political Instability in Latin America." *Western Political Quarterly* 9 (March 1956): 21-35.
248. ──────. "Violence and Politics in Latin America." *The Sociological Review* 2 (1967): 119-32.
249. Kornhauser, W. *The Politics of Mass Society*. New York: Free Press, 1959.
250. Kryzanek, M. J. "Political Party Opposition in Latin America." Ph.D. dissertation, University of Massachusetts, 1975.
251. Kuhn, T. *The Structure of Scientific Revolutions*. Chicago: Univ. Press, 1971.
252. "Labour Legislation and Collective Bargaining in Latin America." *International Labour Review* 84 (Oct. 1961): 269-91.
253. Lafaye, J. "The Spanish Diaspora: The Enduring Unity of Hispanic Culture." Washington: Wilson Center, Latin American Program, 1977.
254. Landsberger, H. A., ed. *The Church and Social Change in Latin America*. Notre Dame: Univ. Press, 1970.
255. ──────. "The Labor Elite: Is It Revolutionary?" in 273.
256. Lanning, J. T. *Academic Culture in the Spanish Colonies*. London: Oxford, 1940.
257. LaPalombara, J. "The Utility and Limitations of Interest Group Theory in Non-American Field Situations." *Journal of*

Politics 32 (Feb. 1960): 29-49.
258. LaPalombara, J., and Weiner, M., eds. Political Parties and Political Development. Princeton: Univ. Press, 1966.
259. Lerner, D. The Passing of Traditional Society. Glencoe: Free Press, 1958.
260. Levinson, J., and de Onis, J. The Alliance that Lost Its Way. Chicago: Quadrangle, 1970.
261. Levy, D. "Corporatist and Pluralist Principles in Government-University Relations." Paper presented at the University of Lancaster, Aug. 29-Sept. 1, 1978.
262. Lewis, A. R. The Development of Southern French and Catalan Society, 718-1050. Austin: Texas, 1965.
263. Lewy, G. Constitutionalism and Statecraft during the Golden Age of Spain. Geneva: Droz, 1960.
264. Lieuwen, E. Arms and Politics in Latin America. New York: Praeger, 1960.
265. Lijphart, A. "Consociational Democracy." World Politics 21 (Jan. 1969): 207-25.
266. Lima, A. A. Indicações Políticas. Rio de Janeiro: Civilização, 1936.
267. Linz, J. "An Authoritarian Regime: Spain." In Mass Politics, pp. 251-83. Edited by E. Allardt and S. Rokkan. New York: Free Press, 1970.
268. _____. "From Falange to Movimiento-Organización: The Spanish Single Party and the Franco Regime." In Authoritarian Politics in Modern Society. Edited by S. P. Huntington and C. H. Moore. New York: Basic, 1970.
269. _____. "Spain and Portugal: Critical Choices." Paper presented at the "Mini-Conference on Contemporary Portugal," Yale Univ., March 28-29, 1975.
270. Linz, J., and de Miguel, A. "Within-Nation Differences and Comparisons: The Eight Spains." In Comparing Nations, pp. 267-319. Edited by R. L. Merritt and S. Rokkan. New Haven: Yale, 1966.
271. Lipset, S. M. Political Man. New York: Anchor, 1963.
272. Lipset, S. M., and Rokkan, S., eds. Party Systems and Voter Alignments. New York: Free Press, 1967.
273. Lipset, S. M., and Solari, A., eds. Elites in Latin America. New York: Oxford, 1967.
274. Lodge, G. C. Spearhead of Democracy: Labor in the Developing Countries. New York: Harper & Row, 1962.
275. Logan, R. W. Haiti and the Dominican Republic. New York: Oxford, 1968.
276. López-Pina, A. "Spain as Anti-Model: From the Latin American Area Studies to the Latin Cultures Approach." Ann Arbor: Univ. of Michigan, Dept. of Political Science, May 1973.
277. Lorwin, V. R. "Segmented Pluralism." Comparative Politics 3 (Jan. 1971): 14-75.
278. Lousse, E. Corporativismo Antigo e Moderno. Lisbon: Cruz, 1959.
279. _____. Organização e representação corporativa. Lisbon: Bib. Social e Corporativa, 1959.

280. Lowenthal, A. "The Dominican Republic." In Reform and Revolution. Edited by A. von Lazar and R. R. Kaufman. Boston: Allyn & Bacon, 1969.
281. _____, ed. The Peruvian Experiment. Princeton: Univ. Press, 1975.
282. Lowi, T. The End of Liberalism. New York: Norton, 1969.
283. _____. "The Public Philosophy: Interest Group Liberalism." American Political Science Review 61 (March 1967): 5-24.
284. Lucena, M. de. A evolução do sistema corporativo portugues. Lisbon: Perspectivas e Realidades, 1976.
285. _____. "The Evolution of Portuguese Corporatism under Salazar and Caetano," in 524.
286. McAlister, L. N. "Changing Concepts of the Role of the Military in Latin America." Annals 360 (July 1965): 85-98.
287. _____. "Civil-Military Relations in Latin America." Journal of Inter-American Studies 3 (July 1961): 341-50.
288. _____. The "Fuero Militar" in New Spain, 1746-1800. Gainesville: Florida, 1957.
289. _____. "The Military," in 223.
290. _____. "The Reorganization of the Army of New Spain." Hispanic American Historical Review 33 (Feb. 1963): 1-32.
291. _____. "Social Structure and Social Change in New Spain." Hispanic American Historical Review 43 (Aug. 1963): 349-70.
292. _____ et al. The Military in Latin American Sociopolitical Evolution. Washington: Center for Research in Social Systems, 1970.
293. McGovern, G. Revolution into Democracy: Portugal after the Coup. Washington: GPO, 1976.
294. MacKay, A. Spain in the Middle Ages. London: Macmillan, 1977.
295. McLaughlin, M. "Political Parties in Latin America." Amherst: Univ. of Massachusetts, Dept. of Political Science, 1977.
296. Maday, B. C. Area Handbook for Brazil. Washington: American Univ., Foreign Area Studies Div., 1964.
297. Madden, M. R. Political Theory and Law in Medieval Spain. New York: Fordham, 1930.
298. Magalhães, J. C. de. Historia do Pensamento Economico em Portugal. Coimbra: Univ. Press, 1967.
299. Maidenberg, H. J. "Chaos Hovers over Latin Lands." New York Times, Jan. 26, 1970, p. 49.
300. Maier, C. S. Recasting Bourgeois Europe. Princeton: Univ. Press, 1975.
301. Maier, J., and Weatherhead, R. W., eds. Politics of Change in Latin America. New York: Praeger, 1954.
302. Makler, H. "The Portuguese Industrial Elite and Its Corporative Relations," in 524.
303. Maldonado D., M. "La Caída de Juan Bosch y la Política en la República Dominicana." Caribbean Monthly Bulletin 1 (Nov. 1963): 9-12.
304. Malloy, J., ed. Authoritarianism and Corporatism in Latin America. Pittsburgh: Univ. Press, 1977.

305. _____. "Authoritarianism and Corporatism in Latin America: The Modal Pattern," in 304.
306. _____. "Authoritarianism and Corporatism: The Case of Bolivia," in 304.
307. _____, and Thorn, R., eds. Beyond the Revolution: Bolivia since 1952. Pittsburgh: Univ. Press, 1971.
308. _____. Bolivia. Pittsburgh: Univ. Press, 1970.
309. _____. "Bolivia: An Incomplete Revolution," in 557.
310. Mander, J. The Unrevolutionary Society: The Power of Latin American Conservatism in a Changing World. New York: Knopf, 1969.
311. Manoilesco, M. "Le Génie Latin dans le nouveau régime Portugais," VI Congresso do Mundo Portugues. Lisbon: Comissão dos Centenarios, 1940, pp. 621-39.
312. _____. Le Siècle du corporatisme. Paris: Félix Alcan, 1938.
313. Marques, A. H. de O. A History of Portugal. New York: Columbia, 1972.
314. Marsal, J. Cambio Social en America Latina: Crítica de Algunas Interpretaciones Dominantes en las Ciencias Sociales. Buenos Aires: Solar/Hachette, 1967.
315. Martins, H. "Portugal," in 168.
316. Martins, M. B. Sociedades e grupos em Portugal. Lisbon: Estampa, 1973.
317. Martz, J. "Latin American Intellectuals and Latin American Studies: The Structuring and Sociology of Research." Paper presented at the VII National Meeting of the Latin American Studies Association, Houston, Nov. 2-5, 1977.
318. _____. "The Place of Latin America in the Study of Comparative Politics." Journal of Politics 28 (Feb. 1966): 57-80.
319. Martz, J., and Jorrín, M. Latin American Political Thought and Ideology. Chapel Hill: North Carolina, 1970.
320. Masselman, G. The Cradle of Colonialism. New Haven: Yale, 1963.
321. Mecham, J. L. Church and State in Latin America. Chapel Hill: North Carolina, 1966.
322. Medhurst, K. N. Government in Spain. Oxford: Pergamon, 1973.
323. Meisler, S. "Spain's New Democracy." Foreign Affairs 56 (Oct. 1977): 190-208.
324. Mejía, L. F. De Lilís a Trujillo. Caracas: Elite, 1944.
325. Mercier Vega, L. Roads to Power in Latin America. New York: Praeger, 1969.
326. Merêa, M. P. O Poder Real e as Cortes. Coimbra: Univ. Press, 1923.
327. Merkl, P. H. Modern Comparative Politics. Hinsdale: Dryden, 1977.
328. Merryman, J. H. The Civil Law Tradition. Stanford: Univ. Press, 1969.
329. Middlebrook, K. J., and Palmer, D. S. Military Government and Corporativist Political Development. Beverly Hills: Sage, 1975.

330. Miguel, A. de. "Change in the Spanish Social Structure under Francoism." New Haven: Yale Univ., Dept. of Sociology, 1977.
331. Mileur, J. M. The Liberal Tradition in Crisis. Lexington: Heath, 1974.
332. Miller, A. S. The Modern Corporate State. Westport: Greenwood, 1976.
333. Millikan, M., and Blackmer, D. The Emerging Nations. Boston: Little, Brown, 1961.
334. Miró Quesada, F. "The Impact of Metaphysics on Latin American Ideology." Journal of the History of Ideas 24 (Oct.-Dec. 1963): 539-52.
335. Mitchell, C. "Changing Views of Bolivian Politics." Latin American Research Review 14 (Summer, 1979): 297-304.
336. _____. "Factionalism and Political Change in Bolivia." In Factional Politics. Edited by F. B. Belloni and D. C. Beller. Santa Barbara: ABC-Clio, 1978.
337. _____. The Legacy of Populism in Bolivia. New York: Praeger, 1977.
338. Monson, R. A. "Perspectives on Corporatist Approaches to Political Change in Latin America." Paper presented at the Annual Meeting of the Southwestern Political Science Association, Fort Worth, March 28-31, 1979.
339. _____. "Race and Political Development in the Caribbean: Nation-Building in Corporatist Perspective." Plural Societies 7 (Summer, 1976): 49-70.
340. Moody, J. N. Church and Society: Catholic Social Thought and Movements, 1789-1950. New York: Arts, 1953.
341. Moore, B., Jr. Social Origins of Dictatorship and Democracy. Boston: Beacon, 1966.
342. Moreira, V. "Corporativismo: Tradição Cultural e Poder Política." Vertice, June-July, 1974, pp. 461-73.
343. Moreno, F. J. "The Spanish Colonial System: A Functional Approach." Western Political Quarterly 20 (June 1967): 308-20.
344. Morris, J. A., and Ropp, S. C. "Corporatism and Dependent Development: A Honduran Case Study." Latin American Research Review 12 (1977): 27-68.
345. Morris, J. O. Elites, Intellectuals, and Consensus: A Study of the Social Question and the Industrial Relations System in Chile. Ithaca: Cornell, 1966.
346. Morris, J. O., and Cordova, E. Bibliography of Industrial Relations in Latin America. Ithaca: Cornell, 1967.
347. Morse, R. M. "The Heritage of Latin America," in 545.
348. _____. "Recent Research on Latin American Urbanization." Latin American Research Review 1 (Fall, 1965).
349. _____. "The Strange Career of Latin American Studies." The Annals, No. 356 (Nov. 1964).
350. _____. "Toward a Theory of Spanish American Government," in 545.
351. The Movement of Labor Circles in Brazil. Rio de Janeiro: n.p., n.d.
352. Moya Pons, F. Historia Colonial de Santo Domingo. Santiago: Univ. Católica, 1974.

353. Needler, M. *Political Development in Latin America*. New York: Random, 1968.
354. _____. "Political Development and Military Intervention in Latin America." *American Political Science Review* 40 (Sept. 1966): 616-26.
355. Neto, J. B. N. P. "Social Evolution in Portugal since 1945." In *Portugal and Brazil in Transition*. Edited by R. S. Sayers. Minneapolis: Minnesota, 1968.
356. Nettl, J. P. *Political Mobilization*. New York: Basic, 1967.
357. Nettl, J. P., and von Vorys, K. "The Politics of Development." *Commentary* 46 (July 1968): 52-9.
358. Newton, R. C. "The Corporate Idea and the Authoritarian Tradition in Spain and Spanish America." Paper presented at the IV Annual Meeting of the Latin American Studies Association, Madison, May 1973.
359. _____. "On 'Functional Groups,' 'Fragmentation,' and 'Pluralism' in Spanish American Political Society." *Hispanic American Historical Review* 50 (Feb. 1970): 1-29.
360. _____. "Natural Corporatism and the Passing of Populism in Spanish America." *The Review of Politics* 36 (Jan. 1974): 34-51.
361. Nisbet, R. A. *Social Change and History*. London: Oxford, 1969.
362. Nolte, E. *Three Faces of Fascism*. New York: Holt, Rinehart & Winston, 1966.
363. Nowell, C. E. *A History of Portugal*. Princeton: Van Nostrand, 1962.
364. Nuccio, R. "Spain, Latin America and the Myth of Democratic Incapacity." Paper presented at the VII National Meeting of the Latin American Studies Association, Houston, Nov. 2-5, 1977.
365. Nun, J. "The Middle Class Military Coup," in 494.
366. Nunn, F. M. *The Military in Chilean Politics*. Albuquerque: New Mexico, 1973.
367. O'Donnell, G. "Corporatism and the Question of the State," in 304.
368. _____. *Modernization and Bureaucratic Authoritarianism*. Berkeley: Univ. of California, Inst. of International Studies, 1973.
369. Organski, A. F. K. "Fascism and Modernization." In *The Nature of Fascism*, pp. 19-41. Edited by S. J. Woolf. New York: Vintage, 1969.
370. _____. *The Stages of Political Development*. New York: Knopf, 1965.
371. Ornes, G. *Trujillo*. New York: Nelson, 1958.
372. Ortega y Gasset, J. *Invertebrate Spain*. New York: Norton, 1937.
373. Ortigueira, R. "La Desintegración, estado normal de paises en desarrollo." *Journal of Inter-American Studies* 5 (Oct. 1963): 471-94.
374. Osborn, H. *Bolivia*. London: Oxford, 1964.
375. Owen, E. "Recent Latin American Labor Codes." *Inter-American Quarterly* 3 (Jan. 1941): 68-79.

376. Packenham, R. A. "Foreign Aid and the National Interest." *Midwest Journal of Political Science* 10 (May 1966): 214-21.
377. _____. *Liberal America and the Third World: Political Development Ideas in Foreign Aid and Social Science*. Princeton: Univ. Press, 1973.
378. Pahl, R. E., and Winkler, J. T. "The Coming Corporatism." *Challenge*, March-April 1975, pp. 28-35.
379. Palmer, D. S. *"Revolution from Above": Military Government and Popular Participation in Peru*. Ithaca: Cornell Univ., Latin American Studies Program Dissertation Series, 1973.
380. Panitch, L. "The Development of Corporatism in Liberal Democracies." Paper presented at the 1976 Annual Meeting of the American Political Science Association, Chicago, Sept. 2-5.
381. Parry, J. H. *The Spanish Theory of Empire in the Sixteenth Century*. Cambridge: Univ. Press, 1940.
382. Parsons, T. *Societies: Evolutionary and Comparative Perspectives*. Englewood Cliffs: Prentice-Hall, 1966.
383. _____. *The Structure of Social Action*. New York: Free Press, 1968.
384. Payne, J. L. *Labor and Politics in Peru: The System of Political Bargaining*. New Haven: Yale, 1965.
385. _____. "The Politics of Structured Violence." *Journal of Politics* 27 (May 1965): 362-74.
386. Payne, S. *Falange*. Stanford: Univ. Press, 1961.
387. _____. *A History of Spain and Portugal*. Madison: Wisconsin, 1973.
388. Paz, O. "Op-Ed" essay. *New York Times*, Oct. 21, 1973.
389. Pearson, N. J. "Small Farmer and Rural Worker Pressure Groups in Brazil." Ph.D. dissertation, University of Florida, 1967.
390. Perlmutter, A. "The Praetorian State and the Praetorian Army." *Comparative Politics* 1 (April 1969): 382-404.
391. Petras, J. *Political and Social Forces in Chilean Development*. Berkeley: California, 1969.
392. Petras, J., and Zeitlin, M., eds. *Latin America: Reform or Revolution?* New York: Fawcett, 1968.
393. Phelan, J. L. "Authority and Flexibility in the Spanish Imperial Bureaucracy." *Administrative Science Quarterly* 5 (June 1960): 47-64.
394. Picón-Salas, M. *A Cultural History of Spanish America*. Berkeley: California, 1968.
395. Pike, F. "Corporatism and Latin American-United States Relations." *Review of Politics* 36 (Jan. 1974): 132-70.
396. _____. *Hispanismo*. Notre Dame: Univ. Press, 1971.
397. _____. "The New Corporatism in Franco's Spain and Some Latin American Perspectives," in 400.
398. _____. *The United States and the Andean Republics*. Cambridge: Harvard, 1977.
399. _____, ed. *The Conflict between Church and State in Latin America*. New York: Knopf, 1964.
400. Pike, F., and Stritch, Thomas, eds. *The New Corporatism: Social and Political Structures in the Iberian World*. Notre Dame: Univ. Press, 1974.
401. Pinto, J. M. C. *A Corporação*. Coimbra: Coimbra, 1955.

402. Poblete Troncoso, M. "The Enforcement of Labour Legislation in Latin America." International Labour Review 32 (Nov. 1935): 637-64.
403. ──────. "Labour Legislation in Latin America." International Labour Review 17, 2 parts (Jan. 1928): 51-67; and (Feb. 1928): 204-30.
404. ──────. El Movimiento obrero Latinoamericano. Mexico: Fondo de Cultura Económica, 1946.
405. ──────. "Recent Advances in Labour Legislation in Latin America, 1928-1934." International Labour Review 30 (July 1934): 358-80.
406. Poblete Troncoso, M., and Burnett, B. G. The Rise of the Latin American Labor Movement. New York: Bookman, 1960.
407. Polanyi, K. The Great Transformation. New York: Farrar & Rinehart, 1944.
408. Post, G. "Roman Law and Early Representation in Spain and Italy." Speculum 18 (April 1943): 211-32.
409. ──────. Studies in Medieval Legal Thought: Public Law and the State, 1100-1322. Princeton: Univ. Press, 1964.
410. Potash, R. The Army and Politics in Argentina. Stanford: Univ. Press, 1969.
411. ──────. "The Impact of Professionalism on the Twentieth Century Argentine Military." Amherst: Univ. of Massachusetts, Program in Latin American Studies, Occasional Papers Series, No. 3, 1977.
412. Powell, J. D. "Peasant Society and Clientelist Politics." American Political Science Review 64 (June 1970): 411-25.
413. Prebish, R. Transformación y Desarrollo: La Gran Tarea de America Latina. Washington: Inter-American Development Bank, 1970.
414. "Proceedings of the 67th Annual Meeting of the American Society of International Law." American Journal of International Law 67 (Nov. 1973): 198-226.
415. Programa para a democratização da República. Porto: Gonçalves, 1961.
416. Prothro, J. W., and Grigg, C. M. "Fundamental Principles of Democracy: Bases of Agreement and Disagreement." Journal of Politics 22 (May 1960): 276-94.
417. Purcell, J. F. H., and Purcell, S. K. "Mexican Business and Public Policy," in 304.
418. Purcell, S. K. "Decision-Making in an Authoritarian Regime: Mexico." Paper presented at the 1971 Annual Meeting of the American Political Science Association, Chicago, Sept. 7-11.
419. Putnam, R. D. "Toward Explaining Military Intervention in Latin American Politics." World Politics 20 (Oct. 1967): 83-110.
420. Pye, L., and Verba, S., eds. Political Culture and Political Development. Princeton: Univ. Press, 1965.
421. Rachum, I. "The Latin American Revolutions of 1930." Paper presented at Hebrew University, Jerusalem, May 5-12, 1977.
422. Relatorio da Federação de Trabalhadores de Minas Gerais. Belo Horizonte: 1967.

423. Riggs, F. W. *Administration in Developing Countries*. Boston: Houghton-Mifflin, 1964.
424. Rio, A. del. *The Clash and Attraction of Two Cultures: The Hispanic and Anglo-Saxon Worlds in America*. Baton Rouge: Louisiana State, 1965.
425. Rivera, J. *Latin America: A Sociocultural Interpretation*. New York: Appleton-Century-Crofts, 1971.
426. Robinson, R. A. H. "The Religious Question and the Catholic Revival in Portugal, circa 1900-1930." Paper presented at the Workshop on Modern Portugal, Univ. of New Hampshire, Durham, Oct. 10-14, 1973.
427. Rock, D. *Politics in Argentina, 1890-1930*. London: Cambridge, 1971.
428. Rodman, S. *Haiti*. New York: Devin-Adair, 1954.
429. Rodrígues, H. N. *Regime Jurídico das Relações Colectivas de Trabalho*. Coimbra: Atlantida, 1971.
430. Rodrígues, C. "Regionalism, Populism, and Federalism in Argentina, 1916-1930." Ph.D. dissertation, University of Massachusetts, 1974.
431. Rodríguez Demorizi, E. *Sociedades, Cofradías, Escuelas, Gremios y otros Corporaciones Dominicanas*. Santo Domingo: Educativa Dominicana, 1975.
432. Roett, R. *Brazil: Politics in a Patrimonialist Society*. Boston: Alyn & Bacon, 1972.
433. _____. "The Quest for Legitimacy in Brazil: The Dilemma of a Praetorian Army." Paper presented at the 1970 Annual Meeting of the Midwest Association of Latin American Studies, Univ. of Nebraska, Lincoln, Oct. 1-3.
434. Rogowski, R., and Wasserspring, L. *Does Political Development Exist? Corporatism in Old and New Societies*. Beverly Hills: Sage, 1971.
435. Rokkan, S. "Norway: Numerical Democracy and Corporate Pluralism." In *Political Opposition in Western Democracies*, pp. 70-115. Edited by R. Dahl. New Haven: Yale, 1966.
436. Rosenn, K. "Judicial Review in Latin America." *Ohio State Law Journal* 35 (1974): 785-819.
437. Rossell Silva, G. *De la necesidad de legislar sobre el trabajo*. Santiago: Cervantes, 1906.
438. Rostow, W. W. *The Stages of Economic Growth*. Cambridge: Univ. Press, 1960.
439. Rothstein, L. E. "Aquinas and Revolution." Paper presented at the 1976 Annual Meeting of the American Political Science Association, Chicago, Sept. 2-5.
440. Rudolph, L. "Authority and Power in Bureaucratic and Patrimonial Administration." Paper presented at the 1974 Annual Meeting of the American Political Science Association, Chicago, Aug. 29-Sept. 2.
441. Rudolph, L., and Rudolph, S. K. *The Modernity of Tradition*. Chicago: Univ. Press, 1967.
442. Rustow, D. A. *A World of Nations*. Washington: Brookings, 1967.
443. Salazar, A. de O. *Discursos*. Coimbra: Coimbra, 1966 ff.
444. Salisbury, W. T., and Story, J. "The Economic Positions of

Spain and Portugal in 1980." Paper presented at Institute for the Study of Conflict, London, May 29-31, 1975.
445. Sánchez-Albernoz, C. "The Frontier and Castilian Liberties." In The New World Looks at Its History. Edited by A. R. Lewis and T. F. McGann. Austin: Texas, 1963.
446. Sanders, T. "Catholicism and Development." In Churches and States. Edited by K. H. Silvert. New York: American Universities Field Staff, 1967.
447. Saraiva, J. S. O Pensamento político de Salazar. Coimbra: Coimbra, 1953.
448. Sarfatti, M. Spanish Bureaucratic-Patrimonialism in Latin America. Berkeley: Univ. of California, Inst. of International Studies, 1966.
449. Sarmento, A. de M. O Corporativismo Portugues e as postulados da Sociológia Católica. Braga: Cruz, 1964.
450. Sarti, R. "Fascist Modernization in Italy: Traditional or Modern." American Historical Review 75 (April 1970): 1029-45.
451. Schmidt, C. T. The Corporate State in Action. London: 1939.
452. Schmitter, P. "Corporatist Interest Representation and Public Policy-Making in Portugal." Paper presented at the 1972 Annual Meeting of the American Political Science Association, Washington, Sept. 5-9.
453. _____. Interest Conflict and Political Change in Brazil. Stanford: Univ. Press, 1971.
454. _____. "Military Intervention, Political Competitiveness, and Public Policy in Latin America: 1950-1967." In Armies and Politics in Latin America, pp. 113-64. Edited by A. Lowenthal. New York: Holmes & Meier, 1976.
455. _____, ed. Military Rule in Latin America. Beverly Hills: Sage, 1973.
456. _____. "Paths to Political Development in Latin America." In Changing Latin America. Edited by D. Chalmers. New York: Academy of Political Science, Columbia Univ., 1972.
457. _____. "The 'Portugalization' of Brazil." In Authoritarian Brazil. Edited by A. Stepan. New Haven: Yale, 1973.
458. _____. "Still the Century of Corporatism?" Review of Politics 36 (Jan. 1974): 85-131.
459. Schneider, J. O. "Fundador do Movimento Circulista no Brasil." Rio de Janeiro, 1964. (Mimeographed.)
460. Scott, R. E. "The Government Bureaucrats and Political Change in Latin America." Journal of International Affairs 20 (1966): 289-308.
461. Seligman, L. G. "Elite Recruitment and Political Development." Journal of Politics 16 (Aug. 1964).
462. Serrão, J. "Decadencia e Regeneração no Portugal Contemporaneo." Paper presented at the Workshop on Modern Portugal, Univ. of New Hampshire, Durham, Oct. 10-14, 1973.
463. Shonfield, A. Modern Capitalism. London: Oxford, 1965.
464. Shulman, M. D. "On Learning to Live with Authoritarian Regimes." Foreign Affairs 55 (Jan. 1977): 325-38.
465. Silvert, K. Chile. New York: Holt, Rinehart & Winston, 1965.
466. _____. "The Cost of Anti-Nationalism: Argentina," in 471.

467. ———. The Conflict Society: Reaction and Revolution in Latin America. New York: American Universities Field Staff, 1966.
468. ———. "National Values, Development, and Leaders and Followers." International Social Science Journal 15 (1964): 560-70.
469. ———. "Politics and the Study of Latin America." Paper presented at the 1973 Annual Meeting of the American Political Science Association, New Orleans, Sept. 4-8.
470. ———. "The Politics of Social and Economic Change in Latin America," in 545.
471. ———, ed. Expectant Peoples: Nationalism and Development. New York: Vintage, 1967.
472. Slater, J. The United States and the Dominican Revolution. New York: Harper & Row, 1970.
473. Smith, R. S. The Spanish Guild Merchant. Durham: Duke, 1970.
474. Soares, G. A. D. "Latin American Studies in the United States." Latin American Research Review 11 (1976).
475. Spiro, H. J. "The Primacy of Political Development." In Africa. Edited by H. J. Spiro. New York: Random, 1966.
476. Stein, S. J., and Stein, B. H. The Colonial Heritage of Latin America. New York: Oxford, 1970.
477. Stepan, A. The Military in Politics: Changing Patterns in Brazil. Princeton: Univ. Press, 1971.
478. ———. "The New Professionalism of Internal Warfare and Military Role Expansion." In Authoritarian Brazil. Edited by A. Stepan. New Haven, Yale, 1973.
479. ———. "Political Development: The Latin American Tradition." Journal of International Affairs 20 (1966): 223-34.
480. ———. State and Society: Peru in Comparative Perspective. Princeton: Univ. Press, 1978.
481. Stevens, E. "Mexico's PRI: The Institutionalization of Corporatism," in 304.
482. Tanzi, H. J. "La doctrina de los juristas hispanos sobre el poder político y su influencia en américa." Boletin Histórico, Sept. 1970, pp. 328-49.
483. Tarso, P. de. Os Cristãos e a Revolução Social. Rio de Janeiro: Zahar, 1963.
484. Taylor, C. "Interpretation and the Sciences of Man." In Social Structure and Political Theory. Edited by W. E. Connolly and G. Gordon. Lexington: Heath, 1974.
485. Tôrres, J. C. de O. Historia das Ideias Religiosas no Brasil. São Paulo: Grijalbo, 1968.
486. U.S. Dept. of Labor. Labor Law and Practice in Brazil. Washington: GPO, 1967.
487. Urrutia, M. The Development of the Colombian Labor Movement. New Haven: Yale, 1969.
488. Ussach, S. "The Portuguese Presidential Election of 1958." Amherst: Univ. of Massachusetts, Dept. of Political Science, 1974.
489. Vance, C. R. "Human Rights Policy." Washington: Dept. of State, Bureau of Public Affairs, Office of Media Services, 1977.

490. Vaz, H. C. de L. "The Church and Conscientizaçao." *America*, April 26, 1968.
491. Véliz, C. "Centralism and Nationalism in Latin America," in 545.
492. _____. *The Centralist Tradition in Latin America*. Princeton: Univ. Press, 1980.
493. _____, ed. *Obstacles to Change in Latin America*. London: Oxford, 1965.
494. _____, ed. *The Politics of Conformity in Latin America*. London: Oxford, 1967.
495. Vernengo, R. "Freedom of Association and Industrial Relations in Latin America." *International Labour Review*, 2 parts, 73 (May 1956): 451-82; and 74 (June 1956): 592-618.
496. Viana, S. "O Sindicato no Brasil." Rio de Janeiro, 1953. (Mimeographed.)
497. Vianna, F. J. de O. *Instituições Políticas Brasileiras*. Rio de Janeiro: Olympio, 1955.
498. Vicens Vives, J. *Historia social y económica de España y America*. Barcelona: 1957-59.
499. Viera, E. A. *Oliveira Vianna e o estado corporativo*. São Paulo: Grijalbo, 1976.
500. Viera, V. P. *Organização Professional e Representação de Classes*. São Paulo: 1933.
501. Wagley, C. *The Latin American Tradition*. New York: Columbia, 1968.
502. _____, ed. *Social Science Research on Latin America*. New York: Columbia, 1964.
503. Walker, N. A. de. "Corporativismo y Clase Trabajadora." *Desarrollo Economico* 8 (July-Dec. 1968): 313-48.
504. Warden, M. D. "Freedom and Tyranny: The Political Philosophy of Donoso Cortes." Unpublished ms., 1971.
505. Weber, M. *The Theory of Social and Economic Organization*. New York: Oxford, 1947.
506. Weinstein, M. *Uruguay: The Politics of Failure*. Westport: Greenwood, 1975.
507. Welles, S. *Naboth's Vineyard: The Dominican Republic, 1844-1924*. New York: Payson & Clarke, 1928.
508. Wheeler, D. L. "The Portuguese Revolution of 1910." *Journal of Modern History* 44 (June 1972): 172-94.
509. _____. "Portuguese Elections and History." Durham: Univ. of New Hampshire, Dept. of History, 1975.
510. _____. *Republican Portugal*. Madison: Wisconsin, 1978.
511. Whitaker, A. "The Argentine Paradox." *Annals* 334 (March 1961).
512. Wiarda, H. J. *The Aftermath of the Trujillo Dictatorship: The Emergence of a Pluralist Political System in the Dominican Republic*. Gainesville: Univ. of Florida, Dept. of Political Science, 1965.
513. _____. *The Brazilian Catholic Labor Movement*. Amherst: Univ. of Massachusetts, Labor Relations and Research Center, 1969.
514. _____. "The Catholic Labor Movement in Brazil." In *Contemporary Brazil*, pp. 323-47. Edited by W. Tyler and H. J.

Rosenbaum. New York: Praeger, 1972.

515. _____. "The Changing Political Orientation of the Church in the Dominican Republic." A Journal of Church and State 7 (Spring, 1965): 238-54.

516. _____. "Constitutions and Constitutionalism in the Dominican Republic: The Basic Law within the Political Process." Law and Society Review 2 (June 1968): 385-405.

517. _____. "The Context of United States Policy toward the Dominican Republic: Background to the Revolution of 1965." Cambridge: Harvard Univ., Center for International Affairs, 1966.

518. _____, ed. The Continuing Struggle for Democracy in Latin America. Boulder: Westview, 1980.

519. _____. Corporatism and Development: The Portuguese Experience. Amherst: Univ. of Massachusetts Press, 1977.

520. _____. "Corporatism and Development in the Iberic-Latin World: Persistent Strains and New Variations." Review of Politics 36 (Jan. 1974): 3-33.

521. _____. "Corporatism in Iberian and Latin American Political Analysis: Criticisms, Qualifications, and the Context and 'Whys' of the Debate." Comparative Politics 10 (Jan. 1978): 307-12.

522. _____. "Corporatism Rediscovered: Right, Center, Left Variants in the New Literature." Polity 10 (Spring, 1978): 416-28.

523. _____. "Corporatist Theory and Ideology: A Latin American Development Paradigm." Journal of Church and State 13 (Winter, 1978): 29-56.

524. _____. "The Corporatist Tradition and the Corporative System in Portugal." In Contemporary Portugal, pp. 89-122. Edited by L. Graham and H. Makler. Austin: Texas, 1979.

525. _____. "The Corporative Origins of the Iberian and Latin American Labor Relations Systems." Studies in Comparative International Development 13 (Spring, 1978): 3-37.

526. _____. Critical Elections and Critical Coups: State, Society and the Military in the Processes of Latin American Development. Athens: Ohio Univ., Center for International Studies, 1979.

527. _____. "Cuba: Is It also Corporatist and Bureaucratic-Authoritarian?" Amherst: Univ. of Massachusetts, Dept. of Political Science, 1978.

528. _____. "The Development of the Labor Movement in the Dominican Republic." Inter-American Economic Affairs 20 (Summer, 1966): 41-63.

529. _____. Dictatorship and Development: The Methods of Control in Trujillo's Dominican Republic. Gainesville: Univ. of Florida Press, 1968.

530. _____. "Dictatorship and Development: The Trujillo Regime and Its Implications." Social Science Quarterly 48 (March 1968): 548-57.

531. _____. Dictatorship, Development, and Disintegration: Politics and Social Change in the Dominican Republic. Ann Arbor: Xerox University Microfilms Monograph Series, 1975.

532. _____. "The Dominican Republic: Dictatorship, Development, and Disintegration." In Political Systems of Latin America, pp. 184-200. Edited by M. C. Needler. Princeton: Van Nostrand, 1970.
533. _____. The Dominican Republic: Nation in Transition. New York: Praeger, 1969.
534. _____. "The Dominican Republic: The Politics of Frustrated Revolution," in 557.
535. _____. "The Dominican Revolution in Perspective: A Research Note." Polity 1 (Fall, 1968): 114-24.
536. _____. "Elites in Crisis: The Decline of the Old Order and the Fragmentation of the New in Latin America." Columbus: Ohio State Univ., Mershon Center, 1970.
537. _____. "The Ethnocentrism of the Social Sciences: Implications for Research and Policy." Cambridge: Harvard Univ. Center for International Affairs, 1980.
538. _____. "From Fragmentation to Disintegration: The Social and Political Effects of the Dominican Revolution." America Latina 10 (April-June 1967): 55-71.
539. _____. "The Latin American Development Process and the New Developmental Alternatives: Military 'Nasserism' and 'Dictatorship with Popular Support.'" Western Political Quarterly 25 (Sept. 1972): 464-90.
540. _____. "Latin American Intellectuals and the 'Myth' of Underdevelopment." Paper presented at the VII National Meeting of the Latin American Studies Association, Houston, Nov. 2-5, 1977.
541. _____. "The Latin Americanization of the United States." New Scholar 7 (1978): 51-85.
542. _____. "Law and Political Development in Latin America." American Journal of Comparative Law 19 (Summer, 1971): 434-63.
543. _____. "Political Culture and National Development: In Search of a Model for Latin America." Latin American Research Review 13 (1978): 261-66.
544. _____. "The Political Economy of Latin American Development: The Mercantilist Model." Paper presented to the Joint Seminar on Political Development, Center for International Affairs, Harvard University, and Center for International Studies, MIT, Feb. 27, 1980.
545. _____, ed. Politics and Social Change in Latin America: The Distinct Tradition. Amherst: Univ. of Massachusetts Press, 1974.
546. _____. "The Politics of Civil-Military Relations in the Dominican Republic." Journal of Inter-American Studies 7 (Oct. 1965): 465-84.
547. _____. "Portugal: The Two Revolutions." Paper presented at the Annual Meeting of the International Studies Association, Toronto, Feb. 25-29, 1976.
548. _____. "The Portuguese Corporative System: Basic Structures and Current Functions." Iberian Studies 2 (Autumn, 1973): 73-80.

549. _____. "Review of Political Development in Latin America." Journal of Politics 31 (Aug. 1969): 821-22.
550. _____. "Spain and Portugal." In Western European Party Systems, pp. 298-328. Edited by P. H. Merkl. New York: Free Press, 1980.
551. _____. "Toward a Framework for the Study of Political Change in the Iberic-Latin Tradition: The Corporative Model." World Politics 25 (Jan. 1973): 206-35.
552. _____. Transcending Corporatism? The Portuguese Corporative System and the Revolution of 1974. Columbia: Univ. of South Carolina, Institute of International Studies, 1976.
553. _____. "The Transition to Democracy in Portugal: Real or Wishful?" Paper presented to the Joint Seminar on Political Development, Center for International Affairs, Harvard Univ., and Center for International Studies, MIT, Dec. 8, 1976.
554. _____. "Trujilloism without Trujillo." The New Republic, Sept. 19, 1964, pp. 5-6.
555. _____. Trujillo's Dominican Republic: A Case Study in the Methods of Control. Gainesville: Univ. of Florida, Dept. of Political Science, 1962.
556. _____. "The United States and the Dominican Crisis: Background to Chaos." Caribbean Monthly Bulletin 2 (July 1965): 5-8.
557. Wiarda, H. J., and Kline, H. F., eds. Latin American Politics and Development. Boston: Houghton-Mifflin, 1979.
558. Wiarda, H. J., and Kryzanek, M. J. "Dominican Dictatorship Revisited: The Caudillo Tradition and the Regimes of Trujillo and Balaguer." Revista/Review Interamericana 7 (Fall, 1977): 417-35.
559. Wiarda, H. J., and Wiarda, I. S. "The Churches and Rapid Social Change: Observations on the Differences and Similarities between Protestants and Catholics in Brazil." Journal of Church and State 12 (Winter, 1970): 13-39.
560. Wiarda, H. J., and Wiarda, I. S. "Revolution or Counterrevolution in Brazil?" Massachusetts Review 8 (Winter 1967): 149-65.
561. Wiarda, I. S. Acción Democrática of Venezuela: The Political Party as a Factor in the Modernization and Integration of a Developing Country. Gainesville: Univ. of Florida, Dept. of Political Science, 1968.
562. Wilenius, R. The Social and Political Theory of Francisco Suárez. Helsinki: Societas Philosophica Fennica, 1963.
563. Willems, E. Latin American Culture. New York: Harper & Row, 1975.
564. Williams, E. J. "Latin American Catholicism and Political Integration." Comparative Political Studies 2 (Oct. 1969).
565. _____. Latin American Christian Democratic Parties. Knoxville: Tennessee, 1967.
566. Winch, P. The Idea of a Social Science. London: Routledge & Kegan Paul, 1958.
567. Wise, G. S. Caudillo. New York: Columbia, 1951.
568. Wolf, E. R., and Hansen, E. C. "Caudillo Politics: A Structural Analysis." Comparative Studies in Society and History 9

(Jan. 1967): 168-79.
569. Worcester, D. C. "The Spanish American Past: Enemy of Change." Journal of Inter-American Studies 11 (Jan. 1969): 66-75.
570. Worcester, D. C., and Schaeffer, W. The Growth and Culture of Latin America. New York: Oxford, 1970.
571. Yañez, A. Al filo del agua [The Edge of the Storm]. Austin: Texas, 1963.
572. Zariski, R. Italy: The Politics of Uneven Development. Hinsdale: Dryden, 1977.
573. Zavala, S. New Viewpoints on the Spanish Colonization of America. Philadelphia: Pennsylvania, 1943.
574. Zea, L. The Latin American Mind. Norman: Oklahoma, 1963.